the witches' ENCYCLOPEDIA of magical PLANTS

© Jessica Weiser

About the Author

Sandra Kynes is an explorer of history, myth, and magic. Although she is a member of the Order of Bards, Ovates, and Druids, she follows her own Goddess and faery-centered path. She likes to develop creative ways to interact with the world (and otherworld) and integrate them into her spiritual path and everyday life. Her unique views and methods form the basis of her books, which serve as reference material for Pagans and anyone interested in experiencing spirituality and magic in a different way.

In addition to her books, Sandra's work has been featured in numerous Llewellyn almanacs, *Sage Woman*, *The Magical Times*, *The Portal*, and *Circle* magazines, and *The World Ocean Journal*. She writes the "Plant Magic" blog on PaganSquare blog space.

Sandra has lived in New York City, Europe, England, and now mid-coast Maine where she lives with her family and cats in a mid-nineteenth-century farmhouse surrounded by meadows and woods. She loves connecting with nature through gardening, hiking, bird watching, and kayaking. Visit her website at www.kynes.net.

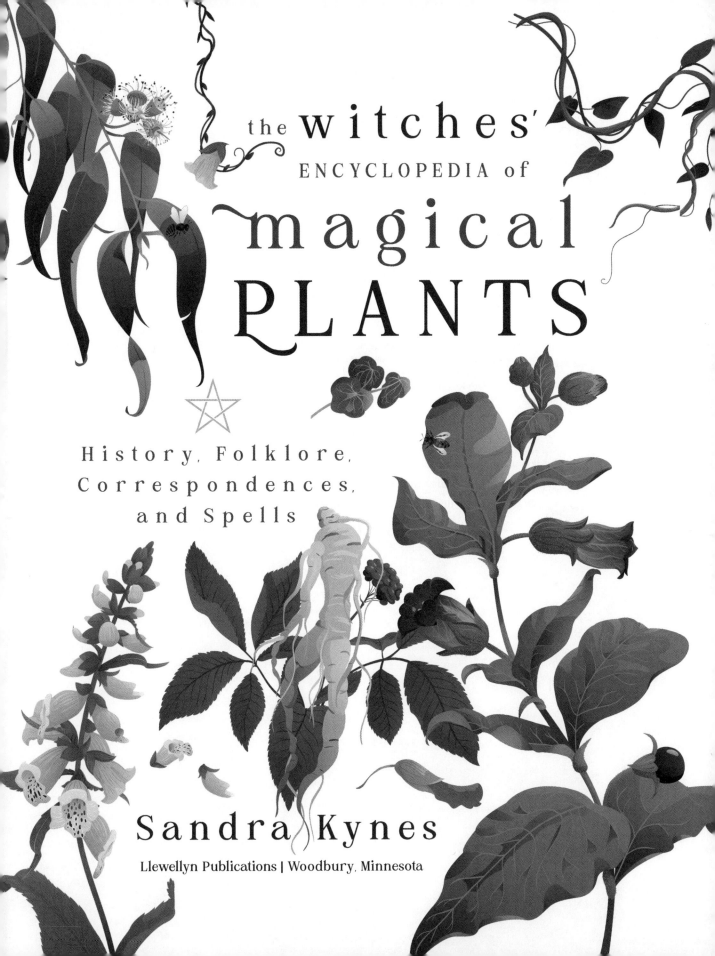

the witches'
ENCYCLOPEDIA of
magical
PLANTS

History, Folklore, Correspondences, and Spells

Sandra Kynes

Llewellyn Publications | Woodbury, Minnesota

FIRST EDITION
First Printing, 2024

Book design by R. Brasington
Cover design by Kevin R. Brown
Editing by Marjorie Otto
Interior illustrations by Llewellyn Art Department

Llewellyn Publishing is a registered trademark of Llewellyn Worldwide Ltd.

Library of Congress Cataloging-in-Publication Data (Pending)
ISBN: 978-0-7387-7548-7

Llewellyn Publications
A Division of Llewellyn Worldwide Ltd.
2143 Wooddale Drive
Woodbury, MN 55125-2989
www.llewellyn.com

Printed in the United States of America

Other Books by Sandra Kynes

Magical Faery Plants (2022)

Tree Magic (2021)

Beginner's Guide to Herbal Remedies (2020)

Magical Symbols and Alphabets (2020)

Llewellyn's Complete Book of Essential Oils (2019)

365 Days of Crystal Magic (2018)

Crystal Magic (2017)

Plant Magic (2017)

Bird Magic (2016)

Herb Gardener's Essential Guide (2016)

Star Magic (2015)

Mixing Essential Oils for Magic (2013)

Llewellyn's Complete Book of Correspondences (2013)

Change at Hand (2009)

Sea Magic (2008)

Your Altar (2007)

Whispers from the Woods (2006)

A Year of Ritual (2004)

Gemstone Feng Shui (2002)

Disclaimer

The material contained in this book is for informational purposes only. It is not intended to be a medical guide or a manual for self-treatment. This book is sold with the understanding that the publisher and author are not liable for the misconception, misinterpretation, or misuse of any information provided. Use caution, as some plants mentioned within this book may be harmful or poisonous in various forms or uses.

Dedication

With this book, I hope to honor all of the witches, wise women, and cunning folk of the past whose wisdom lives on.

Contents

Introduction   1

A...9
B...31
C...59
D...97
E...111
F...119
G...131
H...145
I...167
J...171
K...177
L...181
M...201
N...225
O...229
P...235
Q...257
R...261
S...269
T...295
U...309
V...313
W...321
Y...329
Z...333

Appendix A: Powers and Attributes   337
Appendix B: Plants by Other Associations   351
Appendix C: Deities   357
Bibliography   363
Index   377

Introduction

While humans have relied on plants for everything—food, medicine, fiber for clothing, wood to build shelters, raw materials for daily life—there seems to be something more, something mystical, about plants that touches the psyche. Throughout most ancient cultures, people believed plants to be magical and, in many cases, used them as much for ritual as they did for medicine and food. The presence of plants in ancient tombs attests to their power beyond mundane purposes. Plants were integral components of spiritual and magical practices in cultures worldwide and throughout time.

Historical Perspective

The ancient Egyptians believed that deities were embodied in the smoke and fragrance of temple incense. Burning plant material provided a connection between the physical and spiritual. It also enhanced magic. Dating to the sixteenth century BCE, the Ebers Papyrus is the oldest written record of Egyptian use of plants. Along with the physical details of plants, the manuscript contains spells and incantations.

The Babylonians and Sumerians prized certain plants and used them as offerings for their deities. The Assyrians were fond of aromatics for religious rituals as well as personal use, and the Mesopotamians used ceremonies and special incantations when gathering herbs. By the second century BCE, there was a thriving trade in herbs and spices among Asia, India, the Middle East, and Europe.

Some of the earliest texts from India, the Vedas (c. 1500 BCE), contain praises to the natural world along with details about plants. Chinese herbalists influenced the practices of Japan and Korea as fifth-century Buddhist monks transported spiritual and herbal information with them on their travels.

Phoenician merchants were instrumental in bringing herbal treasures from the Far East to Europe, most notably to the Greeks and Romans.

Called *rhizotomoki*, "root gatherers" or "root cutters," the herb merchants of ancient Greece kept information about the properties of herbs.[1] Said to be a somewhat secretive profession, legend has it that the sorceress Circe and the centaur Chiron were rhizotomoki. Greek physician and botanist Pedanius Dioscorides (c. 40–c. 90 CE) compiled the first herbal manuscript in Europe, *De Materia Medica*, "The Material of Medicine," which served as a major reference for centuries. Another influential writer was the Roman naturalist and historian Pliny the Elder (c. 23/24 CE–79 CE). Eight of his thirty-seven volumes dealt with plants and were a valuable resource for herbalists well into the seventeenth century.

Elsewhere in the world, the Aboriginal people of Australia developed a sophisticated understanding of plants. In South and Central America, the Maya, Inca, and Aztec had herbal traditions that were intertwined with their religious rites. On the other side of the Rio Grande, plants were integral for both healing and spiritual ceremonies of the Indigenous people throughout North America.

After the decline of the Roman Empire, Europe entered a period of uncertainty, and monasteries became centers of stability and learning. Monks who had translated copies of ancient manuscripts had also learned from local healers and offered medical assistance; however, most of the populace turned to the people who had always been there helping and sharing information, the midwives and folk healers. They were the ones

whom villagers trusted and went to for medicine, divination, and advice. In the power vacuum left by the Roman Empire, the Church sought to hold onto and increase its control over people's lives and the traditional folk healers became a convenient scapegoat. The fear mongering of the witch trials and demonization of witches were methods for discouraging people from questioning authority. The use of plants, potions, and other items became a way to identify witches. Unfortunately, we know the tragedy that followed. To compound the problem, the emerging medical establishment sought to take healing out of the hands of those they regarded as uneducated, most of whom were women. And of course, women were not permitted to attend the burgeoning universities and medical schools that supported this new regime.

Despite the social turmoil and threats to personal safety, the knowledge and old ways survived in the hands of those who managed to stay quiet and keep under the Church's radar. They helped the people who did not live close enough to monasteries where monks could help them or who could not afford the fees of university-trained doctors. Those who were brave enough to carry on the practices that had been used for centuries kept wisdom alive. Ironically, there were some unwitting allies such as English botanist and herbalist Nicholas Culpeper (1616–1654) who published an herbal treatise *The English Physician* intended for laypeople. As a child he started learning about plants from his grandmother and eventually became an outlier to the medical establishment.

Even though the Church officially condemned magical practices, some members flirted with them. It wasn't just lowly monks tucked away in remote monasteries who took part in a clerical

1. Chevallier, *The Encyclopedia of Medicinal Plants*, 247; Lawrence, *Witch's Garden*, 13.

underground that explored the realm of magic. A medieval grimoire known as the *Grand Albert* is often attributed to German friar and bishop Albertus Magnus (c. 1200–1280) who explored and wrote about his interests in botany and alchemy. Freewheeling abbots, such as Johannes Trithemius (1462–1516) who wrote about alchemy and astrology, had to relocate from time to time to avoid scrutiny. When the young Heinrich Cornelius Agrippa of Nettesheim (1486–1535) turned to Trithemius for advice about what he wanted to pursue, the abbot encouraged him to continue his occult studies.

Plants were an integral part of magic work. Agrippa's work on natural magic and astrology involved the use of plants to draw down the energy and power of the planets and stars. His work also included gemstones, which were often boosted through the power of plants. Medieval magicians used suffumigation (burning plant material to produce clouds of smoke and fumes) not only to contact but also to conjure spirits, faeries, and sometimes demons to do their bidding. The Bodleian Library in Oxford, England, has a manuscript by English antiquarian and astrologer Elias Ashmole (1617–1692) that contains conjurations of faeries and spirits for ceremonial magic. Although the common concept of alchemy is the transmutation of base metal into gold, Swiss physician and alchemist Theophrastus Bombastus von Hohenheim (1493–1541) who called himself Paracelsus, noted that the quest of alchemy was originally focused on plants and the search for the elixir of life.[2]

While the "educated" followed their high-minded pursuits, magical practices were also widespread among the healers, wise folk, and ordinary people. Plants were easy to come by and were used for the practical purposes of healing, divination, protection, removing curses or negative influences, and many other situations that were important to everyday life. Today it would be labeled as *low magic*, as opposed to *high ceremonial magic*, but historically, plant magic was part of people's lives. Then and now, for many of us, the magical use of plants is part of everyday life.

Plant Names

Common names and folk names are easy to remember, but they are a source of confusion because some names have been given to multiple plants and many plants have multiple names. In addition, folk names are sometimes applied incorrectly causing even more confusion. Keep in mind that two plants may share a folk name, but it does not mean that all folk names apply to both plants. While this may seem minor, it is important to know which plants we are using because some are extremely toxic and can be dangerous to handle or fatal to ingest. For safety reasons, it is important to also know the botanical (genus and species) names when studying or purchasing plants or plant material. But don't worry, you don't have to memorize scientific names, just jot them down in your journal or grimoire along with their common and folk names.

Genus and species are part of a complex naming structure devised by Swedish naturalist Carl Linnaeus (1707–1778), whose work became the foundation for the identification system used today. Latin is used most often for botanical names because during Linnaeus' time it was a common language for those engaged in scientific research. Over time, as new information was

---

2. Sonnedecker, *History of Pharmacy*, 40.

discovered, plant names were changed to reflect the new data. This is why botanical names often have synonyms. The antiquated names are not completely dropped because they aid in identification. For example, common moonwort is noted as *Botrychium lunaria* syn. *Osmunda lunaria*. Occasionally, the use of synonyms is the result of scientific disagreement.

The first word in a botanical name is the plant's genus, which is often a proper noun and always capitalized. The second word, the species name, is an adjective that usually provides something descriptive about the plant. For example, in coriander (*Coriandrum sativum*) the species name means "cultivated."[3]

Occasionally, there may be a third word preceded by "var." indicating that it is a variety of a species. For example, bitter almond is *Prunus dulcis* var. *amara*. A third word may also indicate a cultivar, or more appropriately, a cultivated variety. This type of plant was created in the garden and not found naturally in the wild. The cultivar name is written in single quotes. The Tinkerbelle lilac is an example: *Syringa* x *microphylla* 'Baibelle.' The letter "x" indicates that the plant is a hybrid, a cross between two plants. The letter *f* in a name means *forma* or form and indicates a more subtle variation such as white-flowered foxglove *Digitalis purpurea* f. *alba*.

Helpful Words, Terms, and Historical Periods

Some words often appear in plant names such as *wort* as in Saint John's wort. This comes from the Old English *wyrt*, meaning "plant" or "herb."[4] *Bane* is another, as in wolfsbane and henbane. It is an Anglo-Saxon word for poison and was incorporated into the names of some plants as a warning.[5]

The term *vulgaris*, as in thyme (*Thymus vulgaris*), means that it is common. *Officinale* and *officinalis*, as in dandelion (*Taraxacum officinale*) and vervain (*Verbena officinalis*), means that the plant is (or was when it was named) officially recognized as a medicinal plant. The Latin *folia* and *folium* means "foliage" and is found in the American beech (*Fagus grandifolia*) meaning "large foliage" and yarrow (*Achillea millefolium*) meaning "thousand-leafed." Table 1 provides a few botanical terms that are useful to know.

Helpful Botanical Terms

Axil	The area of a plant between a stem or branch and a leaf stem
Bract	A modified or specialized leaf situated at the base of a flower
Catkin	A thick cluster of tiny flowers; male catkins are usually larger than female catkins and pendulous; female catkins are most often upright
Lobed	A leaf with deeply indented edges, such as oak or maple tree leaves
Rhizome	An underground stem that is usually considered as a type of root
Sepal	The outermost part of a flower that protects the young bud

3. Cumo, *Encyclopedia of Cultivated Plants*, 436.

4. Durkin, *The Oxford Guide to Etymology*, xxxviii.

5. Storl, *The Herbal Lore of Wise Women and Wortcunners*, 234.

Toothed	A leaf with jagged edges; also called serrated
Whorl	A circular or spiral growth pattern of leaves, needles, or flower petals

Greek	1200 BCE–323 CE
Inca	1438–1532
India / Indus Valley	3000 BCE–1300 BCE
Maya	2600 BCE–900 CE
Medieval/Middle Ages	475 CE–1400
Olmec	1200 BCE–400 BCE
Persian	550 BCE–330 BCE
Renaissance	1400–1600
Roman Empire	753 BCE–476 CE
Tudor England	1485–1603
Victorian	1837–1912
Viking Era	793–1066

In addition to botanical terms, you will find the two common spellings of *faery* and *fairy* throughout this book. The word *faery* indicates actual beings and their world; *fairy* refers to the imaginary beings and their land in stories of entertainment. That said, where the traditional and customary spelling is *fairy* in plant names (such as fairy flax, fairy bells, fairy cups) and other terms (such as fairy ring, fairy horse, fairy path), I have maintained the conventional spelling.

Table 2 contains a listing of time periods and approximate dates (sources vary) of empires and eras mentioned throughout this book. I included this to add perspective to the historical information in the plant entries and because I don't expect most people to be a nerdy history buff like me. They are listed alphabetically for ease of use.

Time Periods and Ancient Civilizations

Anglo-Saxon	410 CE–1066
Assyrian	1365 BCE–609 BCE
Aztec	1325–1521
Babylonian	1894 BCE–539 BCE
Celts	1200 BCE–60 CE
Chinese	1600 BCE–220 CE
Crusades	1095–1291
Egyptian	4300 BCE–30 BCE
Elizabethan	1558–1603

Plant Tools

Bringing plants into our homes conveys their energy into our personal environments and magic work. A potted plant placed on an altar can amplify the focus of a ritual. A twig, flower, piece of fruit, or any part of a plant chosen for an attribute or association can magnify your intent and the energy of a spell. We can use plants (and their parts) as is or we can make them into tools or purchase something made from plant material.

Wands, walking sticks, and magic staffs are easy to make and can be as simple or elaborate as you like. In addition to tree branches, wands and staffs can be made from any woody shrub or plant. Small items and boxes made of wood can also serve a magical purpose. Instead of a crystal, a plant pendulum can be created with a small piece of wood or bundle of herbs.

A wreath isn't just for hanging on your door at Yule. A small one can be placed on your altar around the base of a candle or other object. It can be made from a slender twig or long flower stem by winding it into shape and tying it in place. Leaves and flowers can be hung in bundles and individually dried or pressed. A method called *rubbing* is a way to save the image of a leaf in a journal or Book of Shadows.

The use of oils has been an integral part of magical practices for centuries. Essential oils, infused oils, hydrosols, and flower essences provide a way to maintain tradition while giving your magic and spiritual practices new depth. These can be used for preparing candles, anointing for blessings, as well as consecrating magic and divination tools. If bathing before ritual or magic work is part of your practice, adding an oil to the water or applying it your body aids in purification and helps to set intention.

Scent is also a tool used in the form of incense, diffusing essential oil, or burning dried plant material. Scent can stimulate, inspire, and enchant us. Although smell is not our most acute sense, it is closely linked with memory and emotion. It can transport us back to childhood or to other realms by retrieving a total experience of feelings, imagery, and sounds. Scent also provides the ability to connect with the spirit world.

Symbolism

In ritual and magic we often use various parts of plants because of their symbolism. For example, flowers are often used for love and sex magic, seeds for fertility, and fruit for abundance and manifestation. In addition to using a certain type of plant, you may find that coordinating a particular plant part with your purpose can add power to your spells and rituals.

Residing under the earth, roots provide grounding energy and stability for our rituals and magic work. They offer access to the underworld, making them useful for connecting with ancestors, spirits, or chthonic deities. As a symbol of longevity, roots encourage us to hold secrets when bidden.

Wood and bark from trees or the woody parts of other plants provide protective energy to rituals, spells, and charms. In addition to being a gauge of growth, they can aid us in manifesting our growth. Being at the center or encircling a plant, wood and bark provide balance and strength.

From the moment they burst forth in the spring until the wind whisks them away in the autumn, leaves enfold the world with aerial enchantment. Leaves personify energy and growth and give our magic and personal endeavors an encouraging boost. They also provide protection and concealment. Whether they are flashy or subtle, flowers are the crowning glory of plants. They represent beauty with the goals of attraction, sex, and fertility. Flowers and leaves add potency and fragrance to magic work.

Fruit symbolizes fruition, manifestation, completion, and success. Fruit is the personification of abundance and represents an increase in power or energy. Use fruit to increase what you have and to gain what you seek.

Seeds and nuts move between the worlds, carried on a breeze, or snuggled into the earth, they represent beginnings, changes, and cycles. They also represent duality such as the alternation between life and death, light and dark.

About this Book

I feel that I stand on the shoulders of Scott Cunningham (1956–1993), whose *Encyclopedia of*

Magical Herbs has been a go-to source for decades for many of us who follow a magical path. His work has been an inspiration to me and I hope that my work will inspire others.

Many of the plants included in this book are well known for their use in magic, a few are a bit obscure, and several are common garden or houseplants that have come into magical use in modern times. Houseplants are convenient, especially for apartment dwellers, as many people either have them or can easily acquire them.

Each plant profile includes botanical, common, and folk names, and a plant description. I have included the more widely known common and folk names and some that are fanciful. While some plants may have the same folk name, they may have a slightly different spelling. For example, bird's eye and bird's eyes or fairy wand and fairy's wand, self heal and self-heal.

Cautions are included in each profile and pertain only to humans. Many plants that are safe for us are toxic to our pets; it is important to check. Although many plants are well known and generally safe to consume, others are sometimes sold as tea or herbs, but may not be safe to ingest. Always err on the side of caution and do not consume anything that may not be safe, especially during pregnancy and breastfeeding or if you have a medical condition. When using essential oils, check the manufacture's information as they often have their own precautions. Handling and using plants must be done with common sense and safety. When in doubt about identifying plants in the wild, it is safer to use photographs to represent them (magic is about intention). I have also noted threatened and endangered species as well as those regarded as invasive; you will need to check their status in your area if you intend to

gather plants from the wild and/or plant them in your garden.

Each profile includes historical information and folklore. I wanted to go beyond the commonly known stories to show the rich background of plants and I thoroughly enjoyed the research that was involved. Following a botanical trail with its twists and turns sometimes felt as challenging as untangling the canes of a blackberry bush. Occasionally, when it seemed that I had gone down a rabbit hole to a dead end, a little gem from a plant's history would emerge and give me another trail to follow. As you read the entries, you may find that the historical context of a plant sparks something for you, making it more meaningful for your magic and everyday life. Another note of interest is that many of the plants that were used against witches were also said to have been used by them. While many plants have much more to their stories, I had to limit the amount to share in order to have space for as many entries as possible.

Correspondences, attributes, and other associations are a part of each profile, too, and come from a range of traditions and sources. When more than one plant is included in a profile, I have noted where a correspondence or attribute applies specifically to one. The appendices also include this distinction. Appendix A is a listing of plants according to their powers and attributes. Appendix B contains listings by elements, astrological signs, and planetary/solar system associations. Appendix C is a listing of deities and the plants associated with them.

The ogham alphabet is included in the correspondences because of its association with trees and its use in magic. Information about the ogham comes from medieval sources such as *The*

Book of Ballymote, Auraicept na n-Éces or "Scholar's Primer," and several others. In addition to the character names varying within and between these books, they were often translated differently. For example, the name *Beith* is most widely used for the character that represents the letter *B*. However, the *Auraicept* contains the names *Beithe*, *Beithi*, and *Bethi*, and in his influential book *The White Goddess*, Robert Graves (1895–1985) used the name *Beth*. As a result, Beith and Beth are in common use. Similarly, the names *Huath* and *Uath* are most commonly used (representing the letter *H*) but occasionally you may see the Gaelic *hÚath*. In cases where some ogham character names have a wide range of spellings, I have limited them to two. In addition to older names, two ogham characters have been reinterpreted with new meanings and names added. *Ebad Ebhadh* also became *Koad/Grove* to represent more than one tree and *Emancoll/Amhancholl* also became *Mór* and associated with the sea.

As is often the case, we may want to work with a plant that does not grow where we live. As an aid, each profile includes suggestions for items that can be purchased. This information is not intended as a comprehensive list, but as a starting point for what you may find on the market. Last but not least, each profile includes suggestions for magical and ritual use.

Overall, this book is intended as a learning and reference tool to support you in your magic work and spiritual path. Learning and working with plants connects us more closely with all the wise folk who have gone before us as we carry on their timeless traditions. Getting to know the green world and working with plants helps us to grow as individuals and to discover unique ways of self-expression in the craft.

Acacia

Cat Claw Acacia (*Senegalia greggii* syn. *Acacia greggii*); also known as devil's claw

Gum Arabic (*A. nilotica* syn. *Vachellia nilotica*); also known as babul acacia, thorn mimosa

Red Acacia (*A. seyal* syn. *V. seyal*); also known as shittah tree, whistling thorn, whitethorn

The gum Arabic tree has globes of golden-yellow flowers and long thorns that grow in pairs. The red acacia has globes of bright yellow flowers and long thorns. With flattened, spreading crowns and fern-like feathery leaves, they are iconic landmarks of the African savannah. The cat claw acacia has yellowish-white flowers and small, gray-green leaves that grow in clusters among thorns shaped like a cat's claws.

History and Lore

Throughout the ancient world from Africa and the Middle East to India, acacia gum served as sacred incense. The Hindus used acacia wood for ritual fires and the Hebrews forbid secular use of it. Because it survived in the harshest conditions, the tree symbolized immortality and the afterlife to the Egyptians. Known as the staff of the dead, a large acacia branch was often placed in graves. In some tomb inscriptions, Osiris was referred to as "the solitary one in the acacia."[6] According to myth, acacia wood was used to construct Osiris's sacred barge. A type of mistletoe (*Loranthus acacia*) is specific to acacia trees and commonly found on them throughout the Middle East.

....

6. De Cleene and Lejeune, *Compendium of Symbolic and Ritual Plants in Europe*, 67.

Magical Connections

Element/s	Air
Astrological influence	Aquarius, Leo; Mars, Sun
Deities	Astarte, Brahma, Diana, Ishtar, Isis, Neith, Osiris, Ra
Other associations	The afterlife, Lughnasadh, Samhain
Powers and attributes	Abundance, ancestors, awareness, balance/harmony, consecrate/bless, death/funeral practices, divination, healing, inspiration, love, negativity, prosperity/money, protection, psychic abilities, purification, relationships, spirituality, wisdom
Available for purchase	Powdered gum Arabic; gum nuggets; pieces or powdered bark

Spells and Rituals

Boost the energy of protection spells by incorporating a picture of acacia thorns. To consecrate and cleanse ritual space, burn a couple of gum nuggets and waft the smoke in a circle. Use acacia to honor your ancestors at Samhain.

Aconite

Monkshood (*Aconitum napellus*); also known as blue rocket, friar's cap, helmet flower, wolf root, wolfsbane

Wolfsbane (*A. lycoctonum*); also known as monkshood, northern wolfsbane, white-bane, yellow monkshood/wolfsbane

These plants are known for their distinctive, elongated flowers that grow in clusters atop graceful stems. The leaves have deeply cut lobes. Wolfs-bane flowers are yellow or whitish yellow, and sometimes purple. Its leaves are light green. Monkshood flowers are dark blue-violet and its leaves are dark green.

Caution: All parts of these plants are extremely toxic and fatal if ingested; wear gloves to handle as poisoning can occur through broken skin.

Aconite

History and Lore

There is a great deal of confusion about these two plants because they look so similar and their names have been used interchangeably for centuries. Dedicated to Hecate, the Greeks attributed some illnesses to aconites and used the plants for euthanasia. In the narrative poem *Metamorphoses* by Roman poet Ovid (43 BCE–17 CE), the sorceress Medea caused aconites to sprout from the spittle that fell from Cerberus, the triple-headed dog of the underworld. Medea is also blamed for using it to poison Theseus, the mythical king and founder of Athens. The Anglo-Saxons reputedly used aconite to poison their arrows for wolf hunts. During the Middle Ages in Europe, the aconites were regarded as witches' plants and believed to be an ingredient in the legendary flying ointment.

Magical Connections

Element/s	Water
Astrological influence	Capricorn, Mars (wolfsbane); Saturn
Deities	Hecate, Medea, Shiva, Thor
Other associations	The otherworld
Powers and attributes	Consecrate/bless, death/funeral practices, negativity, peace, prophecy, protection, relationships, skills, strength, support
Available for purchase	Flower essence; seeds

Spells and Rituals

In the garden, aconite provides protection for the home and dispels negative energy. Sprinkle your ritual and magic tools with flower essence to consecrate them or store them with a small pouch of seeds. Working with aconite aids in dealing with the darker side of self.

Adder's Tongue

Common Adder's Tongue (*Ophioglossum vulgatum*); also known as adder's tongue fern, devil's tongue, English adder's tongue, serpent's tongue, southern adder's tongue

Yellow Trout Lily (*Erythronium americanum*); also known as yellow adder's tongue, dogtooth violet, fawn lily

Although common adder's tongue is a fern, it doesn't look like a typical one. It has one pointed, oval leaf-like frond and one yellowish-green, spike-like frond, which is a seed stalk. The seeds form in segments that look like a double row of beads. The yellow trout lily has a pair of mottled leaves (spotted like the fish) at the base of a stalk that bears a solitary, yellowish flower. The drooping flower has dark, protruding stamens. The name *dogtooth violet* refers to the shape of its white root/bulb.

Caution: In some areas, these plants are regarded as endangered or threatened species.

History and Lore

During the Middle Ages in Europe and Britain, common adder's tongue was used medicinally and regarded as particularly potent for healing when gathered during a waning moon. It was believed to be especially good for curing venomous snakebites. Made with adder's tongue and olive oil, the green oil that English herbalist and botanist John Gerard (1545–1612) recommended for wounds was also reputedly used by witches when casting spells. Considered a love herb and aphrodisiac, German women sewed dried pieces of the plant into the hems of their skirts. In nineteenth-century America, yellow trout lily was also regarded as an aphrodisiac.

Magical Connections

Element/s	Water
Astrological influence	Moon
Powers and attributes	Communication, courage, divination, dream work, emotions, healing, sex/sexuality, spirituality, strength
Available for purchase	Trout lily bulbs

Spells and Rituals

Use yellow trout lily flowers to support divination and lunar magic. If you find them in the wild where they are endangered, take a moment or two to sense their energy, and then state your purpose for seeking their aid. Send them healing, supportive energy before leaving.

African Violet

African Violet (*Saintpaulia ionantha*)

African violets come in a wide variety of sizes, shapes, and colors. This species is the quintessential plant with rounded, slightly fuzzy, dark green leaves that grow from a center crown. Stalks with clusters of purple flowers also grow from the center. Given the right conditions, it can bloom all year as a houseplant.

History and Lore

The African violet was brought to the attention of Europeans by Baron Walter von Saint Paul-Illaire (1860–1940), a German serving as regional commissioner in an area now part of Tanzania. Because of his interest in botany, he took samples back to a friend at the Royal Botanical Gardens in Hanover, Germany. It didn't take long for the African violet to become a popular and beloved houseplant. The species name was derived from either the Greek *ionantha* or Latin *ionanthus*, meaning "violet-color flowers."[7]

Magical Connections

Element/s	Water
Astrological influence	Venus
Powers and attributes	Abundance, balance/harmony, consecrate/bless, family and home, growth, love, spirituality
Available for purchase	Flower essence; houseplant

Spells and Rituals

Closely associated with the home, African violets lift the energy and invite blessings inside. Position a flowering plant wherever you want to get energy moving. Place one with dark blue or purple flowers on your altar to raise the spiritual vibration of meditation or ritual.

Agrimony

Common Agrimony (*Agrimonia eupatoria*); also known as cocklebur, fairy's wand, golden rod, liverwort, sticklewort, stickwort

Agrimony leaves consist of lance-shaped leaflets that are deeply veined and coarsely toothed. Stems growing two to four feet tall hold dense clusters of yellow, five-petaled flowers. The whole plant is slightly aromatic and the flowers have a

---

7. Neal, *Gardener's Latin*, 69.

richly scented, slightly spicy odor. Seed capsules form burrs.

History and Lore

Agrimony was used medicinally in the Middle East and by the Greeks and Romans. In addition to healing, the Anglo-Saxons used it in an ointment for protection against poison and evil spirits. According to medieval legend in Western Europe and Britain, witches used agrimony to cast spells as well as to break them. It was also an ingredient in a potion that enabled a person to see witches. On the island of Guernsey, agrimony was one of many ingredients in a charm to wear around the neck for protection against spells. Regarded as a highly magical plant in Scotland, it was used to cure elf shot, which was believed to be an invisible magical weapon used by elves to cause disease. For love divination, two small leafy branches were placed under the pillow to bring dreams of a future husband. Hanging a sachet of dried agrimony in the home was said to protect it against evil spirits.

Magical Connections

Element/s	Air, earth
Astrological influence	Cancer, Taurus; Jupiter, Mercury
Magical entities	Elves, faeries
Powers and attributes	Balance/harmony, banish, dream work, family and home, healing, hexes, negativity, protection, purification, release, spirit guides/ spirits
Available for purchase	Flower essence; cut, dried leaves; seeds

Spells and Rituals

To send a hex back to its origin, burn three handfuls of dried leaves, one at a time, as you visualize the energy returning to its source. If you find agrimony burrs, place a few on your altar to purify the space for magic or ritual. Also use the burrs for banishing spells.

Alder

Black Alder (*Alnus glutinosa*); also known as aller, common alder, European alder
Red Alder (*A. rubra*); also known as Oregon alder
Smooth Alder (*A. serrulata*); also known as hazel alder, tag alder

Alder trees have rounded, glossy green leaves; the black alder leaves are notched at the tip. Appearing before the leaves develop, the male catkins are slender and drooping, the female catkins are pinecone-like and called *cones* and *black knobs*. Alder trees often have multiple trunks.

History and Lore

Throughout Europe and the British Isles, the alder has been considered a highly magical tree. The *Silva Gadelica*, a medieval collection of Irish folklore, contains the poem "The Lay of the Forest Trees" in which the alder is described as the warrior witch of the forest. In other Irish legends, alder is said to be protected by faeries and can provide access to their realm. In Denmark, faeries were believed to live in or under alders. Germanic people used alder wood for sacred fires, especially when making sacrifices to deities. While the Germans and Belgians hung leafy sprigs on their houses and stables to keep witches away, they also believed that witches used alder for weather spells. In Austria, drinking wine in which a piece of alder bark had been boiled was believed to counteract a love potion. The English decorated sacred wells with the female catkins, however, in Somerset it was said that a person would disappear if they walked through an alder copse at night.

Magical Connections

Element/s	Air, fire, water
Astrological influence	Aries, Cancer, Pisces; Mars, Moon, Venus
Deities	Cailleach Bheur, Freya, Manannán Mac Lir, Minerva, Pan, Venus
Magical entities	Elves, faeries, unicorns
Other associations	Ostara
Ogham	Fern ⊤⊤⊤
Powers and attributes	Banish, clarity, death/funeral practices, divination, dream work, healing, intuition, knowledge, luck, negativity, prophecy, protection, renewal, see faeries, spirit guides/spirits, strength (black), transformation
Available for purchase	Flower essence; charcoal; wood chips

Spells and Rituals

To boost the energy of a banishing spell, burn a few male catkins. For a protective travel charm, place a female catkin/cone in a decorative bag to take with you or to keep in your car. To enhance rituals, magic work, or divination sessions, burn a couple of wood chips beforehand.

Alkanet

Alkanet

Common Alkanet (*Anchusa officinalis*); also known as bugloss, common bugloss

Dyer's Alkanet (*Alkanna tinctoria* syn. *Anchusa tinctoria*); also known as bird's eye, dyer's bugloss, orchanet, Spanish bugloss, true alkanet

Common alkanet is an erect plant with hairy stems and leaves. Growing in clusters, the cup-shaped flowers are purplish-blue with white centers. The stems of dyer's alkanet sprawl across the ground and are dense with hairy, oblong leaves. Its cup-shaped flowers are bright blue with darker centers. They grow in small clusters at the tips of the stems.

History and Lore

The common name for these plants comes from the Arabic *al-hinna,* "the henna," which was Anglicized to *alkanna* and *alkanet.*[8] Henna (*Lawsonia inermis*) was sometimes used as a substitute for alkanet, although not in Europe where henna was

....
8. Dobelis, *Magic and Medicine of Plants,* 82.

expensive. From Europe to the Middle East to India, Alkanet root was widely used as a pigment for everything from cosmetics to fabric to wood. Like litmus, the color from dyer's bugloss is red in an acidic environment but blue in alkaline. Alkanet was used medicinally by the Romans, and naturalist Pliny the Elder noted that dyer's bugloss in wine increased happiness. In medieval Europe, the root was used as a good luck charm. In the American magical tradition of hoodoo, alkanet is an ingredient in red fast luck oil, an attraction oil for making things happen quickly in your life, especially when it comes to luck and success.

Magical Connections

Element/s	Earth, water
Astrological influence	Taurus; Jupiter, Venus
Powers and attributes	Happiness, luck, prosperity/ money, protection, success
Available for purchase	Cut, dried root; powdered root

Spells and Rituals

To jump-start a spell, mix the powdered root with your favorite oil and dab it on a candle or other object to be used in magic. Carry a piece of root in your wallet or purse as a charm to attract financial prosperity and success.

Allspice

Allspice (*Pimenta officinalis*, syn. *P. dioica*); also known as Jamaican pepper, myrtle pepper, pimenta, pimento berry, pimento leaf

Allspice is an evergreen tree with dark green, oval leaves that grow four to eight inches long. When crushed, the leaves have a clove-like fragrance. Clusters of small, white flowers grow at the ends of branches. The green, pea-sized berries turn brown as they ripen.

History and Lore

The genus name *Pimenta* comes from the Spanish *pimienta* for "black pepper," so named because the dried berries resemble peppercorns.[9] Although Christopher Columbus (1451–1506) is attributed with "discovering" allspice on one of his journeys to the New World, the Indigenous people of the West Indies and Central America had been using it for medicinal and culinary purposes for many centuries. The Maya also added it to smoking tobacco, and it was used in the embalming process by the Maya and Aztec.

Magical Connections

Element/s	Fire
Astrological influence	Aries, Scorpio; Mars
Deities	Aphrodite, Oshun, Venus, Yemaya
Other associations	Samhain
Powers and attributes	Abundance, consecrate/bless, courage, determination, fertility, growth, healing, love, luck, negativity, prosperity/money, purification, relationships, spirituality
Available for purchase	Essential oil; flower essence; whole or ground dried berries; dried leaves

---

9. Small, *Top 100 Exotic Food Plants*, 47.

Spells and Rituals

Associated with spirituality and purification, allspice brings powerful energy when consecrating amulets, altars, and ritual space. For luck, carry a dried berry with you. When meditating on your purpose in life, dab a little of the flower essence over your third eye chakra.

Almond

Bitter Almond (*Prunus dulcis* var. *amara* syn. *P. amygdalus* var. *amara*); also known as wild almond

Sweet Almond (*P. dulcis* var. *dulcis* syn. *P. amygdalus*, *Amygdalus communis*)

Reaching about fifteen feet tall, the almond tree has lance-shaped leaves that are medium green and lighter underneath. The fragrant, five-petaled flowers are pale pink to white. The green, oblong fruit has a velvety texture and holds the seed/almond.

Caution: Raw bitter almonds are lethal to ingest; the seeds and leaves of *Prunus* species produce cyanide in the digestive tract.

History and Lore

In ancient Greek rituals, crushed almonds were mixed with water to represent the semen of Zeus. Symbolizing fertility, almonds were scattered at weddings to bring blessings and fertility. The Greeks also believed that bitter almond prevented intoxication. Marzipan, a confection made with sugar, honey, and almond meal, was used by the Germans during the Middle Ages for love spells and as a maternity charm. To the French, almonds were a symbol of happy marriage. In northern Italy, almond branches were used as divining rods to find hidden treasure. Tantric Hindus associated the almond shape with the yoni, female genital symbol, one of the two primal powers (Shiva linga and Shakti yoni, male and female) that form the greater symbolism of cosmic consciousness and existence.

Magical Connections

Element/s	Air, fire
Astrological influence	Aquarius, Gemini, Virgo; Jupiter, Mars, Mercury, Sun, Venus
Deities	Astarte, Attis, Cybele, Hermes, Mercury, Shakti, Shiva, Thoth, Venus, Zeus
Magical entities	Faeries
Other associations	Ostara, Beltane
Powers and attributes	Abundance, awareness, creativity, divination, fertility, happiness, hope, intuition, knowledge, love, luck, prosperity/money, protection, renewal, sex/sexuality, spirit guides/spirits, spirituality, wisdom
Available for purchase	Almonds; almond milk; sweet almond oil; almond flour

Spells and Rituals

To honor the God during rituals or to boost a fertility spell, use almond milk as a libation. Open your awareness for divination or when communicating with spirits by placing a dab of almond oil on your third eye chakra. To add a bit of tradition to a love spell, include marzipan.

Aloe

Aloe Vera (*Aloe vera* syn. *A. barbadensis, A. vulgaris*); also known as Mediterranean aloe

Arabian Aloe (*A. rubroviolacea*)

Aloe is an evergreen succulent with spiny-edged leaves that can grow up to two feet long from a center base. Arabian aloe leaves have reddish spines along the edges that turn slightly violet red in the winder. Aloe leaves contain a pale, translucent gel that is used for healing.

Caution: The yellow sap called *bitter aloe* that is exuded at the base of the leaves should not be used on the skin or ingested.

History and Lore

Mentioned in Sumerian and Egyptian healing texts, aloe was used medicinally throughout the Middle East and North Africa. Associating it with immortality, the Egyptians used aloe in the embalming process. It was also used for the living and reputedly it was one of Cleopatra's beauty secrets. In the Middle East, leaves were hung over the entrances to homes to keep evil spirits and ghosts from entering and to bring good luck. The Greeks and Romans used aloe for treating wounds. As a symbol of bitterness, it was customary for Arabs to plant aloe at the foot of graves. Muslims hung a leaf over a doorway to show that a person had made the pilgrimage to Mecca.

Magical Connections

Element/s	Water
Astrological influence	Cancer, Libra, Pisces; Jupiter, Moon, Venus
Other associations	The afterlife
Powers and attributes	Balance/harmony, death/funeral practices, family and home, healing, loss/sorrow, love, luck, peace, protection, purification, security, sex/sexuality, success, support, wisdom
Available for purchase	Fresh leaves; cut, dried or powdered leaves; aloe gel

Spells and Rituals

For esbat rituals, sprinkle dried, powdered leaves around the base of a white candle on your altar to aid in drawing down the wisdom of Luna. To raise protective energy for your home, break open the end of a leaf and dab a little of the clear gel over each exterior doorway.

Amaranth

Foxtail Amaranth (*Amaranthus caudatus*); also known as hanging amaranth, love-lies-bleeding, tassel flower, velvet flower

Purple Amaranth (*A. blitum* syn. *A. lividius*); also known as Guernsey pigweed, livid amaranth

The foxtail amaranth is an upright plant that can grow eight feet tall. It has drooping, tassel-like clusters of red flowers and light green, lance-shaped leaves. Not as attractive as many of its cousins, purple amaranth grows to about three feet tall when erect, but it is often prostrate. It has clusters of small, white flowers that grow on spikes. The leaves are somewhat egg shaped with a notch at the end.

History and Lore

The Greeks and Romans cultivated purple amaranth and hung wreaths of it in temples to honor deities. As a symbol of immortality and the afterlife, it was also used to decorate tombs. According to Greek legend, the mourners at Achilles's funeral wore chaplets of amaranth. Into the late Middle Ages in Europe, a garland of amaranth was often used to honor kings and princes, which led to the belief that such a crown could bestow fame and fortune on anyone. Foxtail amaranth was an important food crop in Mexico and South America. Along with human sacrifice, the Aztec used amaranth in rituals to honor deities. The seeds were also left as offerings for wandering ancestral spirits and have been found in 2000-year-old tombs in Argentina.[10]

Magical Connections

Element/s	Fire
Astrological influence	Aquarius, Leo; Saturn, Sun, Venus
Deities	Artemis, Chalchiuhtlicue, Chicomecoatl, Demeter, Huitzilopochtli, Xiuhtecutli
Other associations	The afterlife, the otherworld
Powers and attributes	Balance/harmony, death/funeral practices, emotions, healing, loss/sorrow, prosperity/money, protection, relationships, release, spirit guides/spirits
Available for purchase	Flower essence; dried flowers; seeds

Spells and Rituals

Sprinkle a handful of seeds around a candle on your altar to enhance contact with spirits. When dealing with the loss of a loved one or healing from a romantic breakup, anoint your forehead with flower essence as you acknowledge the ending and prepare to move on.

Amaryllis

Barbados Amaryllis (*Hippeastrum equestre* syn. *H. puniceum*); also known as Barbados lily, house amaryllis, orange lily

Johnson's Amaryllis (*H.* x *johnsonii*); also known as red lily, St. Joseph's lily

The amaryllis is popular for its large lily-like flowers that grow on stalks one to two feet tall. The strap-like leaves are about eighteen inches long. The Barbados amaryllis flower is orange-red with a yellowish-white star in the center and two to four flowers per stem. Johnson's amaryllis has bright red flowers with a white star in the center and six flowers per stem.

Caution: These plants are toxic if ingested.

History and Lore

The genus name *Hippeastrum* means "knight's star" and refers to the shape of the fully opened flower, which resembles the brooch of certain orders of knighthood.[11] The common name comes from the confusion and scientific disagreement about the relationship of these plants to the true amaryllis, which is the belladonna lily (*Amaryllis belladonna*). Even though the belladonna lily is often noted as the source of poison for arrows that were used by the Indigenous people of the West Indies, it was most likely the Barbados ama-

---

10. Kiple, *The Cambridge World History of Food*, 76.

11. Gledhill, *The Names of Plants*, 200.

ryllis that supplied the poison because the bella-donna lily is native to Africa.

Amaryllis

Magical Connections

Element/s	Earth
Powers and attributes	Fertility, love, sex/sexuality
Available for purchase	Flower essence; bulb

Spells and Rituals

Although amaryllis does not have a history of magical use, the phallic stalk and flower bud are an excellent symbol of fertility for Ostara, Belt-ane, or sex magic any time of year. They take six to eight weeks to flower, so plant a bulb four to five weeks beforehand for the phallic bud stage.

Anemone

Poppy Anemone (*Anemone coronaria*); also known as crown anemone, Grecian windflower, Spanish marigold, windflower

Wood Anemone (*A. nemorosa*); also known as devil's bite, evening twilight, fairy wind-flower, lady's chemise, wood windflower

The poppy anemone flower is cup shaped with colors that range from red, pink, purplish blue to white; all have dark centers. The flower stem rises above a clump of parsley-like leaves with a small whorl of leaves just under the flower. The star-shaped wood anemone flowers are white inside with a ring of yellow at the center and tinged pink or purple on the outside. The petals have delicate veining patterns. The leaves are lobed and grow in a whorl around the stem.

Caution: Anemones are toxic if ingested; may irritate the skin.

History and Lore

While the Romans regarded the anemone as a lucky flower, the Egyptians associated it with ill-ness, possibly because of the irritant it contains. In Eastern Europe, it was regarded as a flower of the dead. Even though it was often considered bad luck, the Germans sometimes wore a wood anemone as an amulet for protection against sorcery. Although anemones were used to deter witches, they were sometimes known as *hexen-blumen* "witches' flowers" and said to be used by witches for magic. Both the Germans and Eng-lish believed that picking the flowers would bring on a thunderstorm and taking them into the house would attract lightning. According to English legend, the patterns on wood anemone flowers were painted by faeries.

Magical Connections

Element/s	Air, fire
Astrological influence	Aries, Scorpio; Mars
Deities	Adonis, Aphrodite, Brigid, Flora, Venus
Magical entities	Faeries
Powers and attributes	Balance/harmony, courage, creativity, determination, emotions, healing, inspiration, loss/sorrow, love, luck, protection, relationships, wishes
Available for purchase	Flower essence is made from both of these anemones; bulbs

Spells and Rituals

For luck, blow on the first wood anemone flower you see in the spring and make a wish. When dealing with emotional upheaval or any type of loss, gaze at a picture of wood anemones and then visualize a soft, white light surrounding you with healing energy.

Angelica

Garden Angelica (*Angelica archangelica*); also known as masterwort, Norwegian angelica, wild celery

Wild Angelica (*A. sylvestris*); also known as woodland angelica

Garden angelica has towering, purplish stalks and large, bright green leaves that are lobed and coarsely toothed. Tiny white or greenish flowers grow in globes or umbrella-shaped clusters. The seeds are ribbed on one side and pale, brownish yellow. Wild angelica is shorter than its garden cousin with smaller flower heads that are more numerous. Its leaves are not lobed.

History and Lore

Angelica has been used medicinally and magically for centuries. The Anglo-Saxons wore a piece of root on a string around the neck for protection from enchantment, spirits, and harm from witches. It was used to protect cattle from elf shot, which was believed to be an invisible magical weapon used by elves to cause disease. Angelica was sometimes placed on children to help keep them out of trouble. In southern England, the plants were hung at the entrance to Romani camps to prevent dark spirits from gaining access. Angelica was believed to be especially useful against dark magic. In North America, the Cherokee and Delaware used the plant to ward off evil spirits.

Magical Connections

Element/s	Fire
Astrological influence	Aries, Leo; Sun
Deities	Venus
Magical entities	Faeries
Other associations	Beltane, Imbolc, Samhain, Walpurgis

Powers and attributes	Balance/harmony, banish, bind, consecrate/bless, courage, divination, growth, healing, hexes, inspiration, knowledge, manifest, negativity, peace, protection, renewal, spirituality, strength, success
Available for purchase	Essential oil; cut, dried root

Spells and Rituals

Burn pieces of dried root to break a hex or to banish any type of negativity. Smoke from the burning root is also ideal for consecrating ritual space. Write a goal or something you seek on a piece of paper and burn it with some angelica root to bring it to fruition.

Anise

Anise (*Pimpinella anisum*, syn. *Anisum officinalis*); also known as aniseed, sweet cumin

Anise is an erect, branching plant that grows about two feet tall. Its lower leaves are round with toothed edges; the upper leaves are narrow and feathery. Yellowish-white, five-petaled flowers grow in umbrella-shaped clusters at the tops of the stems. The small, flat seed is oval and ridged. Anise has a sweet fragrance and a taste similar to licorice.

History and Lore

As a culinary herb and medicinal herb, the Greeks and Romans used anise in after-dinner cakes to aid digestion. Mixed with wine, anise was used as a cure for asp snakebites. Anise was also used as an aphrodisiac. Greek philosopher Theophrastus (c. 372–c. 287 BCE) noted that anise seeds kept by the bedside at night resulted in sweet dreams. The Romans followed suit and placed a sprig of leaves beside the pillow to ward off bad dreams. As a highly prized commodity, they also used anise seeds to pay taxes. In medieval England, anise was believed to avert the evil eye.

Magical Connections

Element/s	Air
Astrological influence	Gemini, Leo, Pisces; Jupiter, Mars, Mercury
Deities	Apollo, Hecate, Hermes, Mercury
Other associations	Walpurgis
Powers and attributes	Awareness, banish, consecrate/bless, divination, dream work, emotions, hexes, love, negativity, nightmares, prophecy, protection, psychic abilities, purification, sex/sexuality, spirit guides/spirits
Available for purchase	Essential oil; whole or ground seeds; anise seed tea

Spells and Rituals

Diffuse a little essential oil to heighten awareness when working with spirits. The scent is a powerful ally for divination and dream work. Make a wreath with a long stem or two, and then hang it wherever you need to clear away negative energy.

Apple

Orchard Apple (*Malus domestica* syn. *M. communis*); also known as silver bough

Apple trees have distinctively crooked trunks. The pointed, oval leaves range from yellowish green to dark green on top and lighter underneath. The five-petaled flowers are white to pinkish white and grow in clusters.

Caution: Ingesting the seeds produces a form of cyanide in the digestive tract.

History and Lore

Associated with the legendary Avalon, the apple was a supernatural fruit of knowledge, magic, and prophecy to the Celts. Throughout folklore, the apple has been regarded as especially magical to the English, Irish, Germans, Scandinavian, and Breton people. In one version of Merlin's story, he is not in a crystal cave but waits and watches from a magical apple tree.[12] In medieval France and Germany, the apple was a symbol of erotic love and used as an aphrodisiac. It is also a symbol of marriage and remains part of wedding customs in parts of Germany. Apples, apple peels, and seeds were used in love prophecy in England, France, Germany, and Belgium. Marking the end of Yuletide in England, the ritual of wassailing consisted of dipping branch tips into a bowl of spiced cider and asking the spirit of the tree and/or orchard to bless future harvests.

Magical Connections

Element/s	Air, water
Astrological influence	Aquarius, Cancer, Libra, Taurus; Jupiter, Venus
Deities	Aphrodite, Apollo, Athena, Badb, Balder, Ceres, Demeter, Diana, Dionysus, Eros, Freya, Hera, Idunn, Macha, Manannán Mac Lir, Minerva, Rhiannon, Venus, Zeus
Magical entities	Elves, faeries, pixies and colt pixies, unicorns
Ogham	Quert / Cert ⦀⦀⦀⦀⦀
Other associations	The afterlife, the otherworld, Beltane, Lughnasadh, Samhain, Yule
Powers and attributes	Abundance, ancestors, bind, consecrate/bless, creativity, death/funeral practices, divination, dream work, fertility, happiness, healing, love, luck, prosperity/money, relationships, renewal, security, sex/sexuality, spirit guides/spirits, strength, success, wisdom
Available for purchase	Fresh or dried fruit; apple juice or cider; flower essence

Spells and Rituals

Burn a small piece of apple wood to scent your home and attract abundance. Use the color of an apple to give a spell a magical boost. Use a red apple for love, passion, and desire; a yellow or golden apple for success; and a green apple for abundance and prosperity.

---

12. Markale, *Merlin Priest of Nature*, 118.

Apricot

Apricot (*Prunus armeniaca*); also known as Armenian plum, Chinese apricot

The apricot tree has toothed leaves that are rounded at the base and pointed at the tip. Its five-petaled flowers are white or pinkish. The fleshy fruit is pale orange-yellow with velvety skin. The oval stone/pit contains a kernel from which oil is extracted.

Caution: The kernels/seeds are toxic if ingested and can be fatal; the seeds and leaves of *Prunus* species produce cyanide in the digestive tract.

History and Lore

In northeastern China, apricots were believed to bestow the power of prophecy. In Greek mythology, the apricot is one of the contenders for being the mythical golden apples in Hera's garden. Called *melon* and *malum* by the Greeks and Romans, respectively, "apples" referred to almost any type of large, round fruit.[13] In Syria and Egypt, dried apricots were pressed and rolled into thin sheets called *moons* and *moon of the faithful*.[14] Because of the fruit's evocative cleft and texture of its skin, the apricot has been a symbol of female genitalia throughout the Middle East and Europe. In medieval France, *abricot* was a slang word for vulva.[15]

Apricot

Magical Connections

Element/s	Water
Astrological influence	Taurus; Neptune, Sun, Venus
Deities	Aphrodite, Venus
Powers and attributes	Balance/harmony, changes/transitions, creativity, defense, determination, divination, fertility, happiness, knowledge, love, peace, prophecy, purification, relationships, renewal, sex/sexuality
Available for purchase	Fresh or dried fruit; apricot kernel oil; juice; wine

13. De Cleene and Lejeune, *Compendium of Symbolic and Ritual Plants in Europe*, 91.

14. Denker, *The Carrot Purple and Other Curious Stories of the Food We Eat*, 13.

15. Staub, *75 Remarkable Fruits for Your Garden*, 21.

Spells and Rituals

Well known for its connection with love, apricot is instrumental for bringing lovers together; use the flowers in a handfasting ceremony or when celebrating anniversaries. Although its energy is gentle, apricot can be a catalyst for changes that usher in renewal for any type of fresh start.

Arnica

Mountain Arnica (*Arnica montana*); also known as leopard's bane, mountain daisy, sneezewort, wolf's bane, wolfsblume

Arnica has round, hairy stems and grows up to three feet tall. The bright green upper leaves are toothed and slightly hairy; the lower leaves have rounded ends. The daisy-like flowers are bright yellow-orange and are two to three inches wide.

Caution: All parts of the plant are toxic if ingested; prolonged external use can cause skin irritation; arnica should not be used on broken skin.

History and Lore

Despite its toxicity, arnica has had a long use in European folk medicine. In Germany it was gathered at Midsummer for magical purposes and hung on houses for protection against lightning, hail, and fire. Because the name for the plant was misunderstood or mistranslated as *wolfsleiche*, which means "wolf's corpse," many erroneous legends were perpetuated.[16] German mystic and herbalist Hildegard von Bingen (1098–1179) also related arnica to wolves by calling it *Wolfesgelegena*. The name *leopard's bane* is a case of misidentification because arnica looks similar to

....
16. Bäumler, *Heilpflanzenpraxis Heute*, 65.

great leopard's bane (*Doronicum pardalianches*). While arnica does not have the power to dispatch a great cat, Hildegard noted that it was an aphrodisiac and used in love magic. In nineteenth-century New England, a remedy for sprains called *toad ointment* included arnica and, yes, toads.

Magical Connections

Element/s	Water
Astrological influence	Saturn
Deities	Hecate
Powers and attributes	Confidence, divination, love, peace, protection, psychic abilities, purification, security, sex/sexuality, spirit guides/spirits
Available for purchase	Dried flowers; seeds; oil

Spells and Rituals

For love spells, include a candle that was prepared with arnica oil. Use the seeds for a protection spell by sprinkling them at the corners of your property as you visualize their energy creating a dome of safety. Raising energy inside your home with arnica helps quell restless spirits.

Asafoetida

Asafoetida, Asafetida (*Ferula assa-foetida*); also known as devil's dung, devil's incense, hing, stinking gum

Reaching up to nine feet tall, asafoetida has a thick central stem and numerous smaller branches. It has parsley-like leaves and pale, greenish yellow flowers that grow in pom-pom clusters. The reddish brown fruit is flat and oval. The large, fleshy root contains a thick, milky gum resin that hardens when dried. The gum resin has a pungent, sulfurous odor.

History and Lore

The Babylonians, Greeks, Romans, and people of India used asafoetida as a spice. The gum resin was such a highly prized condiment that the Persians called it *food of the gods*.[17] Despite the fact that it produces a rank scent when burned, asafoetida has been used as ritual incense. According to Persian and Hindu mythology, the plant sprang up where the semen of a fertility god had touched the earth. Both Paul Sédir—pseudonym of Yvon Le Loup (1871–1926) French mystic, professor, and author—and German scholar and occult writer Heinrich Cornelius Agrippa noted that medieval alchemists and magicians burned the resin to manifest spirits. In Germany and Colonial Pennsylvania, a lump of resin was worn around the neck as an amulet to keep evil spirits, witches, and ghosts away. Burying lumps of resin under the doorsill of a cowshed was said to prevent a witch from entering.

Magical Connections

Element/s	Fire
Astrological influence	Gemini; Mars, Pluto
Deities	Cernunnos, Kali, Pan
Powers and attributes	Banish, fertility, healing, hexes, negativity, protection, purification, spirit guides/spirits
Available for purchase	Pieces or powdered gum resin

17. Orr, *The New American Herbal*, 88.

Spells and Rituals

To counter spells against you, sprinkle a circle of asafoetida, stand in the middle, and visualize a veil of energy rising around you, swirling, and then moving out of sight taking all negativity with it. To encourage a spirit to leave, place a jar with asafoetida where you sense its presence.

Ash

Black Ash, Swamp Ash (*Fraxinus nigra*); also
   known as basket ash, brown ash
Common Ash, English Ash (*F. excelsior*); also
   known as European ash, Venus of the woods
White Ash, American Ash (*F. americana*); also
   known as cane ash

Ash leaves are composed of lance-shaped leaflets with serrated edges. The small, greenish flowers produce clusters of seeds that remain on the tree throughout the winter. Also called *keys* and *samara*, the flat seeds have a straight wing, unlike the curved maple seed wing.

History and Lore

The ash was regarded as a sacred tree by the Greeks, Romans, and Scandinavians. According to Norse mythology, the giant ash *Yggdrasil* connected the nine realms of the universe. The Germans also venerated ash and favored the wood for bows, arrows, and shields. In Ireland and parts of Britain, a place where ash, oak, and hawthorn grew was said to make the faery realm visible. While ash was also believed to be protected by faeries, in Somerset a pointed ash stick was used as an amulet against them and witches too. Residents of the Austrian Tyrol and southern Germany believed that witches lived or gathered under ash trees. In Wales and parts of England, ash leaves with an even number of leaflets were considered lucky—similar to four-leaf clovers—and used in love charms and for divination. Carrying a few ash seeds in a pocket was also regarded as lucky.

Magical Connections

Element/s	Air, earth, fire, water
Astrological influence	Capricorn, Libra, Taurus, Virgo; Mercury, Neptune, Sun, Uranus
Deities	Ares, Bel/Belenus, the Dagda, Freyr, Frigg, Holle, Macha, Manannán Mac Lir, Mars, Minerva, Nemesis, Neptune, Odin, Poseidon, Thor
Magical entities	Elves, faeries, Vila (Serbian mountain nymphs)
Ogham	Nuin ⵔⵔⵔⵔⵔ
Other associations	Asgard, home of the Norse gods; Ostara, Walpurgis, Beltane
Powers and attributes	Awareness, changes/transitions, communication, creativity, divination, dream work, fertility, focus, healing, hexes, inspiration, intuition, love, luck, negativity, prophecy, prosperity/money, protection, see faeries, strength, wisdom
Available for purchase	Flower essence; baskets made of ash twigs

Spells and Rituals

For dream work or journeying, keep a small ash twig nearby to enhance your awareness and aid in opening other realms. To increase the energy of a spell, carve ash's ogham on a candle, and then make a circle with ash keys around the base.

Aspen

European Aspen (*Populus tremula*); also known as common aspen, quaking aspen
Quaking Aspen (*P. tremuloides*); also known as American aspen, aspen poplar, mountain aspen, quaking poplar, shivering tree, trembling aspen

Aspen trees have rounded to nearly heart-shaped leaves that are dark, glossy green and flutter in the slightest breeze giving the impression that they are trembling. The long, green catkins produce tiny, cottony seeds. Aspens are a type of poplar.

History and Lore

According to *Cormac's Glossary* (an Irish/Latin dictionary compiled around 900 CE) a rod of aspen called a *fé* was used to measure a newly dug grave to ensure that its occupant would fit.[18] To keep a suspected witch in the grave, Russians laid an aspen rod on top of the soil or used it to pierce the deceased's heart. In medieval England, aspen was sometimes used as arrow shafts even though the wood is light and soft. Physician and botanist John Gerard noted that aspen was used medicinally; like willow, its bark contains the anti-inflammatory agent salicin. In northern England, aspen was also used for magical healing by pinning a lock of hair to the tree.

Magical Connections

Element/s	Air, water
Astrological influence	Aquarius, Capricorn, Libra; Mercury, Saturn, Venus

---

18. Chormaic, *Cormac's Glossary*, 75.

Deities	Apollo, Danu, Frigg, Gaia, Hecate, the Morrigan, Odin, Persephone, Tyr, Zeus
Ogham	Edad / Edhadh ‖‖‖ Ebad / Ebhadh also called Koad / Grove ✳
Other associations	The otherworld, Mabon
Powers and attributes	Ancestors, communication, courage, death / funeral practices, determination, divination, healing, hexes, knowledge, negativity, peace, prosperity / money, protection, renewal, success
Available for purchase	Flower essence; cut, dried leaves, pressed leaves

Spells and Rituals

To break a hex, crumble and burn a dried leaf as you visualize sending the energy back to its source. To attract prosperity, keep a pressed leaf in your checkbook. Place a twig on your altar to aid in connecting with your ancestors.

Aster

China Aster (*Callistephus Chinensis*); also known as annual aster, powder puff aster

Italian Aster (*Aster amellus*); also known as fall aster, European Michaelmas daisy, Italian starwort

New York Aster (*A. novi-belgii*); also known as fellowship aster

Aster

These plants have upright, branching stems and daisy-like flowers with yellow centers. The Italian aster has dark green, oval leaves and deep, violet-blue flowers. The New York aster has gray-green leaves and large, pinkish-lavender flowers. China aster has toothed, oval leaves and white to violet flowers that look like pom-pom balls.

History and Lore

According to Greek mythology, asters were formed from Virgo's tears that fell as stardust. The Greeks used aster as an antidote for snakebites and burned it to drive away serpents. Roman poet

Virgil (70–49 BCE) noted that Italian asters were used as wreaths and placed on temple altars to honor deities on festival days. In medieval France and Germany, aster leaves were burned to ward off evil spirits. The flowers were used as a love talisman and in Germany they served as a daisy-like love oracle.

Magical Connections

Element/s	Water
Astrological influence	Sagittarius, Virgo; Venus
Deities	Venus
Magical entities	Faeries
Other associations	Mabon
Powers and attributes	Clarity, consecrate/bless, creativity, dream work, focus, inspiration, intuition, love, negativity, protection, psychic abilities, truth
Available for purchase	Dried flowers; seeds; flower essence

Spells and Rituals

Place a dab of flower essence on your third eye chakra to bring clarity and focus to psychic work. When seeking the truth in a situation, hold a handful of flowers as you meditate. Scatter a handful of petals on your doorstep to invite blessings into your home.

Avens

Wood Avens (*Geum urbanum*); also known as bennet, blessed herb, clove root, colewort, gold star, herb bennet, rams' foot, wild rye

Resembling an old-fashioned rose, wood avens has small, yellow flowers with rounded petals. The bushy, green flower center develops into a seed cluster that is a round, spiky burr. The leaves are pointed, coarsely toothed, and heavily veined. The roots have a spicy fragrance that resembles cloves. Avens can grow twelve to eighteen inches tall.

History and Lore

Avens root was believed to have significant magical power in Europe during medieval times, especially for abundance and safety. It was used in medicinal remedies and worn as a charm around the neck to ward off disease. This amulet was also believed to provide protection from demons, dangerous beasts, and monsters. In addition to medicinal uses, the English and Germans used the roots to flavor ale. Thirteen-century architects used the flower in ornamental carvings. In England and America, sprigs were hung over doorways to ward off evil spirits and to prevent the devil from entering. Growing it near the house was said to be equally effective. In late nineteenth-century America, it was believed that two people holding avens leaves could communicate telepathically over a distance.

Magical Connections

Element/s	Fire
Astrological influence	Pisces; Jupiter
Powers and attributes	Abundance, hexes, love, protection, purification
Available for purchase	Flower essence; cut, dried roots; seeds

Spells and Rituals

Press and dry a few flowers to use as a love charm. Boil a handful of dried roots, and then use the liquid to purify ritual space. Use several spiky seed balls to counter a jinx or negative magic sent your way.

Avocado

Avocado (*Persea americana*); also known as alligator pear, butter pear, Spanish pear

The avocado is an evergreen tree with glossy, lance-shaped leaves. The small, pale green to yellowish-green flowers grow in loose clusters at the ends of branches. The green, pear-shaped fruit has a rough texture and turns brown when ripe. It produces one large seed.

History and Lore

Avocado was an important food crop in Mesoamerica and South America that was often given as a tribute to overlords. According to legend, the name *avocado* came about because Spanish explorers had trouble pronouncing the Aztec name for it. Usually hanging in pairs, the Aztecs unabashedly called the fruit *ahuacatl*, "testicle."[19] In addition to providing strength, eating avocados was believed to increase a man's virility and make him more vigorous in general. Not only was eating the fruit an aphrodisiac, but the aroma of a ripening avocado was regarded as powerfully erotic. When writing of his voyages, English buccaneer William Dampier (1651–1715) perpetuated the legacy by noting that the avocado incited lust.

Magical Connections

Element/s	Earth
Astrological influence	Libra; Venus
Powers and attributes	Abundance, fertility, healing, love, prosperity/money, sex/sexuality, strength, success
Available for purchase	Fresh fruit; oil

Spells and Rituals

Given its history, avocado is a perfect fruit to include in spells having to do with love, sex, and passion. Peel off the skin, and then slowly eat the fruit as you visualize making love with the person you want to attract. As part of a healing spell, prepare a green candle with avocado oil.

19. Small, *Top 100 Food Plants*, 75.

Bamboo

Black Bamboo (*Phyllostachys nigra*); also known as
running bamboo

Common Bamboo (*Bambusa vulgaris*); also
known as golden Hawaiian bamboo

Giant Bamboo (*Dendrocalamus giganteus*); also
known as dragon bamboo

Bamboo is a tall, woody grass with long, narrow
leaves. Common bamboo can reach sixty feet tall
with culms (stalks) about four inches in diameter.
Largest is the giant bamboo, which can grow up
to eighty feet tall with twelve-inch culms. Black
bamboo reaches about twenty-five feet with two-
inch culms that often arch over.

History and Lore

Despite its extensive mundane use, bamboo was
considered sacred in many Asian cultures. While
temple priests in China originally used bamboo
sticks for divination, similar sticks were used in
later centuries for fortune telling. Most often called
kau cim and *chi chi* sticks, they were also known
as the Oracle of Kuan Yin.[20] In China, pieces of
bamboo were burned to ward off evil spirits and
negative influences. The Tibetans and Indonesians
also believed in its power to ward off evil spirits. In
the West Indies, black bamboo was regarded as an
aphrodisiac and used in love potions. It also served
as a magic charm.

---

20. Lucas, *Bamboo*, 82.

Magical Connections

Element/s	Air
Astrological influence	Sun
Deities	Hina, Izanami, Kuan Yin, Thoth
Powers and attributes	Adaptability, balance/harmony, courage, divination, dream work, happiness, hexes, love, luck, negativity, peace, protection, strength, wisdom, wishes
Available for purchase	Fresh shoots; cut, dried leaves; a wide range of products are made from bamboo

Spells and Rituals

To invite luck and harmony into your home, hang a bamboo flute or stick above the front door. When making a wish, hold a bamboo stick in your hands as you visualize it coming true. To enhance your divination sessions, store your tools in a box made of bamboo.

Barberry and Oregon Grape

Barberry, Common Barberry (*Berberis vulgaris*); also known as berberry, dragon grape, European barberry, sow berry

Oregon Grape (*B. aquifolium* syn. *Mahonia aquifolium*); also known as blue barberry, holly-leaved barberry

Growing up to ten feet tall, barberry is a spreading shrub with drooping stems that form arches. It has oval leaves with finely serrated margins and thorns that grow in groups of three at the branch joints. Its yellow, cup-shaped flowers grow in drooping clusters and the elongated, oval fruit is red. Oregon grape reaches up to six feet tall and has shiny leaves with pointed, wavy margins that resemble holly. Its yellowish-green flowers are cup shaped and grow in clusters. The purple or blue-black berries resemble grapes.

Caution: All parts of these plants are mildly toxic if ingested.

History and Lore

Barberry was used medicinally by the ancient Greeks, Romans, and Egyptians. In medieval Europe, barberry was said to ward off evil and in England it was believed that cutting the shrub down could break a spell. A superstition persisted among English and French farmers that barberry could damage wheat and rye if it grew near the crops. During the Middle Ages in France, a law banned the planting of it near grain fields. In the Pacific Northwest of America, Oregon grape was used medicinally by the Karuk, Samish, and Sanpoil people.

Magical Connections

Element/s	Earth
Astrological influence	Scorpio, Taurus; Jupiter, Mars, Venus
Powers and attributes	Abundance, clarity, healing, negativity, prosperity/money, protection
Available for purchase	Flower essence; dried fruit; pieces of root; powdered root

Spells and Rituals

A dried root of either plant can be worn as a protective talisman or several placed around your property to dispel negative energy and attract abundance. When making important decisions, especially financial, hold several berries while meditating to bring clarity for your choices.

Basil

Basil

Holy Basil, Tulsi (*Ocimum sanctum* syn. *O. tenuiflorum*); also known as sacred basil, tulasi
Sweet Basil (*O. basilicum*); also known as common basil, French basil

Common basil has oval leaves with a distinctive downward curl; they are yellow-green to dark green and very fragrant. Growing in clusters, the flowers are white, pink, or purple. Holy basil has veined, oval leaves that are green or purple and somewhat toothed. Tight whorls of purplish flowers grow at the ends of stems.

History and Lore

Venerated as one of the most sacred herbs in India, holy basil was grown in temple gardens.

The roots were dried and made into beads to adorn statues of deities. In Hindu tradition, a sprig of basil was placed on the chest of a dying person and was included on the funeral pyre.[21] In Persia, sweet basil was often grown in cemeteries and in Egypt it was placed in tombs. It was also associated with death in Crete. The Greeks and Romans believed it caused madness. During the Middle Ages in Europe, sweet basil was hung in the home for protection from misfortune, disease, and witches. In Tudor England it was presented as a love token. Regarded as an aphrodisiac in Italy and Romania, sweet basil was used in love spells.

Magical Connections

Element/s	Fire
Astrological influence	Aries, Leo, Scorpio; Mars, Pluto, Venus
Deities	Krishna, Lakshmi, Venus, Vishnu
Other associations	The afterlife, Imbolc, Samhain
Powers and attributes	Courage, death/funeral practices, divination, focus, happiness, healing, hexes, love, luck, negativity, peace, prosperity/money, protection, psychic abilities, success, trust
Available for purchase	Cut, dried leaves and seeds; essential oil; flower essence from holy basil

Spells and Rituals

To aid mental and energetic concentration, inhale the scent of basil before a divination session or

---

21. De Cleene and Lejeune, *Compendium of Symbolic and Ritual Plants in Europe*, 54.

when working to develop psychic abilities, especially clairvoyance. Brew an infusion with the leaves, and then sprinkle a bit of it in each room to promote a peaceful household.

Bay

Bay, Laurel (*Laurus nobilis*); also known as bay laurel, Roman laurel, sweet bay, true laurel

Bay is an evergreen shrub with dark green, leathery leaves that are sharply pointed and commonly used in cooking. The small flowers are greenish yellow and grow in clusters. The oval berries are small and turn bluish black when ripe.

History and Lore

Bay was sacred to the Greeks and Romans who used it in purification rituals. To ward off illness, evil spirits, and ghosts, the Greeks hung leafy branches over doorways. They also wrote magic charms against illness on bay leaves. Regarded as a powerful aid for prophecy, the priestesses of Delphi reputedly wore bay leaves or held one in the mouth to aid visions. For divination, branches and leaves were burned and omens sought in the smoke and sparks. In England, bay was used as a charm to attract love as well as to bring a stray lover back. On Valentine's night a sprig under the pillow was believed to foster romantic dreams. Herbalist Nicholas Culpeper noted that bay could ward off the influence of witchcraft.

Magical Connections

Element/s	Air, fire
Astrological influence	Gemini, Leo, Pisces; Sun
Deities	Adonis, Apollo, Artemis, Asclepius, Bacchus, Balder, Ceres, Cernunnos, Daphne, Diana, Dionysus, Gaia, Helios, Hermes, Mars, Mercury, Ra, Vesta
Magical entities	Elves, faeries
Other associations	Litha, Saturnalia
Powers and attributes	Abundance, banish, creativity, defense, divination, dream work, healing, hexes, intuition, justice/legal matters, love, negativity, peace, prophecy, prosperity/money, protection, psychic abilities, purification, release, security, success, wisdom, wishes
Available for purchase	Dried leaves, whole or powdered; essential oil; hydrosol

Spells and Rituals

To keep negative energy from entering your home, sprinkle crumbled leaves around the exterior. To enhance defensive magic, burn a dried leaf. For support during divination, use essential oil to prepare a candle for your session. Bay leaves hung in the kitchen invite abundance.

Bean

Fava Bean, Broad Bean (*Vicia faba* syn. *Faba vulgaris*); also known as common garden bean, broad vetch, English bean, mojo beans
French Bean, Common Bean (*Phaseolus vulgaris*); also known as haricot, navy bean, white kidney bean

Fava bean leaves have three to seven oval leaflets; the common bean has three. Both have pea-like flowers that grow in clusters. Fava flowers are white to purplish; French bean flowers are white, pink, or purplish. Both plants have cylindrical, oblong seedpods. Fava beans are flattened and irregularly shaped; French beans are kidney shaped.

History and Lore
The ancient Greeks, Romans, and Egyptians believed that fava beans held the souls of the dead and that the dead sometimes waited in bean fields for reincarnation. Greeks and Romans offered beans to the deceased at funerals, in Egypt they were offered to deities. Regarded as especially appropriate food for mourning, the French and Italians served beans at funerals well into the nineteenth century. To the Romans, the scent of the flowers was so intoxicating that it could cause someone to behave foolishly, the English believed the scent was an aphrodisiac. The Dutch and Belgians regarded the scent as dangerous and believed that falling asleep in a bean field could bring on madness, nightmares, or even death. While Roman poet Ovid noted that witches put beans in their mouths to call up the spirits, in Wiltshire, England, spitting beans at a witch reputedly removed the power of her spells. In Italy, a bean was carried in the wallet for luck.

Magical Connections

Element/s	Air, Water
Astrological influence	Gemini, Libra, Virgo; Mercury, Saturn
Deities	Apollo, Carna, Ceres, Dionysus
Magical entities	Faeries

Powers and attributes	Courage, creativity, death/funeral practices, luck, negativity, psychic abilities, relationships, skills, spirituality, strength, truth, wisdom
Available for purchase	Flower essence; fresh or dried beans

Spells and Rituals
When seeking the truth in a situation, hold a couple of beans in your upturned palms as you meditate. At Samhain or whenever a loved one passes, place a few beans or picture of the flowers on your altar as an offering to wish them well on their journey.

Bedstraw
Fragrant Bedstraw (*Galium triflorum*); also known as sweet bedstraw
Lady's Bedstraw, Yellow Bedstraw (*G. verum*); also known as curdwort, fleawort, Frigg's grass, maid's hair

Bedstraw flowers have four pointed petals and are known for their pleasant fragrance that gets stronger as they dry. The leaves grow in whorls around branch nodes of the main stem and along the branches. Lady's bedstraw has delicate lance-shaped leaves and tiny, yellow flowers that grow in branching, elongated clusters. Fragrant bedstraw leaves are elliptical and wider at the leaf tip. Clusters of one to three greenish white flowers grow at the leaf axils.

History and Lore
Since the time of ancient Greece, lady's bedstraw was used medicinally and as a substitute for rennet in the cheese-making process. In medieval

Europe, both lady's and fragrant bedstraw were used as strewing herbs to freshen homes and, as their name suggests, stuff mattresses. According to legend, a nuptial bed of bedstraw would bless the couple with many children. In Scandinavia and Eastern Europe, a mattress of bedstraw was believed to ease childbirth and provide a calming effect for mother and infant. According to English herbalist John Gerard, the root added to wine or the fragrance of the flowers was enough to stir up lust. Lady's bedstraw was used in love potions and for marriage divination. In Romania, both Midsummer's Day and lady's bedstraw are called *Sânziene*. Faeries are called *Sânzienele* and are said to increase the healing potency of the herbs they bless on this day.[22]

Magical Connections

Element/s	Water
Astrological influence	Venus
Deities	Frigg
Magical entities	Faeries
Other associations	Midsummer's Eve and Day
Powers and attributes	Abundance, fertility, love, peace
Available for purchase	Flower essence; cut, dried flowers; seeds

Spells and Rituals

To invite abundance and peace into your home, hang small bundles of bedstraw in areas of the house used by all members of the family. Throw a handful into the Midsummer's bonfire or place it on your altar to honor the fae.

Bee Balm

Scarlet Bee Balm, Scarlet Bergamot (*Monarda didyma*); also known as bergamot, bergamot mint, gold Melissa, Indian nettle, monarda, Oswego tea

Purple Bee Balm, Wild Bergamot (*M. fistulosa*); also known as horsemint

Growing three to four feet tall, bee balm has square stems and lance-shaped leaves. The rounded flower head has a distinctive array of tubular florets. Scarlet bee balm flowers are red and the plant's scent is similar to the bergamot orange (*Citrus bergamia*). Purple bee balm flowers range from lavender to purple; its scent is spicy and minty.

History and Lore

Both scarlet and purple bee balm were used medicinally by the Cherokee, Chippewa, Meskwaki, Ojibwe, Teton Dakota (Lakota), and other tribes throughout North America. The leaves of purple bee balm were used for purification in sweat lodges. The Oswego made a beverage with scarlet bee balm that became popular with English settlers after the incident in Boston Harbor ended their supply of tea. While the flowers were used in posies, in England they were said to be unlucky to keep in the house because it was believed they would cause sickness or even death. However, carrying a leaf in the pocket or purse was said to bring financial prosperity.

22. Mallows and Brummel, *Romania*, 102.

Magical Connections

Element/s	Air
Astrological influence	Gemini, Virgo; Mercury, Moon, Venus
Powers and attributes	Clarity, focus, peace, prosperity/money, purification, success
Available for purchase	Flower essence; essential oil; cut, dried leaves; dried flowers; seeds

Spells and Rituals

For a purification bath, sprinkle a handful or two of dried flowers and/or a few drops of essential oil in the tub. When you need to bring clarity and focus for decision-making or other endeavor, place a dab of essential oil on your third eye chakra.

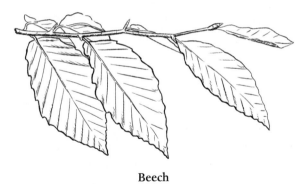

Beech

Beech

American Beech (*Fagus grandifolia*); also known as white beech

European Beech (*F. sylvatica*); also known as common beech

The European beech has pointed, rounded leaves; the American tree's leaves are more oval with a gentle taper. After turning brown, the leaves stay on the tree through winter. Flower clusters form into spiky balls, and then develop into nuts encased in spiny, woody husks. The edible nut has a triangular shape.

History and Lore

To the ancient Greeks and Romans, beech was an auspicious tree. Highly regarded by the Romans, the wood was used to make ritual libation bowls and jugs for presenting offerings to deities. According to legend, Bacchus drank from a beech goblet. Not only did the sacred grove of Zeus at Dodona contain oak and beech, according to Greek legend the oracle of the grove dwelled in a great beech tree. Similarly, Norse people regarded the tree as sacred and believed that it served as an oracle of Thor. Sticks of beech wood were frequently used for runic writing. The Swiss, Germans, and Belgians believed it was a tree of weather and harvest predictions. Like hazelnuts, beechnuts were believed to impart wisdom and used as amulets in England.

Magical Connections

Element/s	Fire, water
Astrological influence	Gemini, Sagittarius, Virgo; Jupiter, Saturn
Deities	Apollo, Athena, Bacchus, Cerridwen, Diana, Dionysus, Freya, Frigg, Holle, Loki, Odin, Thor, Zeus
Ogham	Emancholl / Amhancholl also called Mór ▦ Ifin ᛥ Uilleann / Uilleand ᚖ
Other associations	Litha, Midsummer's Eve, Samhain

Powers and attributes	Abundance, ancestors, creativity, fertility, healing, knowledge, luck, manifest, prophecy, prosperity/money, protection, psychic abilities, renewal, transformation, wisdom, wishes
Available for purchase	Beechnut oil and flower essence are made from the European beech

Spells and Rituals

To honor your ancestors, place beech leaves on your Samhain altar. Use a cluster of beechnuts as an offering when seeking abundance. To foster second sight, eat a few beechnuts as you work on your psychic abilities. To promote stability, place a twig in a prominent location in your home.

Belladonna Lily

Belladonna Lily (*Amaryllis belladonna* syn. *Callicore rosea*); also known as Cape belladonna, Jersey lily, magic lily, naked lady, true amaryllis

This plant produces flat, strap-like leaves during late autumn that die back in the spring. In late summer, bare flower stems emerge and produce two to twelve lily-like flowers. The flowers are white, pink, or slightly purple.

Caution: Belladonna lily is toxic if ingested.

History and Lore

Although there has been confusion and scientific disagreement about the belladonna lily's relationship with plants commonly called *amaryllis*, it is now the only species in the *Amaryllis* genus. While this plant is often noted as the source of poison for arrows used by the Indigenous people of the West Indies, it was most likely the Barbados amaryllis (*Hippeastrum equestre*), which is native to that region. However, the belladonna lily was widely used for arrow poison in the Congo of Africa. While the plant is not related to deadly nightshade (*Atropa belladonna*), its name may be the reason it was considered unlucky in England to take into the house. Sources vary as to the genus being named for a nymph in Greek mythology or a beautiful shepherdess in Roman poet Virgil's pastoral poems.

Magical Connections

Element/s	Water
Astrological influence	Moon
Powers and attributes	Changes/transitions, love, purification, renewal
Available for purchase	Flower essence; bulbs

Spells and Rituals

The belladonna lily is a flower of renewal especially as it rises from the ground on its own unaccompanied by leaves. Place a vase of flowers or a picture of them on your altar to aid in transitions or to initiate a new phase in your life. Use dried flowers in a sachet as a love charm.

Benzoin

Benzoin, Sumatra Benzoin (*Styrax benzoin*); also known as Benjamin tree, gum Benjamin, styrax

Siam Benzoin (*S. tonkinensis*); also known as gum benzoin, Laos benzoin, styrax

These shrubby trees have pointed, oval leaves that are heavily veined. The white, five-petaled flowers hang in drooping clusters. The gum or resin is obtained by piercing the bark. These trees differ in their locale of origin and the chemical compounds in their resin.

Caution: The resin from these trees should not be confused with the chemical color additive called *benzoin*.

History and Lore

Benzoin resin was burned as incense in the Middle and Far East to fumigate and perfume temples, elevate spiritual awareness, and provide a link with the spirit world. Believed to have magical properties, it was burned in Malaysia to curse spirits. The ancient Egyptians used benzoin for incense and perfumery, and in early medieval times, Arabian and Russian physicians used it medicinally. The Arabs also used it for ritual and religious purposes. In Central and Eastern Europe, benzoin was believed to have the power to banish evil spirits and ward off demons.

Magical Connections

Element/s	Air, water
Astrological influence	Capricorn; Mars, Mercury, Saturn, Sun, Venus
Deities	Aphrodite, Mut, Venus
Powers and attributes	Awareness, banish, changes/transitions, focus, hexes, love, protection, purification, spirit guides/spirits, spirituality
Available for purchase	Essential oil; powdered gum; resin oil; resin pieces

Spells and Rituals

Use benzoin for focus and psychic protection during astral work and when contacting the spirit realm. It also aids in reaching higher levels of consciousness. A powerful ally for magic, it can increase the rate of success for spells. Use it as incense to banish anything unwanted.

Bergamot
Bergamot Orange (*Citrus bergamia* syn. *C. aurantium* var. *bergamia*)

The bergamot orange is a small tree with glossy leaves that are tapered at the bottom and pointed at the tip. The white flowers are star-shaped and grow in clusters. The fragrant, pale yellow or greenish yellow fruit is slightly flattened, pear shaped, and bumpy.

History and Lore

The bergamot orange is believed to be a hybrid of the lemon (*C. limon*) and the bitter orange (*C. aurantium*). The common name comes from the Italian *bergamotto*, which was derived from the Turkish word *beg-armudi*, "prince's pear."[23] For a time, the fruit was referred to as bergamot pear. Used for perfumery in France since the seventeenth century, bergamot provides the distinctive aroma of Earl Grey tea.

Magical Connections

Element/s	Air
Astrological influence	Mercury, Sun
Powers and attributes	Confidence, luck, prosperity/money, protection, spirit guides/spirits
Available for purchase	Essential oil; fresh fruit; seeds

23. Small, *North American Cornucopia*, 105.

Spells and Rituals

Diffuse a little essential oil to aid in contacting and communicating with spirits. Use the scent on your body for psychic protection when dark powers seem to cast a shadow. Include the fruit in spells to attract luck and build wealth.

Betony

Wood Betony (*Betonica officinalis* syn. *Stachys officinalis*); also known as bishop's wort, common hedgenettle, devil's plaything, purple betony, woundwort

Betony has dark green, oval leaves with ruffled edges. The two-lipped, rosy-lavender flowers grow in tight clusters on spikes eighteen to twenty-four inches tall. The flower spikes are unusual with a section of bare stem below the main flower cluster followed by a smaller, lower cluster of flowers.

History and Lore

As a medicinal herb, betony was valued by the ancient Romans and Celts. In addition to healing, the Anglo-Saxons used it for protection against "frightful goblins."[24] By day, betony was worn around the neck as a charm against evil; at night it warded off bad dreams. In medieval England, betony was grown in the garden or rubbed on windowsills and doorframes to protect a home from witchcraft and sorcery. It was grown in cemeteries to keep souls in their place and prevent them from turning into wandering ghosts. Applied to the forehead, betony was said to rid a person "possessed of devils."[25] A belief persisted that a stag would search for betony if a hunter had wounded it.

24. Watts, *Elsevier's Dictionary of Plant Lore*, 31.
25. Folkard, *Plant Lore, Legends and Lyrics*, 251.

Magical Connections

Element/s	Fire
Astrological influence	Aries, Cancer; Jupiter, Mercury
Deities	Amun, the Dagda, Zeus
Other associations	Midsummer's Eve
Powers and attributes	Banish, challenges/obstacles, clarity, dream work, healing, loss/sorrow, love, negativity, nightmares, protection, purification, spirit guides/spirits
Available for purchase	Flower essence; cut, dried leaves and stems; seeds

Spells and Rituals

Dab a little flower essence on your forehead to ward off bad dreams. To enhance dream work, observe the optical pattern of a flower spike as you twirl it between your thumb and index finger, and then place it on your bedside table overnight.

Bilberry

Bilberry (*Vaccinium myrtillus*); also known as blaeberry, crowberry, European blueberry, heath berry, whortleberry

Bilberry is a low-growing shrub that is easily mistaken for American highbush blueberry (*V. corymbosum*). Bilberries are usually darker blue, almost purple when ripe, and smaller than blueberries. Growing only fifteen inches tall, bilberry's small, bright green leaves are egg shaped with serrated edges. The drooping, globular flowers range from greenish yellow to slightly reddish to rosy with a greenish tinge.

Bilberry

it was customary to pick bilberries and flowers and place them as an offering on the cairn (burial mound) at the summit of Knockfierna. According to Celtic lore, Knockfierna had been the home of Donn Fírinne, one of the Tuatha Dé Danann and a faery king. As with other types of berries, places where bilberries grew were regarded as liminal spaces where faeries were often encountered.

Magical Connections

Element/s	Fire, water
Astrological influence	Pisces, Sagittarius; Jupiter
Deities	Lugh
Magical entities	Faeries
Other associations	Lughnasadh
Powers and attributes	Dream work, family and home, healing, hexes, love, luck, manifest, prophecy, prosperity/money, protection, success
Available for purchase	Cut, dried leaves; dried berries; leaf tea; jam

History and Lore

The Anglo-Saxons called the plant *heorotberge*, "hart's berry" because it seemed to be a favorite of deer.[26] In the north and west of Britain, moorland tea was brewed from bilberry leaves, heather tops, and several other herbs. According to Irish lore, bilberry was an indicator for the autumn harvest: an abundance of berries meant the harvest would be good, not so many meant the opposite. As part of the Lughnasadh festivities in County Limerick,

Spells and Rituals

To aid in making a dream come true, write a keyword or two on a picture of bilberry fruit. Hold the picture between your hands as you visualize a positive outcome. Boost the energy of your Lughnasadh ritual by placing a few bilberries or a teaspoon of bilberry jam on your altar.

Bindweed

Field Bindweed (*Convolvulus arvensis*); also known as creeping Jenny, devil's guts, hellweed,

....
26. Hall, *Concise Anglo-Saxon Dictionary*, 154.

small bindweed, thunder flower, wild morning glory

Hedge Bindweed (*Calystegia sepium* syn. *Convolvulus sepium*); also known as bearbind, devil's garters, greater bindweed, hedge bell, old man's nightcap, wild morning glory

Close cousin to the morning glory (*Ipomoea purpurea*) and High John (*I. purge*), bindweeds have twining stems that climb anything nearby or they sprawl across the ground. The leaves vary from oblong to arrow shaped. The flowers are funnel shaped and open for only one day; occasionally they open in bright moonlight. Field bindweed flowers are usually white, but sometimes with pink patterns. Hedge bindweed flowers are white to pale pink and sometimes pale pink with white stripes. Its stems can be reddish.

Caution: All parts of these plants, especially the roots and seeds, are toxic if ingested.

History and Lore

Bindweed's negative reputation comes from its tendency to strangle neighboring plants and deplete the surrounding soil of nutrients. In England, witches reputedly cast spells on people by wrapping a bindweed stem nine times around a poppet representing the chosen individual. Spell work with bindweed was said to be especially effective three days before a full moon. Children in Scotland were warned not to pick the flowers of field bindweed because it would bring on a thunderstorm. Young women were also warned to not pick them because it would cause the death of a boyfriend.

Magical Connections

Element/s	Air, water
Astrological influence	Aquarius, Gemini; Mercury, Saturn
Powers and attributes	Bind, changes / transitions, strength
Available for purchase	Flower essence; cut, dried stems and leaves

Spells and Rituals

Because bindweed stems spiral widdershins (counterclockwise) around things, use it when working widdershins. Let it grow around an outdoor altar but keep it in check so it doesn't interfere with your garden. Bindweed is ideal for knot magic and handfasting ceremonies.

Birch

American White Birch, Paper Birch (*Betula papyrifera*); also known as canoe birch, silver birch

European White Birch, Silver Birch (*B. pendula* syn. *B. alba*); also known as common birch, lady of the woods

Both of these trees have slender, often multiple, trunks with peeling white or pale bark. The leaves are triangular or heart shaped with serrated edges. In early spring, birches produce drooping, yellowish-brown male catkins and upright, greenish female catkins.

History and Lore

Highly regarded in Central and Northern Europe, the birch tree was associated with birth as well as rebirth after death. In Scandinavia and Germanic areas of Europe, the tree was believed to hold the spirits of ancestors. Birch was used in purification and initiation rites of Siberian shamans. On Walpurgis in Sweden, branches were placed in front of homes to deter witches. In England, crossed twigs were hung over doorways for protection against enchantment. Despite using birch branches to thwart witches, during the Middle Ages in France witches were said to use them for weather magic and to fly. Called *grave brooms* in Ireland, bushy branches were used to cover the deceased enroute to the cemetery.[27] Dense tangles of birch branches were also known as fairy's brooms. In Scotland, a spirit known as the Ghillie Dhu is said to live in birch woods.

Magical Connections

Element/s	Water
Astrological influence	Capricorn, Sagittarius; Jupiter, Moon, Sun, Venus
Deities	Angus Mac Og, Cerridwen, the Dagda, Freya, Frigg, Lugh, Thor
Magical entities	Faeries, Ghillie Dhu, Lieschi
Ogham	Beith / Beth T
Other associations	Imbolc, Ostara, Walpurgis, Beltane, Litha, Midsummer's Eve, Yule
Powers and attributes	Ancestors, banish, changes/transitions, clarity, death/funeral practices, divination, fertility, focus, growth, healing, hope, inspiration, intuition, love, negativity, protection, purification, renewal, wisdom
Available for purchase	Essential oil is made from the silver birch; flower essence is also made from the silver birch

27. Fry, *Burial in Medieval Ireland 900-1500*, 126.

Spells and Rituals
As part of a love spell, place several pieces of bark in a sachet to use as a charm. Because the bark of the American birch has a smooth inner surface and often peels off the tree in big pieces, it can be used to write a spell or charm.

Bistort
American Bistort (*Bistorta bistortoides* syn. *Persicaria bistortoides*, *Polygonum bistortoides*); also known as western bistort, snakeweed
Common Bistort, Meadow Bistort (*B. officinals* syn. *Persicaria bistorta*, *Polygonum bistorta*); also known as adderwort, dragonwort, snakeroot, snakeweed

Common bistort forms large clumps of lance-shaped leaves. Resembling a bottlebrush, dense clusters of tiny white or pink flowers grow on spikes two to three feet tall. American bistort is very similar with white flowers. Both plants flower on and off from late spring to early autumn.
Caution: Abortifacient.

History and Lore
Through the centuries in Western Europe and the British Isles, bistort was used medicinally for a wide range of ailments; however, for certain cures in northern England it had to be picked during a full moon in order to be effective. In sixteenth-century France, bistort was believed to aid conception and was worn as an amulet. Despite its depiction amongst plants symbolizing fertility in one of the unicorn tapestries and its subsequent association with fertility, bistort is an abortifacient. For a protective travel charm in Ireland, a few flowers were picked just before going

on a journey and taken along in the pocket. In Scotland, the leaves were tied into a cloth to undo a spell. Burning the root and wafting the smoke around was said to rid a house of ghosts.

Magical Connections

Element/s	Earth
Astrological influence	Aquarius, Virgo; Saturn
Other associations	Ostara
Powers and attributes	Bind, challenges/obstacles, changes/transitions, death/funeral practices, divination, knowledge, negativity, psychic abilities, purification, release, support
Available for purchase	Flower essence; cut, dried root; seeds

Spells and Rituals

To purify an area for ritual, sprinkle dried flowers and leaves as you cast a circle. Afterwards, sweep up the pieces and burn them. Strew dried pieces of root in front of your home or place it under the doormat to repel negative energy.

Bittersweet

American Bittersweet (*Celastrus scandens*); also
 known as false bittersweet
European Bittersweet (*Solanum dulcamara*); also
 known as amara dulcis, bitter nightshade,
 bittersweet nightshade, woody nightshade
Bittersweet is a woody vine. The American plant has pointed, yellowish-green leaves and clusters of greenish white flowers. In the autumn, yellow-orange petals surround the red berries. The dark green leaves of the European bittersweet have a large, arrow-shaped center lobe. Its star-shaped flower has a prominent, yellow cone at the center and purple, backward-arching petals. The berries turn from green to yellow, then orange, and finally red.

Caution: Berries and leaves of the European bittersweet are toxic if ingested and sometimes fatal. The berries of American bittersweet are toxic if ingested. Handle all parts of these plants with care.

History and Lore

Throughout the British Isles, bittersweet was believed to have the power to remove a witch's spell from a person or animal. In Ireland, garlands of bittersweet were hung around the necks of livestock to keep them safe from spells and harm. Garlands were sometimes worn by people to cure ailments. In England, holly and bittersweet sprigs were attached to a horse's collar to protect it from witchcraft. Dried berries strung together and worn as a necklace was believed to protect children from evil. Regarded as starvation food, the Menominee, Ojibwe, and Potawatomi ate American bittersweet for sustenance during the winter or whenever necessary.

Magical Connections

Element/s	Air
Astrological influence	Aquarius; Mercury, Pluto, Saturn
Deities	Hecate
Other associations	Samhain

Powers and attributes	Banish, death/funeral practices, emotions, family and home, healing, hexes, manifest, peace, protection, release, renewal, truth
Available for purchase	Flower essence is made from European bittersweet

Spells and Rituals

To release toxic emotions, hold three berries between your palms and send your feelings into them; afterwards, bury them outside. On Samhain, place a sprig or two of dried berries on your altar to represent the bitter, sweet sorrow in remembering loved ones who have passed.

Black Cohosh

Black Cohosh (*Actaea racemosa* syn. *Cimicifuga racemosa*); also known as black snakeroot, bugbane, bugwort, fairy candles, rattle weed, squawroot

Standing six to eight feet tall, black cohosh has branching flower stalks topped with long plumes of white flowers, usually three flower heads to a stalk. The flowers develop into seedpods. Its dark green leaves are oblong and irregularly shaped with toothed edges. The gnarled root is dark brown to black.

Caution: Avoid during pregnancy and while breastfeeding.

Black Cohosh

History and Lore

Used medicinally by the Iroquois, Delaware, Algonquin, and Cherokee for a range of ailments, black cohosh is still a popular herb for healing and wellness. The name *cohosh* comes from an Algonquian word meaning "rough," which refers to the texture of the root.[28] In the American magical tradition of hoodoo, black cohosh is used for defense against tricks or conjured problems. At dusk in the woods, a patch of black cohosh

28. Dobelis, *Magic and Medicine of Plants*, 105.

may appear slightly spooky because the stalks of white flowers can look like a gathering of little ghosts. On a breezy day when the plant is in seed it sounds faintly like a rattlesnake.

Magical Connections

Element/s	Fire
Astrological influence	Scorpio; Mars, Pluto
Powers and attributes	Challenges/obstacles, courage, defense, fertility, hexes, love, luck, protection, strength
Available for purchase	Flower essence; cut, dried root; powdered root; seeds

Spells and Rituals

To bolster courage, carry a piece of dried root in a small pouch as an amulet. Black cohosh gives you the pluck to follow your own path no matter what those around you may say. Use the seeds to cast a circle for defensive magic and to remove any type of spell directed at you.

Blackberry

American Blackberry (*Rubus villosus*); also known as bramble, shrub blackberry

European Blackberry (*R. fruticosus*); also known as black heg, bramble, bramble thorn, brambleberry, wild blackberry

Blackberry bushes are sprawling shrubs with woody, arching stems called *canes*. Blackberry leaves consist of three to five coarsely toothed leaflets. Its white, five-petaled flowers grow in clusters at the ends of the stems. Each flower produces a berry, which changes from green to red to black as it ripens. The berry is fully ripe when it is dull black, not glossy.

History and Lore

In the British Isles, the arching canes of blackberry bushes were believed to have magical properties for healing and protection against evil. In the folk medicine of England, Ireland, and the Balkans, crawling under arching canes or gaps in a thicket was believed to cure various ailments. Reputedly in England, planting a blackberry bush on a grave or placing a few canes across it would keep the deceased in place. To protect a barn on the island of Guernsey, a large wreath made with blackberry canes was hung in the rafters to scratch any witch that flew inside. In Brittany, eating blackberries was often avoided because faeries didn't like humans using their magical fruit.

Magical Connections

Element/s	Water
Astrological influence	Aries, Scorpio, Taurus; Moon, Venus
Deities	Brigid, the Dagda, Danu, Freya, Manannán Mac Lir
Magical entities	Elves, faeries, pooka
Ogham	Muin ┼
Other associations	Imbolc, Beltane, Lughnasadh, Mabon, September full moon

Powers and attributes	Abundance, awareness, balance/harmony, challenges/obstacles, communication, death/funeral practices, fertility, growth, happiness, healing, intuition, knowledge, luck, prosperity/money, protection, purification, spirit guides/spirits
Available for purchase	Blackberries; blackberry juice; blackberry wine; dried leaves; blackberry leaf tea

Spells and Rituals

To stimulate protective energy, make a wreath with several prickly canes and hang it above your altar or on your front door. Eat a handful of blackberries before magic work to reach deeper levels of consciousness. Use berry juice to prepare candles when communicating with spirits.

Blackthorn

Blackthorn (*Prunus spinosa*); also known as black haw, blackthorn plum, fairy tree, sloe plum, wild plum, wishing thorn

Blackthorn is a shrubby tree with spiny branches. Its white, five-petaled flowers bloom in early spring before the leaves appear and stand in stark contrast to the dark thorns and bark. Called *sloes*, the blue-black fruit is small and round and ripens in the autumn after the first frost.

Caution: The seeds and leaves of *Prunus* species produce cyanide in the digestive tract.

History and Lore

The Greeks believed that blackthorn provided protection against witches and sorcery. According to Germanic folklore, it sprouted from the blood of a Teutonic warrior. In Eastern Europe, a piece of blackthorn was sewn into clothing for protection. In Ireland, blackthorn was the preferred wood for a walking stick because it could be used to ward off any type of evil, including ghosts. According to legend, faeries known as the *Lunantishee* (Luna sídhe, moon faeries) were guardians of blackthorns. In England, witches reputedly liked this tree, carved spells into its wood, and used the thorns for black magic. However, in Europe a blackthorn branch was used to break a hex and after partially burning it, it was hung in the house for protection. In the Balkans it was believed that a blackthorn stake should be used to impale a vampire.

Magical Connections

Element/s	Earth, fire
Astrological influence	Aries, Scorpio; Mars, Saturn
Deities	Banba, Bel/Belenus, Bertha, Brigid, the Dagda, Holle, Loki, Macha, Ran
Magical entities	Faeries, Lunantishee
Ogham	Straif ᚏ
Other associations	Imbolc, Walpurgis, Beltane, Samhain
Powers and attributes	Authority/leadership, banish, challenges/obstacles, defense, hexes, loyalty/fidelity, negativity, protection, purification, strength, truth
Available for purchase	Flower essence; walking stick; dried sloes are often marketed as blackthorn berries; pieces of bark are often marketed as sloe tree bark

Spells and Rituals

As part of a banishing a spell, crumble and burn a few leaves or draw the ogham on a piece of parchment paper to use instead. To strengthen a spell, include a couple of sloes. Use the thorns for building defensive energy or breaking a spell that was cast your way.

Bloodroot

Bloodroot (*Sanguinaria canadensis*); also known as bloodwort, red puccoon, red root

In the early spring, bloodroot sends up a single leaf from which a flower emerges on a separate stem. The leaf unfurls after the flower blooms. Pale green underneath, the palm-shaped leaves have five to nine lobes and are yellowish green. The flower has a yellow center and eight to sixteen white petals. It opens in the sun and closes at night.

Caution: The plant is toxic if ingested; do not use on the body. It has a threatened or endangered status in some areas; check vendor sources when purchasing any product.

History and Lore

The genus name for this plant was derived from the Latin *sanguis*, meaning "blood," which refers to the reddish-brown or red-orange sap that oozes from the rhizome when cut.[29] More than a sweet-looking little woodland plant, bloodroot was used by the Algonquin, Cherokee, Delaware, Iroquois, and Micmac as a medicinal herb and as a dye for cloth and baskets. The Ojibwe and Powhatan used it for war paint and the Ponca and Algonquin as a love charm.

Magical Connections

Element/s	Fire, Water
Astrological influence	Mars, Moon
Powers and attributes	Abundance, courage, divination, family and home, love, negativity, protection, purification, release, strength
Available for purchase	Flower essence; cut, dried root; powdered root

Spells and Rituals

For esbat and women's rituals, place three flowers on your altar or prepare a candle with the flower essence. Place a few pieces of dried root in a sachet and carry it with you to attract love. If you find bloodroot in the wild, work with its energy and leave an offering.

Bluebell

Common Bluebell, English Bluebell (*Hyacinthoides non-scripta*); also known as fairy bells, harebell, wild hyacinth, wood bells

Virginia Bluebell (*Mertensia virginica*); also known as jacinth and Virginia cowslip

The fragrant common bluebell has pendulous flowers that dangle from slender, arching stems. The tubular flowers are deep, violet-blue. The large, oval leaves of the Virginia bluebell are light to grayish green and somewhat floppy. Growing on nodding stems, the flowers start off pink and gradually turn a vivid shade of light blue as they mature.

Caution: The bulbs can be toxic if ingested.

---

29. Martin, *Wildflower Folklore*, 91.

History and Lore

Throughout the British Isles, the bluebell was reputedly one of the most powerful faery plants and where it grew was said to mark a place of faery magic. According to legend, the flowers were rung like bells to call the fae together, but if a human heard the sound, it meant someone would soon die. Nevertheless, these flowers were believed to aid in seeing faeries. Closely associated with enchantment, some legends indicate that bluebell flowers were used for dark faery magic. In Somerset, going into the woods to pick the flowers risked being pixie-led. In Devonshire it was regarded as unlucky to take the flowers into the house and in Scotland it was considered unlucky to pick them.

Magical Connections

Element/s	Earth, water
Astrological influence	Cancer, Libra; Moon, Saturn
Deities	Apollo, Cronus, Luna, Saturn, Selene
Magical entities	Faeries, pixies
Other associations	Beltane
Powers and attributes	Challenges/obstacles, love, loyalty/fidelity, manifest, nightmares, renewal, see faeries, truth
Available for purchase	Flower essence

Spells and Rituals

To overcome an obstacle, write what you want on a picture of bluebells, and then burn it in your cauldron. Wearing bluebell flowers is said to prompt a person to speak from the heart. Use this judiciously as truth carelessly spoken can seem hurtful.

Bodhi

Bodhi Tree, Sacred Fig (*Ficus religiosa*); also known as banyan fig, bo tree, pipal

Like most figs, the Bodhi is a spreading tree that is usually as wide as it is tall. Unlike other figs, Bodhi leaves are rounded or slightly heart shaped with a long, pointed tip. The small, rounded fruit grow singly or in pairs and turn purple when ripe.

History and Lore

According to Indian mythology, the Bodhi is a cosmic tree at the center of the world. It was generally regarded as protective and a branch placed in front of the door before leaving home was believed to ensure that a person returned safely. Because other fig trees had a phallic association in Europe, Catholic missionaries in India regarded the Bodhi as the devil's tree. Siddhartha Gautama (c. 563/566–486 BCE) found a suitable place for meditation under a fig tree in Bodh Gaya, a small town in northern India, where he achieved enlightenment and became the Buddha. Over time, Bodhi trees were regarded as a symbol of the Buddha's presence. The tree is also sacred in Hinduism and Jainism. Carved bodhi seeds are strung together to make mala beads for meditation.

Magical Connections

Element/s	Air, water
Astrological influence	Jupiter, Venus
Deities	Buddha, Vishnu

Powers and attributes	Ancestors, awareness, balance/harmony, knowledge, peace, psychic abilities, spirituality, transformation, truth, wisdom
Available for purchase	Flower essence; mala beads; seeds

Spells and Rituals

Prepare a candle with the flower essence to heighten your awareness when developing your psychic abilities. Hang a string of Bodhi mala beads as high in your house as you can to foster a sense of peace and harmony.

Bog Myrtle

Bog Myrtle, Sweet Gale (*Myrica gale*); also known as bayberry, candleberry, gale, golden willow, moor myrtle

Bog myrtle is a bushy shrub that reaches a height of only two to four feet. Its foliage is dark green to grayish green and sweetly scented. The oval leaves have broad tips that taper at the base; they grow in a spiral around the branches. Upright yellow-orange (male) and red (female) flowers develop into clusters of pointed, egg-shaped seeds.

Caution: Abortifacient.

History and Lore

Bog myrtle was picked for luck in Scotland, but in Ireland the plant was sometimes considered unlucky, especially if you stepped on it. In many areas of Scotland, bog myrtle was used to keep mischievous faeries away. However, in the formerly Pictish areas, the faeries reputedly wore badges of bog myrtle sprigs. In Yorkshire, the leaves were used as a substitute for hops in a brew called *gale beer*. In England, Wales, and France bog myrtle was added to beer for flavor.

Bog Myrtle

Magical Connections

Element/s	Water
Astrological influence	Venus
Magical entities	Faeries
Powers and attributes	Adaptability, defense, determination, dream work, focus, inspiration, luck, peace, prosperity/money, protection, purification, relationships

| Available for purchase | Flower essence; essential oil; cut, dried leaves; seeds Although bog myrtle is also known as bayberry, most bayberry candles are made from the wax of myrtles (M. pensylvanica and M. cerifera). |

Spells and Rituals

Diffuse a little essential oil in your work area when you need to focus your attention. For support in dream work, place a few seeds in a sachet to hang on your bedpost. Burn a pinch of dried leaves for protection spells to raise defensive energy and to purify your space.

Borage

Borage (*Borago officinalis*); also known as bee
    bread, bugloss, burrage, star flower

The hallmark of this garden favorite is its intensely blue, star-shaped flowers that grow in drooping clusters. The gray-green leaves are pointed and have prominent veins. The hollow, upright stems and leaves are covered with tiny hairs. Growing one to three feet tall, the sprawling, drooping branches give the plant a round appearance.

History and Lore

From ancient Greece to modern Wales, borage has been known as the herb of gladness. In addition to a range of medicinal purposes, the Greeks used borage to flavor wine. Roman naturalist and historian Pliny the Elder called the plant *Euphrosinum* because it was said to bring happiness.[30] Medieval herbalists in Europe used borage for a range of ailments. Borage tea was the preferred

beverage in England before a jousting tournament to bolster the strength and bravery of competitors. Crusaders reputedly added it to wine. The flowers were also added to wine in Lebanon where they were believed to be an aphrodisiac.

Magical Connections

Element/s	Air, Fire
Astrological influence	Aquarius, Leo; Jupiter
Powers and attributes	Awareness, changes/transitions, courage, divination, emotions, happiness, inspiration, loss/sorrow, peace, protection, psychic abilities, security, strength
Available for purchase	Borage seed oil; flower essence; cut, dried leaves; seeds

Spells and Rituals

Before any type of psychic work, prepare a candle with the seed oil to aid in expanding awareness. Call on the power of borage to help initiate changes in your life by floating several flowers in a bowl of water while you visualize what you seek.

Boxwood

Common Box, English Boxwood (*Buxus sempervirens*); also known as American boxwood, box, box tree

Growing as wide as it does tall, boxwood has dense, evergreen foliage that is often used for topiary. It has small, oval leaves and rounded clusters of yellowish flowers. The seed capsules have three horn-like protrusions and turn brown when mature.

---

30. Bonar, *Herbs*, 50.

History and Lore

The name of this tree comes from its popular use by the ancient Greeks and Romans for making boxes. Associated with death in the north of England, mourners carried sprigs in funeral processions. Sprigs were also placed in graves. During the Middle Ages in Europe, the wood was used as an amulet against witchcraft. Box was also used in potions to remove hexes. In Germany, a branch was placed on the roof of a new house for protection against natural and supernatural calamities as well as to invite happiness to the occupants. In Brittany, boxwood was placed on baby cradles to keep faeries from substituting a changeling. At the beginning of spring in other areas of Europe, a box branch replaced the holly sprig of winter for protection against a range of goblins and malicious faeries. The Welsh used sprigs to dress wells on New Year's Eve.

Magical Connections

Element/s	Earth
Astrological influence	Mars
Deities	Aphrodite, Apollo, Circe, Cybele, Hades, Pluto, Venus
Magical entities	Faeries
Other associations	Ostara, Beltane, Samhain, New Year's Eve

Powers and attributes	Ancestors, death/funeral practices, defense, divination, fertility, happiness, hexes, love, luck, prophecy, prosperity/money, protection, renewal
Available for purchase	Seeds; candle rings and door wreaths made from leafy branches; the wood is widely used for figurines

Spells and Rituals

For help in removing a hex, use a box branch to "comb" your aura with downward strokes as you visualize all influence and negativity being swept away. To strengthen the energy of your divination tools, store them with a piece of boxwood.

Bracken

Bracken Fern, Western Bracken Fern (*Pteridium aquilinum* syn. *Pteris aquilina*); also known as brake fern, female fern, trows' caird

Reaching about four feet tall, bracken fern has triangular fronds that rise directly from its deep roots. The fronds commonly tilt backwards to an almost horizontal position. The spore cases appear in rows near the margins of the frond leaflets. In the early spring, bracken ferns emerge with multiple fiddleheads on their stalks.

Caution: Bracken fiddleheads should not be eaten.

History and Lore

In England and Ireland, it was believed that fern seeds (spores) gathered on Midsummer's Eve could make a person invisible. This is because the seeds were believed to be invisible except when falling from the plant. Invisibility also applied at Samhain in Ireland and carrying the seeds were believed to bring luck. In Celtic myth, a fern was proof that a person had visited the faery realm. In England it was believed that hanging a fern root in the house would protect it from lightning. In Scotland, witches were said to avoid the plant. The roots were also used in love charms and for divination. According to German lore, the seeds were said to shine like gold on Midsummer's Night.

Magical Connections

Element/s	Air, earth
Astrological influence	Gemini; Mercury
Magical entities	Faeries
Other associations	Midsummer's Eve, Mabon, Samhain, Walpurgis
Powers and attributes	Abundance, divination, dream work, focus, hexes, love, luck, negativity, prophecy, protection, psychic abilities, release, trust
Available for purchase	Dried fronds

Spells and Rituals

Closely aligned with the elements air and earth, ferns can lighten and lift energy as well as keep you grounded. To clear negative energy and banish unwanted spirits, burn a small piece of dried frond. Also use a frond in protection spells against hexes. Kiss a fern leaf to seal an oath.

Broom

Common Broom, Scotch Broom (*Cytisus scoparius*); also known as besom, broom straw, golden rod, ling

Broom is a hardy, multi-stemmed, evergreen shrub that can reach eight feet tall and wide. The yellow and orange flowers are fragrant. The lower leaves consist of three leaflets, while the upper leaves are single. When mature, the silky, gray-green seedpods turn black and snap open with a popping sound to eject the small, black seeds. Broom is easily confused with gorse (*Ulex europaeus*).

Caution: All parts of the plant are toxic and can be fatal if ingested; do not burn, as the smoke is also toxic.

History and Lore

On the night before a wedding, it was customary in northern Scotland for the bride to keep a branch of broom in her room to ensure fertility. Branches of green broom were used at Romani weddings for the couple to jump over. According to English legend, witches favored broom for their besoms and used it for wind magic. Although branches were used as a household broom, sweeping with flowering branches was said to bring bad luck. The Welsh used broom as a sleep charm. In Ireland, a solitary bush was said to be a gathering place of faeries, who reputedly used broom in spells. In Italy, broom was burned to keep witches away.

Magical Connections

Element/s	Air
Astrological influence	Aries; Mars, Sun
Magical entities	Faeries
Other associations	Samhain
Powers and attributes	Banish, challenges/obstacles, communication, creativity, death/funeral practices, determination, fertility, focus, healing, intuition, negativity, protection, purification, release, strength
Available for purchase	Flower essence; dried bunches of flowers are marketed as broom bloom

Spells and Rituals

To remove anything unwanted from your life, cast a circle, and then use several branches like a broom as you visualize sweeping it away. For support during difficult times, place a few dried flowers where you will see them often and be reminded of your inner strength.

Bryony

Black Bryony (*Tamus communis* syn. *Dioscorea communis*); also known as black bindweed, devil's cherry, lady's seal, mandrake

Red Bryony (*Bryonia dioica* syn. *B. cretica* subsp. *dioica*); also known as mandrake, red-berried white bryony, white bryony

White Bryony (*B. alba*); also known as devil's turnip, hedge grape, snake berry, womandrake

These plants are climbing vines that have long, divided taproots. White and red bryony have light colored roots, coiling tendrils, leaves with five lobes, and yellow-green, five-petaled flowers. White bryony has black berries; red bryony's berries are bright red. Black bryony has black roots, heart-shaped leaves, and five-petaled, yellow or greenish yellow flowers. Its berries are red.

Caution: All of these plants are toxic and can be fatal if ingested; may irritate the skin.

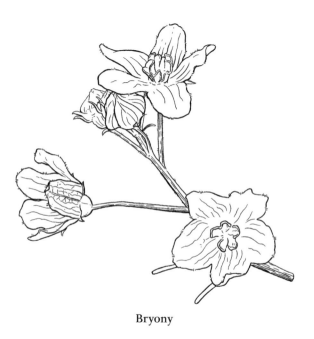

Bryony

History and Lore

Also spelled *briony*, white and red bryony were associated with witchcraft and black magic in England and Europe. As a result, these plants were considered unlucky to take indoors. Witches could reputedly grow the plants without dirt and use them in spells to harm enemies. Because the roots of all three species resemble mandrake, medieval herbalists used them as a substitute to fetch higher prices. In addition, the roots were often doctored to look more authentic. In England, a necklace of beads made with polished white bryony root was used to ward off the evil eye. In Cambridgeshire, a dried root of white bryony was kept with money in an old stocking under the mattress to increase savings.

Magical Connections

Element/s	Fire
Astrological influence	Capricorn, Leo; Mars, Mercury
Powers and attributes	Abundance, fertility, luck, prosperity/money, protection
Available for purchase	Cut, dried root; seeds

Spells and Rituals

To help increase wealth, place a small pouch of dried root with your financial papers. A piece of polished root can be worn as a talisman for luck. For protection, bury a root under your front steps or scatter pieces around your property.

Buckthorn

Alder Buckthorn (*Frangula alnus* syn. *Rhamnus frangula*); also known as berry-bearing alder, breaking buckthorn, black dogwood, false buckthorn

Common Buckthorn (*R. cathartica*); also known as European buckthorn, hartsthorn, purging buckthorn, ramsthorn, waythorn

Common buckthorn's oval leaves are toothed and curl inward. Its yellow-green flowers have four petals. Alder buckthorn leaves are oval and heavily veined. Its greenish white flowers have five triangular petals. Common buckthorn has thorns; alder buckthorn does not. Both trees have black, berry-like fruit.

Caution: The berries and bark are toxic if ingested.

History and Lore

In ancient Athens, it was believed that during an event known as the commemoration of the dead, the deceased would walk the earth. Buckthorn branches were placed at entrances to bar them from entering homes and temples so they would return to their graves. Centuries later in Europe, branches were hung as a talisman in windows and beside doors to repel witches, vampires, demons, and sorcerer's spells. A necklace of buckthorn bark was believed to prevent a person from being possessed. In Germany, it was considered prudent to carry a buckthorn walking stick to strike a witch or demon should the occasion arise. The Mongols used alder buckthorn wood to carve images of their deities.

Magical Connections

Element/s	Fire, water
Astrological influence	Libra; Mars, Saturn
Other associations	Samhain
Powers and attributes	Banish, defense, hexes, justice/legal matters, negativity, protection, wishes
Available for purchase	Pieces of bark; powdered bark

Spells and Rituals

Place twigs in the shape of a pentagram on your altar for protection when engaging in magic. Cast away a handful of powdered bark as part of a banishing ritual or when counteracting a hex. When making a wish, toss three berries into a fire as you visualize it coming true.

Burdock

Greater Burdock (*Arctium lappa*); also known as
    Billy buttons, bur, burweed, cockle buttons
Lesser Burdock, Common Burdock (*A. minus*);
    also known as burweed, button-bur

Growing up to eight feet tall, greater burdock has purplish stems and elongated, heart-shaped leaves with wavy edges. Lesser burdock is smaller, only reaching forty inches tall. Its leaves are lance shaped and often toothed. Both plants have clusters of thistle-like, purple flowers. The round, spiky seedpods called *burrs* turn brown and remain on the plant until they get attached to passing animals or people.

Caution: Burdock is somewhat similar in appearance to common cocklebur (*Xanthium strumarium*), which is toxic.

History and Lore

In England's country village tradition, the Burry Man (who may have represented the Green Man) wore a costume covered with burrs and walked around town to symbolically catch any evil in the area.[31] Burrs were also used in a form of divination to tell if someone had a sweetheart. The leaves were used in love potions to stimulate lust. In Cornwall, pixies were said to use burrs in pranks to tangle the manes of colts. In Albania, burdock leaves were used in exorcism rites if a person was believed to be under the influence of an evil forest spirit.

Magical Connections

Element/s	Water
Astrological influence	Libra, Sagittarius, Taurus; Venus
Magical entities	Faeries, pixies
Powers and attributes	Balance/harmony, banish, defense, divination, healing, love, negativity, peace, protection, purification, release
Available for purchase	Cut, dried leaves; cut, dried root; dried root powder

Spells and Rituals

To remove something that you no longer want in your life, wear work gloves, and collect a few burrs. Meditate on what you want to remove as you roll the burrs between your hands to break them up. Take the pieces outside and toss them to the wind.

Buttercup

Creeping Buttercup (*Ranunculus repens*); also
    known as butter flower, crow flower, elf
    goblets
Meadow Buttercup, Tall Buttercup (*R. acris*); also
    known as butter flower, crazies, fairy basins,
    tall buttercup

Reaching less than a foot tall, creeping buttercup's leaves are deeply lobed and heavily veined. The meadow buttercup grows up to three feet tall. Its leaves are similar but have more of a feathery appearance. Both plants have shiny, cup-shaped

---

31. Vickery, *Vickery's Folk Flora*, 110.

flowers with five rounded, slightly overlapping petals. They are, of course, the color of butter.

Caution: These plants should never be ingested; although the sap can cause skin irritation and blistering, the toxins they contain evaporate as the plant dries out.

History and Lore

In the English Midlands, the odor of the meadow buttercup was believed to cause madness. In other areas of the country, the flowers were worn in a pouch around the neck to cure lunacy. Even though cows avoid buttercups because of the acrid taste, there was a long-held belief that butter was yellow because cows ate them. On Midsummer's Eve, garlands containing buttercups were placed on cows to bless the milk. In Ireland, pulling up buttercups in someone else's field reputedly made their cows give less milk. Although some legends note that faeries drink dew from small buttercups, the flowers were traditionally placed on doorsteps and windowsills on May Eve to protect against their mischief.

Magical Connections

Element/s	Water
Astrological influence	Aries; Mars
Magical entities	Faeries
Powers and attributes	Abundance, adaptability, divination, dream work, emotions, happiness, love, manifest, prosperity/money, spirituality, success, truth, wisdom
Available for purchase	Flower essence; dried, pressed flowers

Spells and Rituals

To deepen spiritual commitment and open your heart and mind for ancient wisdom, place a bowl of buttercup flowers on your altar while meditating. When fresh flowers are not available, gaze at a picture of them.

Butterwort

Common Butterwort (*Pinguicula vulgaris*); also known as bog violet, Kerry violet, marsh violet, mothan, Valentine's flower

Butterwort is a carnivorous plant with a star-shaped base of fleshy, yellow-green leaves that roll inward at the edges. A sticky substance on the leaves traps insects. Several stems, four to eight inches tall, rise from the center of the leaves. Each curved, leafless stem has one drooping, purple flower. The flower has a three-lobed upper lip and a slightly longer two-lobed lower lip.

History and Lore

Butterwort was regarded as magically powerful throughout the Scottish Highlands. It was considered an all-purpose protector that worked against witches, faeries, hunger, drowning, and lack of love. It was used with gorse and juniper as a charm against witchcraft. Along with pearlwort (*Sagina procumbens*), butterwort is one of two plants thought to be the mystical herb of Scotland called *mothan*, which was said to provide protection from witches, faeries, and fire. In parts of England, it was believed that if a cow ate butterwort, it would be safe from elf shot, an invisible magical weapon used by elves to cause disease. In Ireland, it was believed that the cow was protected from faery spells and if a person ate cheese made from the milk, he or she would also have protection. According to Norwegian lore, placing butterwort under the bed pillow and thinking about someone before going to sleep was said to bring dreams about that person.

Magical Connections

Element/s	Water
Magical entities	Faeries
Powers and attributes	Adaptability, awareness, challenges/obstacles, determination, dream work, family and home, healing, hexes, love, luck, negativity, prophecy, protection, support
Available for purchase	Seeds

Spells and Rituals

When facing problems, hold a picture of butterwort while meditating on how to meet the challenges. To clear away negative energy, tie butterwort flowers together like a daisy chain to make a ring and hang it in your home wherever it is needed.

Cabbage

Green Cabbage (*Brassica oleracea* var. *capitata*);
  also known as colewort
Red Cabbage (*B. oleracea* var. *capitata f. rubra*);
  also known as purple cabbage
White Cabbage (*B. oleracea* var. *capitata* f. *alba*);
  also known as Dutch cabbage

Known as head cabbage, the succulent leaves of cabbage are covered with a waxy coating and layered into a densely packed sphere. After the head matures, a stalk emerges from the center and grows two to four feet tall. Clusters of yellow, four-petaled flowers sprout at the top of the stalk and develop into seedpods.

History and Lore

The Greek and Roman belief that cabbages were harmful to grapevines gave rise to the notion that cabbage was a remedy for intoxication. Cabbage was eaten more for medicinal purposes rather than food. The Anglo-Saxons also used it mainly for remedies. However, by medieval times in the British Isles and Europe cabbage had become a dietary staple. A symbol of fecundity, it was customary in France to serve newlyweds cabbage soup after the wedding night. In Ireland and Scotland, cabbage was used for love divination at Samhain. To the Pennsylvania Germans, finding two shoots from one root was considered lucky, however, two heads on one plant was an omen of death. According to English lore, witches and faeries were said to use cabbage stalks to fly.

Magical Connections

Element/s	Water
Astrological influence	Cancer, Scorpio (green); Jupiter (red), Moon
Magical entities	Faeries
Powers and attributes	Fertility, luck
Available for purchase	Fresh heads; seeds

Spells and Rituals

As part of a fertility spell, write the importance of mother/fatherhood on a piece of paper, and then wrap it in a couple of cabbage leaves. Place it on your altar until the leaves have dried out, and then burn the bundle. For a good luck amulet, carry an uneven number of seeds in a small pouch.

Cacao

Cacao (*Theobroma cacao*), also known as cocoa, chocolate

Cacao is a small tree with large, glossy leaves. Its yellow flowers grow in clusters on the trunk and main branches. The oblong, brown or reddish pods contain seeds (also referred to as beans) and a sweet, buttery pulp. Chocolate is produced from the beans, which also contain fat from which cocoa butter and white chocolate are made. The spelling *cacao* refers to the raw beans and *cocoa*, a product made from the beans.

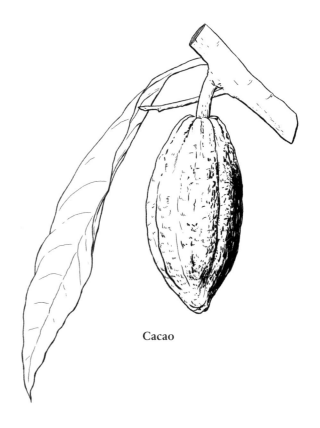

Cacao

History and Lore

Most of us would agree with Swedish botanist Carl Linnaeus who gave cacao the genus name *Theobroma*, which translates as "food of the gods."[32] The Maya, Aztec, and Olmec regarded it as a sacred plant. According to Mayan and Aztec mythology, cacao was a gift from the feathered serpent god. The seeds were used as offerings to deities, often sprinkled with blood from priests who ceremonially cut themselves. Cacao was used in spicy, bitter ceremonial beverages taken by men and priests, but considered too intoxicating for women and children. It was given to victims prior

32. Foster and Johnson, *National Geographic Desk Reference to Nature's Medicine*, 106.

to sacrifice. The Maya used it as a stimulant before events, either chewing the leaves or brewing them as a tea. Throughout Mesoamerica cacao beans were used as currency. Introduced into Europe in the sixteenth century, the Aztec belief that cacao was an aphrodisiac lingered. In present-day Mexican Day of the Dead celebrations, cacao is offered to loved ones on home altars and at gravesites.

Magical Connections

Element/s	Fire, water
Astrological influence	Mars, Moon (white chocolate), Venus
Deities	Kukulcan, Quetzalcoatl
Powers and attributes	Happiness, love, prosperity/money, sex/sexuality
Available for purchase	Chocolate; cacao beans; cacao nibs; cocoa butter

Spells and Rituals

Follow age-old tradition and include chocolate in love spells or sensually eat some with your lover. Wrap a cacao bean in the highest denomination bank note you have to attract prosperity and wealth. Place a round piece of white chocolate on your esbat altar.

Cactus

Desert Prickly Pear (*Opuntia phaeacantha*); also
    known as devil cactus, nopal, paddle cactus,
    tulip prickly pear
Melon Cactus (*Melocactus matanzanus*); also
    known as Turk's cap cactus
Saguaro (*Carnegiea gigantea*)

The prickly pear has flat, oblong, blue-green pads speckled with tufts of spines. They produce yellow, red, or purple flowers and plump, cylindrical fruit that is red or purple. The melon cactus is one of the smallest cacti; rounded and ribbed with tufts of large spines. Older plants develop a red or white structure on the top where pink or red flowers sprout. The iconic saguaro can reach fifty feet tall and live for two hundred years. Tree-like and columnar, its large arms bend upward. It develops white flowers and red fruit at the tops of the arms.

History and Lore

In Aztec legend, a prickly pear was one of the signs given by their gods for finding a place to settle. When cacti were imported into Europe in the sixteenth century, they were viewed with suspicion. One belief was that eating the fruit would turn a person's urine red. In Hungary, it was considered bad luck to have any type of cactus in the house. However, in England, watering a house cactus on Christmas morning was said to bring good luck. In Brazil, if a melon cactus thrown onto a roof took root, it would bring good luck and ward off witches, as well as bad storms.

Magical Connections

Element/s	Water
Astrological influence	Mars
Powers and attributes	Abundance, determination, healing, luck, protection
Available for purchase	Flower essence; cactus juice

Spells and Rituals

For protection spells, include a few of the needle-like spines. Using tweezers, carefully remove a few from different areas of the plant. The spines can be buried at the corners of your house or wrapped in a small sachet that can be hung inside.

Camellia

Chinese Camellia (*Camellia sinensis* syn. *Thea sinensis*); also known as tea plant
Japanese Camellia (*C. japonica*); also known as common camellia, rose of winter

The Chinese camellia has glossy, oval leaves with serrated edges. Its small flowers are white or pinkish with yellow centers. The round fruit bears two to five triangular seeds. Black, white, green, and oolong tea are made from the leaves of this plant. The Japanese camellia has rose-like flowers up to five inches wide. They are commonly white, pink, or red with yellow at the center.

History and Lore

Camellia was a traditional offering to the gods when making special requests during Chinese New Year ceremonies. According to Japanese legend, samurai planted red camellias where their ancestors were buried because the flowers drop intact instead of shedding petals and would decorate the graves. Other legends note that samurai did not like camellias because the fallen flowers resembled severed heads. By the nineteenth century, Victorian enthusiasm for tea and beautiful flowers rehabilitated the symbolism of the camellia and it became an emblem of romance and lovers' devotion.

Magical Connections

Element/s	Fire, water
Astrological influence	Scorpio; Moon, Venus
Deities	Kuan Yin, Parvati
Powers and attributes	Abundance, awareness, confidence, courage, death/funeral practices, love, manifest, prosperity/money, spirituality, strength, trust, truth, wishes
Available for purchase	Flower essence; green tea seed oil; camellia oil/tsubaki oil; black, white, green, and oolong tea; seeds

Spells and Rituals

Drink a cup of tea before an important event to bolster your confidence. To spark romance, use a red camellia in love spells. Place a white flower or a picture of one on your altar during esbat rituals to aid in drawing down the energy of the moon.

Camphor

Camphor Tree (*Cinnamomum camphora* syn. *Laurus camphora*); also known as camphorwood, laurel camphor, true camphor, white camphor

Cousin to the cinnamon tree, camphor has oval, pointed leaves that are bronze to reddish before turning dark green. Groups of flower stems bear clusters of small, yellowish, or greenish white flowers. The round berries are dark blue to black.

Caution: The fruit, leaves, and roots are toxic if ingested.

History and Lore

Camphor was used by the ancient Egyptians in the embalming process and by medieval Arabs for perfumery and as a culinary flavoring. During the Middle Ages throughout Europe, it was used medicinally and as a fumigant against the plague.

Wearing a piece of camphor served as an amulet to keep evil spirits away. It was used in Hindu religious rituals and burned as an expression of devotion. In Malaysia when anything was taken from a camphor tree, it was customary to leave a food offering for the spirit that looked after the tree. The Japanese believed that the spirit of the camphor tree had power over the elements.

Magical Connections

Element/s	Air, fire, earth, water
Astrological influence	Cancer, Pisces; Moon
Deities	Krishna, Kuan Yin, Shiva, Vishnu
Powers and attributes	Banish, divination, focus, negativity, past-life work, purification
Available for purchase	Essential oil; flower essence; incense; seeds

Spells and Rituals

Camphor has strong cleansing and banishing properties that are instrumental in clearing away negative energy. It aids in keeping the mind focused in the present as well as awakening past-life memories. Use it to support moon and element magic.

Campion

Red Campion (*Silene dioica*); also known as bachelor's buttons, devil's flower, fairies' pinks, ragged Robin, Robin Hood

White Campion (*S. latifolia* syn. *S. alba*); also known as thunder flower, thunderbolts

The long, tubular campion flower has five, deeply notched petals. Red campion flowers are a distinctive pinkish-red color and its leaves are oval with pointed tips. White campion has lance-shaped leaves and white flowers. The two plants often hybridize and produce flowers in various shades of pink. The seed capsules are barrel-shaped.

History and Lore

Because of its association with faeries, snakes, and thunder, picking campion flowers was said to result in bad luck in the British Isles. Not only could picking the white flowers bring thunder, but also lightning and even death by lightning. Red campion was regarded as a faery plant on the Isle of Man and picking it was said to bring their wrath. Elsewhere, picking the flowers was believed to cause the death of one's mother. In Wales, picking either color flower was said to bring an attack of snakes. Also regarded as a faery plant in England, red campion was associated with the good-natured, but often mischievous faery Robin Goodfellow.

Magical Connections

Element/s	Earth
Astrological influence	Mars
Deities	Cernunnos, Pan
Magical entities	Faeries
Powers and attributes	Challenges/obstacles, clarity, courage, creativity, determination, focus, healing, inspiration, knowledge, love, manifest, protection, support, wisdom
Available for purchase	Flower essence; seedpods; seeds

Spells and Rituals

For personal support in getting through a difficult situation, carry a small pouch of seeds. To aid in bringing your plans to fruition, write a couple of keywords on a picture of red or white campion as you visualize your dreams coming true.

Caraway

Caraway

Common Caraway (*Carum carvi*); also known as meridian fennel, Persian cumin, Roman cumin

Looking like a small version of Queen Anne's lace, caraway has feathery, light green leaves that are smaller on the upper stalks. It has small umbrella-like clusters of white flowers with five petals that are notched at the tip. The slightly crescent-shaped seeds have ridges.

History and Lore

During the Middle Ages throughout Europe, caraway seeds were valued for medicinal purposes, but in northern countries they became more widely used for baking. Caraway was *the* seed in seed cake and in parts of England it was customarily served at funerals. Caraway seeds were believed to protect against witchcraft, hexes, and sorcery and were sometimes sprinkled in coffins to protect the dead. In German-speaking areas of Europe, the seeds were sometimes baked into bread to "drive away dwarfs and demons."[33] Regarded as an aphrodisiac, caraway was used in love potions to attract a lover or for help in retaining a relationship. There was also a wide-spread belief that anything containing caraway could not be taken, which resulted in seeds being placed in valuable objects and fed to poultry to keep them safe.

Magical Connections

Element/s	Air, fire
Astrological influence	Gemini, Virgo; Mars, Mercury
Deities	Artemis, Hermes, Mercury
Powers and attributes	Changes/transitions, confidence, death/funeral practices, love, loyalty/fidelity, protection, relationships, secrets, sex/sexuality
Available for purchase	Essential oil; seeds

....

33. Németh, *Caraway*, 186.

Spells and Rituals

Caraway is effective when there is a problem in keeping or retaining things, including magical tools as well as secrets. To help renew a relationship, serve seed cake, especially when celebrating anniversaries. Use the essential oil to initiate changes in your life.

Cardamom

Green Cardamom (*Elettaria cardamomum*); also known as queen of spices, true cardamom

Cardamom is a reed-like plant that can grow up to fifteen feet tall. It has long, lance-shaped leaves and yellowish flowers marked with a striking mauve veining pattern. The flowers mature into pods containing reddish brown oblong seeds. The highly aromatic seeds have a warm, slightly pungent flavor.

History and Lore

Cultivated since ancient times in China and India, cardamom was hailed as the queen of spices. In India, it was used as incense and as an aphrodisiac. In the Middle East, cardamom was used in religious rites. After encountering it during their forays in the Mediterranean, ninth-century Vikings took cardamom to Scandinavia where it became a popular ingredient in mulled wine, pastries, and bread. Regarded as a witches' plant in medieval Europe, cardamom was the ingredient called *the fire of Venus* in love potions.[34] In West Africa, if witchcraft was suspected in a death, a relative chewed a few seeds, and then placed them in the mouth of the deceased. This was a signal to the person's spirit that they could seek vengeance.

....
34. Rhind, *Fragrance and Wellbeing*, 207.

Magical Connections

Element/s	Earth, fire, water
Astrological influence	Aries, Cancer, Pisces, Taurus; Venus
Deities	Aphrodite, Circe, Hecate, Krishna, Medea, Rama
Powers and attributes	Balance/harmony, changes/transitions, clarity, confidence, courage, creativity, divination, focus, healing, love, relationships, sex/sexuality, strength
Available for purchase	Essential oil; whole pods; whole seeds; ground seeds

Spells and Rituals

To enhance the power of love spells, burn a few cardamom seeds as you prepare your magical space. Diffuse a little essential oil in the bedroom to stimulate passion. For clarity in divination, place a few seedpods on your altar or table. Also do this when you need to focus on studies.

Carnation

Carnation (*Dianthus carophyllus* syn. *D. coronaries*); also known as clove pink, gillyflower
Common Pink, Garden Pink (*D. plumarius*); also known as feathered pink, wild pink
Sweet William (*D. barbatus*); also known as lady's tuft

Dianthus flowers have serrated petals and slender leaves that are usually gray-green. Carnation flowers are the largest with ruffled layers of petals. They can be white, pink, red, or yellow. The common pink has five petals in a combination of pink, red, and white with a dark center. These flowers have a spicy, clove-like scent. Sweet William flowers grow in densely packed, flattened clusters. They are bicolor in shades of red, pink, white and often have a contrasting center.

History and Lore

Dedicated to Zeus and Jupiter, the name *Dianthus* comes from Greek meaning "divine flower."[35] The ancient Greeks and Romans used carnations in garlands at festivals and in funeral wreaths. It was a predominant garland flower during the Middle Ages throughout Europe. A symbol of love and sexual promise in medieval Italian art, the pink was also believed to be an aphrodisiac. For love magic in the state of Tyrol, Austria, pinks were placed on windowsills and worn in buttonholes. In southern Germany and France, pinks were also used medicinally. Used to flavor beer and wine in Elizabethan England, carnations were also worn as a protective amulet.

Magical Connections

Element/s	Fire
Astrological influence	Aries, Capricorn, Sagittarius; Jupiter, Saturn, Sun
Deities	Jupiter, Zeus
Other associations	The otherworld (white carnation)
Powers and attributes	Awareness, balance/harmony, confidence, consecrate/bless, death/funeral practices, fertility, healing, love, luck, nightmares, peace, protection, relationships, renewal, sex/sexuality, strength, truth
Available for purchase	Essential oil; flower essence; dried flowers; seeds

Spells and Rituals

For aid in strengthening confidence when seeking new employment, carry a few seeds in your pocket or purse. Wear a carnation or pink to stimulate love interest. To boost passion, place a vase of cut flowers in the bedroom. When seeking truth, hold a white carnation and meditate.

Catnip

Catnip (*Nepeta cataria*); also known as catmint, catnep, cat's fancy, catwort, field balm

Reaching up to three feet tall, catnip is a perennial herb with triangular, grayish green leaves that are heavily veined and toothed. The white flowers are marked with purple spots and grow in dense whorls at the end of the main stem and branches.

History and Lore

Catnip has been a popular garden herb for culinary and medicinal purposes since the time of the Roman Empire. According to a French legend, chewing the root provided courage and was used by executioners before carrying out their duties. In Tudor England, catnip was popular as an afternoon tea before trade with the East made black tea (*Camellia sinensis*) available. English herbalist Nicholas Culpeper recommended mixing catnip with wine as a remedy for some ailments. It was also added to pillow stuffing as a sleep aid. Medieval French and German magicians knew it by the occult name *bieith* as noted in the *Grand Albert* grimoire.[36]

---

35. Cumo, *Encyclopedia of Cultivated Plants*, 218.

36. Sédir, *Occult Botany*, 135.

Magical Connections

Element/s	Air, water
Astrological influence	Cancer, Libra, Pisces; Mercury, Venus
Deities	Bast, Sekhmet
Other associations	Samhain
Powers and attributes	Abundance, awareness, courage, dream work, family and home, fertility, happiness, healing, love, luck, peace, protection, psychic abilities, spirit guides/spirits, strength
Available for purchase	Essential oil, cut, dried leaves; seeds

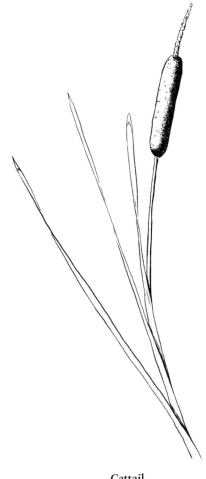

Cattail

Spells and Rituals

Catnip is effective for increasing psychic abilities and for bonding psychically with a cat. Use it as a charm to attract luck as well as love. Catnip enhances courage when called upon to provide protection. To contact benevolent spirits, sprinkle dried leaves on your altar.

Cattail

Common Cattail (*Typha latifolia*); also known as cat-o'-nine-tails, fairy woman's spindle, false bulrush, great reed mace, water torch

Native throughout most of the world, cattails usually reach four to eight feet tall and have flat, blade-like leaves. Its large, brown, cylindrical flower spike stays on the plant until autumn before breaking up into downy white fluff.

History and Lore

Cattails served many domestic needs for centuries in the British Isles. Soaked in fat, the flower spike provided a cheap alternative to candles and the downy fluff was used to stuff pillows. The roots and young shoots were often used for food. In Ireland, cattail is regarded as a faery plant. In Scotland, cattail was used as a charm against illness, but it had to be picked at midnight on Midsummer's Eve and wrapped in a shroud. In parts of England, cattail was believed unlucky to take into the house. In North America, the Apache use cattail pollen to bless girls during their coming-of-age ceremony as well as to bless young children.

Magical Connections

Element/s	Water
Astrological influence	Pisces, Sagittarius, Scorpio; Mars, Saturn
Deities	Coventina, Geb, Inanna, the Morrigan, Pan, Rhiannon
Magical entities	Faeries
Other associations	Imbolc, Samhain
Powers and attributes	Abundance, ancestors, confidence, consecrate/bless, determination, family and home, growth, healing, inspiration, loyalty/fidelity, protection, sex/sexuality, support
Available for purchase	Dried cattails; cattail pollen flower essence; pollen

Spells and Rituals

To consecrate an altar, especially for a healing ritual, sprinkle a pinch of pollen in each of the cardinal directions. For aid in connecting with ancestors on Samhain, include a couple of stalks in your ritual. Place a flower spike in the kitchen to foster family loyalty.

Cedar

Atlas Cedar (*Cedrus atlantica*); also known as
  Atlantic cedar, blue Atlas cedar

Cedar of Lebanon (*C. libani*); also known as Lebanese cedar

Eastern Red Cedar (*Juniperus virginiana*); also
  known as red juniper

Western Red Cedar (*Thuja plicata*); also known as
  giant cedar

The needles of the cedar of Lebanon grow in clusters that spiral around the branches. The Atlas cedar's short needles curve toward the tips of branches. Both trees have cylindrical cones that sit upright on the branches. Although not true cedars, the red cedars of North America were regarded as sacred. Instead of needles, they have fans of scale-like foliage.

History and Lore

Throughout the Middle East, cedar wood was burned as sacred offerings and in Tibet it was used as temple incense. The Egyptians used the resin to make sacred perfumes and incense for offerings to deities. They also used cedar as part of the embalming process to purify the body of the deceased and prepare the soul for the afterlife. Regarding the wood as sacred, the Romans used it for statues of deities and ancestors. In North America, red cedar wood was burned for purification rites by many Indigenous people including the Delaware, Kiowa, and Lakota. Tribes of the Northern Plains used cedar to repel ghosts. The legendary thunderbird was said to nest in a cedar tree. European settlers in the Ozarks used witch pegs, three-pronged pieces of cedar driven into a garden path, to keep witches away from their houses.

Magical Connections

Element/s	Air, earth, fire, water
Astrological influence	Aries, Sagittarius, Taurus; Jupiter, Mercury, Sun
Deities	Arianrhod, Artemis, Astarte, Baal, Brigid, Ea, Odin, Osiris, Persephone, Ra
Magical entities	Elves, faeries, phoenix, thunderbird, unicorn
Other associations	The afterlife, Imbolc, Beltane, Mabon, Yule
Powers and attributes	Abundance, ancestors, dream work, healing, hexes, justice / legal matters, love, loyalty / fidelity, prosperity / money, protection, psychic abilities, purification, spirit guides / spirits, spirituality, transformation
Available for purchase	Essential oil; incense; cedarwood boxes; figurines and other objects

Spells and Rituals

Use cedarwood incense or essential oil to stimulate dream work and strengthen psychic abilities. Include the foliage to boost the energy of love spells. The scent of cedar can facilitate contact with spirits. When dealing with legal matters, carry an amulet made of cedarwood.

Celandine

Greater Celandine (*Chelidonium majus*); also
    known as devil's milk, swallowwort, tetterwort, true celandine, wartwort
Lesser Celandine (*Ficaria verna* syn. *Ranunculus ficaria*); also known as crazies, crowfoot, golden stars, pilewort, raven's foot

Greater celandine is a sprawling plant that reaches two feet tall. Its bright, yellow flowers have four petals and grow in loose clusters. The leaves are gently lobed with wavy margins. The stems contain a yellow-orange sap. Lesser celandine is a mat-forming plant with irregularly lobed leaves that have a reddish-brown splotch at the center. Its yellow, daisy-like flowers grow on individual stems.

Caution: Greater celandine is highly toxic and can be fatal if ingested; lesser celandine is toxic if ingested.

History and Lore

The Anglo-Saxons used greater celandine roots in charms against dwarfs and the sap on arrows to poison prey. Resembling cow udders, the roots of lesser celandine were hung in barns in Scotland to encourage cows to produce more milk and to keep faeries from meddling with it. Sometimes called *caeli donum*, "a gift from heaven," greater celandine was used by medieval alchemists in Germany and reputedly bestowed the ability to predict the future.[37] It also served as an amulet for legal success and protection against imprisonment.

Magical Connections

Element/s	Earth, fire
Astrological influence	Aries (lesser), Leo (greater); Mars, Sun (greater)
Magical entities	Dwarfs (greater), faeries (lesser)

---

37. Kear, *Flower Wisdom*, 126.

Powers and attributes	Challenges/obstacles, dream work, happiness, hope, justice/legal matters, knowledge, prophecy, protection, release, success
Available for purchase	Flower essence; cut, dried leaves and stems

Spells and Rituals

For help in overcoming a problem, press a celandine leaf in a book and keep it in your wallet until the situation is resolved. To release something unwanted from your life, crumble a handful of dried leaves and scatter them outdoors as you slowly turn in a circle.

Celery

Garden Celery (*Apium graveolens* var. *dulce*)
Wild Celery (*Apium graveolens*); also known as
   marsh parsley, smallage

Celery is an erect plant with deeply lobed and coarsely toothed leaves. The grooved stems of wild celery are thin and wispy; garden celery has thick, chunky stems. White or greenish white flowers grow in small umbrella-shaped clusters. The ribbed seeds are brown and tan. Wild celery has a stronger odor.

History and Lore

In ancient Greece, celery was associated with the cult of the dead and eaten at funerals. The leaves were scattered on graves and sometimes made into wreaths to adorn the deceased. Even though it was a symbol of mourning, celery also represented victory and wreaths were used to deck monuments of warriors. While German alchemists and magicians used it to conjure spirits, celery was also used to keep evil spirits away.

It was generally believed that seeing the spectral Wild Hunt would cause blindness unless a person could obtain celery from one of the riders. Placing it in pigsties and cowsheds was said to prevent animals from being bewitched. In northern Germany, brides wore a sprig of celery in their clothes as a charm to keep their husbands faithful. It was also believed to be an aphrodisiac.

Magical Connections

Element/s	Fire, water
Astrological influence	Leo; Mercury, Moon
Deities	Hades, Hera, Hercules, Juno, Pluto, Poseidon
Powers and attributes	Awareness, creativity, death/funeral practices, divination, healing, hexes, loyalty/fidelity, protection, psychic abilities, sex/sexuality
Available for purchase	Essential oil; whole or crushed seeds; fresh celery

Spells and Rituals

To hone divination skills or enhance psychic abilities, eat a stalk of garden celery before sessions. Use celery seeds in sex magic to increase passion and fidelity. Burn a few seeds for protection or to counteract any magic used against you.

Centaury

Common Centaury, European Centaury (*Centaurium erythraea* syn. *C. minus*, *Erythraea centaurium*); also known as bitter herb, centaur's hoof, centaury gentian, feverwort

Reaching about a foot tall, centaury has star-like flowers that grow in loose clusters at the tops of the stems. The five-petaled flowers are light pink to reddish with yellow centers and open only on sunny days. The oblong leaves are gray-green and form a rosette at the base of the plant and grow in pairs up the stems.

History and Lore

Centaury's original botanical name of *Chironia centaurium* was in honor of Chiron the centaur. According to Greek mythology, Chiron used the plant to heal himself after being wounded with a poisoned arrow. Centaury was highly prized and used medicinally by the Greeks, Romans, and Egyptians. The Anglo-Saxons combined it with wine for treatment of snakebites and with vinegar to counteract other poisons. Medieval magicians in France were said to use it to create visions and witches in Germany to increase their psychic abilities. In Ireland, centaury could reputedly counteract magic and repel evil spirits. It was considered especially powerful if picked on Beltane.

Magical Connections

Element/s	Fire
Astrological influence	Leo, Sagittarius; Jupiter, Saturn, Sun
Deities	Adonis, Apollo, Horus, Ra
Magical entities	Chiron
Powers and attributes	Banish, consecrate/bless, healing, intuition, knowledge, luck, negativity, protection, psychic abilities, skills, strength
Available for purchase	Cut, dried stems and leaves marketed as centaury herb; powdered herb; flower essence; seeds

Spells and Rituals

To boost magical energy for spells and ritual, pick three flowering sprigs for your altar. Spread them fan-like with their stems touching and flowers toward you. When developing a new skill, place a small jar of powdered herb in your workspace to enhance your ability.

Chamomile

Chamomile

German Chamomile (*Matricaria recutita* syn. *M. chamomilla*); also known as blue chamomile, mayweed, true chamomile, wild chamomile
Roman Chamomile (*Chamaemelum nobile* syn. *Anthemis nobilis*); also known as common

chamomile, English chamomile, sweet chamomile, true chamomile

German chamomile is an erect plant with branching stems. Roman chamomile is a spreading plant with stems that creep along the ground. Both chamomiles have small, daisy-like flowers with white petals and yellow centers. German chamomile flowers are less fragrant than the apple-scented Roman. Both plants have feathery leaves.

History and Lore

Chamomile was used medicinally for a range of ailments by the ancient Egyptians, Greeks, and Romans. While the Anglo-Saxons called it *may-the*, in northern areas of Europe the plant was known as Balder's brow.[38] In medieval England it was a popular strewing herb for pest control and scenting the air. In England, Belgium, Italy, and Germany it was believed to be most powerful if picked at Midsummer. Chamomile was customarily thrown into the Midsummer bonfire for protection and prosperity. Used in healing charms, chamomile was reputedly powerful enough to ward off spells. However, in Prussia it was said that after Midsummer, witches would fly over chamomile in gardens to take its power. Throughout most of Germany, a wreath of chamomile hung on Midsummer's Eve protected a house from thunderstorms and wearing a sprig at any time of year would protect a person from bewitchment. Small bunches were hung from the ceilings in northern German homes for witch detection, reputedly they would sway and betray the presence of a witch entering the house.

38. Pollington, *Leechcraft*, 138.

Magical Connections

Element/s	Air, water
Astrological influence	Cancer, Leo; Mercury, Sun
Deities	Balder, Cernunnos, Ra
Magical entities	Faeries
Other associations	Litha, Midsummer's Eve, Walpurgis, Yule
Powers and attributes	Abundance, confidence, consecrate/bless, divination, dream work, emotions, healing, hexes, intuition, love, negativity, peace, prosperity/money, protection, psychic abilities, purification, release
Available for purchase	Essential oil; tea made from leaves and flowers; dried flowers; seeds

Spells and Rituals

To enhance dream work, drink a cup of chamomile tea before going to bed. Also drink it before divination sessions to hone your intuition. To counteract hexes, use two stems of German chamomile to create the letter *X* on your altar.

Cherry

Black Cherry (*Prunus serotina*); also known as rum cherry, wild cherry
European Bird Cherry (*P. padus*); also known as hackberry, hagberry, Mayday tree, witches' tree
Sweet Cherry, Bird Cherry (*P. avium*); also known as mazzard, merry-tree, wild cherry

The black cherry has clusters of white flowers and purplish black fruit. Its oblong leaves have pointed tips and tapering bases. The sweet cherry has white flowers that grow singly or in clusters and oval, dark green leaves with toothed edges. Its fruit is cherry red. The European bird cherry has white flowers that grow in pendulous clusters. Its dark green leaves are pointed. The red fruit turns black as it ripens.

Caution: The seeds and leaves of *Prunus* species produce cyanide in the digestive tract.

History and Lore

Since the Middle Ages throughout Europe, cherry fruit has been associated with virginity as well as fertility and seduction. Similar to the English custom of wassailing apple trees, the French would drink a toast to cherry orchards. Cherry trees also had a dark side. The Danes believed that demons often lived in cherry trees. On certain nights of the year, Albanians burned cherry branches to destroy any evil spirits that might prevent the tree from blooming and producing fruit. Because of the acrid odor of bird cherry bark, the tree was associated with witchcraft in areas of Scotland and in Germany it was known as *hexenbaum*, "witches' tree."[39] In England, the odor was believed to keep the plague at bay and pieces of bark were placed over doorways. In Belgium it was used for protection from witches and sorcery.

Magical Connections

Element/s	Fire, water
Astrological influence	Aquarius, Aries, Libra, Taurus; Mercury, Venus
Deities	Artemis, Flora, Mars, the Morrigan, Pan, Persephone, Thor

Magical entities	Elves, phoenix, unicorn, Vila
Powers and attributes	Abundance, awareness, balance/harmony, challenges/obstacles, creativity, divination, fertility, happiness, knowledge, love, luck, manifest, peace, renewal, spirituality, transformation, wisdom
Available for purchase	Fresh or dried cherries; cherry juice; pieces of dried bark from the black cherry; flower essence

Spells and Rituals

Use two cherrystones as a charm to attract romance. Include cherry blossoms in a bridal bouquet to foster happiness and make your dreams come true. During divination sessions, burn a small piece of cherry bark to heighten awareness and foster wisdom.

Chervil

Garden Chervil (*Anthriscus cerefolium* syn. *Scandix cerefolium*); also known as French parsley, true chervil

Sweet Cicely, Sweet Chervil (*Myrrhis odorata* syn. *S. odorata*); also known as garden myrrh, myrrhis, Spanish chervil

Chervil plants have finely divided, fern-like leaves and grooved stems and branches. The tiny, white flowers grow in flat, umbrella-like clusters. The seeds look like caraway but are longer and thinner. Garden chervil grows one to two feet tall; sweet cicely two to four feet tall. Chervil has an anise like scent although sweet cicely is sometimes thought to smell faintly like myrrh.

---

39. Friend, *Flowers and Flower Lore*, 538.

History and Lore

Chervil was highly prized by the ancient Egyptians who placed baskets of seeds in tombs. The Romans used it medicinally and were responsible for the plant's spread throughout Europe and Britain. The Anglo-Saxons used chervil medicinally and as an ingredient in healing charms to ward off demons and sickness. In England, mixing it with pig's dung was part of a spell to cure injuries and lameness caused by witches. Dried leaves were burned like incense after a death to ease grief and to aid in contacting the deceased. Chervil was also used to sooth bad dreams.

Magical Connections

Element/s	Air
Astrological influence	Jupiter, Mercury
Deities	Ceres
Powers and attributes	Happiness, loss/sorrow, nightmares, renewal, spirit guides/spirits
Available for purchase	Cut, dried leaves; seeds

Spells and Rituals

Sprinkle dried leaves on the grave of a loved one to wish them well in the next life. When dealing with any type of loss, bury a handful of leaves to symbolically lay your burden to rest and make way for a new cycle in your life.

Chestnut

Horse Chestnut (*Aesculus hippocastanum*); also known as candle tree, Roman candles

Sweet Chestnut (*Castanea sativa* syn. *C. vulgarus*); also known as European chestnut, Spanish chestnut

The sweet chestnut has dark green, oblong leaves and upright flowers that are yellow to greenish. Encased in pairs by a spiny round husk, chestnuts are flat on one side and rounded on the other. Horse chestnut flowers are white with a reddish or yellow tinge at the base and grow in showy, upright clusters. Its dark green leaflets are arranged in a fan shape. The nuts are commonly called *conkers*.

Caution: The nuts from the horse chestnut are toxic if ingested.

History and Lore

The chestnut was important enough to the Celts of Wales to be used in place of the highly esteemed hazelnut. Similarly in some parts of Ireland, chestnut branches were placed in cattle barns on Beltane for protection if hawthorn wasn't available. According to English legend, the horse chestnut would light up its flowers like candles so faeries would not have to travel home in the dark after their nightly revels. The sweet chestnut was used in love divination. Reputedly, if a man carried a sweet chestnut in his pocket, it would improve his romantic prospects. A horse chestnut in the pocket was a good luck charm.

Magical Connections

Element/s	Air, fire, water
Astrological influence	Cancer, Gemini, Sagittarius, Virgo; Jupiter, Sun
Deities	Artemis, Boann, Diana
Magical entities	Elves, faeries

Other associations	Beltane, Yule
Powers and attributes	Abundance (sweet), banish (horse), consecrate/bless, divination (horse), family and home, healing, hexes, justice/legal matters, love, luck, peace, prosperity/money, protection, strength, wishes
Available for purchase	Flower essence; chestnuts

Spells and Rituals

To ward off a potential hex, paint your initials on the flat side of a chestnut, and then hold it as you visualize energy from the chestnut surrounding you like a protective husk. To enhance divination sessions, place a horse chestnut on your table or altar.

Chickweed

Common Chickweed (*Stellaria media*); also known as bird weed, satin flower, starweed, starwort, white bird's eye, winterweed

This delicate, lanky annual has sprawling, tangled stems that create a dense mat, which can extend more than two feet in diameter. Its small, oval to egg-shaped leaves grow in pairs. The tiny, white, star-shaped flowers have five petals that are deeply divided giving the appearance of ten. After blooming, they develop into oval seed capsules.

History and Lore

Chickweed became a popular medicinal remedy for a wide range of ailments during the Middle Ages in England and Ireland. Because the flowers open on sunny days but close in the rain or when the sky is overcast, the plant served as a type of weather divination in England: if the flowers were wide open it wouldn't rain for at least four hours, if they were shut it would rain soon. In the Fenlands, chickweed was grown in flowerpots to attract luck to the home. It was also said that when gathered with the dew still on it, crushed and applied to the face any woman would become beautiful.

Magical Connections

Element/s	Water
Astrological influence	Gemini, Libra, Pisces; Jupiter, Moon
Deities	Dian Cécht
Powers and attributes	Emotions, family and home, fertility, love, loyalty/fidelity, negativity, purification, relationships, support
Available for purchase	Flower essence; cut, dried leaves marketed as chickweed tea

Spells and Rituals

To aid in releasing anger, sprinkle a handful of flowers in your bath water. For esbat rituals, hold a sprig in each hand to draw down lunar energy. Place a sachet under your bed as part of a fertility spell or to foster fidelity. To dispel negative energy, burn a few dried leaves.

Chicory

Common Chicory (*Cichorium intybus*); also known as blue sailors, coffeeweed, succory

Chicory has a rough, stiff stem and spreading, angular branches. The lower leaves are long, narrow, coarsely toothed, and reminiscent of dandelion. Sparse leaves on the branches are smaller. Chicory's sky-blue flowers have rayed petals with ragged ends. Growing in clusters of two or three, the flowers open and close at the same time every day. Pink or white flowers are rare.

Chicory

History and Lore

Because chicory was believed to have the power to bestow invisibility, it was sometimes used as a motif on banners to keep English and European Crusaders safe as they traveled and fought in the far-off lands of the Middle East. Drinking chicory tea before crystal gazing was said to enhance a person's abilities. The Germans used the seeds in love potions and a piece of root was carried in a pocket for luck. The root was used as an amulet in France to ward off spells and evil spirits. In England, chicory was believed to be especially lucky for finding treasure and opening locks. The catch, however, was that it had to be gathered on St. James Day (July 25) in silence using a gold knife. Speaking during the process would cause the death of the gatherer.

Magical Connections

Element/s	Air
Astrological influence	Aries, Virgo; Mercury, Sun, Uranus
Powers and attributes	Abundance, banish, challenges/obstacles, clarity, defense, divination, luck, prosperity/money, release, secrets, spirit guides/spirits, spirituality
Available for purchase	Dried, ground root; flower essence, seeds

Spells and Rituals

For help in finding your spiritual path or purpose in life, sprinkle a pinch of dried root on your altar before meditation. Burn a piece of root with a little incense to bring clarity to divination sessions. Carry a piece of dried root to help remove obstacles and banish turmoil from your life.

Chili Pepper

Cayenne Pepper (*Capsicum annuum* var. *cayenne*); also known as bird pepper, capsicum, red chilies

Jalapeño Pepper (*C. annuum* var. *jalapeño*); also known as chipotle

Paprika Pepper (*C. annuum* var. *paprika*)

These well-known peppers are distinguished by the amount of capsaicin they contain; capsaicin is the compound that makes them hot. The plant grows to about three feet tall with angular branches giving it a bushy appearance. The five-petaled flowers are white to yellowish-white and develop into peppers. Cayenne is long and slim, jalapeño is less slim and oblong, and paprika is squat and lobed.

Caution: Wear gloves when handling these peppers; consume in small amounts.

History and Lore

Quite appropriately, the genus name *Capsicum* comes from the Greek *kapto*, meaning "to bite."[40] Although chili peppers were cultivated in Africa and India for thousands of years, they didn't catch the attention of Europeans until Columbus's New World "discoveries." In Europe and the Americas, hanging a wreath or strand of chili peppers is said to attract luck. Because they are hot, chili peppers are regarded as an aphrodisiac. In Hungary, it was believed that peppers provided protection from the evil eye and vampires. In the American magical tradition of hoodoo, cayenne is used as a hot-foot charm to keep people away from you and/or your home.

Magical Connections

Element/s	Fire
Astrological influence	Aries; Mars
Powers and attributes	Challenges/obstacles, courage, defense, hexes, love, loyalty/fidelity, luck, negativity, protection, sex/sexuality, strength
Available for purchase	Fresh or dried whole peppers; flaked or powdered

Spells and Rituals

To spice up a relationship, include chili peppers in a love charm. For defensive magic, scatter pepper flakes at the corners of your property. Hang a strand as a talisman to attract luck and aid in overcoming problems. Add a small red pepper to your Yule wreath to foster love and loyalty.

Chinaberry

Chinaberry Tree (*Melia azedarach* syn. *M. sempervirens*); also known as bead tree, Indian lilac, Persian lilac, pride of India

Reaching up to fifty feet tall, the Chinaberry tree has reddish brown bark often with light brown spots. Its coarsely serrated leaflets are lance shaped and taper to a point. The five-petaled flowers are pink to lavender and grow in loose clusters. The round, yellowish berries are about the size of marbles. Growing in clusters, the berries stay on the tree through the winter.

Caution: All parts of the plant are toxic if ingested.

History and Lore

According to Chinese legend, the phoenix and unicorns enjoyed eating Chinaberry leaves, but dragons were said to dislike the tree or were frightened by it. In India, Chinaberry was regarded as the female counterpart to the Bodhi tree (*Ficus religiosa*). The dried seeds were made into beads and often dyed different colors. Garlands of beads were hung in doorways to ward off illness. Introduced into North America in the eighteenth century, the use of Chinaberry seeds for beads caught on and they were carried as good luck charms and worn as amulets to cure disease.

---

40. Coombes, *Dictionary of Plant Names*, 47.

Magical Connections

Element/s	Earth
Astrological influence	Taurus; Saturn
Magical entities	Dragons, phoenix, unicorns
Powers and attributes	Banish, changes/transitions, healing, luck
Available for purchase	Cut, dried bark; beads; seeds

Spells and Rituals

When you need any type of healing, hold a necklace or several beads as you meditate on the outcome you seek. Wear or carry the beads with you until you sense a change in energy. Use thick thread to braid three strands of beads together for a good luck charm.

Chive

Chinese Chives (*Allium tuberosum*); also known as Chinese leek, garlic chives

Wild Chives (*A. schoenoprasum*); also known as flowering onion, onion chives

Wild chives consist of slender, cylindrical leaves that grow directly from the bulb. Dense globular clusters of pale purple to pink flowers grow on individual stems up to eighteen inches tall. The leaves of Chinese chives are wider and flat. It has white, star-shaped flowers in rounded, flat-topped clusters. Wild chives have a mild onion taste; Chinese chives have a mild garlic taste.

History and Lore

Chives have been used for medicinal and culinary purposes in China for about five thousand years. Since the time of ancient Greece through the nineteenth century, chives were thought to be an aphrodisiac in Europe. The Romans had a few medicinal uses for them including an antidote to poison. However, according to English herbalist Nicholas Culpeper, chives gave off what he called "hurtful vapours to the brain, causing troublesome sleep" and that only an alchemist could safely prepare remedies with them.[41] In Devonshire, chives were said to be used as musical instruments by the faeries. In Romania, the Romani used chives in fortune telling and hung them in the home to ward off illness and evil spirits.

Magical Connections

Element/s	Fire
Astrological influence	Sagittarius; Mars
Magical entities	Faeries
Powers and attributes	Negativity, protection
Available for purchase	Fresh or dried leaves; dried flowers; flower essence; seeds

Spells and Rituals

Hang a dried bunch of chives with flowers wherever you sense negative energy in your home. As a protective charm, grow them in your garden or in a flowerpot on a windowsill. Clip several long leaves to use in knot magic.

41. Culpeper, *The English Physician*, 88.

Chrysanthemum

Common Chrysanthemum (*Chrysanthemum morifolium*); also known as florist's chrysanthemum, garden mum, mums, pot mum

Garland Chrysanthemum (*Glebionis coronaria* syn. *C. coronarium*); also known as crown daisy, edible chrysanthemum

The common chrysanthemum is a well-known perennial that reaches between one to three feet tall. It has dark green, deeply lobed leaves. The dense, globular flower heads can be white, yellow, orange, or reddish orange as well as various shades of purple. Looking more like a daisy, the garland chrysanthemum has white and yellow or just yellow flowers. It reaches two to three feet tall and has deeply lobed leaves.

History and Lore

The garland chrysanthemum was grown by the ancient Egyptians, who used it to make wreaths and bouquets to place in shrines and adorn statues of deities. Regarded as one of Medea's plants, in Greece the flower was believed to protect against black magic and bewitchment. Although in Japan the common chrysanthemum represented the sun and life, in Europe it was used to honor the dead and became known as *Fiori dei Morte*, "flower of the dead" in Italy.[42] Because of this association, it was sometimes considered unlucky to take inside the home. Despite this, the flower became a symbol of cheerfulness and optimism to the Victorians.

....
42. Kear, *Flower Wisdom*, 116.

Magical Connections

Element/s	Fire
Astrological influence	Leo; Mercury, Sun
Deities	Amaterasu, Apollo, Athena, Hecate, Medea
Other associations	Samhain
Powers and attributes	Consecrate/bless, death/funeral practices, family and home, happiness, inspiration, loss/sorrow, love, protection, release, truth
Available for purchase	Flower essence; dried common chrysanthemum flowers; seeds

Spells and Rituals

Place a white chrysanthemum on your altar when seeking truth; a yellow one to aid in recovering from slighted love. Remove the petals from a flower and scatter them across a stream or pond as you visualize releasing unwanted things from your life.

Cinnamon

Cassia Cinnamon (*Cinnamomum. cassia* syn. *C. aromaticum*); also known as bastard cinnamon, Chinese cinnamon

Ceylon Cinnamon (*C. zeylanicum* syn. *C. verum*); also known as true cinnamon

The lance-shaped leaves of these trees start out pinkish or reddish, and then turn green and leathery. Growing at the ends of the stems, clusters of yellow-white flowers mature into purplish-blue berries. Like cloves, the young flowers of the cassia tree are picked and dried and used as a spice. The most widely used cinnamon spice comes from the bark.

Caution: Consuming excessive amounts of cassia or cinnamon can be toxic.

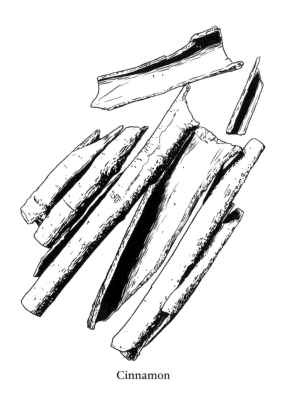

Cinnamon

History and Lore
One of the world's oldest spices, cinnamon was a valuable commodity for the Phoenicians and Arabs in trade with the Egyptians, Greeks, and Romans. The Egyptians used it in the embalming process and the Romans for decorating temples. According to Greek legend, the phoenix constructed its nest with cinnamon twigs. On the island of Rhodes, cinnamon oil was used during wedding ceremonies to anoint the bride's hands. The Hebrews valued both cinnamon and cassia. Cassia was regarded as sacred in China where, according to legend, eating the spice from a gigantic cassia tree bestowed immortality. During the Middle Ages in Europe, it was especially popular for spicing wine.

Magical Connections

Element/s	Fire
Astrological influence	Aries, Capricorn, Leo; Jupiter, Mercury, Sun
Deities	Aphrodite, Apollo, Asclepius, Dionysus, Helios, Horus, Jupiter, Mercury, Ra, Venus
Magical entities	Phoenix
Powers and attributes	Awareness, changes/transitions, consecrate/bless, healing, love, luck, prosperity/money, protection, psychic abilities, purification, sex/sexuality, spirituality, strength, success, wishes
Available for purchase	Essential oil; flower essence; bark, pieces or powdered; cassia buds

Spells and Rituals
Use the essential oil for candle magic to spark awareness and stimulate psychic abilities, especially clairvoyance. To make a wish, take a handful of powdered cinnamon outside and blow it away as you visualize what you want to come true.

Cinquefoil
Creeping Cinquefoil, European Cinquefoil
    (*Potentilla reptans*); also known as five-fingers, five-leaf grass
Dwarf Cinquefoil (*P. canadensis*); also known as running five-fingers

Creeping cinquefoil has yellow, five-petaled flowers that resemble small, wild roses. Stalks with a single flower or leaf rise from the stems, which grow along the ground. Leaves consist of five or seven oval, coarsely toothed leaflets. Dwarf cinquefoil is smaller, has similar flowers, and wedge-shaped leaflets.

History and Lore

While cinquefoil was used for protection against witches in medieval Europe, in England it was believed that witches rubbed cinquefoil on their bodies to produce a trancelike state. It was also said to be an ingredient in a witches' brew that also contained deadly nightshade (*Atropa belladonna*) and hemlock (*Conium maculatum*). Witches were also said to use cinquefoil in spells and love potions. The French believed that cinquefoil was an ingredient in witches' flying ointment. In Wales, people dug up a root on May Eve and tucked it into their clothing for luck. Although in England faeries were said to be fond of cinquefoil's little rose-like flowers, both the flowers and leaves were used to break faery spells.

Magical Connections

Element/s	Earth, fire
Astrological influence	Taurus; Jupiter, Mercury
Magical entities	Faeries
Other associations	Beltane
Powers and attributes	Authority/leadership, communication, defense, divination, dream work, hexes, inspiration, luck, negativity, prosperity/money, protection, relationships
Available for purchase	Dried leaves and roots are marketed as cinquefoil herb

Spells and Rituals

To break a hex or any form of negative magic sent your way, make an infusion of cinquefoil leaves. Without straining out the plant material, take it outside and pour it on the ground as you visualize the energy returning to the sender.

Clove

Clove (*Syzygium aromaticum* syn. *Eugenia caryophyllata*)

Native to Indonesia, the clove tree is an evergreen with a pyramidal shape. It has fluffy, white flowers that grow in clusters and large, bright green leaves. The familiar clove is a dried, unopened flower bud.

History and Lore

Derived from the French *clou* or the Latin *clavus*, both meaning "nail," an early Chinese name for cloves meant "sweet smelling nail."[43] While the ancient Egyptians, Greeks, and Romans used cloves, this highly prized spice didn't make its way into northern Europe until the Middle Ages. French and German alchemists and magicians used it with several minerals to work with the spirits of the dead. In northern India, cloves were used in exorcisms. A necklace of cloves was placed on children to protect them from evil and illness. In parts of Indonesia, cloves were worn in nose and lip piercings to prevent possession by demons.

Magical Connections

Element/s	Air, earth, fire
Astrological influence	Aries, Leo, Pisces, Sagittarius, Scorpio; Jupiter, Mars, Mercury, Sun

43. Weiss, *Spice Crops*, 106.

Deities	Apollo, Horus, Osiris, Ra
Powers and attributes	Banish, creativity, emotions, happiness, healing, hexes, love, negativity, prosperity / money, protection, purification, relationships, sex / sexuality, spirituality
Available for purchase	Essential oil from the clove bud; whole or ground cloves

Spells and Rituals

Clove increases spiritual vibrations making it useful for purifying sacred space. When used in candle magic, it removes negativity and fosters happiness. Clove supports emotional and sexual healing and strengthens relationships.

Clover

Red Clover (*Trifolium pratense*); also known as broad clover, shamrock, purple trefoil

White Clover (*T. repens*); also known as moon clover, shamrock, trefoil

White clover has tiny, white to pale pink flowers in spherical clusters. Although the leaves usually consist of three leaflets, they occasionally produce four or more. The red clover's pink, tubular flowers are clustered into a dome shape. The leaves of both plants have a V-shaped marking in the center.

History and Lore

In England, wearing a sprig of red clover leaves reputedly brought good luck and provided protection from witches. Wearing a clover leaf in a shoe was part of a love spell. Despite the power of three, the four-leaf clover has been regarded as especially lucky to the English and Irish. As a magic talisman, it enabled the wearer to see faeries and to enter the faery realm. In Somerset finding a four-leaf clover meant you would meet your true love. In Wales, finding one during the month of May was a charm against witchcraft. In the Scottish Highlands a four- or five-leaf clover was considered extremely lucky and used as a charm against evil spells. In Ireland, clovers in the *Trifolium* genus are known as shamrocks.

Magical Connections

Element/s	Air, earth
Astrological influence	Gemini (white), Sagittarius (red); Mercury
Magical entities	Elves, faeries, Gwydion
Powers and attributes	Hexes, love, loyalty / fidelity, luck (four-leaf & red), peace, prosperity / money, protection, see faeries (four-leaf), success
Available for purchase	Flower essence; cut, dried red clover flowers; seeds

Spells and Rituals

As part of a spell to attract love, pick enough flowers to tie end-to-end and make a crown to wear. After your magic work is finished, place the crown over your bedpost for three nights. If you find a four-leaf clover, place it in a special spot outside as an invitation to the faeries.

Club Moss

Common Club Moss, Running Club Moss (*Lycopodium clavatum*); also known as foxtail, ground pine, staghorn moss, vegetable sulfur, wolf claw

Fir Club Moss (*Huperzia selago* syn. *L. selago*); also known as northern fir moss, selago

Despite its name, club moss is not a true moss. With needlelike or scale-like leaves, club moss looks like tiny pine trees. Common club moss has branching stems that are covered in tiny, soft green leaves. Club shaped spore cases rise above the branches on separate stems. Fir club moss has a dense growth of stems. Its leaves grow in whorls around the stems and in tufts at the top. Its spores are produced without cases at the leaf axils.

Caution: These plants are unsafe to ingest.

History and Lore

Roman naturalist and historian Pliny the Elder noted that club moss was used as a protective amulet. Known as selago, fir club moss was an important herb of the Druids and was said to bestow the power to understand birds and animals. In parts of England, common club moss was placed in front of houses on Beltane for faeries to dance upon. In Poland, club moss was worn as an amulet for protection from witches and spells and to remove evil spirits. Bunches were hung on barns to protect cattle. In Germany and Sweden, club moss was used to make wreaths for festivals. The spores were said to have aphrodisiac qualities.

Magical Connections

Element/s	Water
Astrological influence	Moon
Magical entities	Faeries
Other associations	Beltane, Samhain
Powers and attributes	Luck, prosperity/money, protection
Available for purchase	Cut, dried stems and leaves; whole dried stems;

Spells and Rituals

Place a little dried club moss in a small pouch to use as a good luck charm. As part of a spell to attract prosperity to your home, tie a bundle of stems with green yarn and hang it in your kitchen or by a fireplace hearth.

Coconut

Coconut Palm (*Cocos nucifera*)

The coconut palm is a slender tree that grows about eighty feet tall. The leaves of its crown can grow up to twenty feet long. The trunk is ringed with the bases of old leaves. Large clusters of coconuts turn brown as they mature and develop a thick fibrous husk over a hard shell.

Coconut

History and Lore

The coconut has been likened to a monkey face because of its three indentations called *eyes*. The name *coconut* was derived from the late fifteenth-century Portuguese word *coco* meaning, "grimace" or "goblin."[44] In Samoa, fallen coconuts were not picked up because it was believed that they belonged to magic spirits and doing so might result in a spirit taking revenge. In Malaysia, a coconut that lacked three eyes was considered a powerful charm against enemies. Regarded as a fruit of deities in India, breaking one open was used in place of sacrifice to the goddess Kali. Coconut was offered to Ganesh, the elephant-headed god of fortune, when asking for his blessings.

Magical Connections

Element/s	Air, fire
Astrological influence	Leo, Sagittarius, Scorpio; Jupiter, Mars, Moon, Sun
Deities	Ganesh, Hina, Kali, Sarasvati, Shiva, Vishnu
Powers and attributes	Abundance, consecrate/bless, family and home, healing, hope, intuition, protection, purification, sex/sexuality, spirituality, success
Available for purchase	Coconuts; coconut milk; dried coconut meat slices, cubes, or flakes; coconut shell beads; coir, fibers from the coconut shell husk

Spells and Rituals

For success in any type of endeavor, wear a string of coconut shell beads or carry them in your pocket or purse. To attract abundance, sprinkle a handful of coconut flakes across the threshold of

....
44. Morton, *Cupboard Love*, 87.

your front door. For protection, place a string of nine coconut beads in your home.

Coltsfoot

Coltsfoot (*Tussilago farfara*); also known as butterbur, coughwort, foalswort, horsehoof

Coltsfoot sends up yellow, dandelion-like flowers early in the spring. Like dandelions, coltsfoot flowers turn into fluffy, white seed balls. The rounded, hoof-shaped leaves have downy undersides. Because the leaves open after the flowers go to seed, it is sometimes difficult to identify this plant.

Caution: Coltsfoot is unsafe to ingest.

History and Lore

The ancient Greeks and Romans used coltsfoot medicinally and by the Middle Ages throughout Europe it was so well known as a cure-all that in place of apothecary shop signage the yellow flower was painted on the doorsteps or doorposts. After having his asthma cured with coltsfoot, an archbishop in sixteenth-century Scotland accused his healer of using witchcraft. In some areas of England, coltsfoot was associated with witches who were said to put it in love potions. Used in weather divination, rain was indicated when the downy seeds were seen floating on the air without a breeze to carry them. In Victorian England, the flower was a symbol that justice would be done.

Magical Connections

Element/s	Water
Astrological influence	Libra, Taurus; Venus
Deities	Brigid, Epona

Powers and attributes	Divination, dream work, family and home, healing, justice/legal matters, love, negativity, peace, prosperity/money, protection, psychic abilities
Available for purchase	Flower essence; cut, dried leaves; dried flowers; seeds

Spells and Rituals

To increase psychic abilities and enhance your visionary experiences, place three flowers in a sachet to wear during divination sessions. To honor Epona, pick four leaves and press them in a book. When the leaves are dry and flat, place them on your altar to represent hoof prints.

Columbine

Garden Columbine, Common Columbine (*Aquilegia vulgaris*); also known as dancing fairies, granny's bonnet, night caps, rock bells

Wild Columbine, Red Columbine (*A. canadensis*); also known as culverwort, dancing fairies, rock bells

Columbine has drooping, bell-like flowers with distinctive, backward-pointing spurs. They grow on long, branching stalks that are one to three feet tall. The flowers give way to seeds that look like clusters of small, upright peapods. The wild columbine has red and yellow flowers with long spurs. Garden columbine has violet-blue flowers with short spurs. Columbine's medium-green leaves are rounded and lobed.

Caution: All parts of the plant are toxic if ingested.

History and Lore

Columbine flowers spark the imagination: the spurs have been likened to an eagle's talons and groups of flowers have been thought to resemble a flight of doves. The Italian derivation *columbina* was a pet name for a ladylove and meant "little dove" or "young coquette."[45] The Saxons called this plant *culverwort*, from their word *culfre*, which means "dove" or "pigeon."[46]

While these are endearing associations, in England the horn-shaped flower spur also gave columbine an association with cuckoldry. During medieval times, horns were a symbol of disloyalty and an unfaithful wife. Because of this, it was an insult to give a woman columbine because it inferred that she had loose morals. It was bad luck to give to a man. To the Victorians, columbine represented desertion. However, in North America wild columbine was associated with the better side of love and the seeds were used by the Meskwaki, Omaha, Pawnee, and Ponca in love charms.

Magical Connections

Element/s	Water
Astrological influence	Venus
Magical entities	Faeries
Powers and attributes	Balance/harmony, consecrate/bless, courage, creativity, emotions, family and home, inspiration, love, negativity, peace, purification, release, spirituality, support, trust
Available for purchase	Flower essence; seeds

45. Kear, *Flower Wisdom*, 95.
46. Hall, *A Concise Anglo-Saxon Dictionary*, 61.

Spells and Rituals

To bolster courage and balance emotions, tuck a few seeds in your pocket on days when you need support. Infuse a few seedpods in olive oil, and then use the oil to prepare candles for love spells. To deepen your spiritual commitment, place a picture of columbine on your altar.

Comfrey

Common Comfrey (*Symphytum officinale*);
  also known as ass ear, blackwort, boneset, knitbone

Growing up to three feet tall, comfrey has upright stems with dark green, lance-shaped leaves that are heavily veined. Its creamy-yellow to purplish, bell-shaped flowers hang in drooping clusters and bloom from May to September. The flowers mature into small, glossy-black fruits.

Caution: Comfrey is considered unsafe to ingest; may irritate the skin when handled.

History and Lore

Herbalists from the ancient Greeks and Romans to medieval times considered this plant a master healer. Throughout Europe, comfrey was attributed with the power to heal broken bones and to remedy internal injuries. The plant was introduced into England by returning crusaders who had learned about it on the battlefield. In the nineteenth century, a comfrey bath was believed to restore virginity. The thinking was that if it could repair bones, it could restore the hymen. In Norfolk, it was added to pig feed to keep the animals from being bewitched.

Magical Connections

Element/s	Air, earth, water
Astrological influence	Capricorn, Gemini; Jupiter, Saturn
Powers and attributes	Abundance, banish, bind, consecrate/bless, family and home, healing, peace, protection, psychic abilities, release, security, strength
Available for purchase	Flower essence; infused oil; pieces or powdered root; cut, dried leaves

Spells and Rituals

Planting comfrey in several places around the garden will bring stability to your household. Burn small pieces of dried root to boost the energy of spells that banish or bind. To aid in safe and easy travel, place a dab of flower essence or infused oil on your forehead.

Coriander

Coriander, Cilantro (*Coriandrum sativum*); also known as Chinese parsley

The name *coriander* refers to the seeds and *cilantro* to the lower leaves, which resemble parsley. The upper leaves are delicate and fern-like. The small flowers range from white to pink to pale lavender. They have five petals and grow in umbrella-shaped clusters. The ball-shaped seeds are golden brown.

History and Lore

The Greeks and the Romans used coriander medicinally and to flavor wine. The Chinese associated it with immortality, the Egyptians placed it in tombs, and in India it is still used as an offering to deities. In the Middle East coriander was regarded as an aphrodisiac and during the Middle Ages and Renaissance in Europe it was an ingredient in love potions. Medieval German magicians and alchemists used coriander to conjure spirits. The seeds were used as charms against witches and evil spirits in Europe and in North Africa they were credited with repelling demons. In some areas of Morocco, people fumigated their homes with coriander for protection against malevolent jinn. According to legend in the Hindu Kush of northern Pakistan, coriander was cultivated by the mountain faeries.

Magical Connections

Element/s	Fire
Astrological influence	Aries, Leo; Mars, Saturn, Venus
Magical entities	Faeries, jinn
Powers and attributes	Balance/harmony, changes/transitions, consecrate/bless, divination, dream work, emotions, fertility, healing, love, peace, protection, secrets, security, sex/sexuality
Available for purchase	Essential oil; flower essence; whole or ground seeds; cut, dried cilantro

Spells and Rituals

Use the essential oil to consecrate charms and amulets. Coriander seeds are instrumental for raising healing energy, especially for emotional balance. Tuck a couple of cilantro leaves under your pillow to dream about romance.

Cornflower

Cornflower (*Centaurea cyanus*); also known as bachelor's buttons, bluebottle, knapweed, little blue heads, witches' bells, witches' needles

Cornflower is prized for its stunning, sapphire blue flowers, which are occasionally purple or white. The slightly raggedly flower head consists of small florets with rays of petals that surround a darker often purplish center. The lower leaves are oblong and toothed; upper leaves are smaller and lance shaped. Covered with a loose down, the plant has a dull gray appearance.

History and Lore

Both the Greek and Roman names for cornflower translate as "plant of the centaur."[47] Like centaury (*Centaurium erythraea*), cornflower was reputedly used by Chiron to heal the wound of a poison arrow. In Switzerland, cornflowers were used for love divination by picking and wearing two young buds. If only one opened, a romance would be one-sided, but if both opened love would be shared. Elsewhere in Europe, the flower was used like a daisy to test a lover's loyalty by pulling off the petals one-by-one. Young women in England wore the flowers to indicate that they were eligible for marriage.

47. De Cleene and Lejeune, *Compendium of Symbolic and Ritual Plants in Europe*, 194.

Cornflower

Magical Connections

Element/s	Earth, water
Astrological influence	Aquarius, Capricorn, Libra, Taurus; Saturn, Venus
Deities	Flora
Magical entities	Chiron

Other associations	Beltane, Mid-Summer's Eve
Powers and attributes	Divination, happiness, hope, love, loyalty/fidelity, negativity, peace, protection, psychic abilities, truth
Available for purchase	Flower essence; hydrosol; dried florets; seeds

Spells and Rituals

To attract happiness and peace to your home, walk through your house and sprinkle a little cornflower hydrosol in each room. Prepare a candle with the flower essence before a divination session to enhance your psychic skills.

Cow Parsley

Cow Parsley, Wild Chervil (*Anthriscus sylvestris*); also known as cow weed, devil's parsley, fairy lace, gypsy lace, hedge parsley, hemlock

Growing up to five feet tall, cow parsley has a ribbed, hairy stalk and sharply lobed, fern-like leaves that give the plant a delicate airiness. The white, slightly notched flowers have green centers and grow in lacy, flat clusters. The narrow, egg-shaped fruit matures from greenish to yellowish and eventually black when it splits into a pair of seeds.

Caution: Although cow parsley leaves have a featherier appearance and its stalks are ribbed, it is easily confused with hemlock (*Conium maculatum*), which is extremely poisonous.

History and Lore

This plant earned its common name because cows and other livestock are fond of eating it. Associated with the devil in England, cow parsley was reputedly used by witches. According to some legends, picking it could bring bad luck or even death. A widespread belief was more specific noting that taking it indoors would cause a person's mother to die. Cow parsley was used to break faery spells and enchantment, and although it was noted to be effective, it was often blamed for provoking subsequent faery attack.

Magical Connections

Element/s	Fire
Astrological influence	Mars
Magical entities	Faeries
Powers and attributes	Balance/harmony, courage, emotions, family and home, healing, hexes, love, negativity, peace, protection, strength
Available for purchase	Flower essence is marketed as wild chervil; seeds

Spells and Rituals

Give lunar magic a boost by placing a cluster of flowers on your esbat altar. To enhance feelings of peace and bring your energy into alignment, put a dab of flower essence on your third eye chakra before meditation. Grow cow parsley in your garden to attract faeries.

Cowslip

Common Cowslip, English Cowslip (*Primula veris*); also known as candle of the woods, fairy basins, fairy bells, fairy cups, fairy flower, key flower, luck flower

The cowslip has drooping clusters of funnel-shaped flowers on an erect stem that rises above a rosette of base leaves. The leaves are oval and wrinkly. The honey-scented flowers are lemon yellow with a reddish spot at the base of each petal.

History and Lore

With dangling flowers that resemble a set of old-fashioned keys, Norse legend notes that they belonged to Freya. Like its cousin the primrose (*Primula vulgaris*), cowslip was known as key flower and luck flower in Germany where it was believed to have the power to unlock an enchanted castle, a secret place, or treasure chest. In English weather lore, short flower stalks indicate a dry summer without warmth until the flowers are done blooming. The flowers blooming in winter was regarded as a death omen. Faeries reputedly made cowslip wine for their revels on Midsummer's Eve. In European legend, the reddish spots on the flower petals occurred where elves had touched them.

Magical Connections

Element/s	Water
Astrological influence	Aries; Venus
Deities	Bertha, Freya
Magical entities	Elves, faeries
Other associations	The afterlife
Powers and attributes	Divination, healing, love, peace, prosperity/money, protection, secrets, spirit guides/spirits, strength, trust
Available for purchase	Flower essence; dried flowers; seeds

Spells and Rituals

For love divination, make a tissy ball by tying flower heads close together along a length of yarn, and then pulling the ends together to make a ball. Say the name of someone you are interested in each time you toss the ball into the air. When it falls apart, that's the name of your true love.

Crabapple

American Crabapple, Sweet Crabapple (*Malus coronaria* syn. *Pyrus coronaria*)

European Crabapple, Wild Apple (*M. sylvestris*); also known as scrog, wild crabapple

The crabapple is a small tree with a short, crooked trunk and a showy display of fragrant flowers that can range from white to pink to almost rosy. It has oval leaves and its small branches have short thorns. The fruit turns dark red as it ripens.

Caution: Ingesting the seeds produces a form of cyanide in the digestive tract.

History and Lore

With an important place in Celtic mythology, crabapples were considered a fruit of knowledge, magic, and prophecy. Emain Ablach (also spelled *Eamhain Abhlach*) the Place of Apples where crab apples grew was an otherworld home to faeries as well as the sea god Manannán Mac Lir. The Anglo-Saxons used crabapples medicinally. When they arrived in England, eighth-century Vikings called the tree *scrabba* or *scrab*, which evolved into or was mistaken for the word *crab*.[48] In medieval England, the fruit was known as *sur appel*, "sour apple."[49] Crabapples were used for love divination and when eaten with cucumber and cheese

48. Staub, *75 Remarkable Fruits for Your Garden*, 55.
49. Hooke, *Trees in Anglo-Saxon England*, 249.

before going to bed, they reputedly inspired erotic dreams.

Magical Connections

Element/s	Air, water
Astrological influence	Aquarius, Cancer, Libra, Taurus; Venus
Deities	Aphrodite, Apollo, Athena, Badb, Cailleach Bheur, Diana, Dionysus, Eros, Flora, Freya, Hera, Lugh, Macha, Manannán Mac Lir, Rhiannon, Venus, Zeus
Magical entities	Elves, faeries
Ogham	Quert / Cert ⊥⊥⊥⊥⊥
Other associations	The otherworld, Beltane, Lughnasadh, Samhain, Yule
Powers and attributes	Abundance, ancestors, death/funeral practices, divination, healing, knowledge, love, prophecy, prosperity/money, protection, wisdom
Available for purchase	Fresh or dried fruit; flower essence

Spells and Rituals

For magical protection, cast a circle with a branch, and then hang it over your altar. When making an important decision, hold a crabapple leaf in each hand as you meditate. To honor your ancestors at Samhain, place a circle of crabapples on your altar.

Cress

Garden Cress, Cress (*Lepidium sativum*); also known as pepperweed, poor man's pepper

Lamb's Cress, Hairy Bittercress (*Cardamine hirsute*); also known as bittercress, land cress

Water Cress (*Nasturtium officinale* syn. *Rorippa nasturtium-aquaticum*); also known as fen cress, watergrass, well cress

Most types of cress have white, four-petaled flowers. Garden cress is slender and erect with lobed, curly leaves; its flowers can be pinkish. Its seedpods are round, flat, and notched. Lamb's cress has a base rosette of rounded leaves with flower stems rising above it. The purplish green seedpods look like flowerless stems. Watercress is an aquatic plant that forms bushy colonies. It has dark green, oval leaflets and sickle shaped seedpods.

History and Lore

Garden cress has been cultivated since ancient times around the Mediterranean and has been found in Egyptian tombs. The Greeks called it *cardamom of Hecate* and *cress of Medea* and used the seeds to create smoke and fumes for magical rituals.[50] Both the Greeks and Romans believed that watercress improved the brain. In Devon, eating it was believed to make a person more intelligent. Because it grows in wells and streams, the magical realm of water, watercress was a source of power to some of the heroes in Irish legends. According to Irish and Scottish Highland lore, witches cut off the tops of watercress for use in charms to steal milk. Lamb's cress may be the Anglo-Saxon herb called *lombes cerse*, which was believed to have been created by Woden and used as an ingredient in healing charms to ward off demons and sickness.

---

50. Sédir, *Occult Botany*, 152.

Magical Connections

Element/s	Fire, water (watercress)
Astrological influence	Aries, Sagittarius; Mars, Moon (watercress)
Deities	Hecate, Medea
Powers and attributes	Consecrate/bless, dream work, knowledge, protection, psychic abilities
Available for purchase	Fresh leaves; seeds

Spells and Rituals

Eat cress sprouts while studying for exams to aid in knowledge retention. Place a handful of seeds on your bedside table to foster and enhance precognitive dreams. Burn a few seeds with incense to bless ritual space and tools, and to increase psychic abilities.

Crocus

Saffron Crocus, Autumn Crocus (*Crocus sativus*); also known as true crocus

Wild Crocus, Snow Crocus (*C. chrysanthus*); also known as golden crocus

Woodland Crocus, Early Crocus (*C. tommasinianus*); also known as Tommies

Crocus has chalice-shaped flowers and long, thin leaves that are dark green with a central white or silvery stripe. The woodland crocus ranges from pale lavender to reddish purple with a white throat. The wild crocus is yellowish orange, sometimes with maroon markings. The saffron crocus is lilac-purple with a reddish orange throat. Unlike the others, it blooms in the autumn.

Caution: Overuse of saffron can be toxic. These plants should not be confused with autumn crocus (*Colchicum autumnale*), which is highly toxic.

Crocus

History and Lore

The interior parts (stigmas and styles) of the saffron flower have been used as a spice for many centuries. The Phoenicians used saffron in moonshaped cakes dedicated to Astarte, the Egyptians burned it to honor Thoth. The Romans and Greeks used the flowers to decorate banquette tables and wedding beds. Magicians and alchemists in medieval Germany burned saffron as an ingredient in incense to manifest spirits. Grown since early medieval times in Britain, saffron had some medicinal uses and was believed to be an aid against the plague. The fishermen of Cornwall were not fond of it and believed that taking saffron cakes onboard their boats would jinx the day's catch. In faery lore, the fae were said to prefer the purple woodland crocus flowers. In Morocco, saffron was used as an amulet to ward off malevolent jinn, in charms to ward off evil spirits, and added to ink for writing spells.

Magical Connections

Element/s	Fire (saffron), water
Astrological influence	Leo, Scorpio (saffron); Sun (saffron), Venus
Deities	Astarte, Eos, Hera, Thoth, Zeus
Magical entities	Faeries, jinn (saffron)
Other associations	Litha
Powers and attributes	Banish, divination, dream work, emotions, family and home, fertility, happiness, healing, love, manifest, nightmares, peace, protection, psychic abilities, relationships, sex/sexuality
Available for purchase	Flower essence is made from the woodland crocus and marketed as purple crocus

Spells and Rituals

To bless your home and promote peace, crumble dried flowers and leaves into a powder and sprinkle it at the corners of your house. To enhance psychic abilities, especially clairvoyance, sprinkle a tiny pinch of the powder on an incense charcoal before divination sessions.

Cumin

Cumin (*Cumimum cyminum*); also known as green cumin, Roman caraway, white cumin

Cumin is a small, delicate herb with feathery, threadlike leaves. The flowers can be white or pink and grow in small, umbrella-shaped clusters. The seeds are ridged and crescent shaped.

History and Lore

Cumin has been used for culinary and medicinal purposes for thousands of years. It was mentioned in Egyptian healing texts and found in ancient tombs. According to Pliny the Elder, Greek and Roman students burned the seeds for an aromatic boost to aid their studies. The Arabs used a combination of cumin, pepper, and honey as an aphrodisiac. The plant was a symbol of love and used in love potions during the Middle Ages in Europe. Cumin was also regarded as a reminder of devotion. As such, it was baked into cake to keep a lover faithful or given in bread for a journey to ensure a lover's safe return. This notion of return was extended to animals. It was fed to homing pigeons so they would return and farm animals to keep them from wandering off or being stolen. In German lore, cumin could reputedly keep dwarfs and wood folk away because they were said to have an aversion to its strong odor.

Magical Connections

Element/s	Fire
Astrological influence	Aries, Scorpio, Taurus; Mars, Venus
Magical entities	Dwarfs, wood folk

Powers and attributes	Balance/harmony, banish, changes/transitions, emotions, family and home, knowledge, love, loyalty/fidelity, negativity, protection, purification, release, renewal, spirituality
Available for purchase	Essential oil; whole seeds; ground seeds

Spells and Rituals

To aid in releasing negative emotions, diffuse the essential oil. Place a handful of seeds on your altar during meditation to bring balance between the spiritual and the mundane. Include cumin in spells to increase their effectiveness and when you want to instigate changes in your life.

Cyclamen

Florist's Cyclamen (*Cyclamen persicum*); also known as Persian cyclamen

Wild Cyclamen (*C. hederifolium*); also known as ivy-leaved cyclamen, Persian violet, sowbread

The nodding flowers of cyclamen seem to float above the foliage on graceful stems. Florist's cyclamen flowers range from white through many shades of pinks and reds. The dark green leaves are rounded with various shades of marbling. The delicate wild cyclamen flowers are white or pink. Its ivy-like leaves have variegated patterns in pale green, gray, or silver.

Caution: All parts of the plant, especially the roots, are toxic if ingested; may cause skin irritation.

History and Lore

The ancient Greeks and Romans used cyclamen medicinally and to enhance the effects of wine. Midwives employed it to ease childbirth. Roman naturalist and historian Pliny the Elder noted that growing cyclamen in a garden would protect a household from malicious spells, especially at night while they slept. Regarded as an amulet against harmful potions, it was also believed to heal poisonous snakebites. During the Middle Ages in Europe and England, cyclamen was associated with lust and used as an aphrodisiac. It was also a charm to attract love and was used for love divination. The uncomely folk name *sowbread* comes from the practice of feeding the roots to pigs.

Magical Connections

Element/s	Water
Astrological influence	Leo, Libra; Mars (wild), Sun, Venus
Deities	Apollo, Hecate
Powers and attributes	Confidence, divination, fertility, happiness, love, negativity, nightmares, past-life work, protection, relationships
Available for purchase	Flower essence; tubers/roots

Spells and Rituals

Call on cyclamen's powers of love, passion, and happiness by incorporating it into a handfasting ceremony. Keep the sparks going by strewing a few petals on the table for anniversary dinners. Place a potted plant where you sense negative energy or in the bedroom to ward off bad dreams.

Cypress

Italian Cypress, Mediterranean Cypress (*Cupressus sempervirens*); also known as graveyard cypress, tree of death

The cypress is an evergreen that grows in narrow, columnar form. Its dense, gray-green, scale-like foliage is strongly aromatic when crushed. Its round, knobby cones grow in clusters. After opening in early autumn to shed seeds, the cones stay on the tree for several years.

History and Lore

The Persians regarded this tree as sacred. While the cypress was associated with death and immortality to the ancient Egyptians, it symbolized the finality of death to the Romans. The Greeks hung a bough on a house door to indicate a death in the family. During the Middles Ages in Europe, garlands of cypress branches were draped on coffins and sometimes placed inside. Although it is a tree of death and often represented sorrow, as an evergreen it also represented immortality. Planting two cypress trees near a home was said to bring peace and prosperity and were regarded as symbolic guardians. While the Middle Eastern jinn were said to live in cypress trees, in Europe the elves and faeries made their homes in them.

Magical Connections

Element/s	Earth, water
Astrological influence	Aquarius, Capricorn, Pisces, Taurus, Virgo; Pluto, Saturn
Deities	Apollo, Artemis, Astarte, Cupid, Diana, the Fates, the Furies, Hades, Hecate, Jupiter, Mithras, Pluto, Saturn

Magical entities	Elves, faeries, jinn
Other associations	The afterlife, the otherworld, Samhain
Powers and attributes	Ancestors, awareness, clarity, consecrate/bless, death/funeral practices, defense, divination, focus, growth, healing, justice/legal matters, knowledge, loss/sorrow, past-life work, peace, prosperity/money, protection, renewal, strength, transformation
Available for purchase	Essential oil; boxes or other small items made from the wood

Spells and Rituals

For comfort and healing, especially when dealing with death and loss, diffuse a little essential oil and visualize your ability to cope with the situation. Also use the scent to enhance past-life exploration sessions. To ground excess energy after ritual, burn a small piece of cypress wood.

Daffodil

Common Daffodil, Wild Daffodil (*Narcissus pseudonarcissus*); also known as daff-a-down-dilly, gold bells, narcissus, wild jonquil

Forming clumps and often carpeting the ground, daffodil reaches up to fourteen inches tall. It has narrow, gray-green leaves that grow from the base of the stem. The flower consists of pale yellow petals that create a corona around the darker yellow trumpet. The two shades of yellow is an easy way to distinguish this wild daffodil from its garden relatives.

Caution: All parts of the plant, especially the bulb, are toxic if ingested.

History and Lore

The Egyptians included daffodils in funerary wreaths because they believed that the scent was evocative of the underworld. According to Greek myth, daffodils were said to have carpeted the blessed otherworld of Elysian Fields. In other legends, these trumpet-shaped flowers heralded Persephone's return and the beginning of spring. In medieval Britain, the first daffodil seen in spring was said to bring luck. However, it was a death omen if a daffodil drooped its flower toward a person. Wherever they grow wild, daffodils were said to indicate the location of an ancient sacred site or a magical place. They were a favored flower to wear in chaplets at festivals. In Germany, a daffodil bulb worn in a piece of cloth under the clothing was believed to rid a person of evil spirits.

Magical Connections

Element/s	Water
Astrological influence	Leo, Sagittarius; Sun, Venus
Deities	Bacchus, Ceres, Demeter, Dionysus, the Fates, Hades, Persephone
Magical entities	Faeries
Other associations	The afterlife, the otherworld, Ostara
Powers and attributes	Clarity, consecrate/bless, death/funeral practices, family and home, love, luck, negativity, nightmares, peace, protection, relationships, renewal, security, spirit guides/spirits
Available for purchase	Flower essence; dried flowers

Spells and Rituals

Although the daffodil is associated with death, it carries the energy of rebirth and renewal and works well for the Ostara altar. To clear negative energy from your property, dip a daffodil flower in a bowl of water, and then sprinkle it around outside your home.

Daisy

Common Daisy, English Daisy (*Bellis perennis*); also known as bairnwort, day's eye, wild daisy

Ox-eye Daisy (*Leucanthemum vulgare* syn. *Chrysanthemum leucanthemum*); also known as moon daisy, Midsummer daisy

The common daisy is a small, white flower with a yellow central disc. Its small, spoon-shaped leaves grow in rosettes at the base of the stems that are one to four inches tall. The ox-eye daisy is also white with a yellow central disc, but it grows up to three feet tall. Long, lance-shaped leaves grow from the base while small, toothed leaves grow along the flower stems.

Daisy

History and Lore

Daisies were used in divination of one's love affairs in England, France, and Belgium by performing the familiar one-by-one plucking of petals. To dream of love, English women placed a daisy root under the bed pillow. In some parts of Britain daisy chains were placed around children's necks for protection from faery abduction, in other areas this was done to seek blessings from the fae. In Ireland, daisy chains were called *fairy chains*, and according to legend, faeries used them in spells and charms. In Germany, the oxeye daisy was used for decoration on the summer solstice. In Bavaria, daisies picked between noon and one o'clock on Midsummer's Day were wrapped in paper and used as protective talismans for travel.

Magical Connections

Element/s	Water
Astrological influence	Cancer, Taurus; Moon (ox-eye), Sun, Venus
Deities	Aphrodite, Artemis (ox-eye), Freya, Ostara, Thor, Venus, Zeus
Magical entities	Faeries
Other associations	Beltane
Powers and attributes	Awareness, challenges/obstacles, consecrate/bless, creativity, divination, dream work, family and home, fertility, healing, love, loyalty/fidelity, luck, protection, skills, strength, truth
Available for purchase	Flower essence; dried flowers; seeds

Spells and Rituals

Use the ox-eye daisy on your esbat altar, as it is associated with Artemis and the moon. Place a few flowers under your pillow to enhance dreams and to aid in interpreting messages received during sleep. Place a small daisy chain over your child's bed and ask for the faeries' blessings.

Damiana

Damiana (*Turnera diffusa* syn. *T. aphrodisiaca*, *Damiana aphrodisiaca*); also known as Mexican holly, old woman's broom

Damiana is a wild shrub that can grow up to six feet tall. The lance-shaped leaves are coarsely toothed and heavily veined. Growing at the ends of the branches, the yellow flowers have five rounded petals that are slightly notched.

Caution: Damiana should not be ingested during pregnancy or while nursing.

History and Lore

The Indigenous people of Mesoamerica used damiana medicinally for a range of ailments, but most often for dealing with sexual issues for both men and woman. The Aztec, Maya, and others also used it as an aphrodisiac. For ceremonial purposes, the Guaycura tribe of Mexico's Baja Peninsula made a type of liquor with damiana. Today, known as liqueur Guaycura de damiana or simply damiana liqueur, it is sold in a bottle shaped like a seated woman and said to represent the Inca goddess of fertility. In the American magical tradition of hoodoo, damiana is dedicated to Erzulie, the voodoo Lwa, a goddess or spirit of love, and used for love, luck, and sex magic.

Magical Connections

Element/s	Fire
Astrological influence	Mars

Deities	Erzulie, Pachamama
Powers and attributes	Love, psychic abilities, sex/sexuality
Available for purchase	Flower essence; essential oil; cut, dried leaves; seeds; incense; liqueur

Spells and Rituals

Share damiana tea or liqueur with your lover to enhance sexual pleasure (beforehand, check all precautions). Sprinkle a handful of leaves across your altar or table when engaging in psychic work to increase your abilities.

Dandelion

Common Dandelion (*Taraxacum officinale*);
also known as devil's milk-pale, fairy
clocks, golden sun, wild endive, wishes,
witch-gowan

Jagged, deeply toothed leaves form a rosette base from which the flower stems rise. The flat, yellow flower radiates outward, and then develops into a round seed head.

History and Lore

In the British Isles, it was commonly believed that making a wish and blowing the seeds off the fluffy white head would make it come true. By whispering into the seed head and then blowing in the direction of one's lover, dandelions were said to carry amorous messages. In various legends, dandelions were either faeries in disguise or they held the spirits of faeries and blowing on a seed head would reputedly release a faery from capture. In parts of England, seeds floating on the air were called *fairies* and it was considered lucky to catch one. It was customary when a single seed was seen floating on the wind to catch it, make a wish, and then let it go. Dandelions gathered on Midsummer's Eve were used to ward off witches. In Scotland, plants that yield a milky juice are allied with Brigid. In France, placing a dandelion leaf under the bed pillow was said to bring dreams of a future husband.

Magical Connections

Element/s	Air
Astrological influence	Aquarius, Aries, Libra, Taurus; Jupiter, Mercury
Deities	Brigid, Hecate
Magical entities	Faeries
Powers and attributes	Authority/leadership, awareness, balance/harmony, clarity, communication, divination, healing, love, negativity, prophecy, protection, psychic abilities, skills, spirit guides/spirits, wishes
Available for purchase	Flower essence; dried flowers; dandelion leaf tea; dried roots.

Spells and Rituals

Extract the root of a small dandelion, let it dry out, and then burn it to honor Hecate, or use it as an amulet. To make a wish, pick a seed head on a moonlit night so you will have the power of Luna to aid you.

Date

Common Date Palm (*Phoenix dactylifera*)

Reaching up to eighty feet tall, the date tree's trunk is marked by the bases of old leaf stems.

The leaves on its crown can grow up to sixteen feet in length. Long spikes of flowers produce clusters of fruit. Over a thousand dates can grow in a single cluster.

History and Lore

Herbalists and naturalists from ancient Greece to medieval Europe regarded the date palm as a go-to tree for healing. The fruit was regarded as an aphrodisiac. The Greeks and Romans planted date palms around temples and shrines. Considered the king of the oasis, it was revered by Arabs. The Assyrians used date wine in prophecy rituals. During the Middle Ages in Europe, a polished date seed was worn as an amulet against spells. On the island of Sicily, it was believed that three palm leaves and the proper incantation could ward off witches. Because it was a symbol of life and rebirth, Swedish naturalist Carl Linnaeus gave it the genus name *Phoenix*.

Magical Connections

Element/s	Air, fire
Astrological influence	Leo, Sagittarius, Scorpio; Jupiter, Mars, Moon, Sun
Deities	Amun, Aphrodite, Apollo, Artemis, Asherah, Astarte, Diana, Dumuzi, Hecate, Helios, Hermes, Inanna, Isis, Leto, Mercury, Nike
Powers and attributes	Abundance, banish, challenges/ obstacles, courage, fertility, healing, love, luck, negativity, prophecy, protection, sex/ sexuality, spirituality, success, transformation
Available for purchase	Dried fruit; flower essence

Spells and Rituals

For a fertility spell, prepare a candle with the flower essence and incorporate several dates into your ritual. Dry a date seed and carry it in your pocket for help when dealing with problems or to bolster courage. Also keep one with you for luck at an interview and success on the job.

Deadnettle

Purple Deadnettle, Red Deadnettle (*Lamium pur-pureum*); also known as purple archangel

White Deadnettle, Bee Nettle (*L. album*); also known as Adam and Eve, archangel, fairy boots, fairy feet

Although the leaves closely resemble those of the nettle (*Urtica dioica*), they do not sting when touched. Deadnettle's tubular flowers grow in whorls around the stem just above a leaf pair. The white deadnettle flower has an upper hood and a three-lobed lower lip. Red deadnettle flowers are purplish pink and have two lower lobes. The leaves at the tops of the stems are greenish purple.

History and Lore

The dark ends of the four stamens under the upper hood of the white deadnettle flower look like little shoes or feet. According to English legend, these were Cinderella's slippers. Faeries were said to store their shoes in the flowers for safekeeping because it grew amongst stinging nettles. In other lore, because the flower held upside down can resemble two people in bed, it was regarded as lucky for love. The Anglo-Saxons used purple deadnettle for healing and magic. In medieval Europe, both white and purple deadnettle were used for protection against evil and witchcraft.

Magical Connections

Element/s	Air
Astrological influence	Venus
Magical entities	Faeries
Powers and attributes	Challenges/obstacles, determination, family and home, healing, love, luck, protection, relationships, release, secrets
Available for purchase	Flower essence; cut, dried leaves; powdered leaves

Spells and Rituals

For help in overcoming obstacles, use the leaves in a spell to support perseverance. Not only can the root be used as a love charm, but it can also promote healing between lovers after a quarrel. To raise protective energy, plant deadnettle anywhere on your property.

Deer's Tongue

Deer's Tongue (*Liatris odoratissima* syn. *Carphephorus odoratissimus*, *Trilisa odoratissima*); also known as dog-tongue, hound's tongue, vanilla leaf, wild vanilla

Elkweed (*Frasera speciosa* syn. *Swertia radiata*); also known as deer ear, deer's tongue, monument plant

Reaching three to five feet tall, deer's tongue has purplish-brown stems that branch near the top. The base leaves are spatulate or tongue shaped; upper leaves are oval. Purple flowers grow in small clusters on branching stems. When bruised, the plant has a vanilla-like aroma. Elkweed exists as a rosette of large, spatula-shaped leaves for several years (even twenty or more) before sending up an eight-foot-tall flower spire. The fringed flowers are greenish white and dotted with purple. They grow in elongated clusters.

Caution: Deer's tongue may cause liver damage if ingested; large doses of elkweed root can be fatal.

Deer's Tongue

History and Lore

In North America, deer's tongue was used by the Cherokee, Creek, and Choctaw to flavor tobacco or sometimes to remove the harshness from smoking mixtures. It was also used as a contraceptive. The Navajo used elkweed roots medicinally as a sedative and the Apache used the roots for food. Both plants were used by the Cherokee to clear the mind and ward off evil spirits.

Magical Connections

Element/s	Fire
Astrological influence	Aries, Sagittarius, Scorpio; Mars

Powers and attributes	Awareness, love, protection, psychic abilities, sex/sexuality
Available for purchase	Cut, dried leaves and stems; whole dried leaves; seeds

Spells and Rituals

Sprinkle a handful of dried leaves on your altar or table to boost and enhance any type of psychic work. Place the seeds in a sachet to use as a love charm or scatter them under your bed to heighten sex and passion. Use deer's tongue or elkweed to boost protective energy.

Devil's Bit Scabious

Devil's Bit Scabious (*Succisa pratensis* syn. *Scabiosa succisa*); also known as blue bobs, blue bonnets, blue button, curl-doddy, devil's bit, scabious

Reaching up to three feet tall, devil's bit has a base rosette of lance-shaped leaves with purplish blotches. Violet-blue flowers in dense, rounded flower heads sit atop slender, branching stems. The flowers are occasionally pink.

History and Lore

According to widespread belief in England, the root of this plant was longer at one time, but the devil was angry that it was used to heal so many ailments that he took a bite of it leaving a stubby little end. While devil's bit was useless in treating the plague, it was successful against scabies, a skin infestation of the scabies mite. In parts of England, it was believed that picking the flowers would cause the devil to appear beside you or in your dreams. In Ireland, cows that ate devil's bit were said to produce creamy milk. The plant was used in potions to cure the effects of the evil eye or any illness inflicted through magic. According to Irish and Scottish belief, holding the root while reciting the proper chant was said to summon a brownie to do the housework. In Europe, flowers or leaves were worn as an amulet for protection from all forms of evil. In Portugal the plant was included in funeral wreaths.

Magical Connections

Element/s	Earth
Astrological influence	Libra, Taurus; Mercury, Venus
Powers and attributes	Challenges/obstacles, defense, luck, negativity, protection
Available for purchase	Flower essence; seeds

Spells and Rituals

When faced with any type of adversity, dry a piece of root, and keep it on your altar as a talisman. Carry a pressed flower in your wallet for luck. Place a small bowl of seeds wherever you need to clear away negative energy or crush a handful of seeds to include in defensive magic.

Devil's Shoestring

Devil's Shoestring, Hobblebush (*Viburnum lantanoides* syn. *V. alnifolium*); also known as American wayfaring tree, dogberry, mooseberry, tangle-foot, trip-toe, witch-hobble

Devil's shoestring is a sprawling, straggly shrub. Its stems tend to droop downward and take root where they touch the ground, forming snarls of loops that are easy to trip over. Its leaves are oval to round, veined and wrinkled with toothed margins. The white, five-petaled flowers grow in flat-topped clusters from the leaf axils. The clusters have tiny flowers at the center and larger ones at the periphery. The center flowers develop into red, berry-like fruit.

History and Lore
As the word *hobble* in several of this plant's names suggests, the loops of tangled branches formed by this bush can trip up anyone (or thing) who does not tread carefully. The Cherokee believed that planting devil's shoestring next to the front entrance of a dwelling could deter evil spirits. The Iroquois used it as a fertility aid and in love medicine. Devil's shoestring is used in the American magical tradition of hoodoo for protection and in breaking hexes.

Magical Connections

Element/s	Fire
Astrological influence	Jupiter
Powers and attributes	Banish, defense, hexes, luck, negativity, protection
Available for purchase	Cut, dried roots

Spells and Rituals
To make a protective amulet for the home that you can hang over a door, bundle a small handful of roots or short branches together, and then tie them with a piece of red yarn. When seeking new employment, include several leaves or fruit in a spell for luck.

Dill
Dill (*Anethum graveolens*); also known as dilly, European dill, garden dill

Reaching about three feet tall, dill has upright stems and bluish green leaves that are ferny and thread-like. Its yellow flowers grow in large, flat clusters. The tiny, oval seeds are flat and ribbed. The term *dill weed* refers to the leaves. Dill looks very similar to its cousin fennel (*Foeniculum vulgare*). The way to tell them apart is that dill has one stem whereas fennel has multiple stems.

History and Lore
The Egyptians and Scythians included dill in burial preparations and decorations. The Greeks associated it with Dionysus; the Romans with Bacchus who they honored with wreaths of dill. During the Middle Ages in Europe, dill was a popular ingredient in love potions. Regarded as a magician's herb, it was used in spells to deter witches as well as in black magic. Offering a cup of dill tea was believed to take away a witch's power. Bunches were hung in animal sheds in Germany for protection against witches on Walpurgis and fed to cattle at other times to protect them from evil spirits.

Magical Connections

Element/s	Air, fire
Astrological influence	Cancer, Gemini, Leo, Scorpio, Virgo; Mercury
Deities	Adonis, Bacchus, Dionysus

Other associations	Walpurgis
Powers and attributes	Banish, changes/transitions, creativity, defense, divination, hexes, love, manifest, prosperity/money, protection, purification, sex/sexuality
Available for purchase	Essential oil; dried, cut leaves; dried seeds; flower essence

Spells and Rituals

To manifest your dreams, make a wreath with long stems and leaves to hang on your front door. Place a couple of flower heads in your workspace to boost creativity, and on your altar to support divination. Use essential oil to purify ritual and magical tools.

Dittany

Dittany of Crete (*Origanum dictamnus*); also known as hop marjoram, wintersweet

Dittany grows in spreading mounds about twelve inches tall and twice as wide. The downy, rounded leaves are aromatic and sometimes mottled with purple. The tiny, two-lipped flowers are greenish and pink to purple. They bloom in pendant clusters that resemble hops.

History and Lore

In her role as Lucina watching over childbirth, Roman goddess Juno was often represented wearing a circlet of dittany. In mainland Greece and Crete, this plant growing on a grave meant that the deceased was at peace. Dittany was a strong token of love in Crete when it was given as a gift because it grew in remote and often difficult to reach areas. According to English and European legend, deer were said to eat dittany after being shot because it had the power to dislodge arrows. Creating a great deal of smoke when burned, dittany was used by European practitioners of magic to conjure spirits. It was also used to drive away evil spirits. Sorcerers reputedly used dittany for incense during scrying because it was said to provide a glimpse of the future as well as communicate with the otherworld. Dittany was also woven into garlands and worn to enhance clairvoyance.

Magical Connections

Element/s	Water
Astrological influence	Gemini, Libra; Moon, Sun, Venus
Deities	Aphrodite, Artemis, Diana, Juno, Osiris, Pan, Persephone, Venus
Other associations	The otherworld; Samhain
Powers and attributes	Divination, love, psychic abilities, spirit guides/spirits
Available for purchase	Flower essence; cut, dried flowers and leaves; seeds

Spells and Rituals

At Samhain, sprinkle dried flowers and leaves on your altar and in the cardinal directions of your circle to aid in contacting ancestors. To enhance psychic skills, prepare a candle with flower essence before a session. Burn a pinch of dried leaves as incense when working with spirits.

Dock

Dock

Bitter Dock, Broad-leaved Dock (*Rumex obtusifo-
    lius*); also known as docken, wayside dock
Dooryard Dock (*R. longifolius*); also known as
    butter dock, northern dock, yard dock
Yellow Dock, Curly Dock (*R. crispus*); also known
    as curled dock, narrow dock

Dock has large base leaves with smaller ones on
the branching flower stalks, which reach about
three feet tall. Dense clusters of drooping, light
green to pinkish flowers grow in whorls around
the stalks. Dock flowers develop into a papery,
heart-shaped, rusty-brown pod that holds a single
seed. The lance-shaped leaves have wavy edges;
yellow dock's leaves are crinklier and wavier; bitter dock's leaves are wider.

History and Lore

The Anglo-Saxons used dock to ward off elf shot,
which was believed to be an invisible magical
weapon used by elves to cause disease. In Scotland, bitter dock was used in charms to break
faery spells that had been cast on children. The
trows (a type of faery) of the Orkney Islands
were said to ride on the stems as though they
were horses. As a fertility aid in Ireland, a woman
would wear a bag of seeds tied to her left arm.
Young Irish women used dooryard dock in divination to discover who they would marry. According to Tennessee folklore, yellow dock was
believed to provide protection from almost everything, even getting hit by a falling tree.

Magical Connections

Element/s	Air, Earth (yellow)
Astrological influence	Jupiter
Magical entities	Faeries, trows
Powers and attributes	Divination, fertility, healing, hexes, love, prosperity/money, protection
Available for purchase	Flower essence; cut, dried root; seeds

Spells and Rituals

For a protection spell, cut a long flower stalk, and
then hold it in front of you as you walk around
the perimeter of your property. If you live in an
apartment, walk through each room. Place the
stalk near your front door until the flowers dry
out, and then burn them at the next full moon.

Dodder

Chinese Dodder (*Cuscuta chinensis*); also known
   as gold thread, strangle weed
European Dodder, Greater Dodder (*C. europaea*);
   also known as angel's hair, devil's guts,
   devil's net, hellweed, love vine, Venus's hair,
   witches' hair, witches' shoelaces

Dodder is a leafless, rootless, parasitic vine with
threadlike stems that attach to other plants.
Resembling a tangle of spaghetti, the twining
stems spread out and cover its host. The bell-
like flowers have pointed, triangular petals and
grow in dense, rounded clusters. European dodder is reddish orange with pinkish white flowers.
Chinese dodder is yellow with whitish yellow
flowers.

History and Lore
Dodder was used medicinally in ancient China
and Greece and in medieval Europe. Because
it seemed to appear out of nowhere like mistletoe, dodder was considered somewhat holy in
Asia and thought to have the power to hold the
secrets of heaven. It was gathered for use as a
charm and believed to be an aphrodisiac, especially for male virility. Dodder was used in love
potions and for love divination in the Ozarks of
North America. A piece of dodder was thrown
or placed on another plant and if it attached and
grew, love was said to be true. In Europe and the
British Isles, the plant was regarded unkindly and
received many negative folk names because it can
overrun and destroy cultivated crops.

Magical Connections

Element/s	Water
Astrological influence	Saturn
Powers and attributes	Bind, defense, divination, love, sex/sexuality
Available for purchase	Whole seeds; powdered seeds

Spells and Rituals
To counter magic used against you, take a cup
of seeds outside, hold it between your hands as
you recite or sing an appropriate incantation, and
then cast the seeds away from you as you turn in
a circle. Gather several handfuls of dodder to use
in knot magic.

Dogwood

Cornelian Cherry Dogwood (*Cornus mas*); also
   known as cornelian tree, European cornel
Flowering Dogwood (*C. florida* syn. *Cynoxylon
   floridum*); also known as American boxwood,
   false box, pegwood
Mountain Dogwood (*C. nuttallii*); also known as
   Pacific dogwood, Pacific flowering dogwood

The cornelian cherry has yellow, star-shaped flowers that grow in rounded clusters. The edible fruit
is bright red and closely resembles a cherry. The
other two dogwoods are showy attention-getters.
The large, notched white petals are bracts that
protect the tiny cluster of greenish white flowers
at the center. The flowering dogwood has bright
red fruit; the mountain dogwood fruit is orange
to red.

Caution: The fruit of the flowering dogwood is not edible; sources vary about the edibility of the mountain dogwood fruit.

History and Lore

Through the centuries, dogwood was believed to have highly protective powers. The Greeks used the wood of the cornelian cherry for spear shafts, bows, and other weapons. The tree was a protective talisman for the city of Rome. In medieval Germany, a handkerchief that had been dipped in the sap of a dogwood was carried on Midsummer's Day to make a wish come true. In the Balkans, dogwood was worn as a protective amulet and placed in baby cradles to deter witches. In areas of Spain, branches were used as divining rods.

Magical Connections

Element/s	Air, earth
Astrological influence	Jupiter (cornelian), Mars, Moon
Other associations	Ostara, Beltane, Midsummer's Day
Powers and attributes	Banish, creativity, defense, emotions, healing, inspiration, loyalty/fidelity, manifest, protection, wishes
Available for purchase	Flower essence

Spells and Rituals

A good luck charm made of dogwood fosters emotional support. To draw down the power of Luna make a circle with white petals/bracts on your esbat alter. To raise protective energy for your home, place a handful of leaves under your welcome mat.

Dragon's Blood

Dragon's Blood (*Daemonorops draco* syn. *Calamus draco*, *C. draconis*); also known as draconis resina, dragon's blood palm

Young plants resemble a small palm but become climbers and take over nearby trees. It has long, lance-shaped leaves and whorls of black spines on stems that can reach fifty feet long. The cherry-sized fruit is covered with vertical rows of scales and grow in long branching clusters. Resin is secreted from the fruit. The red resin known as dragon's blood is obtained from several different plants.

Caution: Dragon's blood is toxic if ingested. The dragon tree (*Dracaena draco*) and medieval dragon's blood (*Dracaena cinnabari*) are considered vulnerable or threatened species.

History and Lore

According to legend in India, a battle between a dragon and an elephant resulted in the magical substance dragon's blood. The mystique of the mythical beast made the resin an important trade item with the West along with frankincense and myrrh. Although depicted as monstrous in medieval European legend and art, the dragon's body was believed to have magical qualities and powers. Dragon's blood was used as ritual incense and as an offering as well as an amulet for protection. In the American magical tradition of hoodoo, dragon's blood is used to draw money and love and to clear away negative energy.

Magical Connections

Element/s	Fire
Astrological influence	Aries, Sagittarius; Mars, Pluto
Magical entities	Dragons
Powers and attributes	Banish, bind, challenges/obstacles, confidence, consecrate/bless, defense, determination, healing, hexes, love, manifest, negativity, protection, release, security, sex/sexuality, spirituality, success
Available for purchase	Resin pieces and powdered; incense

Spells and Rituals

For any type of spell, burn dragon's blood incense as you visualize a dragon rising in the curling smoke and surrounding you with its power. To banish something, burn incense and visualize what you want to remove being bound to the smoke and carried away.

Edelweiss

Edelweiss, Snow Flower (*Leontopodium nivale alpinum* syn. *L. alpinum*); also known as alpine cudweed, glacier queen, lion foot, wool flower

Occasionally reaching a foot tall, the star-shaped edelweiss has small clusters of yellow disc flowers that are surrounded by white, woolly sepals. Growing close together, each flower has its own separate stem. The gray-green base leaves are lance shaped and velvety.

Caution: Edelweiss is no longer considered an endangered species; however, it is a protected plant in some areas.

History and Lore

According to Swiss legend, after dying of loneliness in her snowy mountaintop home, a young woman was transformed into the edelweiss. It became a symbol of devotion for a man to climb the icy mountains to pick the flower for his sweetheart. Possessing a flower was said to bring luck. Although it was a Christian custom in Switzerland to hang wreaths of edelweiss on porches and windows on Ascension Day (May 26), in the state of Tyrol, Austria, wearing a wreath of it was said to make a person invisible. Edelweiss was also used as a protective charm against lightning. In Germany, it was believed that carrying an edelweiss flower wrapped in white linen in a pocket would provide protection from bullets and daggers.

Magical Connections

Element/s	Fire
Astrological influence	Leo; Jupiter
Powers and attributes	Determination, love, loyalty/fidelity, luck, protection
Available for purchase	Flower essence; dried flowers; seeds

Spells and Rituals

To help you stay the course and get through a difficult time, write a few keywords about it on a picture of edelweiss flowers. Meditate with it, and then place it on your altar until the situation changes. Use a small sachet of dried flowers and seeds as a good luck charm.

Elder

American Elderberry, Canada Elderberry (*Sambucus canadensis*)

European Elder, Black Elderberry (*S. nigra*); also known as ellhorn, fairy tree, lady elder, pipe tree

Elder is a large shrub with oval leaves and small white flowers that grow in large, umbrella-like clusters that can reach up to ten inches across. The flowers give way to large pendulous clusters of bluish black berries. The flowers of the American elderberry have a lemon-like scent; the European elder flowers are musky.

History and Lore

It was commonly believed that an old female spirit lived in elder trees; in Germany this spirit was known as Frau Ellhorn; in Denmark she was *Hyldemoer*, Elder Mother. However, in tenth-century England there was a change from belief in a crone-like tree spirit to the entity being a witch and the elder became associated with black magic. In some areas of England and Europe, the tree itself came to be regarded as a witch. In Oxfordshire it was said that burning elder wood could reputedly cause bewitchment. Despite these beliefs, elder wood was also used as a charm against witches and anything negative in England and Europe. In Germany wreaths were hung on houses as a charm against lightning; in Scotland an elder hedge provided that protection. In Denmark, England, and Scotland, elder trees were believed to make faeries visible.

Magical Connections

Element/s	Air, earth, fire, water
Astrological influence	Mercury, Venus
Deities	Bertha, Boann, Cailleach Bheur, the Dagda, Danu, Freya, Freyr, Gaia, Holle, Hulda, Rhea, Venus, Vulcan
Magical entities	Elves, faeries, Frau Ellhorn, Hyldemoer, will-o-the-wisp
Ogham	Ruis ⫽⫽⫽
Other associations	The Crone; Walpurgis, Beltane, Litha, Midsummer's Eve
Powers and attributes	Abundance, banish, consecrate/bless, creativity, death/funeral practices, defense, dream work, healing, hexes, love, loyalty/fidelity, prosperity/money, protection, purification, see faeries, spirit guides/spirits, spirituality, wisdom
Available for purchase	Elderberry juice; dried elderberries; elderberry seed oil; flower essence

Spells and Rituals

To boost the energy of a love charm, include elderberries. To enhance sleep and dream work, place dried berries in a sachet next to your pillow. Place a picture of elder flowers on your altar to celebrate the power of the Crone.

Elecampane

Elecampane

Elecampane (*Inula helenium*); also known as elf dock, elfwort, horseheal, inula, sun flower

With long, lance-shaped leaves, elecampane's erect stem grows three to six feet tall. The base leaves can grow up to three feet long. Its bright flowers have tangled rays of petals making them look like scraggly, yellow daisies or overgrown dandelions. The flowers are slightly aromatic.

History and Lore

The species name *helenium* is in reference to Helen of Troy from Greek mythology. While legends differ about her association with the plant, elecampane has been generally regarded as lucky. On the island of Guernsey, it was used for love charms; however, it had to be gathered on Midsummer's Eve, mixed with ambergris, and then worn over the heart for nine days. (Ambergris is a waxy substance produced in the digestive tract of sperm whales and is used in perfumery.) In the Balkans, elecampane was sewn into the clothing of children to keep them safe from witches. According to English legend, faeries used elecampane roots in rituals and made garlands with the flowers. The Anglo-Saxons used elecampane to treat elf shot, especially when a man's virility was at stake. Elf shot was believed to be an invisible magical weapon used by elves to cause disease.

Magical Connections

Element/s	Air
Astrological influence	Jupiter, Mercury
Magical entities	Elves, faeries
Powers and attributes	Communication, divination, happiness, healing, intuition, love, luck, peace, protection, psychic abilities, purification, relationships, secrets, sex/sexuality, spirit guides/spirits, truth
Available for purchase	Flower essence; essential oil; dried roots; dried flowers; root extract

Spells and Rituals

For help in resolving sexual issues with your partner, use the essential oil or infused oil from the root to anoint the headboard of your bed. To help sort out problems in a friendship, keep a small sachet of dried flowers with you when you are together.

Elm

American Elm, White Elm (*Ulmus Americana* syn. *U. floridana*); also known as water elm

English Elm, Common Elm (*U. procera*); also known as ellum, elven

Wych Elm, Scots Elm (*U. glabra*); also known as hornbeam, quicken, witch elm, witchwood

Elm leaves are oval, heavily veined, and toothed. Wych elm leaves are wider at the ends. The American elm produces dangling clusters of small, reddish-green flowers. The English and wych elm's reddish-green flower clusters are short and rounded. Called *samaras*, elm seeds are encased in a papery covering.

History and Lore

The ancient Greeks associated the elm tree with Morpheus, the god of dreams. Roman poet Virgil noted that it was a tree of prophecy. Elms were believed to mark the entrance to the otherworld in Greek and Roman myth and to the faery realm in Celtic mythology. Elms were often used as execution trees by the Normans. In Scotland, a twig of wych elm was kept beside a butter churn to prevent faeries from making off with the contents. In Yorkshire, wych elm was attached to horse bridles during travel as a protective charm. An Irish method of curing a man's impotency involved writing his name on an elm stick in ogham and then striking him with it.

Magical Connections

Element/s	Air, earth, water
Astrological influence	Capricorn; Mercury, Saturn
Deities	Ceres, Cerridwen, Danu, Demeter, Dionysus, Gaia, Holle, Juno, Loki, Morpheus, Odin, Ran
Magical entities	Elves, faeries
Ogham	Ailm +
Other associations	The otherworld; Yule
Powers and attributes	Changes/transitions, determination, divination, dream work, healing, intuition, justice/legal matters, love, manifest, negativity, prophecy, protection, psychic abilities, renewal, wisdom, wishes
Available for purchase	Flower essence

Spells and Rituals

As an ally for dream work, place a picture of an elm on your bedside table. During transitions, keep an elm twig on your altar to represent and foster renewal. To raise healing energy, place an elm leaf under a green candle and visualize a large tree spreading its branches to those in need.

Eucalyptus

Blue Gum Eucalyptus (*Eucalyptus globulus*); also known as fever tree, gum tree, southern blue gum, Tasmanian blue gum

Lemon-Scented Gum (*E. citriodora* syn. *Corymbia citriodora*); also known as lemon gum tree, spotted gum

The blue gum eucalyptus has narrow, blue-green to yellowish-green leaves, feathery creamy white flowers, and top-shaped seedpods. Its blue-gray bark peels off in large pieces. The lemon eucalyptus has narrow, tapering leaves that give off a lemony scent when crushed. It has feathery creamy white flowers and urn-shaped seedpods. Its pale bark sheds in curling flakes.

History and Lore

The Indigenous people of Australia have used eucalyptus oil medicinally for centuries and have regarded the tree as particularly sacred. Large, hollow branches are still used to make didgeridoos, a traditional ceremonial and ritual musical instrument. Eucalyptus is also integral to the Aboriginal mythology of the Dreaming, the period of time when ancestral spirits created the world. Panels of bark have served as canvases for Aboriginal artists.

Magical Connections

Element/s	Air, earth, water
Astrological influence	Cancer, Pisces; Mercury, Moon, Saturn, Sun
Deities	Luna, Mercury, Selene, Venus
Powers and attributes	Ancestors, banish, determination, dream work, emotions, growth (lemon), focus, healing, loss/sorrow, negativity, past-life work, protection, psychic abilities, purification, security, spirit guides/spirits, spirituality, wisdom
Available for purchase	Essential oil; leaves; seedpods

Spells and Rituals

The scent of eucalyptus helps to release sorrow and foster security. To facilitate contact with spirits, place a handful of dried leaves on your altar. Any part of the tree can be used to support past-life work. Make a circle on your altar with seedpods to honor your ancestors.

Evening Primrose

Common Evening Primrose (*Oenothera biennis*); also known as evening star, king's cure-all, night light, primrose tree

Evening primrose has a rosette of large base leaves and an erect stem that can reach up to five feet tall. Lance-shaped leaves with wavy edges grow on the flower stems. At dusk, the yellow, four-petaled flowers bloom a few at a time and last only one night. The flowers give way to clusters of oblong seed capsules.

History and Lore

Showing only faded blossoms during the day, evening primrose is a plant of the night. At dusk the yellow flower petals unfurl to welcome the night with its scent and faint light from its slight phosphorescence that can be seen on dark nights. This may account for its use in magic. The plant served as food and medicine for the Cherokee, Apache, and Ojibwe. Colonial settlers adopted its use and evening primrose was introduced into Europe in the early seventeenth century. Its common name comes from the resemblance of its flower to the true primrose (*Primula vulgaris*). Evening primrose was cultivated in France and Germany where according to lore it had a calming effect on vicious animals. The root has a faint odor reminiscent of wine, which gave rise to legends in Europe that evening primrose either countered the effects of wine or made a person want to drink wine. There is still disagreement about the interpretation of its genus name

Oenothera from Greek and whether it means "wine-hunting" or "wine-scented."[51]

Powers and attributes	Balance/harmony, banish, changes/transitions, creativity, family and home, healing, night-mares, protection, purification, security, success, truth
Available for purchase	Oil; dried leaves; seeds; herb tea

Spells and Rituals

For help in finding truth, hold a leaf between your palms as you meditate on the situation. Cut a dried flower stalk to use as a wand for banishing spells. To commemorate the beginning of something new in your life, burn a dried leaf in your cauldron as you visualize the future.

Evening Primrose

Magical Connections

Element/s	Fire
Astrological influence	Venus
Magical entities	Faeries

Eyebright

Eyebright (*Euphrasia officinalis* syn. *E. rostkoviana*); also known as bird's eye, eyewort, fairy flax, joy flower

Common Eyebright (*E. nemorosa* syn. *E. Americana*); also known as wild eyebright

Eyebright is a creeping, semi-parasitic herb about eight to ten inches tall with small, deeply toothed leaves. The white or pinkish flower has an irregular shape with two upper petals that curl backward. The three lower petals are marked with a central yellow spot and purple veins; the middle petal is longer. The flowers are arranged around a densely leafed spike. Common eyebright is a little smaller with slender leaves that are coarsely toothed with brown tips. Its flower colors are a little less striking.

51. Sanders, *The Secrets of Wildflowers*, 255

History and Lore

Although German abbess and herbalist Hildegard von Bingen is credited with recognizing eyebright's healing properties, the plant was not widely used until centuries later. In Ireland, it was believed that eyebright was so powerful that it could not be harmed by anything natural or supernatural. It was used to cure fairy stroke (enchantment) and to ward off the evil eye. During the late Middle Ages, it was believed to bestow second sight. In Scotland, it was believed that carrying a sprig in the pocket would make people tell the truth. Eyebright ale was a popular drink in Elizabethan England.

Magical Connections

Element/s	Air
Astrological influence	Aries, Gemini, Leo, Virgo; Sun
Deities	The Graces
Powers and attributes	Clarity, divination, dream work, happiness, intuition, psychic ability, skills, truth
Available for purchase	Flower essence; cut, dried leaves and stems; seeds

Spells and Rituals

When preparing for any type of psychic work, hold a couple of eyebright flowers against your third eye chakra for several minutes to clear your mind. This plant is especially helpful for cultivating clairvoyant skills.

Fairy Wand

Fairy Wand, False Unicorn Root (*Chamaelirium luteum*); also known as blazing star, devil's bit, helonias root, starwort

Fairy wand has small, white flowers that look like tiny starbursts. Growing in tight clusters, the flowers form spikes between four and eight inches long at the top of the stems. Produced on separate plants, male flowers are white and female flowers are slightly greenish. The male flower spike is larger with a downward curing tip. The dark green base leaves are spoon shaped; the stem leaves are smaller and lance shaped.

Caution: This plant is classified as endangered or threatened in some areas, check before gathering in the wild.

History and Lore

Native to North America, fairy wand was used for a range of ailments by the Cherokee and later by European settlers. Through the centuries this plant has been confused with unicorn root (*Aletris farinosa*) and the words *false* and *true* were variously applied to both plants. The ethereal appearance of its flowers gave it an association with faeries.

Magical Connections

Element/s	Earth
Astrological influence	Venus
Magical entities	Faeries, unicorns

Powers and attributes	Banish, consecrate / bless, emotions, fertility, healing, inspiration, loss / sorrow, love, loyalty / fidelity, protection, purification, sex / sexuality, support, wishes
Available for purchase	Flower essence; cut, dried roots; powdered root. As noted this plant is endangered in the wild, check vendors' sources.

Spells and Rituals

Sprinkle a little flower essence to cast a circle for ritual or to consecrate a special area. When dealing with the loss of a loved one, hold a cup of powdered root between your hands in a private ritual to say goodbye, and then scatter it across the person's grave.

Fennel

Bitter Fennel (*Foeniculum vulgare* syn. *F. officinale*); also known as common fennel, wild fennel
Sweet Fennel (*F. vulgare* var. *dulce*); also known as common fennel, French or Roman fennel

Fennel has a white bulbous base and multiple stalks. The foliage is threadlike; however, bitter fennel's fronds are less divided. The tiny, bright yellow flowers grow in large umbrella-shaped clusters. The flat, oval seeds are light brown and ridged. Both fennels have an anise or licorice flavor, but sweet fennel is, well, sweeter.

History and Lore

In Greek mythology, Prometheus used a stalk of fennel as a torch to bring fire to humans and the plant came to symbolize knowledge of the gods. During the lusty Dionysian celebrations, participants wore crowns of woven stalks and leaves, as did attendees of the Greek Attican mystery plays, dramas that developed from Dionysian rituals. The Anglo-Saxons regarded fennel as a powerfully protective plant that had been created by Woden and used it in healing charms to ward off demons and sickness. In later centuries on Midsummer's Eve, the English hung fennel on house doors for protection against fire and witches. The practice continued into the late medieval period with fennel fronds hung on doors or seeds stuffed in keyholes to deter witches, evil spirits, and ghosts from entering a house. In Germany, fennel was used to drive away dwarfs.

Magical Connections

Element/s	Fire
Astrological influence	Aries, Gemini Virgo; Mercury
Deities	Adonis, Dionysus, Kupala, Odin, Prometheus, Woden
Other associations	Walpurgis, Midsummer's Eve
Powers and attributes	Changes / transitions, clarity, confidence, courage, divination, family and home, fertility, focus, healing, protection, psychic abilities, purification, renewal, security, spirit guides / spirits, strength
Available for purchase	Essential oil; flower essence; seeds

Spells and Rituals

To boost the energy of divination sessions, make a circle with fennel seeds on your altar. Hang several fronds in your home to deter unwelcomed spirits. During times of transition, place a pinch of seeds in a small pouch to keep with you to foster courage and a sense of security.

Feverfew

Feverfew (*Tanacetum parthenium* syn. *Chrysanthemum parthenium*); also known as bachelor's buttons, devil-daisy, featherfew, Midsummer daisy, wild chamomile

Reaching about thirty inches tall, feverfew has branching stems with daisy-like flowers that grow in flat clusters at the top of the plant. The flowers have large, yellow centers and short, white petals. The yellow-green leaves are lobed with rounded segments; the lower leaves are more deeply divided. The plant is strongly aromatic.

Caution: Abortifacient; eating fresh leaves may cause mouth sores.

Feverfew

History and Lore

The species name, *parthenium*, is sometimes attributed to a legend that feverfew was used to treat a worker who fell from the Parthenon in Athens during its construction. However, the complete botanical name translates as "immortal virgin" and links it to the goddess Athena in her epithet Athena Parthenos (virgin).[52] The Anglo-Saxons used feverfew in a charm to heal someone after an attack from a spear-wielding she-elf. Worn as an amulet against the plague in medieval Europe, the odor was believed to ward off evil spirits as well. As its common name suggests, feverfew was used to treat fevers and in England just placing it on a sickbed was believed to be enough to cure.

Magical Connections

Element/s	Water
Astrological influence	Sagittarius; Venus
Deities	Athena Parthenos, Hecate
Powers and attributes	Defense, emotions, healing, love, protection, purification, strength
Available for purchase	Essential oil; flower essence; cut, dried leaves; seeds

Spells and Rituals

Regarded as a powerful healer for thousands of years, feverfew aids in sending healing energy to someone in need. Also helpful in recovering from heartbreak, place a few dried flowers in a small pouch to use as an amulet. Include it in protection spells and in defense against jinxes.

52. Hourihane, *The Routledge Companion to Medieval Iconography*, 448.

Fig

Common Fig (*Ficus carica*); also known as cultivated fig, edible fig, true fig

Sycamore Fig (*F. sycomorus*); also known as Egyptian sycamore, mulberry fig

The fig is a spreading tree that is usually as wide
as it is tall. Its thick leaves have three to five lobes.
The slightly pear-shaped fruit of the common fig
ripens to a maroon-brown color and grows singly. The fruit of the sycamore fig grows in clusters and is smaller than the common fig.

History and Lore

As part of the Greek Eleusinian Mysteries, secret
rites in the veneration of Demeter and Persephone, initiates were said to have been seated at
the spot where the first fig tree was discovered.[53]
Dionysus was often depicted with a crown of fig
leaves and during Bacchanalian festivals women
wore necklaces of figs to symbolize fecundity.
At the start of the New Year, Romans used figs
as temple offerings. Regarding the tree as phallic,
they used its milky sap to represent the semen of
the god Mars. Egyptians cultivated the common
fig and used it for offerings, but the sycamore fig
was more highly revered. Figs were also placed in
tombs because they were considered a suitable
food for the afterlife.

Magical Connections

Element/s	Air, water
Astrological influence	Jupiter, Venus

Deities	Bacchus, Ceres, Demeter, Diony-sus, Hathor, Hermes, Iris, Juno, Mars, Mercury, Nut, Osiris, Perse-phone, Ra, Saturn, Thoth
Other associations	Samhain
Powers and attributes	Abundance, ancestors, balance/harmony, creativity, death/funeral practices, fertility, love, peace, prosperity/money, protection, psychic abilities
Available for purchase	Fresh or dried figs; fig juice

Spells and Rituals

At Samhain, place a fig on your altar to symbolically feed your ancestors. To boost the energy of a
fertility spell, eat a fig as part of the process. Place
a picture of the tree in your workspace to enhance
creativity. Use fig juice as a libation in ritual.

Figwort

Common Figwort, Woodland Figwort (*Scrophu-
laria nodosa*); also known as brownwort,
carpenter's square, fothram, knotted figwort,
poor man's salve, throatwort

Reaching about three feet tall, figwort has square
stems and large, lance-shaped leaves that are
toothed and veined. Loose clusters of tiny, bulbous
flowers grow atop the stems. The upper lip of the
flower is reddish brown with two lobes; the lower
lip has three shorter lobes that are green. The
rounded seed capsule resembles a fig.

Caution: Figwort is considered toxic and should
not be ingested.

---

53. De Cleene and Lejeune, *Compendium of Symbolic and Ritual Plants in Europe,* 252.

History and Lore

The Greeks and Anglo-Saxons used figwort medicinally. The Celts associated it with the flowing of milk and the bounty of the land. In the Hebrides and Isle of Skye of Scotland, figwort was considered a magical herb and used as a charm for protecting cows and ensuring the milk supply. Although in Scotland it was used against faeries, in Ireland it was regarded as a plant of the fae. Its Irish name *fothram* was reputedly derived from *faoi trom* "under elder" and meant that the power of the elder tree was passed to any figwort growing underneath.[54] In England, figwort was hung in the smoke of the Midsummer bonfire to increase its power before being placed in the home or worn as a protective amulet.

Magical Connections

Element/s	Earth, Water
Astrological influence	Cancer, Libra, Taurus; Moon, Venus
Deities	Brigid
Magical entities	Faeries
Other associations	Midsummer's Eve
Powers and attributes	Abundance, happiness, peace, protection
Available for purchase	Cut, dried roots; seeds

Spells and Rituals

Place a handful of figwort roots on your Imbolc altar to invoke and honor Brigid. Make an infusion of the roots on Midsummer's Eve and sprinkle it around your ritual area to invite faeries to your celebration.

Fir

Balsam Fir, Eastern Fir (*Abies balsamea*); also
  known as blister fir
European Silver Fir (*A. alba*); also known as common silver fir

The upper branches of the balsam fir grow at right angles from the trunk, the lower branches droop. Its curved needles are dark green, and its cylindrical cones are grayish green with a slight purple tinge. The European silver fir has grooved, dark green needles and cylindrical cones that turn reddish brown as they mature.

History and Lore

The fir tree was considered the king of the forest in northern Europe and believed to house powerful woodland spirits. As a symbol of rebirth and immortality, Romanians carried boughs of fir at the front of funeral processions. In the historical region of Silesia (now part of Poland, Germany, and the Czech Republic) a fir branch was hung on the stable door on May Day to ensure the health of cattle. Throughout Germany, a small fir was planted near the door of a house where a wedding was going to take place. Fir boughs were traditional Yule decorations that also provided comfort to any elves that may visit the home. In northern Germany, sprigs were attached to the last cow out of the barn when the herd was taken out to pasture in the spring as a fertility charm. As part of the Midsummer's Eve celebrations in the Harz Mountains, it was customary to place flowers in a fir tree or a large cut branch and dance around it.

----

54. Mac Coitir, *Ireland's Wild Plants*, 98.

Magical Connections

Element/s	Air, earth, fire
Astrological influence	Aries; Jupiter, Mars, Saturn, Uranus
Deities	Artemis, Athena, Bacchus, Cybele, Diana, Dionysus, Frigg, Inanna, Isis, Osiris, Pan, Persephone, Rhea
Magical entities	Dwarves, elves, faeries
Ogham	Ailm +
Other associations	The otherworld, Beltane, Yule
Powers and attributes	Awareness, changes/transitions, communication, creativity, death/funeral practices, divination, happiness, healing, hexes, hope (silver), inspiration, peace, protection, purification, renewal, spirit guides/spirits, spirituality, transformation
Available for purchase	Essential oil

Spells and Rituals

The scent of fir aids in connecting with forest spirits. To foster creative expression, hold a cluster of needles during meditation. For a prosperity spell, include a cone. To purify ritual space and aid in grounding energy afterwards, burn a few needles.

Flax

Common Flax (*Linum usitatissimum*); also known as linseed, lint bells

Fairy Flax, White Flax (*L. catharticum*); also known as fairy lint, fairy woman's flax, purging flax

Growing two to three feet tall, flax has lance-shaped leaves and pale blue, five-petaled flowers. Contained in round capsules, the seeds are reddish brown, small, and flat. With delicate stems and growing only three inches tall, fairy flax has narrow, oval leaves. Its slightly bell-shaped flowers are white but yellowish near the base.

History and Lore

The ancient Egyptians used flax fibers to make cloth for clothing and other everyday necessities as well as mummy wrappings. In Norway and Denmark, flax was grown near the home to keep ghosts away and seeds were placed in coffins to keep the deceased's spirit from wandering. In the Basque area of Spain, flax was placed in shoes to protect against bewitchment. Even though there was a general European belief that witches used flax seeds in their brews, witches were also believed to hate flax flowers. Because of this, the flowers were worn as a talisman against witchcraft. According to English legend, the extremely delicate fairy flax was chosen by faeries to make their garments. Throughout the folklore of Europe and the British Isles, many types of fae aided humans with spinning.

Magical Connections

Element/s	Fire
Astrological influence	Mercury
Deities	Athena, Bertha, Brigid, the Fates-Freya, Frigg, Holle, Minerva, the Norns
Magical entities	Faeries the Fates, the Norns

Other associations	Samhain, Walpurgis
Powers and attributes	Abundance, awareness, bind, changes/transitions, divination, family and home, prosperity/money, protection, psychic abilities, renewal, secrets, sex/sexuality, skills, strength, transformation
Available for purchase	Dried stalks with flowers; seeds

Spells and Rituals

Flax brings strength to esbat rituals, aids during major transitions, and is helpful for issues relating to sexuality. Use it in spells to bind or in charms to attract abundance, money, and prosperity. Flax is also instrumental in keeping secrets.

Fly Agaric

Fly Agaric

Fly Agaric (*Amanita muscaria*); also known as deadly amanita, fairy tables, pixie stools, red cap

Fly agaric is the classic toadstool that has a red or orange cap studded with white flakes. The stalk is off white and has a slightly bulbous base. Scientifically, there is no difference between a toadstool and mushroom; however, the term *toadstool* is often applied to poisonous fungi in common speech.

Caution: Fly agaric is extremely toxic if ingested; it is generally recommended to avoid touching it.

History and Lore

For centuries in Europe, fly agaric has been regarded as a witches' plant and reputedly an ingredient in their flying ointment. In legends throughout the British Isles and Europe, fly agaric is found wherever there are faeries. Also associated with elves, these toadstools mark an entrance to their magical realm. During the nineteenth century in Central and Northern Europe, fly agaric was used as a good luck charm and regarded as powerful as a four-leaf clover or horseshoe. According to Germanic myth, it sprouted up where foam from the mouth of Wodan's horse hit the ground. Fly agaric was also said to be gnome houses. The psychoactive compounds in fly agaric were important to shamans in Siberia and the Baltic region for communicating between the worlds. The Greeks believed it was an ingredient in ambrosia, a food of the gods that conferred immortality.

Magical Connections

Element/s	Air
Astrological influence	Aries; Mercury
Deities	Gwydion, Odin, Wodan
Magical entities	Gnomes, faeries, pixies
Other associations	Beltane
Powers and attributes	Awareness, banish, creativity, death/funeral practices, divination, dream work, fertility, knowledge, luck, prophecy, protection, psychic abilities, renewal, secrets, spirit guides/spirits
Available for purchase	Because fly agaric is poisonous, it is best to use it symbolically with pictures and other items such as figurines

Spells and Rituals

Paint a couple of toadstool lawn ornaments the color of fly agaric and place them in your garden to attract faeries and pixies. To remove something unwanted from your life, write a few keywords on a picture, and then burn it as you visualize being free.

Forget-Me-Not

Water Forget-Me-Not (*Myosotis scorpioides*); also known as luck flower, mouse ear, scorpion grass, true forget-me-not

Woodland Forget-Me-Not (*M. sylvatica*); also known as luck flower, mouse ear

Water forget-me-not is beloved for its sky-blue flowers that can sometimes be pink or white. With five petals shaped like mouse ears, the flowers have yellow centers. They grow in clusters that curve downward on stems that are between six to twelve inches tall. The oblong leaves are medium green with a prominent center vein. The flowers of woodland forget-me-not can be pinkish purple.

History and Lore

The forget-me-not is most widely associated with stories and poems about parted lovers and remembrance, however, there is a lot more to this unassuming little flower. Prior to blooming, the flower stalks are tightly curled resembling a scorpion tail, which gave rise to its species name and in England the common name *scorpion grass*. The plant was used to treat scorpion stings and spider bites and for protection from faery mischief. In England and Europe, forget-me-not was regarded as a lucky plant. In Germany, it was considered a talisman for finding hidden treasure. Forget-me-not was planted on graves for commemoration. The ancient Egyptians used it to aid in receiving visions during the month of Thoth by placing the leaves over their eyes. The month of Thoth is approximately September 11 to October 10 on the Gregorian calendar.

Magical Connections

Element/s	Air
Astrological influence	Venus
Deities	Thoth
Magical entities	Elves, faeries, Hollen

Powers and attributes	Adaptability, awareness, balance/ harmony, bind, clarity, communication, focus, loss/sorrow, love, loyalty/fidelity, luck, protection, relationships, secrets, strength, success
Available for purchase	Flower essence; dried flowers; seeds

Spells and Rituals

As part of a ritual with your lover, pick a bouquet of flowers and pass them one-by-one back and forth as you each pledge your faith and support for one another. Use the flower essence to aid in attuning your awareness and energy to faeries.

Forsythia

Border Forsythia (*Forsythia x intermedia*); also
    known ás golden bell

Forsythia is a rambling shrub that can reach eight feet tall and ten feet wide. Beloved by gardeners, its sweeping, arching branches are a hallmark of spring. The yellow flowers grow in clusters making the branches look like golden sprays of sunshine. When the flowers fade, oval-shaped leaves with serrated edges fill in the branches creating a rounded thicket.

History and Lore

This beloved hybrid shrub was created in the early nineteenth-century in Germany from plants of East Asian origin and quickly became extremely popular in European and English gardens. Not long afterwards, it was introduced into North America. Although it does not appear in folklore, it has come to be associated with faeries, which is no surprise since its wildly spreading

branches and bright flowers seem like a perfect place for them to live and hold their revels.

Magical Connections

Element/s	Air, fire
Astrological influence	Sun
Magical entities	Faeries
Other associations	Ostara
Powers and attributes	Balance/harmony, changes/transitions, courage, emotions, family and home, fertility, growth, happiness, healing, spirituality
Available for purchase	Flower essence

Spells and Rituals

Place a picture of forsythia wherever you need to activate and lift energy. To deepen your spiritual connection with nature, hold a flowering branch or place a picture of forsythia on your altar during meditation.

Foxglove

Common Foxglove, Purple Foxglove (*Digitalis purpurea*)
White-flowered Foxglove (*D. purpurea* f. *alba*)
Both plants are also known as dead man's bells, elf gloves, fairy bells, fairy caps, fairy petticoats, folk's glove, fox bells, goblin's gloves, witches' bells, witches' thimbles

Foxglove is a woodland plant that is a beloved addition to the garden. It has drooping, tubular flowers that are usually purplish pink or white.

The interior of the flower has a lace-like pattern. In its first year, the plant only consists of a base rosette of leaves. The second year of growth produces tall spires of flowers that can reach three to five feet high.

Caution: All parts of the plant are toxic and can be fatal if ingested.

History and Lore

Throughout the British Isles, foxglove has been regarded as a faery plant. If a flower stalk was seen bent over, it meant that a faery or pixy was inside one of the blossoms. As bells, the flowers were said to create a magical sound and the spots inside the flowers were said to be where elves had touched them. According to other English lore, the flowers were rung to alert foxes to nearby huntsmen. Witches were also reputedly fond of the flowers and said to wear them on their fingers for decoration. In Staffordshire, taking foxglove flowers indoors was said to give witches access to a house, however, in Ireland they were used as a charm against witchcraft. In some areas of England, white foxglove was regarded as a death omen and picking it was considered unlucky. Although foxglove was used medicinally for a range of issues, its use for treating heart ailments came to the attention of English physician William Withering (1741–1799) from an old wise woman healer.[55]

Magical Connections

Element/s	Water
Astrological influence	Aquarius, Libra; Venus

Magical entities	Elves, faeries, pixies
Powers and attributes	Awareness, balance / harmony, challenges / obstacles, communication, creativity, emotions, healing, intuition, peace, protection, relationships, release, truth
Available for purchase	Flower essence; dried flower stalks, seeds

Spells and Rituals

When facing a challenge, keep a picture of foxglove with you or somewhere where you will see it often. Foxglove can help you befriend faeries that may live in your garden. Without removing a leaf from the plant, hold it between your hands and whisper a greeting to them.

Frankincense

Frankincense (*Boswellia carteri* syn. *B. sacra*); also known as incense tree, olibanum

The frankincense tree has papery, peeling bark and a dense tangle of branches. The oblong leaves grow in groups at the ends of the branches. The small, star-shaped flowers are white with orange and yellow centers. The flowers grow in clusters on long spikes among the leaves. When burned, the tear-shaped grains of resin have a sweet, balsam-like aroma.

History and Lore

Frankincense was commonly burned in temples throughout China and India to deepen meditation and spirituality. The Egyptians burned it for religious offerings because the smoke was believed to facilitate contact with the deity to whom it was

---

55. Dobelis, *Magic and Medicine of Plants*, 188.

presented. The Babylonians and Assyrians burned the resin to honor some of their highest deities. Greeks and Romans also used frankincense as offerings. German herbalist Konrad von Megenberg (1309–1374) noted that frankincense had the power to disperse evil spirits. In medieval Europe, it was used in magical practices to fumigate divinatory mirrors and to mark ritual circles. Carried as a charm, it was said to bring good luck.

Magical Connections

Element/s	Air, fire, water
Astrological influence	Aquarius, Aries, Leo, Sagittarius; Moon, Sun
Deities	Aphrodite, Apollo, Astarte, Baal, Bast, Bel/Belenus, Helios, Ra, Venus
Other associations	Yule
Powers and attributes	Awareness, banish, clarity, consecrate/bless, courage, defense, dream work, focus, growth, happiness, healing, justice/legal matters, love, luck, negativity, past-life work, protection, psychic abilities, purification, spirit guides/spirits, spirituality, success, transformation
Available for purchase	Crystal or powdered resin; essential oil

Spells and Rituals

For support in past-life work, dream work, or developing psychic abilities, burn a few resin crystals before engaging in these practices to reach a higher level of awareness. The scent is also an aid for contacting spirits.

Fumitory

Fumitory

Common Fumitory, Drug Fumitory (*Fumaria officinalis*); also known as fumus, hedge fumitory, lady's lockets, smoke-plant, wax dolls

Fumitory is a wispy, scrambling plant with slender, trailing stems. The leaves are deeply divided and have a slight resemblance to parsley or celery. The stems and leaves are a bluish or slivery green. The delicate, tube-shaped flowers are pink with mauve or purple at the tip.

Caution: All parts of the plant are toxic and can cause uncomfortable side effects if ingested.

History and Lore

Fumitory has been used medicinally since ancient Greek and Roman times. Its common name comes from the Medieval Latin *fumus terrae*, which means "smoke of the earth."[56] According to Greek legend, the plant's seemingly spontaneous growth was attributed to its rising from the earth in the form of smoke. During the Middle Ages in Europe, fumitory was used in exorcisms and witches reputedly burned it to invoke underworld spirits. It was burned to purify and protect a new home as well as scattered about the house for luck. Rubbing fumitory on the shoes was said to bring luck. In Germany, fumitory was used to protect against evil and sometimes known as thunderer's plant.

Magical Connections

Element/s	Earth, fire
Astrological influence	Aries, Capricorn; Jupiter, Saturn
Deities	Demeter, Hades, Hecate, Hel, Osiris, Persephone, Thor
Other associations	The otherworld/underworld; Samhain
Powers and attributes	Ancestors, banish, consecrate/bless, family and home, hexes, luck, negativity, prosperity/money, protection, purification, wisdom
Available for purchase	Powdered or cut, dried leaves and stems

Spells and Rituals

To aid in connecting with ancestors at Samhain, burn a little fumitory in your cauldron and envision the smoke carrying your love to them. A light smoke cleansing with fumitory after ritual or magic helps ground excess energy. Burn dried leaves as part of a spell to counter negative magic.

56. Mac Coitir, *Ireland's Wild Plants*, 190.

Galangal

Greater Galangal (*Alpinia galanga*); also known
as blue ginger, Java galangal, Siamese ginger,
Thai ginger

Lesser Galangal (*A. officinarum*); also known as
chewing John, Chinese ginger, galangale,
Indian root, low John

Known as a mild cousin to ginger, galangal grows
in clumps with long, lance-shaped leaves and
spikes of orchid-like flowers that form in loose
clusters. The flowers are white with red streaks
in the center. The root resembles ginger. As the
name suggests, greater galangal is larger.

History and Lore

Despite its smaller size, lesser galangal was considered more important in India because of its medicinal applications, which were noted in Sanskrit
writings dating to 600 CE.[57] Widely used as a culinary herb in medieval Europe, it was also believed
to be an aphrodisiac. Although both plants are
used in the American magical tradition of hoodoo,
lesser galangal is the one usually referred to as low
John. This relates to John the Conqueror, a mythical person whose spirit was said to live in certain
roots. Galangal root is often carried to overcome
hardship and for luck.

Magical Connections

Element/s	Earth, fire
Astrological influence	Aries, Scorpio; Mars, Sun
Deities	Kupala, Lakshmi

57. Prance and Nesbitt, *The Cultural History of Plants*, 163.

Other associations	Litha
Powers and attributes	Awareness, banish, challenges / obstacles, consecrate/bless, courage, hexes, justice/legal matters, luck, negativity, prosperity/ money, secrets, sex/sexuality, success
Available for purchase	Essential oil; dried root whole, sliced, or powdered

Spells and Rituals

Galangal aids in increasing the power of spells, especially those for banishing. It is especially helpful in returning negativity or enchantments back to those who initiate them. Use a piece of root as an amulet to overcome injustices and succeed in court.

Gardenia

Common Gardenia (*Gardenia jasminoides* syn *G. augusta*, *G. grandiflora*); also known as Cape jasmine

Wild Gardenia (*G. thunbergia*); also known as forest gardenia, white gardenia

Common gardenia is a large shrub with glossy, lance-shaped leaves. The creamy white flowers can be a single bloom with six to eight spreading petals or a double bloom that looks slightly rose-like. The scent is reminiscent of jasmine. The orange fruit is ribbed and oblong. Wild gardenia is larger and more tree-like with glossy leaves that are oval and veined. Its creamy white flowers have six to eight spreading petals and a long, tube-like neck. The hard, egg-shaped fruit is grayish green to yellowish.

History and Lore

Common gardenia has been used in Traditional Chinese Medicine for over two thousand years. The plant reached England in the mid-eighteenth century and America shortly thereafter. It has been widely and wildly popular for perfume. Grown and admired for its beauty and strong, intoxicating fragrance, it became emblematic of the antebellum South. The roots of wild gardenia have been used in the traditional medicine of South Africa, where the tree is also believed to drive away evil spirits and bad people.

Magical Connections

Element/s	Water
Astrological influence	Cancer, Pisces, Scorpio; Moon
Deities	Diana, Isis, Luna, Selene
Powers and attributes	Balance/harmony, emotions, healing, love, peace, spirit guides/ spirits, spirituality
Available for purchase	Flower essence; absolute/essential oil; dried flower petals; dried fruit; seeds

Spells and Rituals

Associated with the moon, the white flowers bring the power of Luna to esbat rituals. Sprinkle petals on your altar or diffuse the scent of gardenia to aid in working with spirit guides and the spirit realm in general. Hold a flower for spiritual meditation.

Garlic

Common Garlic (*Allium sativum*); also known as devil's posy, poor man's treacle, stinking rose, stinkweed

Growing up to two feet tall, garlic has flat, pointed leaves on a stem that sprouts from the bulb. The bulb contains four to fifteen cloves that are encased in papery, white skin. The top of the stem becomes curly with a pointed bulge (the flower bud) and is called a *scape*. The stem straightens as a globe-shaped cluster of small white to pinkish flowers develops.

History and Lore

The Greeks and Romans used garlic medicinally as a cure-all as well as a deterrent to magic and the restless spirits of the dead. The Anglo-Saxons used it to break elf-bonds (enchantment) and to cure insanity. In Central Europe it was believed to provide protection from witches and gnomes. It was placed in the mouth of a corpse in the Balkans to keep vampires away and to keep the deceased in the grave. German miners wore garlic for safety from the spirits that were believed to inhabit mineshafts. Considered a plant of luck, the leaves were woven into thatched roofs in Ireland and hung on fishing boats in Turkey. It was regarded as a charm against poverty in Italy when purchased at Midsummer.

Magical Connections

Element/s	Fire
Astrological influence	Mars
Deities	Circe, Hecate, Lilith
Magical entities	Gnomes
Other associations	Midsummer, Walpurgis,

Powers and attributes	Abundance, banish, courage, healing, hexes, luck, prosperity/money, protection, spirit guides/spirits, strength
Available for purchase	Essential oil; flower essence; fresh whole bulbs; minced cloves; dried flakes and powder; fresh scapes

Spells and Rituals

Instead of carrying a bulb of garlic as an amulet, anoint a picture with flower essence (no odor). To encourage an unwanted spirit to move on, hang a braid of bulbs in the area where its presence is most strongly felt. Include fresh scapes in a spell to attract prosperity and abundance.

Geranium

Garden Geranium (*Pelargonium* x *hortorum*); also known as bedding geranium, storkbill, zonal geranium

Rose Geranium (*P. roseum* syn. *P. graveolens*); also known as Bourbon geranium, storkbill

The flowers and foliage of the garden geranium come in a range of colors. The rounded leaves are veined, have shallow lobes, and often have distinct bands or zones of color. The flowers can be single or double blooms in pink, white, red, or salmon. They grow in rounded clusters. Rose geranium is not the familiar garden plant. Its grayish, silvery leaves are deeply lobed and have wavy edges. The small, pink flowers do not form large flower heads like garden geranium. It is loved and widely used for its rose-like scent.

History and Lore

The genus name comes from the Greek *pelargos* meaning "stork," referring to the long seedpods that resemble a stork's bill.[58] Geraniums have been cultivated throughout Europe since the seventeenth century, grown in the garden for their colorful beauty and to protect the home from evil spirits. During the nineteenth century, French perfumers discovered that the scent of the rose geranium closely matched the expensive attar of rose from the Middle East. For a time, the French island of Réunion (formerly named Bourbon) in the Indian Ocean was the center of the rose geranium universe.

Magical Connections

Element/s	Water
Astrological influence	Aries, Cancer; Mars, Venus
Deities	Minerva
Magical entities	Faeries
Other associations	Walpurgis
Powers and attributes	Balance/harmony, communication, confidence, courage, creativity, emotions, focus, growth, love, protection (red), psychic abilities, purification, relationships, security (pink), sex/sexuality
Available for purchase	Essential oil is made from rose geranium; dried petals

Spells and Rituals

For protection, place a couple of red geraniums on a windowsill in the direction from which you feel a threat. Put a cotton ball doused with essential oil with your ritual and magic tools to cleanse

them. The rosy aspect of this plant enhances the ability to attract love and friendship.

Ginger

Common Ginger (*Zingiber officinale*); also known as ginger root, true ginger

Ginger is a tropical perennial that grows about three feet tall. Its lance-shaped leaves grow in two rows along reed-like stems that sprout from the rhizome. Spikes of greenish yellow flowers grow on separate stems. The thick, branched rhizomes form gnarly clumps.

History and Lore

Ginger was used as temple incense by the Syrians, Egyptians, Greeks, Romans, and the people of India either added to the flames or ground into a paste that was rubbed onto wooden sticks. The paste was also used on statues of deities to honor them. The Romans used ginger to spice wine as did the medieval Italians and French. According to Roman naturalist and historian Pliny the Elder, ginger came from "the fabled land of the Troglodytes" reputedly somewhere in Egypt or Ethiopia.[59] In early medieval Europe, its exotic odor, taste, and rarity made it an alluring aphrodisiac and drinking ginger tea was believed to enhance a man's virility. Regarded as auspicious in parts of central India, ginger was used in religious and marriage rites. In sixteenth-century England, ginger was believed to ward off the plague. In Italy, it was one of the spices used in exorcisms to expel demons. In parts of Thailand, a piece of ginger root on a string was placed on children as a necklace to keep them safe from harmful spirits.

58. Euser, *Bay Area Gardening*, 105.

59. Toussaint-Samat, *A History of Food*, 447.

Ginger

Magical Connections

Element/s	Earth, fire
Astrological influence	Aries, Sagittarius, Scorpio; Mars, Moon
Other associations	The otherworld

Powers and attributes	Consecrate/bless, emotions, healing, hexes, love, negativity, prosperity/money, protection, psychic abilities, purification, relationships, secrets, sex/sexuality, success
Available for purchase	Essential oil; fresh, dried, grated, or ground root

Spells and Rituals

Place a piece of root with your magical tools to consecrate and cleanse them. The healing attribute of ginger helps in dealing with problems, especially in relationships and sexuality in general. For protection, prepare an amulet with the essential oil.

Ginseng

American Ginseng (*Panax quinquefolius*); also
     known as sang
Asian Ginseng (*P. ginseng*); also known as Korean
     ginseng

Ginseng has a single, thin stem with a whorl of leaves at the top. The leaves are palm shaped with three to five leaflets that are pointed and toothed. Small, yellow-green flowers grow in umbrella-shaped clusters that develop into round clusters of red berries. The gnarled root is light tan and often resembles a human body with shoots for arms and legs.

Caution: Ginseng should not be ingested during pregnancy or breastfeeding; American ginseng is an endangered or threatened species in some areas.

History and Lore

Used medicinally for several thousand years in Asia, ginseng was often regarded as a cure-all. In Chinese mythology, the plant was a divine gift to a woman who wanted children. According to Korean legend, it had to be gathered using a wooden knife because metal would damage ginseng's virtues. Other lore notes that the plant glows and moves around at night in the guise of a child or bird to lure plant gatherers to their deaths. During the Middle Ages and early Renaissance in Europe, ginseng was considered an aphrodisiac. Like mandrake, the more human-shaped the root, the higher its value. In North America, the Pawnee, Meskwaki, Delaware, and Mohegan used ginseng medicinally and as an ingredient in love charms.

Magical Connections

Element/s	Fire
Astrological influence	Sun
Powers and attributes	Fertility, healing, love, luck, protection, sex/sexuality, wishes
Available for purchase	Whole, sliced, or powdered dried root; seeds

Spells and Rituals

Wrap a pink or red ribbon around a root to use in a fertility or love spell. Carry a small piece of root in your pocket or purse to attract romance into your life. Go to your favorite outdoor place with a handful of powdered roots, make a wish, and blow it to the wind.

Globeflower

Common Globeflower, European Globeflower (*Trollius europaeus*); also known as goblin flower, troll flower, witches' gowan

Growing about two feet tall, each stem is topped by a single, two-inch wide flower. Resembling a small, yellow cabbage, the ball-shaped flower remains closed or barely opens. The sparse foliage is on the lower part of the stems and comprised of three to five deeply lobed leaflets. Globeflower inhibits growth of nearby plants.

Caution: Globeflower is mildly poisonous and should not be ingested; it may cause skin irritation and burns.

History and Lore

In Scotland, this plant was called *witches' gowan* and the toxic, white sap, *witches' milk*. The term *gowan* was originally a generic folk name for any large yellow flower.[60] According to legend in the Netherlands, elves used globeflowers as cups to prepare poison. Scandinavian myth notes that the plant is poisonous because trolls meddled with the flowers.

Magical Connections

Element/s	Water
Magical entities	Elves, trolls
Powers and attributes	Defense, hexes, negativity, secrets
Available for purchase	Seeds

---

60. Britten and Holland, *A Dictionary of English Plant-names*, 216.

Spells and Rituals

Given its background, globeflower functions easily for magical defense or warding off negative energy. Place a picture of a globeflower on your altar and visualize a ball of soft yellow light encircling you. Whenever you feel in need of help, bring the image into your mind.

Goldenrod

European Goldenrod (*Solidago virgaurea* syn. *S. vulgaris*); also known as golden dust, wound weed, woundwort

Sweet Goldenrod (*S. odora*); also known as anise-scented goldenrod, blue mountain tea

Goldenrod is a clump forming plant with lance-shaped leaves and knotty rhizomes. The European goldenrod grows up to seven feet tall with wand-like clusters of tiny flowers on upright stems. Sweet goldenrod is smaller with flower clusters that grow on the upper sides of plume-like branches. Its leaves smell like anise when crushed.

History and Lore

Used medicinally for centuries in Europe, the Germans called goldenrod *Heidnisch Wundkraut*, "Pagan woundwort."[61] It was used as a charm against a number of ailments and may have been connected with witchcraft, which would account for its association with Paganism. In England, the long stems were used as divining rods to find water as well as gold and silver treasure. According to similar legends, carrying a piece of goldenrod in the pocket helped locate hidden treasure. Wearing a sprig of flowers was said to be an aid for finding a lover. Despite its mostly positive associations, in parts of England goldenrod was

61. Weaver, *Sauer's Herbal Cures*, 24.

regarded as unlucky to grow in the garden or take into the house.

Magical Connections

Element/s	Air
Astrological influence	Venus
Powers and attributes	Challenges/obstacles, divination, healing, loss/sorrow, love, luck, prosperity/money, wisdom
Available for purchase	Dried flowers; dried, cut flowers and stems marketed as goldenrod herb or tea; flower essence from sweet goldenrod

Spells and Rituals

As part of a prosperity spell, burn a pinch or two of dried herb. Cut long stems of flower plumes and place these wherever you need to boost energy in your home, especially when recovering from a loss. Gaze at a picture of goldenrod when seeking inner wisdom.

Goldenseal

Goldenseal (*Hydrastis canadensis*); also known as eyeroot, ground raspberry, Indian paint, Indian turmeric, yellow puccoon, yellowroot

Reaching only about a foot tall, goldenseal has one hairy stem with two leaves that have five to seven lobes. The leaves are large, thick, and wrinkled. It has a single greenish white flower that develops into a red fruit that looks like a raspberry, which is inedible. The plant has a thick, yellow root.

Caution: Abortifacient. The plant is listed as vulnerable, threatened, or endangered in a number of areas; only products made from cultivated goldenseal should be used.

History and Lore

As with Solomon's seal (*Polygonatum biflorum*), goldenseal's name is derived from the root scars that resemble an old-fashioned wax seal. The Iroquois and Cherokee used goldenseal for healing and for ceremonial face paint. They passed their medicinal knowledge along to European settlers. In the American magical tradition of hoodoo, it is used for blessings and prosperity with ginger often used as a substitute.

Magical Connections

Element/s	Fire
Astrological influence	Leo; Sun
Powers and attributes	Consecrate/bless, healing, negativity, prosperity/money, wisdom
Available for purchase	Cut, dried root; powdered root; cut, dried leaves

Spells and Rituals

Place a sachet of dried leaves with your magic tools to consecrate and prepare them for use. To dispel negative energy, use a stem with leaves and waft it like a fan to clear the area. If you find it growing in the wild, hold your palms against the leaves and thank the plant for its wisdom.

Gooseberry

American Gooseberry (*Ribes hirtellum*); also known as swamp gooseberry, wild gooseberry

European Gooseberry (*R. uva-crispa* syn. *R. grossularia*); also known as dog berry, fayberry, goosegogs

Gooseberry is a wide, spiny shrub that produces small, dangling clusters of bell-shaped flowers. The European gooseberry produces pinkish yellow flowers and bristly fruit that look like striped, fuzzy grapes. It has a thorn at the base of each leaf stem. The American plant has greenish white flowers and round, green berries that ripen to a purplish color. It has two or more thorns at the base of the leaf stems. The leaves of both shrubs are lobed and dark green.

Gooseberry

History and Lore

The cat-headed Egyptian goddess Bast was frequently described as having gooseberry-green eyes. The Anglo-Saxons used gooseberry thorns in several healing charms. Since medieval times in Europe, gooseberries have been used to produce a sweet and strong, wine-like ale. In Germany, the spiny branches were placed around cowsheds on Walpurgis and Beltane to keep witches away. My English grandmother pronounced the name *gooz-berry* and said that the faeries were fond of the fruit, which is why they were also known as fayberry. In Scotland and northern England, children were told to stay away from the bushes to avoid being kidnapped by Awd Goggie, the faery that guards the unripe berries.

Magical Connections

Element/s	Water
Astrological influence	Venus
Deities	Bast, Cernunnos, the Morrigan
Magical entities	Faeries
Other associations	Beltane, Samhain, Walpurgis
Powers and attributes	Abundance, challenges/obstacles, fertility, healing, peace, success
Available for purchase	Fresh or dried fruit; jam

Spells and Rituals

When faced with a challenging situation, purchase dried fruit, and wrap three of them in parchment or wax paper (they can be sticky). Hold it between your hands, visualize a resolution, and then place the gooseberries in a kitchen cupboard for three weeks before disposing of them.

Goosefoot

Goosefoot (*Syngonium podophyllum* syn.
   Nephthytis triphylla); also known as African evergreen, American evergreen, arrowhead vine, nephthytis

Young goosefoot plants have upright stems but as they age, they develop climbing stems. The leaves are dark green with silvery-white or cream-colored variegation and go through a dramatic change in shape as the plant matures. The juvenile leaf has a goosefoot or arrowhead shape, it develops lobes, and then matures with multiple leaflets. The plant produces green or greenish white flowers but rarely as a houseplant.

Caution: Goosefoot is moderately toxic if ingested.

History and Lore

Goosefoot is widely used as an ornamental garden plant in tropical regions and elsewhere as a houseplant. The Maya used it medicinally as an ingredient with other plants to treat skin ailments.

Magical Connections

Element/s	Air
Astrological influence	Jupiter
Deities	Freya
Powers and attributes	Changes/transitions, defense, protection
Available for purchase	Houseplant

Spells and Rituals

The shape of the leaves makes this plant an aid for defensive magic and because of the way they develop, the leaves are perfect for initiating changes or weathering transitions. Place a fresh leaf or potted plant on your altar to connect with the energy of the goose-footed goddess Freya.

Gorse

Common Gorse (*Ulex europaeus*); also known as broom, furze, golden gorse, prickly bloom, whin

The branches of this scruffy, evergreen shrub have prickly, half-inch-long spines that grow amongst the needle-like leaves. It produces bright yellow flowers in the spring and summer and often blooms throughout the year.

Caution: Gorse is easily confused with broom (*Cytisus scoparuis*), which is toxic.

History and Lore

Because gorse flowers were used for decoration on Walpurgis in Germany, they gained the reputation of warding off evil and dark influences. In Ireland, a sprig of gorse was worn for luck and to keep a traveler from getting lost. On Beltane a branch was hung over doorways to keep luck inside a house. Due to stories in parts of Britain that small dragons lived in gorse thickets, children were often afraid to pick the flowers or go near the bushes. During the month of May in England, sprigs were placed around containers of milk and butter to protect them from faery mischief. Although the flowers were sometimes called *fairy gold*, placing them in a stream was believed to attract the real thing.

Magical Connections

Element/s	Fire
Astrological influence	Aries; Mars, Sun
Deities	Aine, Arianrhod, Bel/Belenus, the Dagda, Freyr, Jupiter, Lugh, Thor
Magical entities	Faeries
Ogham	Onn ╫
Other associations	Ostara, Walpurgis, Beltane, Lughnasadh, Samhain

Powers and attributes	Banish, defense, determination, divination, hexes, hope, inspiration, love, luck, negativity, prosperity/money, protection, purification, renewal, strength
Available for purchase	Flower essence

Spells and Rituals

As part of a protection spell, carve gorse's ogham on a yellow candle and scatter a few spines around it on your altar. For defense against dark magic and negativity, place gorse spines at each corner of your altar and then visualize a shield of protective energy around you.

Grain

Barley (*Hordeum vulgare*); also known as barleycorn
Maize (*Zea mays*); also known as corn
Oat (*Avena sativa*)
Rice (*Oryza sativa*); also known as Asian rice
Rye (*Secale cereale*)
Wheat (*Triticum aestivum*); also known as bread wheat, wheat corn

Technically, the word *grain* refers to the harvested seeds of these cereal plants of which there are too many to include individual descriptions. While the word *corn* is used in North America for maize, in Europe it refers to whichever is the most important grain of a region.

History and Lore

Throughout the ancient world, grains were important sacred and secular plants. As a symbol of rebirth, the Egyptians provided wheat to the dead. The Greeks, Romans, and people of India used wheat as offerings to various deities. Used in important rites in Asia, rice was sometimes believed to have a soul. In Mexico, and Central and South America, maize was regarded as sacred. Widely believed to bring luck and protection, rye was placed on the threshold or under the rafters of a new home in Germany. In Palestine barley was used as a protective amulet for children. In Europe and the British Isles grains of barley, wheat, rye, and oat were used for a wide range of predictions including love divination. The Dutch used rye to expose a witch.

Regarded as a divine gift by many cultures, bread was believed to have the power to protect against evil spirits, demons, and witches in England, Scotland, Germany, France, and Belgium. The Germans also believed that witches could use bread to cause harm. Considered a bringer of luck in Ireland, bread was used for a range of predictions and in Germany and Scandinavia for love magic. If a piece of bread was dropped on the floor in Transylvania, it has to be picked up and kissed to avoid bad luck.

Straw (the dried stalks of cereal grasses) was also used for making predictions and protective magic in England, Ireland, Belgium, and Germany. Referred to as corpse straw, it was placed under the deceased at funerals in Germany, France, and Belgium to keep evil spirits away and to keep the soul of the person from returning. These are but a few of the beliefs and practices relating to grains. There are so many more associated with harvesting and special feast days that are beyond the scope of this book but I encourage you to investigate areas that interest you.

Magical Connections

Element/s	Earth
Astrological influence	Virgo; Sun (maize, rice), Venus
Deities	Amaterasu (rice), Brigid, Ceres, Centéotl (maize), Demeter, Holda, Inanna, Inari (rice), Isis, Lugh, Osiris, Persephone
Other associations	The afterlife, the otherworld; Imbolc, Lammas, Mabon, Ostara, Samhain, Walpurgis, Yule
Powers and attributes	Abundance, consecrate/bless, death/funeral practices, divination, fertility, hexes, hope, love, luck, prophecy, prosperity/money, protection, renewal, trust, truth
Available for purchase	Dried grains; boxed cereal; straw; dried stalks with grain; oils

Spells and Rituals

When marking a loved one's passing, place a few pieces of straw on your altar to represent their coming into fullness and their new journey in the otherworld. Sprinkle a handful of grain on your altar as an offering to your chosen deity.

Grape

Common Grape, European Wine Grape (*Vitis vinifera*); also known as English grape, wine-bearing grape

Fox Grape, Wild Grape (*V. labrusca*); also known as Concord grape

Grapevines have thick, woody base stems and deeply lobed leaves that can measure up to nine inches across. Spikes of small, greenish white flowers grow in dense clusters along the stems. The fruit grows in inverted pyramidal clusters. The fruit of the common grape is green; the fox grape is blue-black and ripens to dark purple.

Grape

History and Lore

In Greece, Persia, and throughout Asia Minor, the grapevine was highly venerated to the point of cult status. Wine may have been regarded as a gift from the gods because under certain circumstances grapes can ferment on the vine producing ready-made wine, however, people soon figured out how to speed up the process. Cultivating them by the third millennium BCE, the Egyptians also depicted grapes on tomb walls and placed vessels of wine with important burials. For the Babylonians, Egyptians, Phoenicians, Greeks, and Romans, wine was offered to deities and provided a means for communing with them. Wine played an important part in Greek culture and mythology. As the Roman Empire expanded, so did cultivation and enjoyment of wine in Europe and Britain. From ancient times through the Renaissance, wine was included in herbal texts as a remedy for a range of ailments.

Magical Connections

Element/s	Air, fire, water
Astrological influence	Libra; Jupiter, Moon, Sun
Deities	Ariadne, Athena, Bacchus, Bona Dea, Dionysus, Faunus, Hathor, Inanna, Juno, Mabon, Rhea, Saturn, Silvanus, Thor
Magical entities	Faeries, satyrs
Ogham	Muin ┼
Other associations	The otherworld; Mabon
Powers and attributes	Abundance, bind, consecrate/bless, creativity, divination, fertility, growth, happiness, healing, inspiration, love, prophecy, prosperity/money, psychic abilities, sex/sexuality, truth
Available for purchase	Fresh fruit; raisins; grape juice; wine; grapeseed oil

Spells and Rituals

To enhance divination or any type of psychic work, eat three grapes before your sessions. To boost the effectiveness of a binding spell, include a short length of vine or several tendrils. Prepare a candle with grapeseed oil for spells to kindle romance or heighten sexual attraction.

Grass

Couch Grass (*Elymus repens* syn. *Triticum repens*);
  also known as dog grass, Medusa's head,
  witch grass
Quaking Grass (*Briza media*); also known as fairy
  circle, fairy grass, fairy ring

While two members of the extensive botanical family of grasses are highlighted here, the magical information is applicable to all grasses. Reaching up to three feet tall, couch grass forms dense clumps of narrow, flat leaves. The slender seed head resembles a wheat spike. Quaking grass forms dense clumps of narrow, green leaves that grow two to three feet tall. Its dangling seed heads resemble oats and tremble in the slightest breeze.

History and Lore

Throughout Europe and the British Isles, grass was believed to bestow the power to contact supernatural beings and to ward off the evil eye. While in parts of England it was said that witches used it for spells, grass was also used to counteract magic or undo what had been done. The ancient Romans and later the English, Welsh, and Germans used grass in healing practices. In England, grass was used in weather predictions and for love or marriage divination. In Europe and the British Isles, a grass circle indicated a place where faeries, elves, or witches had danced or gathered. In the Netherlands and Germany, children were forbidden to pull up grass from circles because of the magic that could be unleashed. It was believed in France that a person being chased by a wild animal could find refuge in a grass circle. Any type of grass used for animal feed is called *hay*. It was sometimes used as a protective amulet in England and seeing a load of hay drawn by a white horse was considered good luck.

Magical Connections

Element/s	Earth
Magical entities	Elves, faeries
Available for purchase	Flower essence; cut, dried leaves; dried stalks with seed heads; seeds
Powers and attributes	Abundance, challenges/obstacles, communication, divination, happiness, hexes, luck, manifest, negativity, protection, psychic abilities, see faeries, spirit guides/spirits, wishes
Available for purchase	Flower essence; cut, dried leaves; dried stalks with seed heads; seeds

Spells and Rituals

To enhance psychic abilities, braid a small ring of grass to wear on your wrist during sessions. To remove hexes or any type of negativity in your life, dry a handful of grass, and then burn it in your cauldron. Grass is ideal for knot magic.

Groundsel

Common Groundsel (*Senecio vulgaris*); also
  known as birdseed, chickweed, goblin's shaving brush, grundy swallow, lady's finger

Reaching up to fifteen inches tall, groundsel has leaves that are jagged with irregular lobes and coarse teeth. The lower leaves are larger and less deeply lobed. The flower is a yellow disk that sits atop a green cylindrical base looking like an unopened dandelion. It looks even more like a dandelion as the seed head develops with tufts of silky, white hairs.

Caution: Groundsel is toxic if ingested.

History and Lore

Although groundsel was used as a healing herb since Roman times, the plant was generally disliked for its habit of quickly spreading and taking over the ground. In the Fenlands of eastern England, it was believed that witches were responsible for its proliferation. A patch of groundsel was said to mark where witches had met; a small patch indicated where one had urinated. In other areas of England, groundsel growing on a thatched roof was said to indicate where a witch had landed. The leaves were burned and used as a fumigant to drive evil spirits from a house. Placing it in a cowshed in Scotland was a charm to keep witches from stealing milk. In the Highlands, a sprig was worn or the root carried in a pocket as a healing charm and as an amulet to guard against the evil eye.

Magical Connections

Element/s	Water
Astrological influence	Venus
Powers and attributes	Focus, healing, inspiration, negativity, protection, release
Available for purchase	Flower essence

Spells and Rituals

Place a couple of seed heads in your workspace to stimulate ideas or to aid your concentration. Gather a few seed heads, blow on them to scatter the seeds as you visualize releasing something you no longer need in your life.

Hackberry

Common Hackberry (*Celtis occidentalis*); also
    known as American hackberry, nettle tree,
    sugarberry
European Hackberry (*C. australis*); al-mais, Euro-
    pean nettle tree, hagberry, hag brier, mays,
    sugarberry

Hackberry leaves resemble those of the nettle
plant (*Urtica dioica*). The common hackberry has
dull green leaves and small, greenish white flowers. The small, cherry-like fruit is reddish orange
and turns dark purple or blue-black when ripe.
The European hackberry leaves are dark green.
It also has small, greenish flowers and cherry-like
fruit.

History and Lore

In the Middle East, hackberry was known by the
name *al-mais*, which was derived from the Arabic
verb *mayasa* meaning "liberation of the moon."[62]
It was believed that the tree's round fruit only
grew in the moonlight. Because hackberry was
highly revered for protection, small pieces of
wood were used as amulets against evil spirits.
In medieval Europe, hackberry was sometimes
known by its Arabic name but more often it was
called *mays*. The fruit was considered an aphrodisiac. Hackberry trees are frequently host to mistletoe and often have witches' brooms, which are
knotted balls of twigs usually caused by disease
but commonly believed to be bewitched.

....
62. Dundes, *The Evil Eye*, 97.

Magical Connections

Element/s	Fire, water
Astrological influence	Moon
Other associations	Mabon
Powers and attributes	Abundance, adaptability, changes/transitions, creativity, emotions, healing, inspiration, loss/sorrow, manifest, negativity, protection
Available for purchase	Flower essence; seeds

Spells and Rituals

Because of hackberry's historical association with the moon, use the leaves or fruit in esbat rituals to boost lunar energy. For help in weathering transitions in your life, dab a little flower essence on your favorite protective amulet and place it on your altar before wearing it.

Harebell

Harebell (*Campanula rotundifolia*); also known as bluebell, fairy bells, fairy caps, hare's bells, tinkle bell, witch bells, witches' thimble, wood bells

This plant has nodding, blue-violet flowers that are bell shaped. They grow singly or in clusters from slender stems. Grass-like leaves grow on the stems while the rounded leaves at the base of the plant fade away before the flowers bloom. Harebell is frequently confused with the common bluebell (*Hyacinthoides non-scripta*).

History and Lore

In England and Ireland, harebell was associated with faeries and witches who reputedly used it in their flying ointment. As a witch's plant, it was considered unlucky to pick the flowers. According to legend, the flowers rang like bells to warn hares of danger. Because the hare was regarded as a witch's animal, it was also believed that witches used the plant to transform into hares. Harebell flowers were said to provide the faeries with bells, caps, and cups. In some legends, if a soft chiming was heard, it was usually the faeries ringing the flowers. In England, wearing the flower was said to make a person speak the truth. The flower's shade of blue was a symbol of true love.

Magical Connections

Element/s	Water
Astrological influence	Mercury, Venus
Magical entities	Elves, faeries, pixies
Other associations	Beltane
Powers and attributes	Abundance, balance/harmony, challenges/obstacles, clarity, loss/sorrow, love, loyalty/fidelity, negativity, peace, see faeries, spirit guides/spirits, truth
Available for purchase	Flower essence; seeds

Spells and Rituals

Worn by faithful lovers, the flowers are especially suitable for handfasting and personal pledges.

Burn a dried leaf in a spell to help overcome a problem. Sprinkle a circle of seeds on your altar to aid in working with spirit guides.

Hawthorn

Hawthorn

Common Hawthorn (*Crataegus monogyna*); also
   known as one-seeded hawthorn
English Hawthorn (*C. laevigata*); also known as
   haeg, hagthorn
Both trees are known as haw bush, May, Mayblossom, Maythorn, quickthorn, whitethorn,
   wishing tree

Hawthorn's shiny leaves have deep lobes and rounded teeth. The branches are studded with small thorns. Growing in clusters, the five-petaled flowers are white, often with a blush of pink or with a slight purplish tint. Usually called *haws*, the oval, red fruit is also known as pixie pears, and hoggins.

History and Lore
Hawthorn was regarded as a sacred tree by the Greeks, Romans, Celts, and Germanic people. As a symbol of marriage, Greek and Roman brides often wore crowns of hawthorn flowers. Romans attached a sprig of hawthorn to cradles to protect infants. In France, mothers prayed to hawthorns to heal their sick children. Venerated as a faery tree in England and Ireland, hawthorn is believed to mark a threshold to the otherworld and that faeries often dance around them. Cutting down a hawthorn, especially a solitary one, was believed to bring bad luck which is why farmers often plow around them in fields. In the Channel Islands, witches were believed to gather under solitary hawthorns. In England, garlands of hawthorn flowers were hung around doorways of homes and barns to celebrate Beltane but in many areas taking them indoors was believed to bring bad luck. An exception was that a twig cut at midnight on Twelfth Night and kept in the house would bring luck. In Ireland, the blossoms were taken indoors to protect a house from evil. Because they were highly esteemed, hawthorn trees were often situated near sacred wells. In weather lore of Germany and Scotland, the amount of fruit a hawthorn produced indicated the severity of the coming winter.

Magical Connections

Element/s	Air, fire
Astrological influence	Aquarius, Aries, Gemini, Taurus; Mars
Deities	Bel/Belenus, Blodeuwedd, Brigid, the Dagda, Danu, Flora, Frigg, Thor, Zeus
Magical entities	Faeries, pixies
Ogham	Huath / Uath ⊥

Other associations	The otherworld, Walpurgis, Beltane
— Powers and attributes	Ancestors, challenges/obstacles, consecrate/bless, defense, fertility, growth, happiness, hope, love, luck, manifest, negativity, peace, prosperity/money, protection, purification, relationships, see faeries, sex/sexuality, wisdom, wishes
Available for purchase	Dried berries, whole or powdered; cut, dried leaves and flowers

Spells and Rituals

To sanctify ritual space, sprinkle a pinch of powdered haws or a handful of petals on the ground beforehand. In a bridal bouquet, the flowers aid in strengthening the relationship. To attract peace and prosperity to your home, place a line of haws on a kitchen windowsill.

Hazel

American Hazelnut (*Corylus americana*); also
   known as American filbert
Common Hazel (*C. avellana*); also known as cobnut, common filbert, English hazel

The shrubby, multi-trunked hazel tree produces showy yellow-brown male catkins and less prominent, reddish female catkins. The leaves are rounded with serrated edges and a small point at the end. The nut is encased in a shell and a husk.

History and Lore

The hazel was a sacred tree to the Greeks and Romans who used hazelnuts in the mystic rites of Mercury and Apollo. Sacred to Germanic people and dedicated to Thor, it embodied the power of lightning but also provided protection from it. According to Celtic myth, the hazel was an important tree to the Tuatha Dé Danann and sometimes referred to as *bilé ratha* "the venerated tree of the rath" (fort).[63] The nut itself was regarded as a repository of wisdom and is mentioned throughout Celtic lore. It was customary in England to toss hazelnuts into a fire on Samhain for divination. A pointed hazel stick was believed to have the power to fight off the spectral black dog, a phantom in the shape of an unusually large dog with glowing eyes. Regarded as a good omen in Scotland and Ireland, two conjoined hazelnuts were carried as a charm against witchcraft. In Russia, a hazelnut was said to bring luck. Frequently used as a divining rod to find water or treasure in Scotland and Germany, the hazel branch had to be cut from the tree on Midsummer's Eve. In the state of Tyrol, Austria, it had to be cut on Midsummer's Day or Twelfth Night.

Magical Connections

Element/s	Air, fire, water
Astrological influence	Gemini, Leo, Libra, Virgo; Mercury, Sun
Deities	Aphrodite, Apollo, Arianrhod, Artemis, Boann, Danu, Demeter, Diana, Hermes, Manannán Mac Lir, Mercury, Odin, Ogma, Thor, Venus
Magical entities	Elves, faeries, pixies
Ogham	Coll ⊣⊢⊣⊢
Other associations	The otherworld, Beltane, Midsummer's Eve, Mabon, Samhain

63. Mac Coitir, *Ireland's Trees*, 79.

Powers and attributes	Abundance, awareness, banish, changes / transitions, creativity, defense, divination, fertility, healing, inspiration, intuition, knowledge, luck, manifest, past-life work, prosperity / money, protection, psychic abilities, secrets, see faeries, truth, wisdom
Available for purchase	Hazelnuts; hazelnut oil; flower essence

Spells and Rituals

To foster protection and raise defensive energy, hang a hazel stick above your altar or over a doorway. For aid in any form of magic, especially banishing spells, place a circle of hazel leaves or a small wreath made with a pliable branch on your altar.

Heather and Heath

Common Heather (*Calluna vulgaris*); also known
     as common hedder, heath, ling, Scots
     heather
Heath, Winter Heath (*Erica carnea* syn. *E. herbacea*); also known as alpine heath, spring
     heath, winter heath, winter flowering
     heather

The small, bell-shaped flowers of heather and heath range from white, pink, and lilac to purple and reddish. Heath and heather are nearly identical and their names are often used interchangeably, however, there is an easy way to tell them apart. Heath has needle-like foliage and heather has scale-like foliage.

History and Lore

The word *heathen* comes from the Gothic *haithi*, meaning "dwelling on the heath" where Paganism lingered in Scotland long after Christianity was introduced.[64] (Gothic was the fourth-century East Germanic language of the Goths.) Because white heather was relatively rare in the wild in Scotland, it was believed to occur where faeries had rested. Finding it was considered lucky. According to other legends, white heather was believed to bring luck and protection because it was not stained by the blood of the Picts in their battles against the Saxon invaders. In Ireland, the gift of a white heather sprig was considered a declaration of love. In Germany, heather flowers were hung in front of sheds and barns on Walpurgis to protect cattle from witches and at other times of the year to ward off evil in general. While heather was used against witches, they reputedly used it for spells.

Magical Connections

Element/s	Water
Astrological influence	Scorpio, Taurus; Venus
Deities	Arianrhod, Isis, Venus
Magical entities	Faeries, pixies
Ogham	Úr ⵜⵜ
Other associations	Walpurgis, Litha

---

64. Barnhart, *The Barnhart Concise Dictionary of Etymology*, 346.

Powers and attributes	Adaptability, awareness, changes/transitions, clarity, confidence, defense, dream work, family and home, healing, love, luck, manifest, peace, protection, psychic abilities, spirit guides/spirits, trust
Available for purchase	Flower essence; dried heather flowers and plants

Spells and Rituals

When working with your spirit guide, place a sprig of purple flowers on your altar to enhance your contact and create a deeper connection. For a good luck charm, place white flowers in a sachet. To bring clarity and awareness, burn a small sprig before psychic work.

Heliotrope

European Heliotrope, Common Heliotrope
(*Heliotropium europaeum*); also known as scorpion's tail, sun turner, turn-sole, wart grass
Seaside Heliotrope (*H. curassavicum*); also known as salt heliotrope

Growing in rows on curled spikes, heliotrope flowers are white and star-like with a yellow throat. European heliotrope stems are covered in soft, gray-green hairs and its elliptical leaves taper at each end. Seaside heliotrope has smooth stems and bluish green leaves. These plants are very different from the sweet-smelling garden heliotrope (*H. arborescens*).

Caution: All parts of the plant are toxic if ingested.

History and Lore

The Anglo-Saxons used heliotrope as a remedy for poisons and as a charm to calm disorderly horses. The plant was highly prized by medieval magicians in France and Germany who could reputedly magnetize themselves with it (when harvested at the appropriate time) and to aid in gaining esoteric knowledge. In a medieval grimoire attributed to German friar and alchemist Albertus Magnus, an amulet made with a wolf's tooth and heliotrope would cause people to speak kindly of whoever wore it. During the Middle Ages in Europe and England, heliotrope was used for protection against witches, demons, and anyone possessed by evil. It was also believed that placing a sprig under the bed pillow, would bring dreams to locate lost or stolen items. Additionally, heliotrope was used to forecast stormy weather.

Magical Connections

Element/s	Fire
Astrological influence	Leo, Pisces; Sun
Deities	Agni, Amaterasu, Apollo, Hathor, Helios, Mithras, Phoebe, Ra
Other associations	Litha
Powers and attributes	Authority/leadership, awareness, dream work, healing, hexes, prosperity/money, protection, psychic abilities, release
Available for purchase	Flower essence

Spells and Rituals

Use heliotrope to boost the power of protection spells. It is especially helpful when developing clairvoyance; wear a sprig to help hone your skills. To aid dream work in general, place a sachet of flowers or a photograph of either plant under your pillow.

Hellebore

Hellebore

Black Hellebore (*Helleborus niger*); also known as
    black nisewort, Christmas rose
White Hellebore (*Veratrum album*); also known as
    white false hellebore, white veratrum

Black hellebore has dark green leaves that are
deeply lobed and lance shaped. The white flowers
are cup shaped with overlapping petals. The word
black in its name refers to the color of its roots.
White hellebore has pleated, elliptical base leaves.
The erect, branching flower stem carries dense
clusters of white, star-shaped flowers.

Caution: These plants are highly toxic and
can be fatal if ingested; the sap can irritate skin.

History and Lore

Although these plants were sometimes used medicinally, it was a fine line between curing and killing.
The Greeks and Romans used hellebore to protect
cattle from spells, the Romans also used it as a cure
for insanity and the Greeks to cure demonic possession. During the Middle Ages in Europe, the
plant was regarded as highly magical and strewn on
floors to banish evil spirits. Hellebore was also used
in exorcisms. While it was considered bad luck to
pick black hellebore flowers, the plant was said to
protect the house where it grew. It was believed in
France that sorcerers ground the roots into a powder and then scattered it in the air around them
to become invisible. In England, garlands were
placed on livestock to protect them from evil spirits. Although both types of hellebore were used to
ward off witches, they reputedly used black hellebore for hexes and flying.

Magical Connections

Element/s	Water
Astrological influence	Aquarius, Capricorn; Mars, Saturn
Deities	Cronos, Helios, Saturn
Powers and attributes	Banish, challenges/obstacles, courage, death/funeral practices, hexes, protection, spirit guides/spirits
Available for purchase	Seeds

Spells and Rituals

For banishing spells, draw a pentagram in the
air with a long stem of white hellebore flowers. Because black hellebore seems to defy winter, place a picture of it on your altar and call on

Cailleach Bheur, the crone of winter, for protection during storms.

Hemlock

Poison Hemlock (*Conium maculatum*); also
known as cowbane, lace flower, madwort

Hemlock leaves are delicate and fern-like with toothed edges and have an unpleasant, musty odor when crushed. The stems are marked with purple blotches. The white flowers grow in umbrella-like clusters. The fruit is green, deeply ridged, and contains several seeds.

Caution: All parts of this plant are highly toxic and fatal if ingested; toxins can be absorbed through the skin. Hemlock is easily mistaken for Queen Anne's lace (*Daucus carota*).

History and Lore

Hemlock was used in ancient Greece for capital punishment allowing the accused to take his own life; the philosopher Socrates (c. 470–399 BCE) was the most famous. Medieval alchemists and magicians in Germany and France burned hemlock to manifest spirits. The Russians considered it a plant of the devil. In England, witches were said to use hemlock in spells to raise spirits and in potions to poison enemies. Faeries in Scotland were believed to poison their arrows by dipping them in the dew that collected on the plant. The way hemlock's dry stalks often make an eerie rattling sound in the wind seems to emphasis its standing as a plant of ill omen.

Magical Connections

Element/s	Water
Astrological influence	Saturn
Deities	Hecate
Magical entities	Faeries
Powers and attributes	Banish, defense, hexes, negativity, protection, purification, release
Available for purchase	Although it is sometimes recommended for purifying ritual tools, especially knives, hemlock is a plant best used symbolically.

Spells and Rituals

To boost magical defense, write what you want protection from on a picture of hemlock. Keep it on your altar until the need has passed. To purify ritual or magical tools, wrap a picture of hemlock around them. Just before using them, burn the picture in your cauldron.

Hemp

Hemp, Marijuana (*Cannabis sativa*); also known as
cannabis, gallow-grass, neck-weed

Hemp is a slender plant with cane-like stalks that can grow up to twelve feet tall. Its leaves are arranged in a palm shape and heavily veined with toothed edges. The small, greenish yellow flowers grow in a cone-like structure. While hemp and marijuana are the same species, they are differentiated by the amount of THC (tetrahydrocannabinol), the compound that provides a high. The law distinguishes which name applies. CBD (cannabidiol) is derived from both.

Caution: Check the laws in your area.

History and Lore

Hemp has been used in Chinese medicine for thousands of years. In India it was regarded as a protector. In Eastern Europe hemp was used to create a magic circle for healing and in Serbia an object made of hemp was believed to have strong protective powers. In the Balkans, a circle of hemp fibers was burned over a fresh grave to keep the deceased's spirit from wandering as a vampire. In the British Isles, hemp seeds were used for love divination, especially on Midsummer's Eve and Valentine's Eve. Although witches were thought to use hemp for harmful spells, it was used against people suspected of witchcraft. Hemp fibers were commonly used to make gallows rope and in the Fenlands of Cambridgeshire a hemp stem placed on a doorstep meant the resident was wished dead.

Magical Connections

Element/s	Water
Astrological influence	Pisces; Neptune, Saturn
Deities	Bacchus, Dionysus, Indra, Pan, Shiva, Vesta
Other associations	Midsummer's Eve, Valentine's Eve, Samhain
Powers and attributes	Awareness, death/funeral practices, divination, fertility, healing, hexes, love, protection, psychic abilities, sex/sexuality
Available for purchase	Cut, dried leaves; dried flowers; seeds; seed oil; CBD oil; rope; twine; clothing; fabric

Spells and Rituals

As part of a love spell, braid a length of hemp string, wear it throughout the remainder of your magic work, and then burn it in your cauldron.

Boost the effectiveness of your favorite amulet or crystal by wearing it on a string of hemp. Make a special altar cloth from hemp fabric.

Henbane

Black Henbane (*Hyoscyamus niger*); also known as black nightshade, devil's eye, insane root, stinking nightshade

Henbane has lance-shaped leaves with wavy edges on stalks that reach up to three feet tall. Growing at the base of the upper leaves, brownish yellow, bell-shaped flowers have purple veins and centers. Despite its unpleasant odor, it is often grown as an ornamental garden plant.

Caution: Henbane is highly toxic and can be fatal if ingested.

History and Lore

The ancient Greeks used henbane leaves to crown the dead and decorate graves. Calling it *hennbana* "hen killer," the Anglo-Saxons used it to ward off evil.[65] By the Middle Ages in Europe, it became associated with witches and sorcerers who were believed to use it in spells and to control the weather. Henbane's power was believed to be strongest around the summer solstice. Reputedly, seeds thrown between lovers would cause them to hate each other. Medieval German alchemists and magicians were said to use it to manifest spirits. Called *Hexenkraut*, "witches' herb," accusations that henbane was used in spells to bewitch people were a theme in the 1538 witch trials in Pomerania, Germany.[66] It was also administered to the accused to extract confessions.

65. Pauwels and Christoffels, *Herbs*, 138.
66. De Cleene and Lejeune, *Compendium of Symbolic and Ritual Plants in Europe*, 259.

Magical Connections

Element/s	Earth, water
Astrological influence	Saturn
Deities	Bel/Belenus, Hades, Hecate, Hera, Jupiter, Medea, the Morrigan.
Other associations	The otherworld, Samhain, Summer Solstice
Powers and attributes	Ancestors, awareness, consecrate/bless, death/funeral practices, negativity, spirit guides/spirits
Available for purchase	Flower essence; seeds

Spells and Rituals

Place a circle of seeds on your altar when working with your spirit guides. Because of henbane's association with death, the otherworld, and spirits, dry a stalk of leaves and flowers to place on your altar at Samhain. When honoring your ancestors, write their names on a picture of henbane.

Henna

Henna Tree (*Lawsonia inermis* syn. *L. alba*); also known as Egyptian privet, hina, mendhi

Henna is a small tree that develops spines at the tips of mature branches. The elliptical leaves are glossy green and tapered at both ends. The small flowers can be white, yellowish, or rose-colored and grow in large, pyramidal clusters at the ends of branches. The flowers develop into round, green seed capsules that turn brown.

Caution: Henna is toxic if ingested.

History and Lore

A dull orange to dark red dye is obtained from the henna root and has been used for centuries for dying hair, beards, and even horses' manes in the Middle East and India. Henna has been applied to the body for cosmetic, ritual, and magical purposes. As body paint it was said to bring good luck and to protect against the evil eye and supernatural forces. Garlands of the fragrant flowers are used in Hindu ceremonies and as temple offerings. In Syria, henna was a component in fertility and marriage rituals. Muslims used it for certain festivals and the important rituals of marriage, birth, and circumcision. Traces have been found on the fingernails, palms, and soles of the feet of Egyptian mummies. The Egyptians also used it medicinally and in perfume.

Magical Connections

Element/s	Earth
Astrological influence	Jupiter
Deities	Anat, Parvati
Powers and attributes	Consecrate/bless, fertility, happiness, healing, love, luck, prosperity/money, protection, sex/sexuality, spirituality, wisdom
Available for purchase	Flower essence; whole, cut, or powdered dried leaves; henna oil; henna cone

Spells and Rituals

You don't have to be an experienced artist to apply the magic of henna; just keep in mind that a henna "tattoo" will last for several weeks. As part of a love spell to invite romance into your life, put a dab of henna on your inner thighs or draw a few hearts.

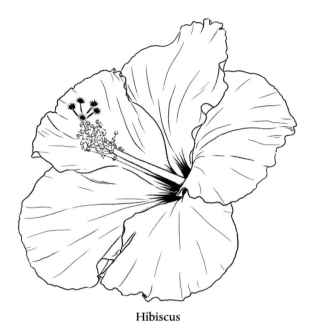

Hibiscus

Hibiscus

Chinese Hibiscus, China Rose (*Hibiscus rosa-sinensis*); also known as Hawaiian hibiscus, rose of China, shoeblack plant

Common Hibiscus, Rose of Sharon (*H. syriacus* syn. *Althaea frutex*); also known as hardy hibiscus, shrub Althea, Syrian hibiscus

Multi-stemmed and shrubby, these hibiscus species have large, funnel-shaped flowers. The red to dark red Chinese hibiscus flowers have ruffled edges and can grow up to six inches wide. Its glossy, oval leaves are slightly pointed and toothed. Common hibiscus flowers can be bluish-mauve, red, pink, or white. The deeply lobed leaves are coarsely toothed.

History and Lore

Hibiscus flowers are traditionally used in Hawaiian leis as a symbol of welcome and joy. According to folklore of the South Pacific islands, a woman wore a red flower behind her left ear when looking for a lover. Worn on the right, meant she already had one, but worn on both sides meant she would like another. In India, the red flowers of China rose were used as religious offerings, however, when bruised the flower turns black and it was believed that witches used them for casting spells. When hibiscus was found growing at crossroads, it was believed that evil spirits could possess anyone who touched the flowers.

Magical Connections

Element/s	Water
Astrological influence	Taurus; Moon (white flower), Venus
Deities	Aphrodite, Diana, Ganesh, Kali, Minerva
Powers and attributes	Creativity, divination, focus, happiness, love, psychic abilities, sex/sexuality
Available for purchase	Flower essence; cut, dried leaves; whole, cut, or powdered flowers; seeds

Spells and Rituals

Include a white hibiscus flower on your esbat altar as an offering to moon goddesses. Place a picture of flowers in your workspace to help get out of a creative rut. Use a red flower as a charm to boost romance. Include hibiscus in divination sessions to keep your mind and energy focused.

Hickory and Pecan

Shagbark Hickory (*Carya ovata*); also known as scalybark hickory

White Hickory (*C. tomentosa*); also known as
    mockernut hickory
Pecan (*C. illinoinensis*)

Hickories are large trees with dense foliage and
wide crowns. The leaves have an uneven number
of lance-shaped leaflets with serrated edges. Male
flowers grow as pendulous, yellow-green catkins;
female flowers sprout as short, greenish spikes at
the ends of young shoots. Hickory nuts are egg
shaped or rounded; pecan nuts are oblong with
one pointed end. The shagbark has long strips of
peeling bark on the trunk.

History and Lore

In post-colonial America, a piece of hickory wood
driven into a doorframe was a charm to keep
a husband from straying. A variation on this to
bring back a lover involved wrapping a piece of
the errant person's hair around a piece of hickory.
In nineteenth-century Pennsylvania, bewitchment
was removed from milk by thrashing the churn or
other vessel with a hickory stick. It was believed
that the witch responsible for meddling with the
milk would have marks on her body. In legends
of the Seneca Nation, people were brought back
to life after their bones were placed beside a great
hickory tree. The Powhatan and other tribes used
the pecan nut to make an intoxicating drink called
Powcohicora, which is the source of the name
hickory.[67]

Magical Connections

Element/s	Air (pecan), earth, fire
Astrological influence	Gemini, Virgo; Jupiter, Mercury, Sun

67. Murray and Pizzorno, *Encyclopedia of Healing Foods*, 441.

Other associations	Mabon
Powers and attributes	Abundance, balance/harmony, changes/transitions, defense, justice/legal matters, loyalty/fidelity, prosperity/money, protection, renewal, security, strength, wishes (pecan)
Available for purchase	Flower essence; nuts; nut oil

Spells and Rituals

As part of a ritual with your partner to renew vows
and express your fidelity, place a small hickory
branch or dowel on the top of your bedroom doorframe. Keep a pecan with your financial papers as
an amulet for abundance and security.

High John

Jalap, High John the Conqueror (*Ipomoea purga*
    syn. *Convolvulus jalapa*); also known as high
    John root, John the conqueror, jalap root

Cousin to the garden morning glory (*Ipomoea
purpurea*), high John is an evergreen vine that can
grow twelve feet long. It has heart-shaped leaves
and purple, trumpet-like flowers. The dried root
resembles testicles.

Caution: High John is toxic and can be fatal
if ingested.

History and Lore

In the American magical tradition of hoodoo,
John the Conqueror is a mythical person whose
spirit was said to live in certain roots that he
created. This legendary person may have been
derived from West and Central African beliefs
or based on an American slave and hero known
as Old John who may have been fictional, or a

hoodoo healer. The word *high* implied authority and strength and in some areas of the American South, the term *high man* was a designation for a conjurer.[68] The root is usually carried in the pocket and rubbed with oils or other substances as needed to keep it potent. It is also used in mojo bag charms. Sources differ about keeping it in a red or green bag.

Magical Connections

Element/s	Earth, fire
Astrological influence	Mars, Sun
Powers and attributes	Authority/leadership, defense, happiness, justice/legal matters, love, luck, prosperity/money, protection, sex/sexuality, spirit guides/spirits, strength, success
Available for purchase	Cut or whole dried root; powdered root

Spells and Rituals

When dealing with a negative spirit, throw a handful of powdered roots out your back door as you tell the entity to leave and never return. Include high John in any type of spell to add strength. Create a mojo bag to carry pieces of root and other herbs for success in a particular endeavor.

Hogweed

Common Hogweed (*Heracleum sphondylium*); also known as beggar weed, cow parsnip, devil's oatmeal, eltrot, gypsy's lace

Hogweed grows between four and six feet tall. Its ridged stem is covered with bristly hairs and ranges from dark green to brownish purple. The leaves are hairy and serrated with three to five lobes. The umbrella-like flower heads have larger petals around the outside edges of each cluster. The flowers are white and often have a pinkish hue. The papery seeds are flat, green discs with reddish markings.

Caution: Hogweed sap is phototoxic, wear gloves to handle this plant. Its larger relative giant hogweed (*H. mantegazzianum*) causes severe reactions and is not safe to touch.

History and Lore

Although the genus name is sometimes attributed to a Greek legend that Heracles discovered hogweed's medicinal properties, it is more likely due to the plant's large size. According to Welsh lore, children who picked the flowers with their left hands would become left-handed. Like other white flowers, in England it was said to be unlucky to take into the home. Nevertheless, the seeds and roots were said to be aphrodisiacs. Hogweed was used in Scotland to break faery spells and to curtail their mischief.

Magical Connections

Element/s	Earth
Astrological influence	Moon
Magical entities	Faeries
Powers and attributes	Fertility, healing, hexes, renewal, sex/sexuality, strength
Available for purchase	Seeds

---

68. Alexander and Rucker, *Encyclopedia of African American History*, 207.

Spells and Rituals

To heighten lunar magic, place a cluster of flowers or a photograph of them on your altar during esbat rituals. As part of a fertility spell when planning a pregnancy, attach three seeds to a picture of a baby cradle.

Holly

American Holly (*Ilex opaca*); also known as
    Christmas holly, prickly holly, white holly
English Holly (*I. aquifolium*); also known as common holly, European holly, hollin

Holly is a large, bushy shrub with distinctive leaves that have wavy margins and sharp spines. English holly has glossy, dark green leaves; the leaves of the American holly are matte green. Small, white flowers grow in clusters.

    Caution: Holly is toxic if ingested.

History and Lore

During the festival of Saturnalia, Romans used holly to decorate their homes and sent sprigs to friends to wish them well. During the Middle Ages, holly branches were placed on houses and barns in Germany, England, and France to protect them from lightning and witchcraft. In England, holly growing next to a house was believed to bring good fortune and protection. For the same purpose, holly wood was used for doorsills in the Fenlands of Cambridgeshire. In other areas of the shire, coachmen carried a whip of holly for protection from witches or placed a sprig on the horse's collar. In Northwest England, a flaming holly branch was carried through the town accompanied by a loud band and fireworks to mark the end of Yule festivities on Twelfth Night. Yule greens were traditionally burned at Imbolc; however, a small piece of holly was sometimes kept for luck and to ward off elf and faery mischief. In the Scottish Highlands, holly was traditionally hung over the door of the cowshed for protection. In Ireland, holly was regarded as a faery tree. The leaves and berries were used for making predictions in England and Ireland.

Magical Connections

Element/s	Air, earth, fire
Astrological influence	Aries, Cancer, Capricorn, Leo, Sagittarius; Mars, Saturn
Deities	Ares, Cailleach Bheur, Cernunnos, the Dagda, Danu, Freyr, Gaia, Holle, Lugh, Saturn, Thor
Magical entities	Elves, faeries, unicorns
Ogham	Tinne ⏗
Other associations	Litha, Midsummer's Eve, Saturnalia, Yule
Powers and attributes	Banish, consecrate/bless, courage, death/funeral practices, defense, divination, dream work, family and home, hexes, intuition, luck, manifest, protection, renewal, spirit guides/spirits, spirituality
Available for purchase	Flower essence

Spells and Rituals

For good luck, tuck a leaf into your purse or wallet. Place three leaves under your front door mat to raise defensive energy around your home. As part of a banishing spell, cut a piece of paper into the shape of a holly leaf, write what you want to achieve on it, and then burn it.

Hollyhock

Common Hollyhock (*Alcea rosea* syn. *Althaea rosea*); also known as althea, rose mallow

With towering stalks up to six or seven feet tall, hollyhock flowers grow individually or in small clusters. The five overlapping petals create a bowl-shaped flower that ranges from white to pink to purplish red. The large, heart-shaped leaves have three to seven lobes and grow up to eight inches long but become progressively smaller toward the top of the stalk.

History and Lore

Like other mallows, the ancient people of China, the Middle East, and Europe used hollyhock for a range of ailments including snakebites and scorpion stings. By the Middle Ages in Europe, it was believed to provide protection from the devil. Grown for beauty, these quintessential cottage-garden flowers were the medieval commoner's roses. A seventeenth-century English recipe listed hollyhock as an ingredient for fairy oil, which when anointed to the eyes made the usually invisible fae visible. With the proper incantation, the oil was also used to conjure a faery named *Elaby Gathon*. Nannies called upon this faery to protect babies as they slept and to prevent bad faeries from substituting changelings.

Magical Connections

Element/s	Water
Astrological influence	Libra; Venus
Magical entities	Faeries

Powers and attributes	Abundance, banish, changes/transitions, emotions, family and home, happiness, prosperity/money, release, see faeries, success
Available for purchase	Flower essence; dried flowers; seeds

Hollyhock

Spells and Rituals

When going through major transitions in your life, keep a photograph of hollyhocks with you to help smooth the way. After moving to a new house, crumble a handful of dried flowers, and then sprinkle them around, inside, and out, to help you and your family feel at home.

Honesty

Honesty, Money Plant (*Lunaria annua* syn. *L. biennis*); also known as devil's penny, dollar plant, lunary, moonflower, moonwort, penny flower, shillings, silver dollars

Reaching about three feet tall, honesty has hairy stems and heart-shaped leaves with coarsely serrated edges and pointed tips. Loose clusters of four-petaled flowers grow atop the stems. The flowers range from deep purple and purply pink to white. The round seeds are visible in the flat, green seedpods that dangle in clusters. After the pods turn brown, the papery covering peels off revealing a translucent, silvery disc. The seed discs shimmer like little moons in the evening light.

History and Lore

Popular in medieval European gardens, this plant's unusual seedpods attracted attention and were said to be powerfully magic. In the Channel Islands, sprigs of honesty were hung in the houses of newlyweds for luck and happiness. Although witches and sorcerers reputedly used the plant, in England it was believed to aid in warding off evil spirits and demons. It also had the reputation of opening doors, breaking chains, and even un-shoeing any horse that stepped on it. Because of its moon-like seedpods, it was thought to be a cure for madness/lunacy. The name *honesty* comes from the Victorian language of flowers.

Magical Connections

Element/s	Water
Astrological influence	Cancer; Moon
Powers and attributes	Clarity, happiness, luck, prosperity/money, protection, truth
Available for purchase	Flower essence; dried stalks with seed pods; seeds

Spells and Rituals

Rest with a dried seed disc over each eye before any type of psychic work to aid in bringing clarity to your sessions. Include several seed discs in a spell or ritual to boost lunar magic. Place a seed disc in your wallet to attract luck and money.

Honeysuckle

Common Honeysuckle, European Honeysuckle (*Lonicera periclymenum*); also known as love bind, wild honeysuckle, woodbine
Italian Honeysuckle, Italian Woodbine (*L. caprifolium*); also known as goat leaf, Italian woodbine

Honeysuckle is a climbing vine with woody stems that grow tightly around anything nearby. It has rounded leaves and whorls of thin, tubular flowers. Common honeysuckle has pale to medium yellow flowers, gray to bluish green leaves, and dark red berries. Italian honeysuckle has pale yellow to pinkish flowers, dark green leaves, and orange-red berries.

Caution: The foliage and fruit of these plants are toxic if ingested; common honeysuckle may cause skin irritation.

History and Lore

Although honeysuckle was used as a cure for the evil eye in Argyllshire, in most of Scotland it was thought unlucky to take the flowers into the home. In the Fenlands of eastern England, the scent of the flowers taken into a house where young girls lived was believed to give them erotic dreams. In Sussex, a honeysuckle "stick" (a hazel branch with spiraling indentations where honeysuckle had grown around it) was believed to guarantee good luck especially in love. Scottish farmers wrapped honeysuckle around a rowan branch and hung it above the barn door on May Day for protection from witches. Honeysuckle growing around the door of a house in Ireland was said to protect it against witchcraft. Although honeysuckle was used against witches it was also believed to be used by them. Janet Stewart stood trial in 1597 in Scotland for using a healing wreath of honeysuckle.[69] As a patient stood in the middle of a room, such a wreath would be passed down around his or her body.

Magical Connections

Element/s	Earth
Astrological influence	Aries, Cancer; Jupiter, Mars, Mercury
Deities	Cerridwen, Gaia, the Morrigan, Venus
Magical entities	Faeries
Ogham	Ebad / Ebhadh also called Koad / Grove ✸ Uilleann / Uilleand ᚌ

Other associations	Ostara, Beltane
Powers and attributes	Abundance, adaptability, bind, clarity, divination, dream work, intuition, love, loyalty/fidelity, luck, prosperity/money, protection, psychic abilities
Available for purchase	Flower essence; essential oil; dried flowers; seeds

Spells and Rituals

To aid in magic or to increase psychic powers, place a handful of flowers on your altar to help tune into a higher level of energy. Place fresh flowers on your bedside table to aid in dream work. A honeysuckle vine growing near the house brings luck.

Hop

Common Hop (*Humulus lupulus*); also known as European hop

Growing about twenty feet long, the hop plant is a climbing vine with angular stems and lobed, heart-shaped leaves. Yellow-green, catkin-like male flowers bloom in branching clusters. Female flowers form a cone-like fruit, which is used for flavoring and preserving beer.

History and Lore

Before their use caught on and were cultivated in Europe, hops were associated with sorcery because brewing and working with herbs was women's work that was perceived as borderline witchcraft. Oddly enough, the Anglo-Saxons included hops

69. Watts, *Elsevier's Dictionary of Plant Lore*, 198.

in a salve to cure sorcery by witches, elves, and goblins. In addition to medicinal use in medieval England, garlands of dried hop vines were hung in the home or a wreath placed over the mantelpiece for good luck. A small pillow of hop flowers was used as a sleep aid and for help in interpreting dreams. As a symbol of hope during Elizabethan times, it was common for a suitor to wear a sprig when visiting the woman of his desire. While Russian brides often wore hop leaves, Tsar Michael Romanov (1596–1645) prohibited the import of hops from Lithuania because witches allegedly put spells on them to spread the plague.

Magical Connections

Element/s	Air, earth, water
Astrological influence	Aquarius, Scorpio; Mars, Pluto
Magical entities	Elves
Powers and attributes	Bind, courage, determination, divination, dream work, fertility, growth, healing, hope, peace, sex/sexuality, skills
Available for purchase	Essential oil; flower essence; whole, cut, or powdered flowers

Spells and Rituals

Because of their association with women's skills and witchcraft, place a circle of hop flowers on your altar for esbat rituals or as an offering to the goddess. Include hops in spells of attraction, especially sexual as well as those that bind people together in a positive way.

Horehound

Common Horehound, White Horehound (*Marrubium vulgare*); also known as bull's blood, eye of the star, hoarhound, seed of Horus

Horehound is a bushy plant with wooly, whitish-gray stems that grow up to three feet tall. The toothed leaves are oval to round, wrinkled, and felty white on the underside. Small, white flowers grow in rounded clusters at the leaf axils. The flowers have a tubular shape; the upper lip has two lobes; the lower lip has three.

History and Lore

The ancient Greeks used horehound medicinally, as did the Egyptians who called it the *seed of Horus*. Horehound was one of the bitter herbs used in the Hebrew ritual of Passover. The Anglo-Saxons used it medicinally for a range of ailments and called it *harehune*; *har* meaning gray, which evolved into *hoar* meaning hoary/white in Old English.[70] During the Middle Ages, horehound was believed to have the power to break magic spells, provide protection from witches, and ward off evil spirits. English physician John Gerard noted that the plant could heal the bites of dogs, especially mad dogs.

Magical Connections

Element/s	Air, earth
Astrological influence	Gemini, Scorpio, Virgo; Mercury
Deities	Horus

---

70. Pollington, *Leechcraft*, 130; Dobelis, *Magic and Medicine of Plants*, 218.

Powers and attributes	Banish, clarity, healing, hexes, protection, strength, wishes
Available for purchase	Cut, dried leaves; seeds

Spells and Rituals

To increase the power of a banishing spell, burn a few leaves and pass your tools through the smoke. Before engaging in hands-on healing, make an infusion with the leaves, and then rinse your hands with it.

Hornbeam

American Hornbeam (*Carpinus caroliniana*); also known as blue beech, ironwood, muscle wood, water beech

European Hornbeam (*C. betulus*); also known as common hornbeam, hard beam, ironwood, muscle wood, yoke elm

Hornbeam trees have multiple trunks and large branches that often have a muscle-like appearance. The trees produce long, yellowish, male catkins and shorter, greenish female catkins; the female catkins develop into clusters of winged nutlets. Mistletoe occasionally grows on hornbeam trees.

History and Lore

According to German mystic and herbalist Hildegard von Bingen, the hornbeam tree could deter and protect against demonic spirits, magic words, and curses.[71] Hildegard also noted that if it were necessary to spend the night in a forest, sleeping under a hornbeam would provide protection. Beliefs were different in Romania where the devil was said to live in a hornbeam tree. Associated with love in France, a twig of hornbeam was hung in front of a sweetheart's door on May Day as a symbol of devotion. Hornbeam was also used in sympathetic magic for healing.

Hornbeam

Magical Connections

Element/s	Fire, water
Astrological influence	Taurus; Saturn
Powers and attributes	Banish, changes/transitions, determination, love, negativity, prosperity/money, protection, release, strength
Available for purchase	Flower essence is made from the European hornbeam

71. De Cleene and Lejeune, *Compendium of Symbolic and Ritual Plants in Europe*, 403.

Spells and Rituals

For a banishing spell, prepare a candle with the flower essence. As part of a prosperity spell, wrap a leaf in the largest denomination of paper money you have and leave it on your altar for three days. To remind yourself that you are strong, keep a small twig in a prominent location.

Houseleek

Common Houseleek, Hen and Chicks (*Sempervivum tectorum*); also known as elf-wand, Jupiter's eye, Jupiter's beard, Thor's beard, thunder plant, welcome-home-husband-however-drunk-you-be

The houseleek is a mat-forming succulent with a rosette of rubbery leaves that are usually pointed and tipped with purple. The main rosette (hen) sends out horizontal stems that form small rosettes (chicks). A thick, scaly flower stalk with pinkish or reddish purple flowers grows from the hen.

History and Lore

Growing in the sand on Roman roof tiles, the houseleek was said to be a gift from Jupiter to protect the home. The Greeks believed it came from Zeus. Whatever it grew on, the structure was believed to be protected from fire and lightning throughout Europe. Readily growing on thatch, in England special nooks were created on other types of roofing where houseleeks could be planted. Houseleek was also said to bring luck to the household and was regarded as a charm against witches and sorcery. Into the twentieth century, it was common practice to take a houseleek from an old roof when moving to a new residence. Widely used medicinally for burns in

Europe and England, it was reputedly used by witches before trial where taking a hot poker in the hands was a common method for determining guilt. On Midsummer's Eve in Italy, houseleeks were used for divination about a future husband.

Magical Connections

Element/s	Air, earth
Astrological influence	Pisces, Sagittarius, Virgo; Jupiter, Venus
Deities	Jupiter, Thor, Zeus
Other associations	Midsummer's Eve
Powers and attributes	Family and home, love, luck, protection
Available for purchase	Flower essence; houseplant; seeds

Spells and Rituals

The houseleek is often kept inside as a houseplant and provides a subtle, decorative way to carry-out magic. Place it near your front door to invite love and luck into your home or move it to a spot where you feel the need for protective energy.

Hyacinth

Common Hyacinth (*Hyacinthus orientalis*); also known as garden hyacinth, jacinth

Hyacinth is a bulbous plant with long, sword-shaped leaves. Separate spikes of tubular flowers with backward curling petals grow in whorls around the stems. The flowers occur in various shades of white, blue, purple, pink, and red and have an intensely sweet scent.

Caution: Hyacinth is toxic if ingested; handling the bulbs may cause minor skin irritation.

History and Lore

The ancient Greeks dedicated the hyacinth to Demeter. Regarded as a flower of death, it was used to decorate memorials. Despite this, brides often wore crowns of hyacinth. According to myth, the flower sprung up where Apollo's young friend/lover Hyacinthos had been accidentally killed. Hyacinthos became a deified mortal carried to heaven by Aphrodite, Artemis, and Athena. Greek physician and botanist Pedanius Dioscorides noted that the plant applied to a child's genitals would delay puberty. In some areas of England, it was considered unlucky to take hyacinth flowers indoors. In France they were worn as a charm to attain friendship.

Magical Connections

Element/s	Water
Astrological influence	Pisces, Virgo; Mars, Saturn, Venus
Deities	Aphrodite, Apollo, Artemis, Athena, Demeter, Hyacinthos
Powers and attributes	Emotions, happiness, loss/sorrow, love (pink), luck, negativity, nightmares, peace, protection
Available for purchase	Flower essence; bulbs

Spells and Rituals

Use pink or red flowers in spells to attract love. When dealing with grief, place a white hyacinth, or picture of one, on your altar to help soothe emotions. To draw off bad dreams, keep one or two bulbs in your bedroom as far away from the bed as possible.

Hyssop

Hyssop (*Hyssopus officinalis*); also known as hedge hyssop

Hyssop has upright, angular stems and grows about two feet tall. Like other members of the mint family its stems are square. Its lance-shaped leaves are dark green and its tiny, purple-blue flowers grow in whorls at the ends of the stems. They bloom from midsummer to early autumn. The stems, leaves, and flowers are aromatic.

Caution: Although used medicinally, high doses can be dangerous.

History and Lore

The ancient Greeks and Romans held hyssop in high regard as a medicinal herb. Its genus and common names come from the Greek word *hussopos*, which means "holy herb," because of its use for cleaning sacred places.[72] In addition, the Romans used hyssop leaves for culinary purposes including a wine they called *Hyssopites*.[73] During the Middle Ages in England, hyssop was rubbed on door frames to keep witches and evil spirits out of a house. In Europe, it was used to ward off the evil eye, magical influences, and to guard against the plague.

72. Kowalchik and Hylton, *Rodale's Illustrated Encyclopedia of Herbs*, 342.
73. Charles, *Antioxidant Properties of Spices, Herbs and Other Sources*, 353.

Magical Connections

Element/s	Air, fire
Astrological influence	Cancer, Sagittarius; Jupiter, Moon
Magical entities	Faeries
Powers and attributes	Changes/transitions, consecrate/bless, fertility, healing, hexes, negativity, peace, protection, purification, sex/sexuality, spirit guides/spirits, spirituality
Available for purchase	Essential oil; flower essence; cut, dried leaves

Spells and Rituals

Infuse hyssop sprigs in olive oil to anoint participants in ritual. To raise spiritual vibrations, burn a leaf or two. Use several stems like a broom to encourage unwanted spirits to move on. Place a sprig under your bed to aid in fertility and vitality as well as any sexual issues.

Immortelle

Immortelle, Helichrysum (*Helichrysum italicum* syn. *H. angustifolium*); also known as curry plant, everlasting, golden eternal flower, Italian strawflower

Immortelle is a two-foot-tall herb with narrow, linear leaves that are silvery green and appear almost white. The plant has a spicy fragrance. The tiny, yellow, button-like flowers look like daisies without white petals and grow in domed clusters.

History and Lore

Immortelle has been an important plant for making wreaths since the ancient Greeks and Romans used it to adorn statues of deities. Because the flowers seem immortal, keeping their color even after being cut and dried, the wreaths were also placed on graves and in tombs. This practice continued for centuries. In Paris, Vienna, and throughout Europe, immortelle wreaths were placed on graves, especially on All Saints' Day and All Souls' Day (November 1 and 2). In Victorian England, wreaths were hung on the front door of a home where someone had died. A wreath was also laid in the grave under the belief that it would hold the spirit of the deceased in place.

Magical Connections

Element/s	Air
Astrological influence	Jupiter, Neptune
Other associations	Samhain

Powers and attributes	Ancestors, death / funeral practices, psychic abilities, spirit guides / spirits
Available for purchase	Essential oil; dried flowers

Spells and Rituals

Include dried flowers on your Samhain altar to aid in connecting with loved ones who have passed. Immortelle helps to ground and center energy after magic or psychic work. Dab a cotton ball with essential oil and store it with your magic tools to increase their effectiveness.

Iris

Blue Flag Iris (*Iris versicolor*); also known as flag lily, wild iris

Common Flag Iris (*I. germanica*); also known as German iris, orris root, purple flag

Yellow Iris (*I. pseudacorus*); also known as flag, sword lily, yellow flag

The iris has three upright petals called *standards* and three lower petals called *falls*. The flat, gray-green leaves are sword shaped. Blue flag is bluish-purple and has narrow standards and falls with yellow veining. Common flag has lilac to purple falls and lighter-colored standards. The yellow iris standards are bright yellow; its falls have brown or violet veining.

Caution: Iris is toxic if ingested; the sap can cause skin irritation.

History and Lore

Named for the goddess Iris who guided souls between the worlds, the Greeks associated this flower with the otherworld. Used in perfumery by the Greeks and Romans, orris root is a powder made from the rootstock of common flag. It is sometimes made from the Florentine iris (*I. florentina*) and sweet iris (*I. pallida*). During the Middle Ages, the Germans and French planted iris bulbs in thatched roofing for fortification to help hold it in place and for protection against witchcraft. The rhizomes were used as a healing amulet against pain. In Ireland, it was believed that a faery changeling baby would turn into a clump of yellow iris if thrown in a stream of running water.

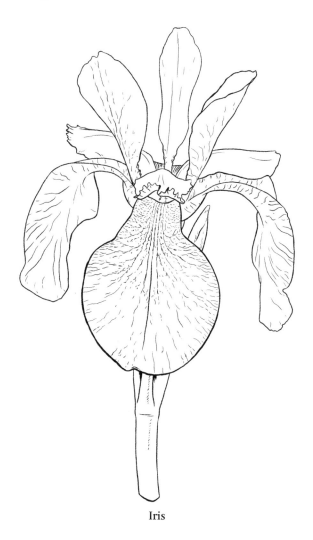

Iris

Magical Connections

Element/s	Water
Astrological influence	Aquarius, Gemini; Moon, Venus
Deities	Hera, Horus, Iris, Isis, Juno
Magical entities	Faeries
Other associations	The otherworld
Powers and attributes	Adaptability, communication, defense, determination, family and home, focus, healing, inspiration, knowledge, love, luck, prosperity/money (blue flag), protection, purification, release, success, wisdom
Available for purchase	Flower essence; dried, cut root; orrisroot

Spells and Rituals

When seeking wisdom, prepare a candle with flower essence just before meditation. Use pieces of dried rhizome or orrisroot in a sachet for love magic or as an amulet for protection. Grow irises in your garden to invite domestic bliss. Burn a dried flower in a spell to bring success.

Ivy

Common Ivy, English Ivy (*Hedera helix*); also known as bindwood, ground ivy, true ivy

Ivy is a woody, evergreen vine that climbs or trails along the ground. Its leaves have three to five lobes. In its juvenile stage, it climbs or spreads. In its adult stage, it becomes more shrub-like and produces clusters of greenish white flowers that develop into blue-black berries.

Caution: All parts of the plant, especially the leaves and berries, are toxic if ingested; sap may cause skin irritation.

History and Lore

Greco-Roman philosopher Plutarch (c. 46–c. 120) noted that ivy was called *chenosiris*, "the plant of Osiris."[74] The Romans believed ivy could bestow the power of prophecy. According to Greek and Roman lore, Bacchus/Dionysus frequently wore crowns of ivy, as did his revelers. In medieval England, wearing a crown of ivy on Beltane Eve was said to enable a person to see witches. Throughout the British Isles, a number of methods were employed with ivy for love divination, mostly on Samhain and New Year's Eve. Strands of ivy were draped over barn doors in Scotland to ward off witches. A piece of woody ivy stem was worn as a good luck charm in the Balkans.

Magical Connections

Element/s	Air, earth, water
Astrological influence	Gemini, Scorpio; Saturn, Venus
Deities	Arianrhod, Bacchus, Cernunnos, Danu, Dionysus, Freya, Hermes, Holle, Loki, Ogma, Osiris, Pan, Persephone, Rhea, Saturn
Magical entities	Faeries, satyrs, Turabug
Ogham	Gort ╫ Ór / Oir ◇ Uilleann / Uilleand ⌒
Other associations	Beltane, Mabon, Saturnalia, Yule

....
74. Wilkinson, *The Manners and Customs of the Ancient Egyptians,* 265.

Powers and attributes	Balance/harmony, bind, divination, growth, inspiration, knowledge, love, luck, negativity, prophecy, protection, renewal, secrets, security, spirituality, transformation
Available for purchase	Dried leaves; flower essence

Spells and Rituals

Place a couple of sprigs on your altar for guidance in your spiritual journey. For a binding spell, make a small wreath with a piece of ivy and place it around the base of a candle. When used on a Mabon altar, ivy represents the balance of light and dark.

Jasmine

Common Jasmine (*Jasminum officinale*); also
   known as poet's jasmine, white jasmine
Winter Jasmine (*J. nudiflorum*); also known as yellow jasmine

Common jasmine is a climbing shrub adored for
the fragrance of its star-shaped flowers, which are
white to pale pink and grow in small clusters. Its
pointed leaves are bright green. Winter jasmine is
a trailing, spreading shrub with arching branches
and small, lance-shaped leaves. The tubular flowers are bright yellow and have no fragrance.

History and Lore

The name of this plant comes from its Persian
name, *yasmin*.[75] According to lore in Malaysia,
the fragrance of jasmine attracts spirits that cure
disease. In China, it was used for culinary and
medicinal purposes as well as incense to honor
the dead. The ancient Egyptians offered jasmine
flowers to their deities, as did the Hindus. Because
its scent is especially strong at night, jasmine was
dubbed "queen of the night" and "moonshine
in the garden" in India where it was traditionally
given at weddings. It was also customary to give
the bride and groom jasmine flowers in Pakistan
and Indonesia. Jasmine also became a bridal
flower in sixteenth-century Italy.

75. Coombes, *Dictionary of Plant Names*, 110.

Magical Connections

Element/s	Air, earth, water
Astrological influence	Cancer, Capricorn, Pisces; Mercury, Moon
Deities	Diana, Rhiannon, Vishnu
Magical entities	Faeries
Powers and attributes	Abundance, bind, communication, creativity (winter), defense, dream work, healing, love, prosperity/money, psychic abilities, sex/sexuality, spirit guides/spirits, spirituality
Available for purchase	Essential oil; flower essence; dried flowers

Spells and Rituals

Diffuse a little essential oil to boost defensive magic or to aid in contacting the spirit realm. Burn dried flowers in spells to attract luck and prosperity as well as to bind a pledge. Place a ring of flowers around the base of a yellow candle on your altar to increase psychic skills.

Jelly Fungus

Fairy Butter, Common Jelly Fungus (*Tremella mesenterica*); also known as yellow witch's butter

Witch's Butter (*Exidia glandulosa*); also known as black witch's butter

Common jelly fungus sometimes looks like a clump of ribbons but mostly it looks like glossy, golden-yellow or orange-yellow blobs. Resembling butter, it is gelatinous when damp but becomes slightly brittle when dry. Witch's butter is very similar, but black.

Caution: Although jelly fungus is edible, never eat it unless a qualified expert has identified it.

History and Lore

According to English legend, yellow jelly fungus was butter that faeries or witches made from the roots of old trees. Similarly in Sweden where it was called *troll smör* "troll butter," witches and trolls were said to have made it.[76] Burning jelly fungus was believed to make a witch confess to accusations. In parts of the British Isles, it was considered lucky to find fairy butter on a house or front gate. However, finding the black witch's butter on a house was an indication of a hex but cutting through it with a hot knife was said to make a witch lift the spell. In Herefordshire, throwing the fungus into a fire was believed to protect against spells and to harm any witch who might cast one. In 1656, jelly fungus was presented as evidence in a witchcraft trial in Wales.[77]

Magical Connections

Magical entities	Faeries, trolls
Powers and attributes	Balance/harmony, banish, healing, hexes, luck, negativity, peace, spirit guides/spirits, support
Available for purchase	Dried fungus

Spells and Rituals

To counteract a hex, write a few keywords on a picture of jelly fungus. After burning it in your cauldron, take the ashes outside, scatter them in a circle, and then cover them with a handful of dirt.

....

76. Friend, *Flowers and Flower Lore*, 535.

77. Roberts and Evans, *The Book of Fungi*, 450.

Place a piece of witches' butter on your altar to aid in banishing unwanted spirits.

Joe Pye Weed

Joe Pye Weed, Gravel Root (*Eutrochium pur-pureum* syn. *Eupatorium purpureum*); also known as jopi, purple boneset, queen of the meadow, sweet Joe Pye weed, trumpet weed

This plant can reach five to seven feet tall and spread two to four feet wide. Its purple-tinged leaves are lance-shaped, coarsely serrated, and grow in whorls along the stem. Tiny pinkish purple flowers grow in domed clusters at the tops of the stems. The seed heads stay on the plant into winter.

History and Lore

The only folklore about this plant is in regard to its name. There are many versions of a story about the name *Joe Pye* originating with an Abenaki or Mohican medicine man of that name who was said to have aided English settlers in colonial New England. On the other hand, the name may have evolved from the word *jopi*, possibly Algonquin for typhoid fever, because the plant was used as a remedy for fevers and simply referred to as jopi.[78]

Magical Connections

Element/s	Water
Astrological influence	Jupiter, Saturn
Powers and attributes	Luck, negativity, spirit guides/spirits, success
Available for purchase	Cut, dried root; seeds

78. Hatfield, *Encyclopedia of Folk Medicine*, 45.

Spells and Rituals

For help in contacting spirit guides, place a vase of fresh flowers on your altar. Carry a piece of dried root to bring luck. Make a sachet with leaves and flowers to include in your bath before a job interview or an important meeting to aid in bringing success.

Jojoba

Jojoba

Jojoba (*Simmondsia chinensis*); also known as coffee bush, deer nut, goat nut, pignut, wild hazel

Growing about eight feet tall, jojoba is a multi-trunked, shrubby tree with an irregular shape. Its oval leaves are leathery and grayish green. Pale green female flowers grow singly and yellowish-green male flowers grow in clusters on separate plants. The oval fruit contains one to three seeds, which are also called *nuts* and *beans*.

Caution: Jojoba is unsafe to ingest.

History and Lore

The Tohono O'odham people of the Sonoran Desert used jojoba seeds for food and the oil for cooking and medicinal purposes. This plant's common name comes from *hohowi*, the O'odham name for it.[79] The Coahuiltecan of Mexico made a drink from jojoba seeds, which European settlers adapted as a substitute for coffee. Other jojoba beverages were used for ritual purposes. There was little commercial interest in the plant until the oil was discovered to be a liquid wax and a good alternative to the expensive sperm whale oil, which was used for lamp oil and making soap.

Magical Connections

Element/s	Water
Astrological influence	Jupiter, Moon
Powers and attributes	Balance/harmony, healing, love, relationships
Available for purchase	Seeds; seed oil

Spells and Rituals

Prepare a candle with jojoba oil to use in a spell to attract love or to heighten romance. Place a few small bowls of seeds throughout your home to get a relationship back on track or for any aspect of life that needs to be brought into balance.

Juniper

Common Juniper (*Juniperus communis*); also known as fairy circles, gin berry, savin

Juniper is a spreading evergreen tree with multiple trunks and brown to reddish brown bark. Young trees have needle-like leaves that develop into scale-like foliage as the tree matures. Technically cones, the round berries turn from green to blue-black and usually have a powdery, white coating.

Caution: Ingesting large amounts of berries can be toxic.

History and Lore

The Greeks and Romans used juniper medicinally and often burned it as incense. Sacred to Germanic people, the berries were called *Heilige Beeren* "holy berries."[80] In Germany it was used during cremations to ward off demons and in Tuscany, boughs were hung on doors to ward off witches. Juniper was used to seal up cracks in the walls of homes in Estonia to prevent evil from entering. In England, the scent of juniper berries was believed to ward off bad luck. Branches were hung in stables to ward off evil spirits and lightning. During the Middle Ages the English and Dutch regarded juniper as a medicinal panacea. Cutting down a juniper in Wales was believed to result in death within a year. In Scotland, branches were used to bless and fumigate homes on New Year's Day.

Magical Connections

Element/s	Earth, fire, water
Astrological influence	Aries, Leo, Sagittarius; Mars, Mercury, Moon, Sun
Deities	Balder, Diana, the Furies, Hecate, Holle, Loki, the Morrigan, Ran
Magical entities	Dragons, dwarves, faeries
Other associations	New Year's Day, Twelfth Night, Walpurgis

79. Greene, Williams, et al., *North American Crop Wild Relatives*, 487.

80. De Cleene and Lejeune, *Compendium of Symbolic and Ritual Plants in Europe*, 364.

Powers and attributes	Abundance, banish, consecrate/ bless, defense, divination, dream work, emotions, happiness, healing, hexes, knowledge, love, negativity, prosperity/money, protection, psychic abilities, purification, secrets, spirit guides/spirits, transformation, wishes
Available for purchase	Dried berries; essential oil

Spells and Rituals

For a charm to attract a lover, string enough berries together to form a circle on your altar. To enhance divination and dream work, have a sachet of dried berries at hand. When seeking knowledge, tie a piece of foliage with dark blue ribbon to hold while meditating.

Kava

Kava (*Piper methysticum*); also known as kava
   root, awa, kava kava, intoxicating pepper

Kava is a vine-like shrub that reaches about ten feet
tall. The glossy, tapering leaves are heart shaped
and heavily veined. Growing on short cylindrical spikes, yellowish-white male and female flowers grow on separate plants. It has a thick, woody
rhizome.

   Caution: Women who are pregnant or breastfeeding should not ingest kava.

History and Lore

Used medicinally and as an aphrodisiac, kava has
been an important social and ceremonial beverage of Pacific Islanders for several thousand years.
Included in Hawaiian initiations, naming ceremonies, and marriages, kava was also used in rituals
to invoke ancestral spirits. Priests divined information by reading the bubbles on the top of the
beverage. In Fiji, the term "drinking kava alone"
meant that a person was practicing witchcraft.[81]
Although legends vary among island societies, the
origin of kava has two types of myths. One is that
kava was a gift from the gods; the other is that it
sprouted from the vagina of a woman's corpse,
which may explain its association with ancestors.

Magical Connections

Element/s	Water
Astrological influence	Capricorn; Neptune, Saturn
Deities	Kanaloa, Kane-Hekili, Lono

81. Lebot, Merlin, and Lindstrom, *Kava: The Pacific Elixir*, 46.

Other associations	Samhain
Powers and attributes	Ancestors, divination, luck, protection, spirit guides/spirits, wisdom
Available for purchase	Cut, dried root; powdered root; essential oil

Spells and Rituals

Place kava roots on your altar at Samhain to honor and commune with your ancestors. Sprinkle a circle of powdered rhizome to cast a circle when contacting spirits. Hold a few pieces of root between your hands before divination to foster wisdom in your session.

Knapweed

Black Knapweed, Common Knapweed (*Centaurea nigra*); also known as bachelor's buttons, clubweed, hardheads, horse knot, loggerheads

Greater Knapweed (*C. scabiosa*); also known as bachelor's buttons, bottleweed, ironhead, loggerheads

Reaching about three feet tall, knapweeds have stiff stems, spherical flower buds, and thistle-like flower heads. They differ from thistles by the lack of prickles and spines. The upper leaves of black knapweed are oblong and narrow, the lower leaves lobed and toothed. The tubular florets of the flower head are pinkish purple, occasionally white. Greater knapweed has deeply lobed leaves with narrow leaflets. The purple florets are fringed at the ends.

History and Lore

Called *knopweed* in Middle English, the words *knop* meant "bud" and *knap* meant "button."[82] Many of the folk names refer to the hard flower buds. Knapweed was widely used for love divination through a number of methods in England. One was for a woman to place a floret in her blouse and think of a prospect; if the flower bloomed, so would love. A daisy-like "he loves me, he loves me not" process was also used. Wearing a knapweed flower indicated a person's eligibility. The seed heads were used for weather prediction.

Magical Connections

Element/s	Water
Astrological influence	Aquarius; Saturn
Powers and attributes	Confidence, determination, divination, healing, love, strength
Available for purchase	Flower essence; dried flowers

Spells and Rituals

To boost divination sessions, especially where love and romance is involved, place two flowers on your altar or table. For aid in raising confidence and the determination to see a situation through, carry a picture of knapweed with you as a talisman.

Knotgrass

Common Knotgrass, Prostrate Knotweed (*Polygonum aviculare*); also known as bird weed, blood weed, hogweed, pigweed, red robin, sparrow's tongue

---

82. Editorial Staff, *Webster's Third New International Dictionary*, 1248, 1251.

Equal-leaved Knotgrass (*P. arenastrum*); also known as oval leaf knotweed, small-leaved knotgrass

Knotgrass/knotweed is named for the knotty joints of its stems, which form mats. Common knotgrass has oval leaves and small clusters of tiny flowers at the base of the leaves. The flowers are white with a pinkish or red tinge. Equal-leaved knotgrass also has oval leaves and its flowers are white and green with a tinge of pink. These plants are not related to the knotweeds in the genus *Fallopia*.

History and Lore

In England, it was believed that a child who ate knotgrass would stop growing. The same applied to young animals. A poppet stuffed with knotgrass was used in magic to gain control of a person. The Anglo-Saxons called the plant *unfortraedde*, meaning "untrodden to pieces" because it couldn't be destroyed by trampling and it seemed almost magically indestructible.[83] If bitten by a poisonous creature, English herbalist Nicholas Culpeper suggested drinking wine that had been boiled with knotgrass. In Iceland knotgrass is called *blood weed* because of the reddish color of the unopened flower buds.

Magical Connections

Element/s	Earth
Astrological influence	Moon, Saturn, Sun
Powers and attributes	Banish, bind, challenges/obstacles, determination, hexes, loss/sorrow
Available for purchase	Cut, dried plant material

Spells and Rituals

As part of a banishing spell or to break a hex, create a special sigil on your altar using the stems. When they dry out, take them outside and burn them. For aid in breaking a bad habit, write what it is on a picture of knotweed, and then put the picture away until the situation has been resolved.

83. Pollington, *Leechcraft*, 133.

Lady's Mantle

Common Lady's Mantle (*Alchemilla vulgaris*); also
    known as dew cup, lion's foot
Soft Lady's Mantle (*A. mollis*); also known as dew
    cup, lion's foot, smooth lady's mantle

Lady's mantle grows in spreading mounds a foot
or more wide. The small flowers grow in clusters
atop branching stems. The rounded leaves have
shallow lobes and a pleated appearance. With a
slightly cupped structure, they hold beads of rain
or dew. Soft lady's mantle has gray-green leaves
and yellowish green flowers. Common lady's
mantle has green flowers.

History and Lore

Medieval German alchemists considered dew to
be especially magical and when collected from
the leaves of lady's mantle it was believed more
powerful for working with metals. The genus
name of lady's mantle was derived from the Arabic *alkemelych* "alchemy."[84] The Anglo-Saxons
used lady's mantle as a cure for bewitchment. In
Scotland and Ireland, it was used to remove faery
enchantment and counteract elf shot, which was
believed to be an invisible magical weapon used
by elves to cause disease. Lady's mantle could
also ward off the evil eye. In Scotland, it was used
in potions to restore a youthful appearance for
both face and breasts. English herbalist Nicholas
Culpeper recommended it for most "female troubles" and to firm sagging breasts. Sleeping with a
lady's mantle leaf under the pillow in Scandinavia
was said to bring pleasant dreams.

84. Hatfield, *Hatfield's Herbal*, 214.

Magical Connections

Element/s	Water
Astrological influence	Venus
Deities	Demeter, Freya, Frigg, Gaia, Rhea, Venus
Magical entities	Faeries
Powers and attributes	Awareness, balance/harmony, challenges/obstacles, changes/transitions, courage, divination, fertility, focus, happiness, healing, love, luck, peace, purification, relationships, spirituality
Available for purchase	Cut, dried leaves; flower essence is made from common lady's mantle; seeds

Spells and Rituals

To help focus attention and energy for divination, hold a leaf between your hands for a few minutes before a session. To support energy for love spells, include dried flowers and/or leaves. Raise energy for full moon or healing rituals by placing a bouquet of flowers on your altar.

Lady's Slipper

Pink Lady's Slipper (*Cypripedium acaule*); also known as Indian moccasin

Yellow Lady's Slipper (*C. parviflorum* syn. *C. pubescens*, *C. calceolus*); also known as American valerian, moccasin flower, nerve-root, whippoorwill's shoe

Lady's slipper produces a solitary flower that has one petal with a pouch-like structure and three thin, twisted sepals that grow out to the sides. The sepals are sometimes called *shoestrings*. Pink lady's slipper's sepals are brown and it has a pair of leaves at the base of the stem. Yellow lady's slipper has purplish sepals and its leaves grow up the stem.

Caution: May cause dermatitis when handled. These orchids are regarded as endangered in some areas. Lady's slippers require highly specific habitat and are difficult to grow; check the reputation of vendors.

History and Lore

According to an Ojibwe legend, the lady's slipper plant first grew in the moccasin prints left in the snow by a young woman who rescued her village by making a difficult journey to obtain medicine. The Ojibwe and other tribes from the upper Midwest through the Northeast used lady's slipper medicinally. While the Meskwaki employed it for love medicine, the Menominee used it "to induce dreams of the supernatural."[85] European settlers in North America found it to be a good substitute for valerian (*Valeriana officinalis*).

Magical Connections

Element/s	Water
Astrological influence	Saturn
Powers and attributes	Awareness, dream work, love, peace, protection
Available for purchase	Flower essence; plants

---

85. Moerman, *Medicinal Plants of Native America*, 146.

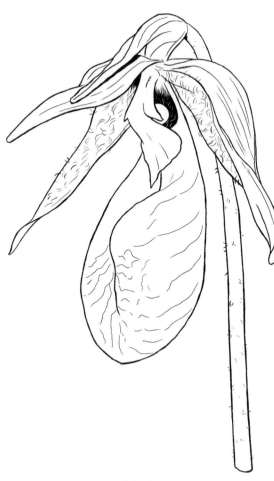

Lady's Slipper

Lady's smock has a rosette of round base leaves and long, narrow leaves on the upper stems. The flowers grow in loose clusters on slender stalks at the tip of the stems. They have four rounded petals that are wider above the middle and sometimes slightly notched at the tip. Usually a pinkish mauve, the flowers are occasionally white.

History and Lore

Looking like little smocks hung out to dry, the flowers were said to be dresses sewn by faeries. Because they were said to be sacred to faeries in England, the flowers were not included in May Day garlands to avoid offending the fae. However, in Oxfordshire it was okay to use the flowers in a garland but it could not be taken into the home because a faery might take the liberty of entering with it. Other stories note that the flowers were not taken inside because witches used them in spells. During medieval times, the word *smock* referred to a woman's undergarment and came to have a promiscuous, and sometimes derogatory, sexual connotation.[86] The association and innuendo was also applied to the flower.

Spells and Rituals

In a love spell, lady's slipper can represent the shoe of the Cinderella (or Cinderfella) you seek. As part of your magic work, cut out an even number of pink flowers from pictures, and then lay them out like footprints across your altar.

Lady's Smock

Lady's Smock, Meadow Cress (*Cardamine pratensis*); also known as bittercress, cuckoo flower, lady's mantle, milkmaids

Magical Connections

Element/s	Water
Astrological influence	Moon
Magical entities	Faeries
Powers and attributes	Divination, fertility, healing, love, sex/sexuality
Available for purchase	Seeds

....

86. Watts, *Elsevier's Dictionary of Plant Lore*, 221.

Spells and Rituals

Include lady's smock in a fertility spell by placing a circle of seeds around the base of a green candle. As part of a love charm, drip a little red candle wax on a picture of lady's smock flowers, and then inscribe your intended's initials into the wax before it hardens.

Larch

American Larch, Tamarack (*Larix laricina*); also known as eastern larch, hackmatack

European Larch, Common Larch (*L. decidua* syn. *L. europaea*); also known as white larch

Larch trees have tufts of gray-green needles that grow in tight, spiraling clusters around the branches. It is the only coniferous tree that is deciduous; the needles turn golden yellow in the autumn before they drop. The cones are small and round.

History and Lore

In fourteenth-century Germany, the larch was considered a guardian tree and a few planks of its wood were built into a house to protect it from fire. Hanging a few twigs on a house also protected it from lightning. Slavic parents protected their children from the evil eye by having them wear an amulet made of larch. Twigs were used to seal doors and windows on Walpurgis for protection against witchcraft in Poland. Regarded as sacred in many areas of the Alps, it was especially revered in the state of Tyrol, Austria, where offerings to deities were placed underneath larch trees. Known as Salgfraulien in Austria, the Salingen are female faeries who are said to be kind to good people but unfriendly to those who are not. In some legends they are said to dress in white and enjoy singing underneath old larch trees.

Common names for the American larch, *tamarack* and *hackmatack*, are corruptions of the Algonquian *akemantak*, meaning "wood for making snowshoes."[87]

Magical Connections

Element/s	Fire
Astrological influence	Jupiter
Magical entities	Faeries, Salingen
Other associations	Walpurgis
Powers and attributes	Healing, intuition, justice/legal matters, knowledge, luck, protection, spirituality, success
Available for purchase	Flower essence; essential oil

Spells and Rituals

To support shamanic work or spiritual practices, burn a small piece of resin. To enhance a spell for success, especially in legal matters, prepare a candle with the essential oil. For a boost in confidence, place a few larch needles in a small pouch to keep with you when you need it.

Larkspur

Forking Larkspur (*Consolida regalis* syn. *Delphinum consolida*); also known as field larkspur, wild larkspar

Giant Larkspur (*C. ajacis* syn. *D. ajacis*); also known as garden larkspur

---

87. Grady, *The Great Lakes*, 97.

Both are also known as knight's spur, lark's claw, rocket larkspur

Larkspur has a distinctive trumpet-shaped flower with a hood at the front and a spur at the back. The leaves are deeply lobed and feathery. Forking larkspur has branching flower stalks, dark blue or purple flowers, and bright green foliage. Reaching four feet tall, giant larkspur has blue-green foliage. Its flowers can be deep blue, pale blue, purple, white, or pink.

Caution: All parts of the plant are toxic, especially the seeds, and can be fatal if ingested.

History and Lore

The giant larkspur is associated in Greek mythology with the story of Trojan War hero Ajax. The flowers were said to grow where his blood touched the ground when he took his own life. A medieval Italian legend noted that larkspur sprang up where three knights wiped their swords on the grass after slaying a dragon. Reputedly, the dragon's blood gave the flower its color and its poison. Medieval witches in England were said to have used the poison in spells. As part of a Midsummer protection spell in Germany, vervain and larkspur were thrown through a wreath of mugwort into the bonfire.

Magical Connections

Element/s	Water
Astrological influence	Mars, Venus
Deities	Apollo
Other associations	Midsummer's Eve

Powers and attributes	Authority/leadership, awareness, courage, loyalty/fidelity, negativity, protection, psychic abilities, spirit guides/spirits, wisdom
Available for purchase	Dried flowers; seeds

Spells and Rituals

For support and wisdom in a leadership role, carry a dried flower in your wallet. To help heighten psychic abilities, sprinkle a circle of seeds on your altar during sessions. Wherever you sense negative energy, make a circle in the air with a flower stalk, and then burn it.

Lavender

English Lavender, True Lavender (*Lavandula angustifolia* syn. *L. officinalis*); also known as common lavender, elf leaf

Spike Lavender (*L. latifolia*); also known as lesser lavender, broadleaved lavender

Lavenders are woody, shrubby evergreens with flower-topped spikes. English lavender has small, purplish lavender colored flowers that grow in whorls atop leafless stems. The slightly fuzzy, needle-like leaves are grayish green or silvery green. Spike lavender's leaves are wider and rougher than English lavender and its gray-blue flowers are smaller.

History and Lore

Used medicinally and for scenting laundry since ancient Greek and Roman times, lavender has been a popular garden plant for many centuries. During the Middles Ages throughout Europe, it was associated with love and thought to be an aphrodisiac. Carrying a flower sprig reputedly enabled a person to see ghosts; used in a potion, a person could see elves. In England, wearing a circlet of flowers and tossing a few sprigs into the Midsummer's Eve bonfire was said to aid in seeing faeries. In Tuscany, lavender was used to counteract the evil eye on children. In Wales, a sprig was worn for luck and sometimes for protection because for some unknown reason it reputedly confused witches and evil spirits.

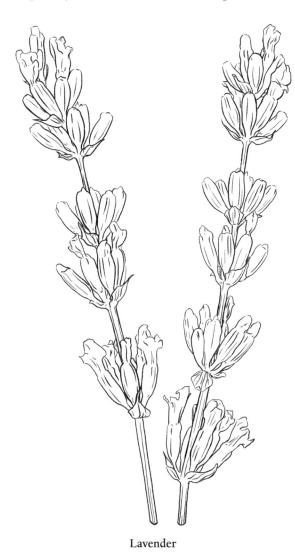

Lavender

Magical Connections

Element/s	Air
Astrological influence	Jupiter (spike), Mercury
Deities	Hecate, Saturn, Vesta
Magical entities	Elves, faeries
Other associations	Midsummer's Eve
Powers and attributes	Awareness, balance/harmony, divination, dream work, healing, intuition, love, loyalty/fidelity, luck, manifest, negativity, peace, protection, psychic abilities, purification, relationships, see faeries, spirit guides/spirits, spirituality
Available for purchase	Essential oil; flower essence; tea; dried flower buds; dried bunches of flowering stems; leaves

Spells and Rituals

The scent of lavender fosters concentration for divination or any type of psychic work and aids in contacting spirit guides. Carry dried flowers in a sachet to promote fidelity in a relationship. Burn dried leaves to release negativity or to provide protection.

Lemon

Lemon (*Citrus limon* syn. *C. limonum*); also known as true lemon

Starting as fragrant reddish buds, the leaves are dark green on top and light green underneath. Sharp thorns line the branches and discourage animals from dining on the tender leaves. The white flowers are tinged with pink and grow singly, in pairs, or in groups of three.

History and Lore

The lemon is believed to be a natural hybrid that developed where the cultivation of citrons (*C. medica*) and limes (*C. aurantifolia*) overlapped in Northeast India and Myanmar (Burma).[88] Arab traders introduced the lemon into the Mediterranean area of Europe during the early thirteenth century. By the late Middle Ages, the fruit became highly valued throughout Europe for medicinal purposes and the blossoms treasured for their fragrance.[89] The lemon was believed powerful enough to protect against poison, the plague, and bewitchment. In India, lemons were used as a cure for the evil eye.

Magical Connections

Element/s	Air, earth, water
Astrological influence	Aquarius, Cancer, Gemini, Pisces; Mercury, Moon
Deities	Anubis, Durga, Hermes, Ma'at, Odin, Parvati, Thoth
Powers and attributes	Abundance, awareness, clarity, divination, fertility, happiness, healing, love, loyalty/fidelity, protection, psychic abilities, purification, relationship, secrets, spirit guides/spirits
Available for purchase	Fresh or dried fruit; lemon juice; flower essence; dried lemon peel; hydrosol; essential oil

Spells and Rituals

To purify magic or ritual tools when you acquire them, dab them with the hydrosol. To amplify energy for moon magic and esbat rituals, use three wheels of sliced lemon to create the triple goddess symbol of a full, waxing, and waning moon on your altar.

Lemon Balm

Lemon Balm, Melissa (*Melissa officinalis*); also known as balm mint, bee balm, common balm, honey plant, sweet balm

Reaching up to three feet tall, lemon balm is a bushy herb with heart-shaped leaves that are crinkly with serrated edges. The leaves have a noticeable lemony scent when brushed against. Small white to yellowish flowers grow in clusters at the leaf axils.

History and Lore

Lemon balm honey has been highly valued since ancient times around the Mediterranean coast where beekeepers have grown it near their hives for over two thousand years. The name *Melissa* is Greek and means "bee."[90] Its medicinal uses were mentioned by both Roman naturalist Pliny the Elder and Greek physician Dioscorides. Lemon balm is reputedly one of the mints consumed by the oracle priestesses in the temple at Delphi. Priestesses who served in the temples of Rhea, Cybele, Demeter, and Persephone were called *Melissae*.[91] Lemon balm was used magically during the Middle Ages in France and Germany. When worn as an amulet, it was said to make a person friendly.

88. Hancock, *Plant Evolution and the Origin of Crop Species*, 229.
89. De Cleene and Lejeune, *Compendium of Symbolic and Ritual Plants in Europe*, 205
90. Castleman, *The New Healing Herbs*, 305.
91. Ransome, *The Sacred Bee in Ancient Times and Folklore*, 96.

Magical Connections

Element/s	Air, water
Astrological influence	Cancer; Jupiter, Moon
Deities	Artemis, Cybele, Demeter, Diana, Kupala, Persephone
Powers and attributes	Clarity, emotions, fertility, focus, healing, love, past-life work, relationships, renewal, spirit guides/spirits, spirituality, success
Available for purchase	Essential oil; flower essence; cut, dried leaves; seeds

Spells and Rituals

Diffuse the essential oil to aid in emotional healing, especially when a relationship ends. Sprinkle a handful of leaves on your altar when preparing for past-life work. Hold a leaf in each hand to focus your mind when exploring your true purpose and seeking renewal.

Lemongrass

East Indian Lemongrass (*Cymbopogon flexuosus*); also known as fever tea

West Indian Lemongrass (*C. citratus*); also known as citronella grass, fever grass

Lemongrass has strap-like leaf blades and grows in large, dense clumps that can reach four to five feet tall and wide. The bulbous bottom of the stalk resembles a large scallion. The small, greenish flowers are tinged with red and grow at the end of a curving stem. As its name implies, lemongrass has a grassy, citrus-like scent.

History and Lore

The ancient Greeks, Romans, and Egyptians used lemongrass for culinary and medicinal purposes. It was widely used for perfumery in the Middle East and India. There is no historical mention of lemongrass in magic work except in the American magical tradition of hoodoo. It is an ingredient in Van Van oil, which is used for cleansing negative energy and spirits from the home. The oil is also used to counteract magic and bring luck.

Magical Connections

Element/s	Air
Astrological influence	Gemini; Mercury, Sun, Venus
Powers and attributes	Clarity, defense, divination, focus, intuition, loyalty/fidelity, luck, negativity, psychic abilities, purification, sex/sexuality, spirit guides/spirits, spirituality, trust
Available for purchase	Essential oil; cut, dried leaves; fresh stalks

Spells and Rituals

Diffuse a little lemongrass essential oil to help open the gates of intuition and to learn to trust what you feel. Prepare a candle with essential oil before divination or psychic work to foster clarity and support clairvoyance. Use lemongrass to aid in contacting spirits.

Lichen

Florida Beard Lichen (*Usnea florida*); also known as old man's beard, tree moss, witches' whiskers

Oakmoss (*Evernia prunastri*); also known as
Mousse de Chene, oak lichen, tree moss,
true oakmoss

Lichens are an unusual combination of algae and
fungi that live in a symbiotic relationship. Florida
beard lichen is pale grayish green with thin, wiry
branches. It grows in clumps that are often topped
with flat discs, which produce spores. Oakmoss
has flat branching stems and grows in bushy
clumps. It ranges from greenish white to yellow-
green and dark green.

History and Lore
The Europeans, Chinese, and Indigenous people
throughout North America have used lichens
medicinally for thousands of years. The Anglo-
Saxons used *Usnea* lichens for elf sickness, ailments believed to have been caused by elves. In
medieval Europe, lichen growing on the bones of
the dead were regarded as particularly potent for
medicinal and magical purposes. During the four-
teenth century in Germany, lichen was believed to
cure epilepsy if it had come from a human skull,
especially if the person had met a violent end.
Such lichen was an ingredient in an ointment
called *weapon salve*. First described by Swiss physician and alchemist Paracelsus, weapon salve was
used in sympathetic magic where the ointment
was applied to the weapon that caused the wound
instead of the wound itself. Lichen was also used
for charms and amulets to attract luck and ward
off negative energy. Baskets of oakmoss have
been found in royal tombs of Egypt. In fifteenth-
century Europe it was used to scent hair; sham-
pooing was not a regular routine. The Spanish
also used oakmoss medicinally as a cure-all.

Magical Connections

Element/s	Earth, water
Astrological influence	Jupiter, Mercury, Moon, Saturn
Magical entities	Forest spirits
Other associations	The otherworld; Samhain
Powers and attributes	Luck, negativity, prosperity/ money, psychic abilities, spirit guides/spirits
Available for purchase	Dried lichen; absolute essential oil

Spells and Rituals
Place lichen on your altar at Samhain to honor
loved ones. Diffuse oakmoss essential oil after
ritual to ground energy. To aid psychic work,
especially clairvoyance, hold a branch with lichen
attached. If you find lichen in the woods, use it to
connect with forest spirits.

Licorice
Common Licorice (*Glycyrrhiza glabra*); also
known as black sugar, licorice root, liquorice,
sweet root, sweet wood, true licorice

Growing three to seven feet tall, licorice has feathery foliage with small oblong leaflets. The bluish
violet to pale blue blossoms resemble sweet pea
flowers and grow on tall spikes. The seedpods
are oblong and turn reddish brown. The root is a
woody, branching rhizome. The scent of licorice
is similar to anise and fennel.

Caution: Licorice root can be toxic when consumed in large amounts; it should not be used during pregnancy or while nursing.

Licorice

History and Lore

Licorice root was used medicinally throughout the ancient world from Europe to the Far East. Greek historian Theophrastus referred to it as Scythian root. Believed to have a calming effect, Roman soldiers chewed it when going into battle. The Egyptians placed licorice in tombs to aid the soul's transition to the afterlife. According to legend in India, the god Brahma condoned its use. Across cultures, licorice had a reputation as an aphrodisiac. In Europe, it was used in love charms and to keep a lover faithful. In sixteenth-century England, sugar and flour were added to the medicinal extract and a popular candy was born. Licorice root is used to dominate another person in the American magical tradition of hoodoo.

Magical Connections

Element/s	Water
Astrological influence	Jupiter, Mercury, Venus
Deities	Brahma, Osiris
Powers and attributes	Bind, healing, love, loyalty/fidelity, peace, sex/sexuality
Available for purchase	Flower essence; cut or whole dried roots; seeds; laces

Spells and Rituals

Use a long licorice lace for knot magic or tie two roots together as part of a love spell. Although licorice is used in magic to control other people, it can be helpful for self-control to empower yourself.

Life Everlasting

Life Everlasting (*Pseudognaphalium obtusifolium* syn. *Gnaphalium obtusifolium*); also known as cudweed, everlasting, Indian posy, rabbit tobacco, sweet everlasting

Pearly Everlasting, Life Everlasting (*Anaphalis margaritacea*); also known as cottonweed, immortelle, moonshine, silver button, silverleaf

The leaves and stems of these plants are densely covered with white, woolly hairs. The layers of tiny, white petals at the base of the flowers are bracts. Life everlasting has narrow, elliptical leaves and small clusters of white, tubular flowers with yellow to brownish tips. Pearly everlasting has slender, pointed leaves. Its flower buds look like clusters of pearls. Once open, the globular flower has a yellowish-brown ring at the center.

History and Lore

Many Indigenous people including the Mohegan, Iroquois, Cherokee, and Chippewa used these plants medicinally as well as for protection from witches, evil spirits, and sorcery. The Creek and Menominee used life everlasting to drive away ghosts and to cure madness. Believing in pearly *everlasting's* mystical power, the Cheyenne used it to purify gifts to ancestral spirits and warriors rubbed it on their bodies for strength and protection. American naturalist Henry David Thoreau (1817–1862) referred to it as "a truly Elysian flower."[92] These plants were introduced into Europe as garden ornamentals. Because the flowers maintain their beauty when dried, they became associated with longevity and immortality.

Magical Connections

Element/s	Earth
Astrological influence	Saturn
Powers and attributes	Banish, courage, healing, protection, purification
Available for purchase	Dried flowers; flower essence; seeds

Spells and Rituals

Keep a small organza bag of dried flowers with you when you need to bolster courage. To remove an unwanted spirit from your home, use dried flowers to cleanse the areas where you feel

its presence. They can also be burned to purify objects for your altar.

Lilac

Common Lilac, French Lilac (*Syringa vulgaris*); also known as blue pipe, French lilac
Tinkerbelle Lilac (*S.* x *microphylla* 'Baibelle' syn. *S.* x 'Bailbelle')

Lilac is a multi-stemmed shrub that is beloved for the fragrance of its four-lobed, tubular flowers that grow in pyramidal clusters. They range from white and lilac to purple. The pointed heart-shaped leaves range from gray-green to blue-green. The Tinkerbelle lilac is a small shrub with deep pink flowers.

History and Lore

In England, it was considered unlucky to wear white lilacs except on May Day. According to other lore, if an unmarried woman wore lilac flowers of any color at any time other than May Day she would never marry. The message when sending lilacs to a fiancée was that the marriage was off. A white lilac flower with five petals instead of four is called a *luck lilac* and said to be a gift from the fae. In Norfolk, purple lilacs were regarded as unlucky because it was a color of mourning. Because of their strong scent, the flowers were often used to line coffins and decorate graves.

Magical Connections

Element/s	Water
Astrological influence	Libra, Taurus; Mercury, Moon, Venus

----

92. Thoreau, *The Writings of Henry D. Thoreau*, 304.

Magical entities	Faeries
Other associations	Beltane
Powers and attributes	Creativity, defense, divination, dream work, focus, happiness, hexes, inspiration, love, luck, negativity, past-life work, peace, prophecy, protection, psychic abilities, spirit guides / spirits, spirituality, wisdom
Available for purchase	Flower essence

Spells and Rituals

For support in psychic work, especially clairvoyance, or to access past-life memories, prepare a candle with the flower essence for your session. To amplify lunar energy, place white lilacs on your altar during an esbat ritual. To foster inspiration, place a twig in your workspace.

Lily

Turk's Cap Lily (*Lilium superbum*); also known as
  American tiger lily, swamp lily, turban lily
White Lily, Madonna Lily (*L. candidum*); also
  known as French lily, Juno's rose, meadow
  lily

Lilies have six-petaled flowers with prominent stamens atop stiff, three- to four-foot-tall stems. The narrow, lance-shaped leaves grow around the stems. The white lily has a trumpet-shaped flower. The orange Turk's cap has reddish brown spots and strongly backward-curving petals. A green streak at the base of each petal forms a star.

History and Lore

The ancient Greeks and Romans used lilies at funerals to memorialize the deceased. According to a Roman legend, all lilies were originally orange until a drop of Juno's milk fell on one creating the white lily. In England, white lilies were hung over doorways to ward off witches and in Wiltshire they were grown in gardens to keep ghosts away. In Europe, the lily was used as an antidote to love potions; however, the dried root was said to be a love charm when worn around the neck. Medieval German alchemists believed the Turk's cap lily could aid in turning base metal to gold. Practitioners of magic burned it for astral materializations.

Magical Connections

Element/s	Water
Astrological influence	Gemini, Pisces, Scorpio, Virgo; Moon
Deities	Artemis, Asherah, Astarte, Ceres, Diana, Eostre, Hera, Isis, Juno, Kuan Yin, Venus
Other associations	The afterlife, the otherworld, Ostara
Powers and attributes	Balance / harmony, changes / transitions, consecrate / bless, death / funeral practices, hope, love (white), manifest (Turk's cap), negativity, peace (white), protection
Available for purchase	Flower essence; bulbs

Spells and Rituals

To aid in transitions or to help initiate a new chapter in your life, place a vase of lilies where you will see them often. Use a flower as a love charm. To define and bless ritual space, hold a flower as you circle the area three times.

Lily of the Valley

Lily of the Valley (*Convallaria majalis*); also
known as fairy cups, fairy ladder, ladder to
heaven, May bells, May lily, muguet

Loved for their powerful scent, the tiny, white, bell-shaped flowers are suspended in a row from one side of an arching stem. Two or three broad, lance-shaped leaves grow from the base of the plant. It produces red berries in the autumn.

Caution: All parts of the plant are toxic and can be fatal if ingested.

History and Lore

In Europe, lily of the valley was gathered on Beltane to decorate maypoles and given as love tokens. In France and Belgium, wearing a sprig of flowers on May Day or giving it as a gift was believed to bring luck for a year. Wearing it at other times in France was said to bring happiness and love. The flowers were used in love potions and to encourage faithfulness. According to legend, the flowers were created from the drops of a dragon's blood that spilled on the ground when it was slain by the Frankish Saint Leonard (496–545 CE) on the south coast of England. In Ireland, taking the flowers indoors or giving them to a friend was considered unlucky possibly because they were often grown in graveyards. In Germany, burying the flowers under a barn threshold would reputedly bewitch the cattle and milk.

Magical Connections

Element/s	Air
Astrological influence	Gemini, Taurus, Virgo; Mercury
Deities	Apollo, Asclepius
Magical entities	Faeries, Salingen
Other associations	Beltane
Powers and attributes	Balance/harmony, challenges/obstacles, clarity, consecrate/bless, courage, defense, emotions, happiness, healing, inspiration, love, luck, peace, protection, skills, spirituality, success
Available for purchase	Flower essence; dried flowers; cut, dried leaves and flowers

Spells and Rituals

For Beltane, include a bouquet of flowers to consecrate your altar, and keep it on hand for magic work later. Dried flowers can be used in spells to heal a rift with a lover or friend. Make a powder from the dried rhizomes to use in charms to overcome challenges and reach goals.

Lime

Key Lime (*Citrus aurantifolia*); also known as
Mexican lime, sour lime, true lime, West
Indian lime
Sweet Lime (*C. limettioides*); also known as Indian
lime, Indian sweet lime, Palestine lime

Lime trees are small with thorny branches and glossy leaves that are often cupped or rolled. The Key lime has elliptical leaves with small, rounded teeth along the margins. Its pale pink to white flowers grow in clusters and its round fruit is green. Sweet lime has serrated, lance-shaped leaves and pure white flowers that grow singly or in clusters. Its oval fruit is pale green to orange-yellow.

Lime

Lime

History and Lore

Limes were used in Sumatra and other areas of Southeast Asia for ceremonial cleansing and consecration. Ceremonial cutting of the fruit was believed to dispel demons and evil spirits. In Malaysia, limes were used to ward off the evil eye. Often used dried in India, the fruit was strung with red chilies and hung in houses and shops to keep evil away. A lime hung over a sick-bed reputedly aided the healing process. Limes were also used in love charms. Arab merchants are credited with transporting limes to the Middle East and Crusaders returning home took them into Europe.

Magical Connections

Element/s	Fire, water
Astrological influence	Leo; Mercury, Sun

Powers and attributes	Consecrate/bless, healing, love, protection, purification
Available for purchase	Flower essence; essential oil; juice; fresh or dried fruit

Spells and Rituals

Lime is a powerful purifier to prepare ritual space and to consecrate tools. To increase the effectiveness of a love spell, include a piece of fresh fruit or flowers. Diffuse a little essential oil to create a protective shield or hang a dried lime and chili pepper where needed.

Linden

American Linden (*Tilia americana*); also known as basswood, bee tree, lime tree

Common Linden, European Linden (*T.* x *europaea* syn. *T.* x *vulgaris*); also known as lime tree

Lindens have dark green, heart-shaped leaves that are heavily veined and pointed at the tips. These trees are most notable for their delicate, creamy white flowers that hang in clusters and sweetly scent the summer air. A pale green bract protects each cluster of pea-sized nutlets.

History and Lore

The linden was considered sacred by the Greeks and Romans. The Romans believed it had the power to counteract poison. Regarded as mystical to the Scythians, nomadic people of the Black Sea region, soothsayers would stand under a linden to make prophecies. In medieval France, it was regarded as a tree of love where couples would make their marriage vows. Despite the belief in Germany that witches gathered under lindens on Walpurgis, branches were used to keep them away from houses. This was done in Austria on Midsummer's Day. A piece of linden bark was used as a talisman against magic and witches in Poland. In southern Germany, dwarves and dragons were believed to live in lindens, in Scandinavia, they were said to be a favorite place for elves that would try to enchant anyone sitting under the tree after dark.

Magical Connections

Element/s	Air
Astrological influence	Gemini, Sagittarius, Taurus; Jupiter, Mercury, Sun
Deities	Arianrhod, Ceres, Eostre, Freya, Frigg, Holda, Lada, Odin, Philyra, Tyr, Venus
Magical entities	Dragons, dwarves, elves, faeries
Other associations	Ostara, Walpurgis, Beltane, Litha
Powers and attributes	Changes/transitions, communication, defense, dream work, justice/legal matters, love, loyalty/fidelity, negativity, peace, protection, strength
Available for purchase	Dried leaves and flowers; flower essence

Spells and Rituals

To attract love and romance, use linden flowers in a spell; use any part of the tree as a charm to enhance fidelity in a relationship. To enhance dream work, place a leaf or a picture of the tree on your bedside table. A picture on your desk helps sharpen communication skills.

Lobelia

Cardinal Flower (*Lobelia cardinalis*); also known as red Betty, red lobelia, slinkweed
Lobelia, Indian Tobacco (*L. inflata*); also known as bladderpod, eyebright, pokeweed

The cardinal flower has unbranched stems topped with spikes of scarlet-red flowers. The tubular flower has three elongated, spreading lower petals and two upper petals that flop out to the sides. The lower stem is lined with narrow, pointed leaves. Indian tobacco has oval, toothed leaves that are larger on the lower stems. The tubular flower has a three-lobed lower lip and an erect two-lobed upper lip. The flowers range from pale blue or lavender to white. Both plants have globular seed capsules.

Caution: Both plants are toxic if ingested; Indian tobacco can be fatal.

History and Lore

The Penobscot, Iroquois, Cherokee, and others used both of these plants medicinally. The Iroquois also used Indian tobacco to counteract sickness caused by witchcraft. The Meskwaki and Pawnee used the roots and flowers for love potions and charms. The Plains Indians used the cardinal flower to counteract approaching storms by throwing it into the air. The Creek used Indian tobacco to ward off ghosts.

Magical Connections

Element/s	Water
Astrological influence	Neptune, Saturn

Powers and attributes	Dream work, hexes, love, purification
Available for purchase	Flower essence; cut, dried leaves; powdered leaves; seeds

Spells and Rituals

A sachet of dried leaves on a bedside table enhances dream work. Include the flowers in a love spell or as a charm to attract romance. Indian tobacco is a plant of dual character that can be used to curse or cure and should be used wisely.

Locust

Black Locust (*Robinia pseudoacacia*); also known
    as false acacia, honey locust, yellow locust
Honey Locust (*Gleditsia triacanthos*); also known
    as sweet bean, sweet locust, thorn tree,
    thorny locust

Both of these trees have feathery leaves and produce legume-like seedpods. The honey locust has small, greenish white flowers and long, twisted seedpods that stay on the tree into winter. It has thorns with three or more points that grow about six inches long. The black locust has fragrant, white flowers in long, drooping clusters and small, sharp spines that grow in pairs. Its seedpods are straight rather than twisted. Despite its name, very little honey is produced from the honey locust; it refers to the sugary-sweet pulp contained in the seedpods.

Caution: The black locust is poisonous if ingested.

History and Lore

The honey locust was used medicinally by the Delaware and Cherokee who also made bows with the wood. The sharp spines were used as sewing needles. According to the folklore of white settlers in Kentucky and Tennessee, a locust tree should be cut back on the dark moon of August to keep it from sprouting. In New England legend, some of the witches in the Salem trials were hanged on a locust tree and more than a century later, locust trees were planted over the graves of several victims.[93] Black locust was introduced into France in the seventeenth century and later became a popular ornamental tree in Europe and England. Locust trees were sometimes regarded as sinister because of their thorns and susceptibility to witches' brooms, a dense tangle of branches that are usually caused by disease but were commonly believed to be bewitched.

Magical Connections

Element/s	Earth, water
Astrological influence	Aries
Deities	Cerridwen, Hecate, the Morrigan
Other associations	Mabon, Samhain
Powers and attributes	Balance/harmony, bind, challenges/obstacles, defense, determination, love, loyalty/fidelity, negativity, protection, secrets, strength
Available for purchase	Flower essence; honey

Spells and Rituals

Dry a few large seedpods to use as rattles for dark moon rituals. As part of a protection spell, place thee thorns on a windowsill pointing in the direction of a threat. To deter negative energy from

---

93. Rosenthal, *Salem Story*, 206.

entering your home, tuck three thorns under your front door mat.

Loosestrife

Purple Loosestrife (*Lythrum salicaria*); also
known as foxtail, purple grass, purple willow
herb, red sally, spiked loosestrife

Reaching four to five feet tall, purple loosestrife has narrow, lance-shaped leaves arranged in pairs that grow in whorls around the stems. The flowers have four to seven petals and grow in clusters along tall spikes. Flower colors range from rosy and red to deep purple even on the same plant.

Caution: Purple loosestrife is classified as an invasive species and is prohibited in some areas.

Loosestrife

History and Lore

Although this plant is not related to yellow loosestrife (*Lysimachia vulgaris*), Greek physician and botanist Dioscorides gave them the same name because he said they both had a calming effect (remove strife) on animals. The Greeks hung garlands of purple loosestrife around the necks of oxen during plowing to keep them pulling together in unison. Used for healing wounds, the genus name of this plant comes from Greek meaning "gore."[94] Gathered on Midsummer's morning in Russia, it was used to ward off witches and provide protection from their spells.

Magical Connections

Element/s	Water
Astrological influence	Mars, Moon
Other associations	Midsummer
Powers and attributes	Peace, protection, wishes
Available for purchase	Flower essence; cut, dried leaves and stems

Spells and Rituals

To aid in making a wish come true, write a few keywords about it on a piece of paper. Sprinkle the paper with dried leaves and/or flowers, fold it, and place it in an envelope. Hold it between your hands as you visualize what you want, and then place the envelope on your altar.

Lords and Ladies

Lords and Ladies, Cuckoo Pint (*Arum maculatum*); also known as Adam and Eve, arrowroot, cuckoo flower, dog's dick, fairy lamps, stallions and mares, wake pintel, wake Robin

Growing up to ten inches tall, the arrow-shaped leaves often have purplish blotches. Rising on a separate stem, the pointed white or purplish structure called a *spathe* (a specialized type of leaf) forms a hood for a cylindrical spike of tiny,

94. Sanders, *Secrets of Wildflowers*, 177.

yellow or purple flowers. The flowers develop into bright red berries.

Caution: All parts of the plant, especially the roots, are toxic if ingested; may cause skin irritation.

History and Lore
Because of the phallic shape of its flower spike, Greek physician and botanist Dioscorides declared the plant an aphrodisiac. Since then, many of its names and associations have been related to sex. The term *pint* is an abbreviation for *pintel*, the Old English word for penis.[95] The word *wake* alluded to an erect penis.[96] In Dorset and other areas of Southwest England, young girls were told not to touch the plant or they would become pregnant. According to legend in the Fenlands of Cambridgeshire, the flowers glowed at night; in fact, the phosphorescence of the pollen gives off a faint light at dusk. In sixteenth-century France, lords and ladies served as a symbol of fertility in several of the unicorn tapestries.

Magical Connections

Element/s	Air
Astrological influence	Aries; Mars
Other associations	Beltane
Powers and attributes	Balance/harmony, creativity, fertility, sex/sexuality
Available for purchase	Cut, dried root; seeds

Spells and Rituals
Lords and ladies is the perfect plant to represent the union of the goddess and god on your Beltane altar. Include a handful of seeds in a fertility spell or place a picture of the plant under your mattress.

Lotus
American Lotus (*Nelumbo lutea*); also known as yellow lotus
Sacred Lotus (*Nelumbo nucifera* syn. *Nelumbium speciosum*); also known as Indian lotus

The cup-shaped flower has a central cone structure that turns into a seedpod. The stalk lifts the flower about six feet above the water. The American lotus is pale yellow. The sacred lotus is usually pink with a yellow center; it can also be white or white with pink at the tips. The round leaves float on the water or rise up to five feet above it.

History and Lore
According to sacred Hindu texts, the lotus symbolizes the womb/yoni and the life-giving power of the primordial mother.[97] In Buddhism, it symbolizes the four elements because after it rises from the mud through water, the flowers lift into the air and face the sun. The Phoenicians associated the lotus with the moon and stars, the Assyrians depicted their moon god sitting on a lotus. The Egyptians regarded it as a type of water lily and used both plants in ritual. In China, incense was offered to the spirit of the lotus to ward off interference by evil spirits.

95. Richardson, *Britain's Wild Flowers*, 170.
96. Watts, *Elsevier's Dictionary of Plant Lore*, 93.
97. De Cleene and Lejeune, *Compendium of Symbolic and Ritual Plants in Europe*, 313.

Magical Connections

Element/s	Air, earth, fire, water
Astrological influence	Cancer; Moon, Sun
Deities	Aphrodite, Apollo, Atum, Brahma, Buddha, Ceres, Demeter, Hathor, Hermes, Horus, Isis, Kuan Yin, Lakshmi, Nefertum, Osiris, Padma, Ra, Thoth, Vishnu
Other associations	The afterlife
Powers and attributes	Awareness, balance/harmony, consecrate/bless, creativity, defense, growth, inspiration, love, peace, purification, sex/sexuality, spirituality, transformation, truth, wisdom
Available for purchase	Flower essence; essential oil; dried seed pods

Spells and Rituals

To heighten your spiritual experiences, place a picture of a lotus flower on your altar during meditation, especially when you are seeking transformation on a deep level. Use the essential oil in a diffuser to consecrate sacred space for ritual.

Lovage

Common Lovage, Garden Lovage (*Levisticum officinale*); also known as love herb, love root

Reaching up to six feet tall, lovage has dark green leaves that are deeply divided and resemble parsley or celery. The tiny, greenish yellow flowers grow in small, umbrella-shaped clusters. The leaves, stems, roots, and seeds have a celery-like flavor.

History and Lore

The Greeks used lovage medicinally, the Romans used it mainly for culinary purposes. Lovage was one of many ingredients in an elaborate concoction that the Anglo-Saxons used to cure elf sickness, ailments believed to have been caused by elves. The Anglo-Saxons were responsible for the plant's association with love because of a phonetic misunderstanding: Their name for the plant *lufestice*, "love pain," sounds very similar to the Latin name, *levisticum*, which referred to the plant's place of origin.[98] The name evolved into *loveache* in Middle English and from there, there was no going back. Although during the Middle Ages throughout Europe it was regarded as an aphrodisiac, lovage was more often used to flavor ale. According to Romanian folklore, lovage was hung on doors and windows or worn on a belt to ward off evil spirits.

Magical Connections

Element/s	Earth, fire
Astrological influence	Pisces, Taurus; Sun, Venus
Powers and attributes	Fertility, love, negativity, protection, purification, relationships, sex/sexuality
Available for purchase	Essential oil; flower essence; cut, dried root; seeds

Spells and Rituals

Diffuse the essential oil to clear away negativity or cleanse an area for magic work. Hold a piece of dried root for a few minutes when you need help in keeping your energy grounded. To promote romance in a relationship, sprinkle a handful of seeds in a circle on your altar.

98. Pollington, *Leechcraft*, 136; Dawson, *Herbs*, 62.

Magnolia

Mexican Magnolia (*Magnolia mexicana* syn.
    Talauma mexicana)
Southern Magnolia (*M. grandiflora*); also known
    as bull bay, evergreen magnolia
Sweet Bay Magnolia (*M. virginiana*); also known
    as swamp magnolia, swamp bay, white bay

Magnolias have oval to elliptical shaped leaves that are medium to dark green and shiny on the upper sides. Sweet bay leaves have a silvery underside; the southern magnolia's leaves are a rusty color. The large cup-shaped flowers are creamy white to yellowish. The Mexican magnolia's flowers are star-shaped with thick petals and often tinged with purple. The cone-like seedpods have bright red seeds.

History and Lore

Considered the most ancient of flowering plants by botanists, the magnolia is an icon of the antebellum South. The Cherokee, Choctaw, and Houma used magnolia medicinally as did the Indigenous people of Mesoamerica. Known in Mexico as *flor de corazon*, "flower of the heart," the Aztec name *yoloxochitl* had the same meaning.[99] While this name is usually attributed to the shape of the unopened flower bud, the romantic fragrance may have had something to do with it too.

Magical Connections

Element/s	Earth, Water
Astrological influence	Capricorn, Libra, Taurus; Jupiter, Saturn, Venus

99. Tucker and Janick, *Flora of the Codes Cruz-Badianus*, 238.

Deities	Aphrodite, Venus
Powers and attributes	Clarity, dream work, love, loyalty / fidelity, protection, purification, sex / sexuality, truth
Available for purchase	Essential oil; flower essence; dried leaves; seedpods

Spells and Rituals

Include magnolia in spells to attract love; dried leaves in a sachet work well as a love charm. Place a seedpod in the bedroom to heighten romance and enhance fidelity with your partner. Diffuse a little essential oil to foster clarity during meditation, especially when seeking self-truth.

Maidenhair Fern

Northern Maidenhair Fern (*Adiantum pedatum*); also known as American maidenhair fern, fairy fern, rock fern

Southern Maidenhair Fern (*A. capillus-veneris*); also known as common maidenhair fern, fairy fern, Freya's hair, hair of Venus, rock fern

Maidenhair fern is popular for its delicate fronds with black or dark purple stems that resemble strands of hair. The southern maidenhair has small, slightly lobed, fan-shaped leaflets. The northern maidenhair has pairs of dark green, wing-shaped leaflets that become progressively shorter toward the tips of the fronds. Both types of maidenhair emerge in the spring as red fiddleheads.

History and Lore

The genus, *Adiantum*, comes from Greek meaning "unmoistened" and it was given this name because of the plant leaves' ability to shed water.[100] The Romans associated maidenhair fern with Venus who, according to myth, arose from the sea with her hair beautifully coiffed and dry. Because the stems resemble strands of hair, the English, Welsh, and Irish believed that the plant could be used as a remedy to keep a person from going bald. According to legend, faeries wore crowns of maidenhair fern for certain festive occasions. Despite its association with good luck, in Norfolk it was regarded as bad luck to take the plant into a house. In the Aran Islands, this fern was used medicinally. In Brazil, if a maidenhair fern wilted when a person looked at it, they were said to be under the influence of the evil eye.

Magical Connections

Element/s	Air, Earth
Astrological influence	Mercury, Venus
Deities	Aphrodite, Venus
Magical entities	Faeries
Powers and attributes	Abundance, banish, defense, divination, focus, healing, hexes, love, luck, peace, protection, psychic abilities, release, security
Available for purchase	Cut, dried leaves; powdered leaves

---

100. Watts, *Elsevier's Dictionary of Plant Lore*, 236.

Common mallow leaves have three to seven shallow lobes and its notched flowers range from rosy to purplish pink with darker streaks radiating from the center. Marshmallow has multiple flower stalks that can reach up to six feet tall. The overlapping petals create a bowl-shaped flower that is pale pink to pinkish white. Its oval leaves are irregularly lobed with serrated edges. The round mallow fruit looks like a little wheel of cheese.

History and Lore

The Greeks planted common mallow on graves and the Egyptians used marshmallow in mortuary garlands. For millennia, marshmallow was used medicinally in India, the Middle East, Europe, and the British Isles. In medieval Europe when trial by fire was used to determine guilt, the gelatinous fluid from the marshmallow root was rubbed on the hands and body for protection. According to Irish legend, the power of mallow was so strong that it could not be harmed by anything natural or supernatural. In Germany, mallow was used to cure someone effected by witchcraft. It was used to remove any affliction caused by faeries on the Isle of Man.

Magical Connections

Element/s	Water
Astrological influence	Moon, Venus
Deities	Althea
Magical entities	Faeries
Other associations	The afterlife, Beltane, Midsummer's Eve

Maidenhair Fern

Spells and Rituals

To help focus your mind and energy for divination sessions or psychic work, place a picture of a maidenhair fern on your altar. As part of a ritual to send healing energy, sprinkle powdered leaves on a plate and write the person's initials in it with your finger.

Mallow

Common Mallow, Wood Mallow (*Malva sylvestris*); also known as buttonweed, cheese plant, fairy cheese, high mallow

Marshmallow (*Althaea officinalis* syn. *M. officinalis*); also known as hock herb, sweet weed, wild mallow

Powers and attributes	Banish, bind, challenges/obstacles, determination, dream work, fertility, healing, hexes, love, nightmares, peace, protection, sex/sexuality, spirit guides/spirits, spirituality
Available for purchase	Flower essence; dried flowers; tea; cut, dried root; seeds

Spells and Rituals

Looking like little round moons, use the fruit in esbat rituals to foster lunar energy and boost your endeavors. As part of a spell to attract love, dab a little flower essence behind your ears. To counteract hexes, burn a couple of leaves in your cauldron.

Mandrake

Autumn Mandrake (*Mandragora autumnalis*); also known as womandrake

Mandrake (*M. officinarum* syn. *Atropa mandragora*); also known as devil's apple, love apple, Mayapple, mandragora, sorcerer's root

Mandrake has a rosette of base leaves that are wrinkled and resemble Swiss chard. The flowers grow in a cluster at the center and the fruit looks like an apple. Mandrake flowers have five petals and are purplish to yellowish green. Autumn mandrake produces purple, six-petaled flowers with a slightly pointed tip.

Caution: All parts of these plants are toxic and can be fatal if ingested.

History and Lore

The magical use of mandrake dates to at least the ancient Greeks. It has been regarded as an aphrodisiac ever since the Egyptians noted that it stimulated love. Mandrake was a symbol of sexuality and fertility in the Middle East. In medieval Europe, the roots were used for love charms and fertility amulets. Because of its human-like form, the root was believed to be sentient and possess an oracular spirit especially if it was found underneath gallows. Such a root was a prized possession because it was believed to attract luck, bring wealth, and predict the future. According to French lore, mandrake could be found growing under oaks that sported mistletoe. The root was sometimes said to be a type of elf in France and in Germany it was sometimes thought to be a devilish spirit in human form or an elf or dwarf that did a witch's bidding. Also in Germany, possessing the root was enough for a woman to be convicted of and executed for witchcraft.

Magical Connections

Element/s	Earth, fire
Astrological influence	Gemini, Taurus; Mercury, Pluto, Saturn, Uranus
Deities	Aphrodite, Circe, Diana, the Fates, Hathor, Hecate, Saturn
Magical entities	Dwarfs, elves
Other associations	Walpurgis
Powers and attributes	Authority/leadership, banish, bind, challenges/obstacles, courage, divination, dream work, fertility, growth, hexes, love, luck, nightmares, prosperity/money, protection, psychic abilities, sex/sexuality, spirit guides/spirits
Available for purchase	Flower essence; seeds

Spells and Rituals

With a history of several thousand years as an aphrodisiac, mandrake is a powerful ally for love spells. For a fertility charm, place a root or picture of one under your bed. Place three leaves on your altar or table to enhance any type of magic work.

Maple

Field Maple (*Acer campestre*); also known as hedge maple, maplin tree, mazer

Sugar Maple (*A. saccharum*); also known as bird's eye maple, hard maple

These maples have gray bark and leaves with three to five lobes. They produce clusters of small greenish yellow flowers that mature into pairs of winged seeds called *samaras* and *keys*. The sugar maple is famous for its fiery autumn colors and the syrup produced from its sap.

History and Lore

The classical name for the tree, *acer*, is Latin meaning "sharp," which may have been derived from the Greek and Roman use of the wood for lances and spears.[101] The Anglo-Saxons used maple for shields. In medieval England, both the tree and a drinking bowl made from a large burl were called *mazer*.[102] The traditional wassail bowl was a mazer. According to legend, passing a child through the branches of a maple could ensure long life, cure illness, and ward off the evil eye. In Germany, a type of faery referred to as the wood folk were believed to have skin like maple bark and clad themselves in moss from the root of the tree.

....

101. Wells, *Lives of The Trees*, 209.

102. Small, *North American Cornucopia*, 651.

Magical Connections

Element/s	Air, earth
Astrological influence	Cancer, Libra, Virgo; Jupiter
Deities	Ares, Athena, Rhiannon, Venus
Magical entities	Fairies, wood folk
Other associations	Mabon, Ostara
Powers and attributes	Abundance, communication, divination, dream work, loss/sorrow, love, prophecy, prosperity/money, release transformation
Available for purchase	Maple syrup; flower essence

Spells and Rituals

To foster prophetic dreams, place three maple seeds in a sachet and hang it on your bedpost. For a spell to attract or rekindle love, press several red leaves, and then scatter them across your altar. When dealing with loss, burn a couple of leaves as you visualize a burden being lifted from you.

Marigold

Common Marigold, Calendula (*Calendula officinalis*); also known as English marigold, goldins, pot marigold, sunflower

This Old World marigold is a daisy-like flower with a central disk and rays of petals that have a yellow-orange-reddish color. A single flower grows on a stem that ranges from eight to twenty inches tall. The oblong leaves have tapering tips. Plants in the *Tagetes* genus are also known as marigolds and their properties are often confused with calendula.

History and Lore

According to Greek mythology, marigolds originated from the tears of Aphrodite after the death of her beloved Adonis. The Romans believed the plant bloomed all year and the name *Calendula* comes from the Latin *calends* meaning "the first of the month."[103] Garlands of flowers were draped as offerings in Hindu temples. Marigolds were also used in Indian weddings. Representing fond memories, the Bavarians planted marigolds in graveyards. In England, they were used for love and marriage divination through dreams. The plant was also believed to have the power to reveal thieves. According to lore, the flowers had the power to ward off witches and holding a bouquet of marigolds was said to make them visible. In Devon, Wiltshire, and Wales marigold was believed to forecast a thunderstorm. Throughout Europe and England, it was used as a medicinal and culinary herb. According to Flemish herbalist Rembert Dodens (1517–1585), alchemists used the seeds in an attempt to make gold.

Magical Connections

Element/s	Fire
Astrological influence	Leo; Sun
Deities	Adonis, Aphrodite, Apollo, Artemis, Diana
Magical entities	Faeries
Other associations	Beltane

Powers and attributes	Consecrate/bless, divination, dream work, happiness, healing, hope, justice/legal matters, negativity, nightmares, prophecy, protection, relationships, see faeries
Available for purchase	Flower essence; calendula (infused) oil; dried flower petals; seeds

Spells and Rituals

To dispel negativity and attract happiness, sprinkle dried flower petals around your property as you visualize light, sunny energy filling your home. To enhance prophetic dreaming, infuse a dream pillow with the flower essence and place it under your pillow.

Marsh Marigold

Marsh Marigold, Kingcup (*Caltha palustris*); also known as broad buttercup, fairy bubbles, goblin flower, May buttercup

With five to nine petals, the large, shiny-yellow flowers grow in clusters on tall stems and resemble their buttercup cousins. The rounded base leaves are often seven inches wide. Leaves on the upper stems are smaller and heart or kidney shaped. It is not related to other flowers known as marigolds.

Caution: The leaves are toxic if ingested; all parts of the plant contain an irritant toxin that can cause inflammation and blistering.

History and Lore

Marsh marigold flowers were collected on May Eve or before dawn on Beltane in Ireland to provide protection from malicious faeries and evil influences. Unlucky to take indoors before May

---
103. Watts, *Elsevier's Dictionary of Plant Lore*, 242.

first, on Beltane they were hung in houses and barns, placed on windowsills, and strewn on doorsteps. In less rural areas, children pushed a flower or two through the letterboxes of people's houses to keep mischievous faeries from entering. Marsh marigold was used similarly for garlands in England. Called the *herb of Beltane* on the Isle of Man, the flowers were used as a charm against faeries and witches on Beltane and as a general protective charm throughout the month of May. The flowers were also placed in a jar of water as a charm against lightning. Marsh marigold was used to protect milk in Scotland.

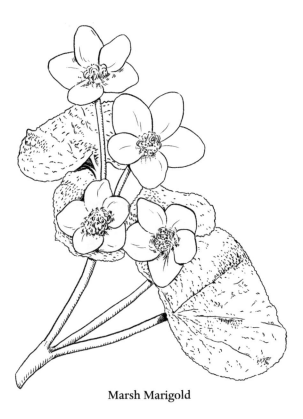

Marsh Marigold

Magical Connections

Element/s	Water
Astrological influence	Sun, Uranus
Magical entities	Faeries
Other associations	Beltane
Powers and attributes	Clarity, growth, healing, inspiration, luck, negativity, prosperity/money, protection, renewal, secrets, spirit guides/spirits, strength
Available for purchase	Flower essence; seeds

Spells and Rituals

To establish a deeper connection with your spirit guides, place several flowers on your altar. For clarity in determining your path for personal growth, place a picture of the flowering plant on your altar and visualize what you want to achieve.

Masterwort

Masterwort (*Peucedanum ostruthium* syn. *Imperatoria ostruthium*); also known as master root

Reaching almost three feet tall, masterwort has clusters of small, white flowers that form large, lacy flower heads. The three-lobed leaves are heavily veined and toothed.

Caution: The sap from this plant may cause dermatitis and/or photosensitivity.

History and Lore

Highly prized for its healing properties during the Middle Ages, the Germans, Danes, and Swedes called this plant *master* and regarded it as divine medicine. Masterwort was believed to be an antidote to poison, including the bite of a rabid dog. It was customary in the state of Tyrol, Austria, to ritually purify the house on Christmas Eve, New Year's Eve, and Epiphany/Twelfth Night by burning dried masterwort root. In England, it was used for culinary and medicinal purposes. The root is used in the American magical tradition of hoodoo for working with spirits to heighten the senses and provide protection. It is the main ingredient in a mixture called *master key oil*, which is used to gain expertise and mastery as well as to unlock personal power.

Magical Connections

Element/s	Fire
Astrological influence	Mars
Other associations	Christmas Eve, New Year's Eve, Twelfth Night
Powers and attributes	Authority/leadership, courage, family and home, intuition, manifest, negativity, protection, purification, skills, spirit guides/spirits, strength, success
Available for purchase	Dried root

Spells and Rituals

When developing talents and learning new skills, keep a picture of masterwort in your pocket as an amulet to boost your abilities and expertise.

Include masterwort in charms to bring success in reaching important goals for you and your family.

Mastic and Pistachio

Mastic Tree (*Pistacia lentiscus* syn. *Lentiscus vulgaris*); also known as gum mastic, lentisco, lentisk, mastic

Pistachio Tree (*P. vera*); also known as green almond, pistachio nut

The mastic tree is a large, evergreen shrub with leathery, oval leaves. It has clusters of tiny, white and red flowers (male) and greenish flowers (female) on separate plants. Female flowers develop into small, bright red berries that turn black when mature. Pistachio is a small tree with gray-green, oval leaflets that are lighter underneath. Clusters of tiny, yellow flowers (male) and brownish green flowers (female) grow on separate trees. The female flowers develop into reddish husks that contain the pistachio nut.

History and Lore

The mastic and pistachio trees were held in high esteem by the Greeks, Romans, and Persians. The Greeks and Romans attributed healing powers to the pistachio. While mastic was a symbol of virginity in Greece, pistachio was an aphrodisiac said to be coveted by the fabled Queen of Sheba. Persian kings regarded it as the nut of paradise. The Egyptians used mastic as temple incense and in the embalming process. In medieval Europe, pistachio was added to sweets and used as a culinary condiment. Used medicinally, the sweet-smelling mastic resin was the original chewing gum used to freshen the breath.

Magical Connections

Element/s	Air
Astrological influence	Jupiter (pistachio), Mercury (pistachio), Sun (mastic)
Deities	Artemis, Bacchus, Diana, Dionysus
Powers and attributes	Clarity, healing, love, purification
Available for purchase	Mastic gum; mastic essential oil; pistachio nuts; pistachio oil

Spells and Rituals

Use mastic as incense to prepare ritual space or for meditation when seeking clarity in a situation. Prepare a light green candle with pistachio oil for a healing ritual. Include pistachio nuts in a spell to attract romance or crush a handful of shells to initiate the end of a relationship.

Mayapple

Mayapple, American Mandrake (*Podophyllum peltatum*); also known as devil's apple, duck foot leaf, hog apple, raccoon berry, wild lemon

Mayapple consists of a single, erect stem that is usually forked. Each stem has an umbrella-like leaf that is deeply divided into five to nine lobes. A white, apple-like flower with a yellow center grows at the fork in the stem and is usually hidden by the leaves. The yellow, oval or egg-shaped berry looks like a small lemon. Mayapple grows in colonies from a single root.

Caution: The unripe fruit and other parts of the plant are toxic and can be fatal if ingested.

History and Lore

Despite one of its common names, Mayapple is not related to the true mandrake (*Mandragora officinarum*). The misnomer came about because both plants were used as purgatives in England. According to Appalachian legend, there were male and female Mayapple plants; the male plant was said to have one leaf stalk, the female two with the flower growing in the crotch of the stalks. Wrapping strands of a couple's hair around a Mayapple root was said to keep them faithful. The Cherokee, Delaware, Iroquois, Osage, and Penobscot used Mayapple medicinally. The Delaware also employed it as a love charm.

Magical Connections

Element/s	Fire
Astrological influence	Mercury
Powers and attributes	Love, negativity, prosperity/money, protection, security
Available for purchase	Flower essence; cut, dried or powdered root (often sold as mandrake)

Spells and Rituals

To raise protective energy around your home, sprinkle a handful of powdered root at the cardinal directions of your property. As part of a love spell, write the name of the person you are interested in on a picture of Mayapple, wrap a piece of your hair around it, and then burn it.

Meadowsweet

Meadowsweet (*Filipendula ulmaria* syn. *Spiraea ulmaria*); also known as bridewort, meadwort, queen of the meadow

Growing up to four feet tall, meadowsweet has toothed leaves with prominent veins and whitish down on the underside. Its tiny, five-petaled flowers are creamy white and grow in loose clusters atop the stems. The flowers have a sweet, almond-like fragrance; the leaves have a sharp scent.

History and Lore

The Anglo-Saxons called this plant *medewyrt*, "meadwort" and, of course, used it to flavor mead.[104] According to Celtic myth, the goddess Aine was traditionally crowned with meadowsweet and gave the flowers their sweet scent. The plant was considered sacred by the Druids. In a legend from the medieval Welsh *Mabinogion*, meadowsweet was one of the plants used by the wizard Gwydion to create Blodeuwedd. Despite its medicinal uses, in parts of England it was considered unlucky to take meadowsweet indoors because it was believed that too much of the fragrance would cause fits. In Ireland, meadowsweet was placed under the bed to cure illness or enchantment caused by faeries. However, faeries were also noted as dancing amongst the meadowsweet in the fields. In Iceland, the leaves were used to determine whether someone was a thief.

Magical Connections

Element/s	Air, water
Astrological influence	Pisces; Jupiter
Deities	Aine, Blodeuwedd, Cú Chulainn, Danu, Gwydion
Magical entities	Faeries

Powers and attributes	Balance/harmony, creativity, divination, family and home, fertility, happiness, healing, inspiration, love, luck, peace, relationships, security, strength, truth
Available for purchase	Flower essence; cut, dried flowers; cut, dried leaves and flowers; flower extract; seeds

Spells and Rituals

To create a sense of harmony and security in your home, place a potpourri bowl of meadowsweet in the dining or living room. Include the fresh flowers in a bridal bouquet to strengthen love and foster a happy marriage. Use dried flowers to scent ritual clothing.

Mesquite

Honey Mesquite (*Prosopis glandulosa*); also known as western honey mesquite

Mesquite (*P. juliflora* syn. *Acacia juliflora, Mimosa juliflora*); also known as ironwood

Mesquites are leguminous trees with twisted trunks, often more than one, and spreading crowns. The branches sport thorns up to two inches long. Growing in pairs, the oblong leaflets give the trees a feathery appearance. Dense, spikey clusters of tiny, pale yellow or yellow-green flowers grow at the ends of branches and resemble bottlebrushes. The long, thin bean pods are green and turn brown when ripe.

History and Lore

Perhaps most widely known as a barbecue flavoring, the use of mesquite dates back thousands of years in Central and South America. The common name was derived from the Aztec word for

---

104. Pollington, *Leechcraft*, 138.

the tree, *mizquitl*.[105] In the Aztec creation myth, when Quetzalcoatl (in his role as god of winds) created the world for the second time, he fed people with the fruit of the mesquite. A cactus spine and mesquite charcoal were used for tattooing by the Yuma during girls' puberty ceremonies. The Moapa crafted arrow tips from fire-hardened mesquite sticks.

Magical Connections

Element/s	Air, Fire, Water
Astrological influence	Moon, Saturn
Deities	Ixtlilton, Quetzalcoatl
Other associations	Beltane
Powers and attributes	Abundance, determination, healing, protection, purification, success
Available for purchase	Flower essence; wood chips; dried bean pods; bean flour

Spells and Rituals

Burn a few wood chips to cleanse an area for outdoor ritual. Use bean pods to increase the power of healing herbs. Tie several bean pods into a bundle with red ribbon or yarn and place it on your altar as a talisman to aid in getting through situations where it is essential to "hang in there."

Milkwort

Common Milkwort (*Polygala vulgaris* syn. *P. oxyptera*); also known as fairy soap, self heal

Heath Milkwort (*P. serpyllifolia*); also known as upland milkwort

105. Martin, *The Folklore of Trees & Shrubs*, 124.

Milkwort is named for its milky white sap. The clusters of flowers are usually blue, but can also be bluish violet, rosy-red, or white. They look like they have wings with two sepals attached to the base of the tubular flower. Common milkwort grows up to ten inches tall with narrow, lance-shaped leaves that alternate up the stem. Heath milkwort is smaller with oblong leaves that grow opposite each other.

Milkwort

History and Lore

In medieval England, mothers drank milkwort tea during lactation because it was believed to increase milk for their babies. In northern areas, garlands of milkwort were carried around the perimeter of properties to bless fields and livestock and for protection against the plague, fire, and wild beasts. Pastures with milkwort were favored in Wales for grazing cows to enhance milk production. In

Scotland, a sprig of milkwort placed in a milk vessel was a charm to remove bewitchment. To protect milk from faery meddling, a hoop made with milkwort, butterwort (*Pinguicula vulgaris*), dandelion (*Taraxacum officinale*), and marigold (*Calendula officinalis*) was placed under a milk pail. In Ireland, the roots and leaves were said to be used by faeries for a lather to wash their hands.

Magical Connections

Element/s	Water
Astrological influence	Moon
Magical entities	Faeries
Powers and attributes	Abundance, balance/harmony, clarity, consecrate/bless, family and home, focus, healing, protection, renewal
Available for purchase	Cut, dried leaves and flowers; dried flower tops; seeds

Spells and Rituals

To bring harmony to the home, especially when dealing with problems, place a handful of dried leaves and flowers in a decorative container in the living room. Keep a jar on the highest shelf in your kitchen to attract abundance. For clarity and focus, meditate with a picture of milkwort.

Mimosa

Cutch Tree, Catechu (*Senegalia catechu* syn. *Acacia catechu, M. catechu*); also known as black cutch, Indian mimosa tree

Mimosa, Silk Tree (*Albizia julibrissin* syn. *Acacia julibrissin, Mimosa julibrissin*); also known as Persian silk tree, silky acacia

Silver Wattle, Mimosa (*Acacia dealbata*); also known as blue wattle

These trees have fern-like leaves and flat, bean-like seedpods. The silk tree has dark green leaves and fluffy, pink powder puff flowers. The silver wattle has blue-green to silvery-gray leaves and fluffy, ball-shaped flowers on short spikes. Neither of these trees have thorns. The cutch tree has short, hooked thorns and pale yellow flowers that grow in cylindrical spikes.

Caution: Silk tree seeds and pods are toxic if ingested.

History and Lore

In India, the silk tree was regarded as lucky and used as a charm against the evil eye. According to myth, the cutch has hooked thorns because the original tree sprang from the claw that a falcon lost while recovering Soma, the drink of immortality, for the gods. Believed to protect against all types of spells, a sprig of cutch was tucked into clothing or hung over the bed. In England, the flowers of the silver wattle were generally considered unlucky to take indoors and, in some areas, it was unlucky to plant the tree in a house garden.

Magical Connections

Element/s	Air, water
Astrological influence	Aquarius, Cancer, Capricorn, Pisces, Virgo; Saturn, Venus
Powers and attributes	Awareness, consecrate/bless, determination, dream work, happiness, intuition, love, luck, peace, protection, psychic abilities, purification, renewal, security
Available for purchase	Flower essence; dried flowers; seedpods; seeds

Spells and Rituals

Use a silk tree flower as a love charm by brushing it across your face several times like a powder puff as you visualize your goal, and then keep it in a sachet. To heighten intuition, hold a couple of leaves between your palms. Place flowers on your altar to raise awareness for ritual.

Mint

Peppermint (*Mentha* x *piperita*); also known as balm mint, brandy mint

Spearmint (*M. spicata*); also known as garden spearmint, green mint

Water Mint (*M. aquatica*)

Mints have square stems and oblong leaves that are deeply veined and toothed. Water mint leaves have a purple tinge and purple veins. Peppermint has tiny, purple, pink, or white flowers that grow in whorls at the tops of the stems. Spearmint has tight whorls of pink or lilac-colored flowers atop the stems. Water mint flowers are pink to lilac and form large, rounded clusters.

History and Lore

Peppermint was considered sacred by the ancient Egyptians and Greeks who placed garlands of it in tombs. Participants in the Eleusinian Mysteries, secret rites in the veneration of Demeter and Persephone, consumed a mint drink or gruel.[106] The Greeks and Romans wore crowns of peppermint at feasts and Roman brides wore garlands called *Corona Veneris,* "crown of Venus."[107] Throughout Europe and the British Isles, mint was regarded as an aphrodisiac and used in love charms. In medieval England, it was often used

as a strewing herb in bedrooms. Spearmint was used to cure the bite of mad dogs. During the Middle Ages in Europe, mint was used to ward off the evil eye and to drive away evil spirits. The Druids regarded water mint as a sacred herb.

Magical Connections

Element/s	Air (spearmint), fire (peppermint), water (spearmint, water mint)
Astrological influence	Gemini; Mercury (peppermint), Venus
Deities	Demeter, Hades, Hecate, Persephone, Pluto, Venus, Zeus
Powers and attributes	Banish (peppermint), focus, healing, love, luck, prosperity/money, protection, psychic abilities (peppermint), purification, strength, trust
Available for purchase	Essential oil; flower essence; fresh leaves; cut, dried leaves; seeds

Spells and Rituals

Purify ritual objects and magic tools by storing them with a sachet that has been sprinkled with essential oil. Include fresh or dried leaves in spells to attract love, luck, and prosperity. Before engaging in divination or any type of work that requires concentration, drink a cup of mint tea.

Mistletoe

American Mistletoe (*Phoradendron leucarpum* syn. *P. flavescens*); also known as oak mistletoe

European Mistletoe (*Viscum album*); also known as all heal, devil's grass, golden bough, witches' broom, witches' nest

Mistletoe's thick, leathery leaves are yellowish green. The small, white or greenish white flowers

106. De Cleene and Lejeune, *Compendium of Symbolic and Ritual Plants in Europe*, 366.
107. Folkard, *Plant Lore, Legends, and Lyrics*, 439.

mature into white or yellowish berries. Although it is semi-parasitic and grows in clumps on tree limbs, these two species of mistletoe are not considered serious threats to their hosts.

Caution: Mistletoe is toxic if ingested.

History and Lore

Mistletoe was revered because of its liminal nature but even more so when it grew on an oak tree, an uncommon occurrence. Oak trees were associated with the most powerful gods in Greek, Roman, Celtic, and Germanic cultures and mistletoe berries were believed to confer the power of fertility because they held the male life-force essence of the god. In Greek and Roman mythology, mistletoe was needed for safe passage to and from the underworld. In Germany, England, Wales, and France, mistletoe was regarded as a plant of good fortune. A sprig was customarily hung in the home for a year and replaced with a fresh one at Yule. In the folklore of Germany, Austria, and Flanders, mistletoe was said to grow where an elf had sat in a tree. It was said in Germany that holding a sprig provided the ability to see and talk to ghosts. In Sweden, mistletoe was gathered on Midsummer's Eve and hung on houses and barns to dispel the power of trolls. A divining rod cut on Midsummer's Eve was said to have the power to find hidden treasure. In Scotland sprigs were placed on cradles to prevent faeries from swapping human infants for changelings.

Magical Connections

Element/s	Air
Astrological influence	Leo; Mercury, Sun

Deities	Apollo, Arianrhod, Asclepius, Balder, Demeter, Freya, Frigg, Hades, Jupiter, Odin, Persephone, Pluto, Venus, Zeus
Magical entities	Elves, fairies
Other associations	The otherworld, Twelfth Night, Litha, Yule
Powers and attributes	Banish, challenges/obstacles, changes/transitions, death/funeral practices, divination, dream work, fertility, love, luck, negativity, protection, purification, renewal, sex/sexuality, spirit guides/spirits
Available for purchase	Cut, dried European mistletoe is marketed as mistletoe herb

Spells and Rituals

To enhance your experiences, hold a sprig of mistletoe before divination or dream work. For fertility spells or to aid sexual issues, place a ring of berries around a green candle on your altar. When dealing with challenges or transitions, hang a sprig over your altar for support.

Moonwort

Common Moonwort (*Botrychium lunaria* syn. *Osmunda lunaria*); also known as grape-fern, moon fern

Moonwort consists of two stems about seven inches tall. One stem has up to nine pairs of fan or half-moon-shaped leaves that often overlap. The other stem spouts branches ladened with round seed capsules. The capsules turn yellow when they mature.

it to extract silver from mercury. To witches and sorcerers, it was known as martagon. According to English and Irish legend, moonwort had a strong effect on metal and could un-shoe a horse that stepped on it. Pushing it into a keyhole was said to open the lock. The faeries of England were believed to use moonwort to enter peoples' homes and to ride it like a horse to their revels. In addition to shining at night, moonwort was said to wax and wane like the phases of the moon.

Magical Connections

Element/s	Water
Astrological influence	Cancer; Moon
Deities	Aine, Ariadne, Arianrhod, Artemis, Diana, Hecate, Luna, Nanna, Rhiannon, Selene, Shiva
Magical entities	Faeries
Powers and attributes	Banish, defense, divination, focus, hexes, knowledge, love, luck, prosperity/money, protection, psychic abilities, purification, release, secrets, security, spirit guides/spirits, truth
Available for purchase	Because of moonwort's endangered status, use photographs to work with it.

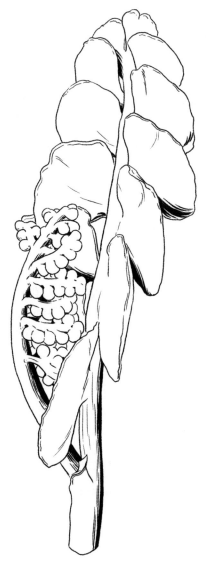

Moonwort

History and Lore

Because of the crescent shape of its leaves, medieval alchemists in Germany believed that moonwort was imbued with the power of the moon and especially potent if gathered in moonlight. Alchemists knew it as lunary and reputedly used

Spells and Rituals

For aid in developing psychic skills, especially clairvoyance, hold a picture of moonwort between your hands before sessions. To draw down the power of the moon for esbat rituals, cut out a sufficient number of leaves from a picture and arrange them in a circle on your altar.

Morning Glory and Moonflower

Common Morning Glory (*Ipomoea purpurea* syn. *Convolvulus purpureus*); also known as tall morning glory

Mexican Morning Glory (*I. tricolor*); also known as grannyvine

Moonflower (*I. alba*); also known as moon vine, tropical white morning glory

The morning glory has heart-shaped leaves and trumpet-shaped flowers. The common variety has purple flowers; the Mexican flowers can be blue, pink, or white. Morning glory flowers open in the morning and close at night or in the rain. Moonflower has rounded leaves with a heart-shaped base. The large white flowers are fragrant and open at dusk.

Caution: All parts of these plants are toxic if ingested and can be fatal.

History and Lore

The Aztec revered morning glory for its hallucinogenic properties and used it to communicate with their deities. The seeds were used for trance in divination and in an ointment to make a person fearless. According to English lore, witches were said to use morning glories and moonflowers in spells. The magical power of moonflowers was regarded as strongest when gathered three days before the full moon.

Magical Connections

Element/s	Water
Astrological influence	Moon (moonflower), Saturn (morning glory)
Magical entities	Faeries
Powers and attributes	Awareness, balance/harmony, banish, bind, changes/transitions, divination, dream work, family and home, happiness, loss/sorrow, peace, security, strength, success
Available for purchase	Flower essence from both plants; seeds

Spells and Rituals

As part of a binding spell, use a long piece of vine to wrap around an object or make a circle with the stem on your altar. Place moonflowers on your esbat altar to honor lunar goddesses and draw down the power of the moon. Enhance dream work by draping a vine above your bed.

Moss

Common Haircap Moss (*Polytrichum commune*); also known as great golden maidenhair, Loki's oats

Sphagnum Moss (*Sphagnum centrale*); also known as bog moss, peat moss

Haircap moss stems are covered with whorls of pointed, dark green leaves. The tan spore capsules are topped with a tuft of hair and grow on separate reddish stems. Sphagnum has upright stems with bundles of branches growing in whorls and a tuft of small branches at the top. The leaves are variously shaped and can be green, yellowish, or reddish.

History and Lore

Throughout the British Isles and Europe, moss was used medicinally and in a range of household items such as mats and padding. In Germany, moss was sometimes a substitute for lichen and used as an ingredient in an ointment called *weapon salve*. It was regarded as especially potent if it had come from the skull of someone who died a violent death. First described by Swiss physician and alchemist Paracelsus, weapon salve was used in sympathetic magic where the ointment was applied to the weapon that caused the wound rather than the wound. On All Saints' Day (November 1) in rural England, it was customary to place a wreath of moss, ivy, and red berries on the grave of a loved one. Although haircap moss was regarded as one of Loki's plants in Norse mythology, it was also dedicated to Sif and Freya. In Germany, faeries known as moss folk or wood folk clothed themselves in moss most often taken from the roots of a maple tree.

Magical Connections

Element/s	Water
Astrological influence	Gemini, Taurus; Saturn
Deities	Freya, Loki, Sif
Magical entities	Faeries, moss folk
Other associations	Samhain
Powers and attributes	Luck, prosperity / money
Available for purchase	Dried and fresh sphagnum; peat moss;

Spells and Rituals

If you have a shady spot in your garden, encourage moss to grow or use a terrarium jar indoors. Outside or in, dedicate it to the fae and use it to aid in contacting them. As part of a money spell, tie a handful of moss with green and gold ribbons.

Motherwort

Common Motherwort (*Leonurus cardiaca* syn. *Cardiaca vulgaris*); also known as cowthwort, heartwort, lion's ear, lion's tail, she-vervain, throw-wort

Growing three to five feet tall, motherwort has a shaggy appearance with mostly drooping leaves and a tuft of them at the top of the stems. The dull green leaves are hairy and have three pointed lobes with jagged edges. Clusters of tiny, white, pink, or purple flowers form wreaths around the stems at the leaf axils. The tube-shaped flower has an erect upper lip and a three-lobed lower lip

Caution: Motherwort can cause contact dermatitis; unsafe to ingest during pregnancy.

History and Lore

From ancient times through the Middle Ages in Europe, motherwort was associated with the heart and used to cure heartburn as well as heartache. The ancient Greeks used motherwort as a sedative, especially for childbirth. Believed to ward off a range of evils, it was worn as a charm and sewn into baby clothes. On the Isle of Man, motherwort and vervain (*Verbena officinalis*) were distinguished as he- and she-vervain, respectively. In the Hebrides, garlands of motherwort were worn on Midsummer's Eve when dancing around the bonfire. Reputed to provide longevity, the Japanese drank it in a beverage.

Magical Connections

Element/s	Water
Astrological influence	Leo; Venus
Other associations	Midsummer's Eve
Powers and attributes	Defense, happiness, love, peace, protection
Available for purchase	Flower essence; cut, dried leaves; seeds

Spells and Rituals

Grow motherwort in your garden or place a small sachet of seeds near your front door to attract peace and happiness to your home. Amplify the magic of Midsummer's Eve by placing several stems on your altar. Use dried leaves in spells to counter any type of negative magic.

Mugwort

Common Mugwort, Common Wormwood
(*Artemisia vulgaris*); also known as felon
herb, motherwort, muggert, silver leaf, wild
wormwood

Growing up to six feet tall, mugwort is a shrubby plant with purplish-brown stems and a sage-like odor. Its deeply lobed leaves are dark green on top and slightly silvery underneath. The small, greenish yellow to reddish brown flowers grow in clusters along the stems.

Caution: Mugwort can be toxic if ingested in large quantities.

History and Lore

From Greco-Roman to medieval times in Europe, mugwort was regarded as a powerful herb and a well-known deterrent to magic. The Germans used it to treat disease caused by spells and to protect people and animals from bewitchment. In Belgium, Denmark, France, and the Isle of Man, it was hung in the rafters to drive witches away as well as to ward off lightning and the plague. Mugwort was used in a potion in Belgium as a cure for bewitchment. The root was worn around the neck as an amulet for protection from poisonous animals and ghosts. Crystal gazers in England were said to drink mugwort tea before sessions to heighten their abilities. While it was used to prevent faery meddling throughout the British Isles, faeries reputedly used it for travel spells. In the British Isles and Germany, mugwort was an important component of Midsummer's Eve to wear, hang in the home or barn, or toss on the bonfire for protection from illness as well as a wide variety of dangers and calamities.

Magical Connections

Element/s	Air, earth, water
Astrological influence	Cancer, Gemini, Libra, Sagittarius, Taurus; Moon, Neptune, Venus
Deities	Artemis, Diana, Hecate, Isis, Thor, Woden
Magical entities	Faeries
Other associations	Samhain

Powers and attributes	Authority/leadership, awareness, banish, consecrate/bless, defense, divination, dream work, family and home, fertility, happiness, love, luck, negativity, peace, protection, psychic abilities, purification, release, spirit guides/spirits, strength
Available for purchase	Essential oil; flower essence; cut, dried leaves and stems; dried stalks

Spells and Rituals

Call on the protective power of mugwort by making a wreath to hang on the most frequently used exterior door of your home. As part of a defensive spell, place two long stems in the shape of an X on your altar. Diffuse a little essential oil to aid divination and psychic work.

Mulberry

Mulberry

Black Mulberry, (*Morus nigra*); also known as Persian mulberry, Spanish mulberry

White Mulberry (*M. alba*); also known as Russian mulberry, silkworm mulberry

The black mulberry has small, green catkins and dark green, heart-shaped leaves. Resembling large blackberries, the green fruit turns red and then black. The white mulberry has yellowish-green catkins and glossy, dark leaves. The fruit is white to pink and sometimes red or purplish black.

History and Lore

In China, the mulberry was regarded as a sacred tree symbolizing cosmic order; however, when planted in front of a house, it was believed to bring sorrow. The Greeks and Romans added mulberries to wine to give it a darker color and to enhance the flavor. While the Romans used the word *morum* for both mulberry and blackberry (*Rubus fruticosus*), the sweet wine they called *moretum* was made from mulberries.[108] Mulberry juice was sometimes used to color attendees' faces at Roman rituals and festivals. The Anglo-Saxon drink of honey and mulberry juice called *morat* was later adopted by the Danes. Used medicinally by the Anglo-Saxons, the unripened fruit had to be picked at night to be effective. Regarded as a tree of good luck in Italy, a piece of twig was carried in the pocket as an amulet.

Magical Connections

Element/s	Air
Astrological influence	Gemini, Virgo; Mercury, Venus
Deities	Athena, Diana, Hermes, Mercury, Minerva, Pan, Venus

---

108. Vickery, *Oxford Dictionary of Plant-Lore*, 250; De Cleene and Lejeune, *Compendium of Symbolic and Ritual Plants in Europe*, 430.

Other associations	Ostara
Powers and attributes	Challenges/obstacles, consecrate/bless, creativity, divination, dream work, inspiration, luck, protection, psychic abilities, secrets, success, wisdom
Available for purchase	Fresh or dried fruit; dried leaves; mulberry juice

Spells and Rituals

To help keep a secret, write a keyword on a picture of a mulberry tree, and then burn it as you think about your pledge. For a protection spell, prepare a candle with mulberry juice. To create sacred space for ritual or magic work, define your circle with a mulberry stick.

Mullein

Common Mullein, Great Mullein (*Verbascum thapsus*); also known as candlewick, flannel leaf, hag's taper, witches' candle

Mullein has a large rosette of oval base leaves that are soft and velvety to the touch. A tall stalk develops in the second year with leaves that taper down in size higher on the stalk. Its yellow, five-petaled flowers are densely packed at the top of the stalk and open a few at a time.

Caution: The seeds and roots are toxic if ingested.

History and Lore

The ancient Romans used the dried flower stalks dipped in tallow as torches. In Greek mythology, mullein was used to fend off enchantment. Even though witches were said to use the stalks as torches and for casting spells, in Ireland carrying a piece of mullein was believed to protect against enchantment and witchcraft. It was used as a charm to see faeries and as an amulet to recover children who had been abducted or enchanted by them. The Anglo-Saxons used a mullein stem as a charm to ward off wild beasts and anything evil. In France, mullein that had been passed through the smoke of the Midsummer's Eve bonfire was believed to protect cattle from sorcery.

Magical Connections

Element/s	Fire
Astrological influence	Aquarius, Libra; Saturn
Deities	Jupiter
Magical entities	Faeries
Other associations	Samhain, Walpurgis
Powers and attributes	Authority/leadership, awareness, banish, courage, defense, divination, healing, hexes, love, negativity, nightmares, protection, psychic abilities, release, security, see faeries, spirit guides/spirits, support
Available for purchase	Flower essence; cut, dried flowers; cut, dried leaves; powdered leaves; seeds

Spells and Rituals

Use the top part of a mullein stalk as a wand in banishing spells. To heighten awareness before divination sessions or magic work, hold a leaf between your palms for a few minutes. Sprinkle dried flowers on your altar to enhance contact with spirits.

Mushroom

Common Puffball (*Lycoperdon perlatum*); also
    known as devil's snuffbox, pixy puff, wolf
    farts

Death Cap Mushroom (*Amanita phalloides*)

Fairy Ring Mushroom, Scotch Bonnet (*Marasmius oreades*); also known as fairy stool, fairy
    table

The puffball has a white stem and a white to
brownish spherical cap with pointy warts that leave
a pattern when they wear off. It releases spores in a
puff of "smoke." Death cap has a yellowish green
to brownish cap, white gills, and white stem. The
young cap is bell-like but becomes flattened. The
cap of the fairy ring is bell-shaped and also flattens
with age. It is usually buff, tan, or reddish with a
white stem. Given their name, it's no surprise that
fairy ring mushrooms often form a circle as they
emerge from the ground. Scientifically, there is no
difference between toadstools and mushrooms.
The term *toadstool* is often applied to poisonous
fungi in common speech.

Caution: The death cap can be fatal if ingested;
while the fairy ring and puffball are edible, never
eat them unless identified by a qualified expert.

History and Lore

The Greeks believed that mushrooms and toadstools were created by lightning. Seeming to
mysteriously appear, the French and Italians
associated mushrooms with negative events and
linked them with the activities of demons and
witches. Puffballs were believed grow where
witches had gathered. In the British Isles, a ring
of mushrooms was said to mark a place where
faeries had danced. The Scots Gaelic word for
mushroom, *Bocán*, also means "hobgoblin" or
"sprite."[109] In Wales, poisonous mushrooms were
called *meat of the goblins*.[110] Associated with fertility in some parts of Germany, mushrooms were
regarded as aphrodisiacs and used in love potions.
People in Yorkshire held the belief that mushrooms came from a stallion's semen.

Magical Connections

Element/s	Earth
Astrological influence	Aries; Mercury, Moon
Magical entities	Faeries, gnomes, leprechauns, pixies
Other associations	Beltane
Powers and attributes	Awareness, courage, creativity, divination, fertility, happiness, psychic abilities, secrets, sex/sexuality, spirit guides/spirits, strength
Available for purchase	Dried mushrooms; figurine

Spells and Rituals

To enhance the power of a fertility spell, include
a picture of a phallic-shaped mushroom. Place a
circle of dried mushroom caps on your altar or
table during divination sessions to increase and
support your psychic awareness. To boost creativity, keep a figurine in your workspace.

109. Mac Coitir, *Ireland's Wild Plants*, 293.
110. Folkard, *Plant Lore, Legends, and Lyrics*, 431.

Mustard

Black Mustard (*Brassica nigra*)

Brown Mustard (*B. juncea*); also known as Chinese mustard, Indian mustard

Yellow Mustard (*Sinapis Alba* syn. *B. alba*): also known as white mustard

Black mustard has oval, lobed lower leaves, and lance-shaped upper leaves. It grows about eight feet tall and has dark brown to black seeds. Brown mustard's leaves are oval and lobed with frilled edges. It grows about six feet tall and has dark brown or yellow seeds. White mustard is about two feet tall with deeply lobed leaves that are heavily veined and pointed. Its seeds are yellow or white. All of these plants have clusters of bright yellow, four-petaled flowers.

Caution: Black and brown mustard are regarded as noxious or invasive weeds in some areas.

History and Lore

Mustard is noted as early as 3000 BCE in Sumerian and Sanskrit texts.[111] Originally used as a medicinal herb by the Greeks and Romans, it was later regarded as an aphrodisiac because it is hot and spicy. According to English folklore, grinding mustard seeds was often done at night by household brownies. In the American South, mustard seeds were used to repel witches and lutins (trickster, elf-like beings). The seeds were scattered across thresholds because it was believed that witches could not cross over them and would have to pick them up one-by-one despite being burned by them. Seeds were also sprinkled under the bed for safety during sleep.

---

111. Cumo, *Encyclopedia of Cultivated Plants*, 670.

Magical Connections

Element/s	Fire
Astrological influence	Aries; Mars
Deities	Asclepius
Powers and attributes	Fertility, healing, justice/legal matters, prosperity/money, protection
Available for purchase	Flower essence; whole or powdered seeds; seed oil; fresh greens

Spells and Rituals

Include mustard seeds in a fertility spell and place a small sachet of them under the bed. Keep a few seeds in your pocket or purse for success when dealing with legal issues. As part of a protection spell, scatter seeds in a circle on your altar.

Myrrh

Common Myrrh (*Commiphora myrrha*); also known as herabol myrrh, true myrrh

Sweet Myrrh (*C. erythraea*); also known as bisabol myrrh, opopanax

These small, thorny desert trees produce a thick, yellow resin that flows from cracks or incisions made in the bark. The resin hardens into a reddish brown tear shape. The leaves consist of three grayish green oval leaflets with the center one usually larger than the other pair. Yellow flowers grow in small clusters at the leaf axils.

Caution: Myrrh is a potential abortifacient.

History and Lore

Myrrh was in high demand throughout the ancient world for sacred and medicinal purposes.

The Romans were known for their use of it in perfumery. The Hebrews used myrrh to anoint sacred objects. The Egyptians used it for ritual purification in temples and as part of the embalming process. Myrrh was an important aromatic offering to deities, especially Isis and Ra. According to Greek mythology, the egg from which the phoenix regenerated itself was made of myrrh resin. In another myth, the god Adonis was born from a myrrh tree. Throughout medieval Europe, myrrh was used as incense to smoke out unwanted spirits. The resin was used medicinally in the Middle East, Belgium, and the Netherlands.

Magical Connections

Element/s	Air, water
Astrological influence	Aquarius, Cancer, Capricorn, Scorpio; Moon, Sun
Deities	Adonis, Aphrodite, Cybele, Demeter, Hecate, Horus, Isis, Juno, Ra, Rhea, Saturn
Magical entities	Phoenix
Other associations	The afterlife, Yule
Powers and attributes	Awareness, banish, consecrate/bless, death/funeral practices, focus, healing, hexes, manifest, negativity, past-life work, protection, purification, release, spirit guides/spirits, spirituality, transformation
Available for purchase	Essential oil; gum resin grains; gum resin powder

Spells and Rituals

When engaging in past-life work, burn a few resin grains to create a protective shield and to heighten awareness. Diffusing a little essential oil during meditation helps release emotional or spiritual blockages that can foster healing and transformation.

Myrtle

Common Myrtle (*Myrtus communis*); also known as Roman myrtle, sweet myrtle, true myrtle

Myrtle is an aromatic, evergreen shrub with glossy, lance-shaped leaves. The showy white flowers have a profusion of long, yellow-tipped stamens in the center. The berries are bluish to purple-black.

Myrtle

History and Lore

Many Greek and Roman deities were crowned with myrtle flowers and leaves as were the Lares (Roman household spirits). Especially associated with Aphrodite and Venus, myrtle became a symbol of love and fertility throughout medieval Europe. In Palestine, bridal couples wore crowns of myrtle and roses, and in England and Germany myrtle was part of the bridal bouquet. It was customary in England to plant a sprig from a wedding bouquet. Greeks and Romans also held the myrtle tree as a symbol of authority.

Regarded as protective, Romans wore a sprig as a talisman while traveling. Myrtle was also associated with death and immortality by the Greeks and Egyptians who used it to adorn graves. The Egyptians also placed it inside tombs to aid the deceased in the afterlife. In France, it was customary to put a branch in the coffin if the tree grew on the deceased person's property.

Magical Connections

Element/s	Water
Astrological influence	Sagittarius, Taurus; Moon, Venus
Deities	Aphrodite, Artemis, Astarte, Athena, Demeter, Dionysus, Eros, Hathor, Ishtar, Mars, Venus
Other associations	The afterlife, the otherworld, Ostara, Litha, Lughnasadh, Mabon
Powers and attributes	Authority/leadership, death/funeral practices, dream work, emotions, family and home, fertility, healing, love, loyalty/fidelity, luck, peace, protection, purification, sex/sexuality
Available for purchase	Dried leaves; essential oil

Spells and Rituals

To help release unsettled emotions, burn a dried leaf as you visualize a burden being lifted. To raise healing energy, make a circle of berries on your altar and leave it in place for three days. For remembrance, place a sprig of leaves next to a picture of a loved one who has passed away.

Nettle
Stinging Nettle, Common Nettle (*Urtica dioica*);
also known as devil's leaf, devil's wort

Growing in dense colonies, nettle can reach up to six feet tall. The leaves have rounded bases and pointed tips and are heavily veined and toothed. Tiny, white or green flowers grow in whorls at the stem tips and at the leaf axils. The stems and leaves are covered with bristly hairs that release an irritant when brushed against.

Caution: The irritant causes a burning, itching sensation that can last from a few minutes to twelve hours or more.

History and Lore
The Greeks and Romans used nettle seeds as a cure for impotence. Germanic peoples used the seeds as an aphrodisiac and the root to increase fertility. Regarded as a protective plant created by Woden, the Anglo-Saxons used nettle as an ingredient in healing charms to ward off demons and sickness. It was also used to soothe the effects of elf shot, which was believed to be an invisible magical weapon used by elves to cause disease. In Denmark, nettles were believed to mark a place where elves lived and a nettle sting was believed to provide protection from sorcery. Nettle was also effective against trolls. In Scandinavia, Russia, Eastern Europe, and Tyrolian Austria, nettles were hung on stable doors at Midsummer to repel evil. During the Middle Ages throughout most of Europe, nettle was believed to protect against witches despite the fact that they were said to use it in potions. In England, Germany, and Tyrolian Italy and Austria, nettle was believed to provide protection from lightning.

Magical Connections

Element/s	Fire
Astrological influence	Aries, Scorpio; Mars, Pluto
Deities	Donar, Thor, Woden
Magical entities	Elves, faeries
Powers and attributes	Banish, confidence, courage, defense, divination, healing, hexes, justice/legal matters, love, luck, negativity, peace, protection, psychic abilities, purification, release, security, sex/sexuality
Available for purchase	Flower essence; cut, dried leaves; nettle leaf tea

Spells and Rituals

To help in dealing with a problematic neighbor, sprinkle dried leaves around your property to deflect negativity. If you are nervous about a meeting, interview, or public engagement, put a dab of nettle infused oil on your soles to bolster confidence and keep your energy grounded.

Nightshade

Black Nightshade (*Solanum nigrum*); also
    known as blackberry nightshade, common
    nightshade
Deadly Nightshade, Belladonna (*Atropa bel-
    ladonna*); also known as banewort, devil's
    cherry, sorcerer's berry, witches' berry

Deadly nightshade is a shrubby plant with broad, oval leaves and drooping, bell-shaped flowers that are reddish purple or greenish purple. Its glossy, black berries are the size of cherries. Black night-shade has lance-shaped leaves with wavy margins. Its white, star-shaped flowers have yellow centers and petals that taper backwards. It has shiny, black berries.

Caution: Deadly nightshade is extremely toxic and fatal if ingested; touching it can irritate the skin; all parts of black nightshade are toxic, except the ripe berries.

History and Lore

Belladonna's dark history stretches back to the ancient Romans who reputedly used it to poison enemies. Along with wine, it may have fueled Bacchanalian orgies. Throughout medieval Europe and noted in the writings of Giambattista della Porta (1535–1615) Italian scholar, alchemist, and occultist, belladonna was believed to be a plant of witches and sorcerers who used it in their legendary flying ointment. French and German alchemists and magicians burned it to manifest spirits. In Normandy, walking barefoot on deadly nightshade was believed to cause a person to go insane and in Scotland it was said to enable a person to see ghosts. Black nightshade was used medicinally by the Anglo-Saxons as well as in healing charms. In Central Europe, it was hung over baby cradles to help them sleep.

Magical Connections

Element/s	Water
Astrological influence	Libra Scorpio; Pluto, Saturn
Deities	Circe, Hecate, Macha
Other associations	The otherworld

Powers and attributes	Creativity, divination, secrets
Available for purchase	This plant is best worked with symbolically

Spells and Rituals

Because of its association with the witches' flying ointment, keep a picture of belladonna with you during journeying or astral work. Similarly, use a picture for help in keeping silent about a secret. If you find either plant in the wild, leave an offering to Hecate beside it.

Nutmeg

Nutmeg

Nutmeg (*Myristica fragrans* syn. *M. officinalis*, *M. aromata*); also known as true nutmeg

The nutmeg tree is a tropical evergreen with glossy, oval leaves and clusters of small, pale yellow flowers. Resembling an apricot, the fruit has a yellowish husk and a large, brown seed, which is the nutmeg. The red netting that covers the nutmeg is mace, an important spice in its own right and is also known as nutmeg flower.

Caution: Excessive use of nutmeg or mace can be toxic and even deadly.

History and Lore

Not surprisingly, nutmeg's species name means "sweet scented."[112] Arab physicians recommended it as a digestive remedy and as an aphrodisiac to boost fertility. In India, nutmeg and mace were used in aphrodisiac potions. Highly prized in France and Germany, nutmeg was included as an ingredient in love potions. Abbess and herbalist Hildegard von Bingen seems to have been aware of nutmeg's drug-like effects when she recommended it as the main ingredient in uplifting little cakes.[113] In Elizabethan England, nutmeg was used in pomanders to ward off the plague. In later centuries it was carried as a lucky charm.

Magical Connections

Element/s	Air (mace), fire
Astrological influence	Leo, Pisces, Sagittarius; Jupiter, Mercury (mace), Moon

112. Neal, *Gardener's Latin*, 54.
113. Rätsch, *The Encyclopedia of Psychoactive Plants*, 608.

Other associations	Yule
Powers and attributes	Awareness, changes / transitions, divination, fertility, focus, healing, hexes, justice / legal matters, love, loyalty / fidelity, luck, prosperity / money, psychic abilities (mace)
Available for purchase	Essential oil; whole, grated, or ground nutmeg; ground mace

Spells and Rituals

Nutmeg increases magical energy and aids in turning enchantment back on the enchanter. Diffuse a little essential oil to increase the power of spells that initiate change in your life. Carry a nutmeg in your pocket or purse when dealing with legal matters.

Oak

Black Oak (*Quercus velutina*); also known as yellow bark oak

English Oak (*Q. robur*); also known as common oak, truffle oak

White Oak (*Q. alba*); also known as ridge oak

The distinctive oak leaf has deep indentations. Black oak leaves have pointed lobes tipped with tiny bristles; white oak leaves are rounded and smooth. The leaves of the English oak have rounded lobes with a pair of smaller ones at the base. The oak nut, or acorn, has a woody cap.

Oak Gall

Also known as: oak apple

Resembling a small, spongy apple, an oak apple is an abnormal growth that forms when an oak apple gall wasp lays eggs in the tree's bark.

History and Lore

Regarded as sacred almost everywhere it grew, the Greeks and Romans associated the oak tree with their most powerful gods, as did the Celts, Germans, and Norse people. In Germany, branches were talismans to ward off witches on Walpurgis. In Italy, the leaves from an oak that had been struck by lightning were used as talismans. Prior to the fifteenth century, Lithuanians left offerings at the base of oaks because they were believed to be the dwelling place of deities. It was customary in England and Ireland to tie a cloth on an oak that grew near a sacred well while asking for blessings, healing, or protection from sorcery. In Somerset it was believed that angry spirits would haunt the trunk of an oak if it had been coppiced (severely cut back to produce new growth resulting in straight sticks for utilitarian purposes). Such a tree was avoided after sundown. In Surrey, oak bark was used in love potions, and in Wales it was believed that rubbing the bark on Midsummer's Day would bring good health for a year. Oak apples were used in England for weather divination and to tell if a child had been bewitched.

Magical Connections

Element/s	Air, earth, fire
Astrological influence	Cancer, Gemini, Leo, Sagittarius, Virgo; Jupiter, Sun
Deities	Ares, Balder, Bílé, Brigid, Cernunnos, the Dagda, Dôn, Herne, Jupiter, Odin, Pan, Perun, Rhea, Thor, Zeus
Magical entities	Dryads, elves, fairies, the Green Man, hamadryads
Ogham	Dair / Duir ⌐⌐
Other associations	The afterlife, the otherworld, Walpurgis, Beltane, Litha, Midsummer's Eve, Lughnasadh, Mabon, Yule
Powers and attributes	Abundance, ancestors, authority/leadership, awareness, confidence, consecrate/bless, courage, defense, determination, fertility, healing, inspiration, justice/legal matters, knowledge, luck, prosperity/money, protection, purification, secrets (white), sex/sexuality, spirit guides/spirits, strength, success, wisdom
Available for purchase	Pieces of bark; flower essence

Spells and Rituals

Place oak leaves on your altar during ritual to represent the God. Invite abundance and bless-

ings into your home by placing three acorn cups on a kitchen windowsill. As a reminder to keep a secret, place three oak leaves where you will see them often.

Olive

Common Olive (*Olea europaea*); also known as European olive

The olive tree has narrow, waxy leaves and clusters of white, four-petaled flowers. The oval fruit contains a single pit. While olive trees become gnarly with age, they can bear fruit for more than a thousand years.

History and Lore

Regarding the olive tree as a gift from the gods, the Greeks crowned statues of deities with olive wreaths and used the oil in sacred rites. In Rome, the wood was used for temple fires when making offerings to deities. A branch was often placed in Greek and Roman graves and wreaths laid on top to help the deceased rest in peace. The Egyptians placed wreaths on mummies to aid them in the afterlife. The Arabs and Hebrews also venerated this tree as did Germanic people who anointed statues of deities with olive oil. According to Italian legends, consecrating a home with olive oil or hanging a branch over the door would deter witches, wizards, and devils.

Magical Connections

Element/s	Air, earth, fire, water
Astrological influence	Aquarius, Aries, Leo; Jupiter, Mercury, Moon, Sun

Deities	Amaterasu, Amun, Apollo, Ashtoreth, Athena, Brahma, Fides, Flora, Hera, Hermes, Horus, Indra, Jupiter, Minerva, Pele, Poseidon, Ra, Saturn, Zeus
Magical entities	Unicorns
Other associations	The afterlife
Powers and attributes	Abundance, consecrate/bless, death/funeral practices, family and home, fertility, healing, hope, love, loyalty/fidelity, luck, peace, prosperity/money, protection, purification, sex/sexuality, spirituality
Available for purchase	Olives; olive oil; dried leaves

Spells and Rituals

For spells to attract love or increase passion, prepare a candle with olive oil. As part of a spell to increase prosperity, place a dab of olive oil on money. To aid in contacting spirits, place a twig on your altar or eat three olives beforehand. Use olive oil to consecrate ritual objects.

Onion

Common Onion (*Allium cepa*); also known as bulb onion, garden onion

The hollow, green leaves sprout from the bulb and taper to a blunt tip. White or pinkish-red flowers grow in a globular cluster atop their own stem. The onion bulb can be yellow, white, or red. The outer layers become dry and brittle.

History and Lore

Egyptians regarded onions as sacred and offered them to deities during religious ceremonies. They were also offered to the dead at funerals and placed in tombs. Dedicated to Isis, onions were sliced to represent various phases of the moon. To the Greeks, the onion was a symbol of fertility and an aphrodisiac. Believing that the odor offended the gods, onions became associated with a demonic underworld in India. In medieval Europe, they were hung over the entrances to homes to ward off the plague and witches, who reputedly did not like them. In Eastern Europe, onions were strung up with garlic to deter vampires. The English used them for weather divination at the winter solstice. In addition to love divination, onions were stuck with pins and roasted to get a wayward lover to return.

Magical Connections

Element/s	Fire
Astrological influence	Mars
Deities	Isis
Powers and attributes	Banish, courage, death/funeral practices, divination, dream work, fertility, healing, hexes, negativity, prosperity/money, protection, secrets, sex/sexuality, spirit guides/spirits, strength
Available for purchase	Fresh, whole, and minced; dried, flaked and powdered; braided onion strings

Spells and Rituals

As part of a money spell, braid a short length of leaves, place it with your financial papers until it is dry and brittle, and then bury it in the ground. To dispel negative energy, crumble a handful of papery onionskins into your cauldron and burn it. Use a sprouted onion in a spell for courage.

Orange

Orange

Bitter Orange (*Citrus aurantium*); also known as
   Seville orange, sour orange
Sweet Orange (*C.* x *sinensis* syn. *C. aurantium* var.
   dulcis); also known as China orange

Orange trees have shiny, oval leaves. Their white, five-petaled flowers are fragrant and grow singly or in clusters. The flesh of the bitter orange fruit is too sour to eat, but the peel is flavorful and aromatic.

History and Lore

Oranges may have been the golden apples of Greek mythology that Gaia presented to Hera on her wedding day. The Greeks and Romans regarded almost any type of large round fruit as apples (*melon* and *malum*, respectively). The first time Italian explorer Marco Polo (1254–1324) saw oranges he called them "apples of paradise."[114] A symbol of fertility in China, oranges were a traditional gift for newlyweds. In the Middle East, the flowers were regarded as an aphrodisiac. Used in love charms in Italy, orange blossoms were an important part of bridal bouquets. In the witchcraft of England and Italy, an orange was used to represent a person's heart. Orange peels were sometimes substituted for apples in southern England for divination concerning love and marriage. The peels of two oranges were removed in a long strip, and then one tossed over each shoulder. Reputedly, the shapes would form the initials of a future husband.

Magical Connections

Element/s	Air, earth, fire, water
Astrological influence	Aries, Leo, Sagittarius; Sun
Deities	Fortuna, Gaia, Hera, Juno, Jupiter, Zeus
Other associations	The otherworld, Litha
Powers and attributes	Abundance, clarity, divination, dream work, fertility, focus, happiness, love, loyalty/fidelity, peace, prosperity/money, protection, psychic abilities, purification, spirit guides/spirits
Available for purchase	Fresh or dried oranges; orange juice; cut or powdered dried peel; flower essence; essential oil

114. Staub, *75 Remarkable Fruits for Your Garden*, 153.

Spells and Rituals

For the summer solstice, place an orange on your altar to represent the power of the sun. To boost the energy of a spell, burn a small piece of dried orange peel. To focus your mind and bring clarity to psychic work, prepare a candle with orange juice.

Orchid

Adam and Eve, Putty Root Orchid (*Aplectrum hyemale*); also known as Adam, Eve, and Son root

Early Purple Orchid (*Orchis mascula*); also known as dog's stones, foxstones, salep orchid, satyrion root

The early purple orchid flower is deep pink with dark spots underneath the white throat. The leaves are usually marked with purple splotches and the root consists of two round tubers, one larger than the other. Adam and Eve orchid has one base leaf and a purplish green flower stalk. The pale green or yellow flowers are purplish toward the tips. The bulbous roots are linked in pairs and sometimes threes.

Caution: The Adam and Eve orchid is toxic if ingested; may cause skin irritation.

History and Lore

The name *orchid* comes from the Greek *orkhis* meaning "testicle" because the roots resemble male genitalia.[115] Regarded as an aphrodisiac, Greek women ate them to increase their sexual appetite. According to Roman legend, orchid roots were the food of satyrs. Originating in the Middle East, a beverage called salep or saloop was made with powdered orchid root, milk, and sugar. The Greeks and Romans enjoyed it as did the Germans and English centuries later. According to medieval European lore, witches used the larger of the two roots for love potions; the smaller one to ease heartbreak. In England, orchid roots were used in love charms. They were also used in divination to see if a romantic affair would have a good outcome and placed under a pillow to dream of a future husband. The root was used in love charms in Ireland and Scotland.

Magical Connections

Element/s	Water
Astrological influence	Libra, Scorpio; Venus
Deities	Bacchus, Dionysus, Pan, Saturn
Magical entities	Satyrs
Powers and attributes	Fertility, love, loyalty/fidelity, luck, psychic abilities, success
Available for purchase	Flower essence; whole or powdered roots

Spells and Rituals

Carry a piece of root as an amulet to attract love or increase fertility. To strengthen commitment with your partner, split a root in half and each keep one in a safe place. To aid in developing and strengthening psychic abilities, hold a root between your hands for several minutes a day.

Oregano and Marjoram

Common Oregano (*Origanum vulgare*); also known as joy of the mountain, shepherd's thyme, wild marjoram

---

115. Mac Coitir, *Ireland's Wild Plants*, 244.

Sweet Marjoram (*Origanum marjorana* syn. *Marjorana hortensis*); also known as joy of the mountain, knotted marjoram, mountain mint

Oregano and marjoram are bushy herbs with oval, gray-green leaves. The small, tube-shaped flowers are white, pink, or purplish and grow in spike-like clusters. Marjoram leaves usually cluster at the ends of the stems; oregano's grow along the entire stem.

History and Lore

The Greeks scented shrouds with these herbs when preparing loved ones for burial and if the plant grew on a grave, it meant that the deceased had found happiness in the afterlife. Reputedly first cultivated by Aphrodite, Greek brides wore garlands of marjoram. Other myths note that she used oregano to heal Trojan hero Aeneas' wounds after the battle of Troy. Both the Greeks and Romans used the flowers in crowns for bridal couples; the plants were believed to be aphrodisiacs. During the Middle Ages in Europe and England, oregano and marjoram were used medicinally. In Germany, these plants were used as a protection charm and hung over a doorway to safeguard a household from witchcraft, ghosts, and goblins.

Magical Connections

Element/s	Air, fire (oregano)
Astrological influence	Aries, Gemini, Libra, Virgo; Mars (oregano), Mercury
Deities	Aphrodite, Kupala, Venus
Other associations	The afterlife, Samhain
Powers and attributes	Death/funeral practices, defense, family and home, focus, happiness, healing, hexes, love, peace, prosperity/money, protection, psychic abilities, purification, release, security
Available for purchase	Essential oil; fresh leaves and stems; cut, dried leaves

Spells and Rituals

Place either herb on your Samhain altar or whenever a loved one dies, to bring comfort and send them on a peaceful journey through the afterlife. To foster security and happiness, grow either plant in your garden or sprinkle the dried herb at the corners of your house.

Pansy

Garden Pansy (*Viola* x *wittrockiana*)

Wild Pansy (*V. tricolor*); also known as Johnny-
jump-up, wild heartsease

Both are also known as forget-me-not, heartsease, kiss-me-at-the-garden-gate, monkey
faces

Pansy flowers can be single or multi-colored and
with or without markings. The most common
type has a dark center called a *face*. The leaves
are oblong to lance shaped and gently lobed. The
garden pansy is a hybrid developed from the wild
pansy. The wild pansy is smaller than its cultivated cousin and often has thin, black lines called
whiskers radiating from the center of its face.

History and Lore

Shakespeare's use of the wild pansy for faery love
spells in *A Midsummer Night's Dream* may have come
from the Celtic practice of brewing a love potion
with the leaves. Believed to be an aphrodisiac, in
England it became associated with Valentine's Day
but was attributed with the dual ability to "cause
love and cure it."[116] Herbalists John Gerard and
Nicholas Culpeper prescribed it in cures for several
ailments including venereal disease. Picking pansy
flowers was believed to have consequences: Picking them on a sunny day could cause the weather
to turn bad but picking one with dew on it could
result in the death of a loved one.

....
116. Watts, *Elsevier's Dictionary of Plant Lore*, 285.

Magical Connections

Element/s	Water
Astrological influence	Saturn
Magical entities	Faeries
Other associations	Valentine's Day
Powers and attributes	Clarity, courage, divination, focus, healing, inspiration, loss/sorrow, love, negativity, peace, renewal
Available for purchase	Flower essence; dried flowers and leaves; heartsease herb; seeds

Spells and Rituals

For help in dealing with the breakup of a relationship, stand outside and hold a bowl of dried flowers as you visualize how you would like to move on. Slowly turn in a circle as you sprinkle the contents on the ground releasing the bonds that held you to the other person.

Parsley

Common Parsley (*Petroselinum sativum*); also known as garden parsley, Italian parsley

Parsley grows in rounded mounds that reach about a foot tall. Its dark green leaves are deeply lobed and can be flat or curly. Tiny, yellow-green flowers grow on separate stalks. The oval seeds are grayish brown and ribbed.

History and Lore

Although the Greeks sometimes wore crowns of parsley at banquets, they associated the plant with Persephone and the underworld and used it to adorn graves. During the summer solstice in Moravia, parsley was given to cows to prevent witches from casting spells on them. In the Pyrenees of France and Spain, parsley boiled in water was given to a person who was thought to have been bewitched. Oddly enough, in some areas of England it was believed that only a witch could grow parsley. Brides in Poland carried parsley to keep evil spirits away, and in Spain to keep witches away. In Germany brides tucked parsley leaves into their skirts as a charm to keep a husband faithful. In England, parsley wine was reputedly an effective aphrodisiac. Alchemists in medieval Germany burned it along with several other herbs to manifest spirits.

Magical Connections

Element/s	Air, fire
Astrological influence	Aquarius, Gemini, Libra; Mercury, Pluto
Deities	Hera, Juno, Jupiter, Persephone, Zeus
Other associations	The afterlife or otherworld; Midsummer's Day, Samhain
Powers and attributes	Changes/transitions, death/funeral practices, emotions, focus, happiness, knowledge, prosperity/money, protection, purification, renewal
Available for purchase	Essential oil; fresh leaves; cut, dried leaves; seeds

Spells and Rituals

More than a dinner plate garnish, parsley is a potent ally for weathering life's transitions and finding emotional balance. Diffuse a little essential oil to aid astral work or burn a pinch of dried leaves to usher in a fresh start. Association with the afterlife makes it appropriate for Samhain.

Passionflower

Passionflower

Blue Passionflower (*Passiflora caerulea*); also
    known as apricot vine, common passion-
    flower, blue crown
Purple Passionflower (*P. incarnata*); also known
    as apricot vine, Mayapple, Maypop, passion
    vine

Passionflower is a vine that climbs with tendrils
or sprawls across the ground. The exotic flowers have a fringe over the petals and an intricate,
antenna-like center. Purple passionflower has a
long, wavy, pink to purple fringe over white petals and dark green, three-lobed leaves. Blue passionflower has white petals and a shorter fringe
with rings of purple, white, and blue. Its leaflets
are arranged in a palm/hand shape. Passionfruit
is egg shaped and somewhat resembles a pomegranate when cut open.

History and Lore

Despite its name, this plant is not connected with
passionate love, but with the Passion of Christ.

When Spanish missionaries first encountered the
passionflower in South America, they believed it
contained symbols relating to the crucifixion of
Jesus. In nineteenth-century England, the flowers were used in wreaths at funerals and engraved
on the glass sides of the horse-drawn hearses.
Because Queen Victoria (1819–1901) liked it for its
decorative value, passionflower became a costly
status symbol to have carved on a tombstone.

Magical Connections

Element/s	Water
Astrological influence	Libra; Venus
Other associations	Samhain
Powers and attributes	Clarity, confidence, dream work, emotions, peace, purification, relationships, spirituality
Available for purchase	Flower essence; cut, dried leaves and stems; whole dried flowers; cut, dried flowers; fruit; fruit juice

Spells and Rituals

Include passionflowers in funeral wreaths for
your loved ones. To enhance dream work, place a
sachet of dried flowers and leaves under your pillow. Gaze at a picture of the flowers during meditation to instill a sense of peace and harmony.

Patchouli

Patchouli (*Pogostemon cablin*); also known as
    pachupat, puchaput

Growing about three feet tall, patchouli is a
shrubby plant with hairy stems and leaves. The
fragrant leaves are oval to slightly heart shaped,
veined, and irregularly toothed. The pale purple

to white flowers grow on short spikes at the leaf axils.

Caution: Patchouli can be toxic if ingested.

History and Lore

Patchouli was used medicinally for thousands of years throughout Asia and the Middle East. In China, it was a base for incense. Patchouli was used in ink for scent and to hold the color. Buddhist monks used the leaves for a purifying bath as well as to wash statues of the Buddha. Persian carpet makers and Indian textile manufacturers used patchouli to perfume and protect their wares from insect damage during transport. In Europe, the fragrance became a hallmark of authentic handmade silks. In most places where it has been used, patchouli has been regarded as an aphrodisiac. Patchouli was *the* scent of the 1960s and 1970s counterculture.

Magical Connections

Element/s	Air, earth
Astrological influence	Aquarius, Capricorn, Scorpio, Taurus, Virgo; Mars, Pluto, Saturn
Deities	Aphrodite, Athena, Buddha, Gaia, Modron, Pan, Shiva, Vishnu
Other associations	The afterlife, the otherworld; Samhain
Powers and attributes	Banish, consecrate/bless, defense, fertility, growth, hexes, manifest, negativity, prosperity/money, purification, sex/sexuality, skills, spirit guides/spirits, spirituality
Available for purchase	Essential oil; cut, dried leaves

Spells and Rituals

Patchouli is a powerful ally for breaking hexes, however, if it is used for negative magic the energy will backfire. Grounding yet enlightening, the scent aids in transcending boundaries and connecting with the otherworld. It aids in communicating with spirits as well as banishing them.

Pea

Garden Pea (*Pisum sativum*); also known as field pea, peas, green pea

Snow Pea (*P. sativum* var. *saccharatum*); also known as Chinese pea pods, mangetout

Sugar Snap Pea (*P. sativum* var. *macrocarpon*); also known as snap pea

The pea has slender stems and tendrils for climbing. The base of the leaf stem has two broad, leaf-like outgrowths. The leaves consist of one to three pairs of oval, dark green leaflets. The flowers can be white, red, or purple. The garden and sugar snap peas have rounded pods; the snow pea pod is flat.

History and Lore

While pea soup was traditionally served after funerals or during deathwatches in Germany, eating peas on the last day of the year was said to bring good luck and fortune. After a wedding, the bride was showered with peas (à la rice). Dwarfs were reputedly fond of peas and said to plunder them from gardens. In France, a pod with nine peas was believed to have special magical powers and an aid for recognizing witches. It was also regarded as good luck. In England, making a wish and throwing a nine-pea pod over the right shoulder was said to make it come true. Peas were used in love and marriage divination in England and Scotland. The Romani placed peas in the graves of loved ones.

Magical Connections

Element/s	Earth
Astrological influence	Jupiter, Venus
Deities	Thor
Magical entities	Dwarfs
Powers and attributes	Creativity, death/funeral practices, divination, fertility, love, luck, prosperity/money, protection, wishes
Available for purchase	Fresh or dried peas; flower essence

Spells and Rituals

As part of a spell to increase prosperity, shell a handful of peas into a bowl, go outside and toss them over your right shoulder as you ask that your finances grow ten times the number of peas. For a boost in creative energy, drape a pea vine over your workspace.

Peach and Nectarine

Common Peach (*Prunus persica* syn. *Amygdalus persica*)

Nectarine (*P. persica* var. *nucipersica*)

These trees have drooping, lance-shaped leaves and pink, five-petaled flowers that grow singly or in pairs. The fleshy fruit is reddish orange and the seed is known as a pit or stone. A peach has fuzzy skin; a nectarine has smooth skin. These trees are so genetically similar that some trees produce both fruit.

Caution: The seeds and leaves of *Prunus* species produce cyanide in the digestive tract.

History and Lore

In China, the peach was a tree of spiritual power and protection. The branches were believed to have the ability to exorcise evil. A pendant made from a peach stone was placed on a child to ward off demons. Both the Greeks and Romans referred to peaches as apples, which is what they called most large, round fruit. Representing immortality to the Egyptians, the mysteries of Osiris rituals were held in sepulchers that had a peach tree growing nearby. Throughout Europe, the fruit was a symbol of female genitals and an ingredient in love potions. Regarded as a tree of prophecy in England, the branches were sometimes used as divining rods.

Magical Connections

Element/s	Water
Astrological influence	Sun, Venus
Deities	Aphrodite, Asherah, Gaia, Harpocrates, Hera, Isis, Venus
Other associations	The afterlife,
Powers and attributes	Banish, death/funeral practices, fertility, happiness, healing, hexes, love, loyalty/fidelity, luck, manifest, negativity, renewal, wisdom, wishes
Available for purchase	Fresh or dried fruit; peach juice; flower essence; peach kernel oil; peach leaf tea

Spells and Rituals

Use a dried blossom in a small sachet as a fertility charm. Rekindle passion and foster fidelity by sensually eating a peach or nectarine with your lover. To help release pent-up feelings, drink a cup of peach leaf tea.

Pear

Common Pear (*Pyrus communis*); also known as
    European pear

The leaves of the pear tree are glossy and oval with a pointed tip. The fragrant, five-petaled flowers are creamy white and sometimes with a tinge of pink. The fruit has a rounded, somewhat teardrop shape.

History and Lore

The pear tree was sacred to the people of Belgium, France, Russia, Germany, and Greece. Ancient poets sang praises about the pear and Greek writer Homer (ninth or eighth century BCE) referred to it as "the fruit of the gods."[117] The Romans enjoyed a beverage of fermented pear juice. In the North Caucasus region of Russia, deities were believed to live in pear trees. Hunters in the French town of Auxerre made offerings with the heads of their quarry to a pear tree. In German-speaking regions of Europe, the tree was believed to have the power of prediction. According to one legend, demons lived in pear trees; others noted that witches met and danced under the trees at midnight. Throughout medieval and Renaissance Europe, the pear was associated with sex because the fruit was suggestive of both female and male genitalia.

Magical Connections

Element/s	Air, earth, water
Astrological influence	Jupiter, Moon, Sun, Venus
Deities	Aphrodite, Apollo, Athena, Helios, Hera, Juno, Minerva, Pomona, Venus
Magical entities	Faeries
Powers and attributes	Bind, consecrate/bless, creativity, healing, justice/legal matters, love, luck, manifest, prosperity/money, protection, sex/sexuality, success, wisdom, wishes
Available for purchase	Fresh or dried fruit; pear juice; pear wine; perry pear cider; flower essence

Spells and Rituals

When seeking justice, place a branch on your altar and ask for wisdom to guide you through the situation. Include a handful of blossoms in spells to attract love or heighten passion. For meditation when dealing with sexual issues, prepare a candle with the flower essence.

Pearlwort

Trailing Pearlwort, Bird-eye Pearlwort (*Sagina procumbens*); also known as beads, bird's eyes, mothan, procumbent pearlwort

Pearlwort is a mat-forming plant with a base rosette of leaves and stems that grow in crisscrossed patterns. Pairs of narrow leaves merge and wrap around the stem. Tiny, white flowers grow at the tips of the stems. The flowers have four white

---

117. Cumo, *Encyclopedia of Cultivated Plants*, 772.

petals and four slightly larger green sepals. The flower buds and seed capsules resemble beads.

Caution: Pearlwort is regarded as an invasive species in some areas.

History and Lore

Along with butterwort (*Pinguicula vulgaris*), pearlwort is one of two plants thought to be the mystical herb of Scotland called *mothan*, which was said to provide protection from witches, faeries, and fire. When hung over a door, pearlwort was also said to keep spirits of the dead from entering a house. It was hung on a house for good luck, too. The English and Scottish people considered pearlwort so powerful that cows that ate the plant were protected from harm, as was anyone who drank the milk. In addition to protection, pearlwort was used for love charms. In England, just wetting the lips with the plant juice was believed to attract a lover. In Scotland, a love charm was made with nine small roots knotted into a ring, and then placed in the mouth before kissing someone who would be bound in love.

Magical Connections

Element/s	Water
Astrological influence	Moon
Magical entities	Faeries
Powers and attributes	Banish, bind, hexes, loss/sorrow, love, luck, negativity, protection
Available for purchase	No products are available

Spells and Rituals

To disarm the effects of negative magic, write the initials of the person originating a spell on a slip of paper. Hold it between your hands as you visualize the person's energy going into the paper. Roll it into a scroll, tie it with a long stem of pearlwort, and then burn it.

Pennyroyal

European Pennyroyal (*Mentha pulegium*); also known as fleabane, pudding grass

The grayish green leaves are lance shaped, heavily veined, and toothed. Small, reddish purple to lilac-blue flowers grow in rounded clusters at the leaf axils. Both foliage and flowers have a strong minty scent. Pennyroyal has two forms: low to the ground and spreading, and upright and lanky.

Caution: Pennyroyal is highly toxic and can be fatal if ingested; abortifacient.

History and Lore

In ancient Greece, pennyroyal was suggestive of sex and a metaphor for a woman's pubic hair. It may be the type of mint used in the drink or gruel consumed by participants during the Eleusinian Mysteries, secret rites in the veneration of Demeter and Persephone. Garlands of pennyroyal may also have been worn as crowns at the feast. The Anglo-Saxons used it for ailments caused by dwarfs. As a medicinal herb, in medieval England pennyroyal was most notably used as an abortifacient and to protect against the plague. Used for protection against the evil eye in Italy and in Morocco, it was also believed to protect people and their livestock from misfortune, but it had to be gathered before Midsummer's Day. Pennyroyal was customarily thrown into the Midsummer's Eve bonfire. German herbalist and abbess Hildegard von Bingen suggested tying pennyroyal to the head to suppress madness.

Pennyroyal

Magical Connections

Element/s	Fire
Astrological influence	Libra; Mars, Venus
Deities	Demeter, Hecate, Persephone
Magical entities	Dwarfs
Other associations	The otherworld; Mabon, Midsummer's Eve, Walpurgis

Powers and attributes	Challenges/obstacles, family and home, healing, hexes, negativity, peace, prosperity/money, protection, purification, sex/sexuality, strength, trust
Available for purchase	Essential oil; cut, dried leaves

Spells and Rituals

To combat negative magic or if you are just feeling jinxed (for whatever reason), sprinkle a handful of dried leaves around the outside of your house and visualize a wall of protection. Mix pennyroyal with barley and water to use as an offering to Demeter.

Peony

Common Peony, Garden Peony (*Paeonia officinalis*)
Wild Peony, English Peony (*P. mascula*)

Peonies have prominently veined, lance-shaped leaves and large, bowl-shaped flowers. Clusters of wedge-shaped seedpods form from the fading flowers. The common peony has red flowers and dark green leaves. The roots are round tubers joined together with root strings. The wild peony flowers are rose pink to deep purplish red and the leaves are light to bluish green. Its roots look like small carrots.

Caution: The roots, flowers, and seeds are toxic if ingested.

History and Lore

According to the ancient Greeks, the peony could glow at night because it came from the moon. They also believed that it could chase away evil spirits and protect the house where it grew, even against lightning. According to Roman naturalist and historian Pliny the Elder and others, a necklace made from the roots warded off nightmares as well as the incubus. Anglo-Saxons wore it to cure lunacy and illness caused by demonic possession. During the Middle Ages in England, a carved root served as a protective amulet against faeries and goblins. The seeds were worn as a necklace to dispel evil spirits and bewitchment. Heavily promoted by physicians in the seventeenth and eighteenth centuries, polished pieces of root were made into beads and worn as an amulet called an *anodyne necklace*. Covering a range of ailments, the necklace was said to also cure the "secret" (venereal) disease.

Magical Connections

Element/s	Fire
Astrological influence	Leo; Jupiter, Sun
Deities	Pan
Magical entities	Faeries
Powers and attributes	Banish, dream work, happiness, healing, hexes, loss/sorrow, luck, negativity, nightmares, peace, prosperity/money, protection, release, spirit guides/spirits
Available for purchase	Flower essence; whole dried flowers; dried petals; seeds

Spells and Rituals

For a good luck charm, dry and polish a piece of root to carry with you. To encourage negative spirits to leave your home, burn a handful of dried flower petals outdoors and waft a little smoke around the exterior of your house

Pepper

Black Pepper, White Pepper (*Piper nigrum*); also known as common pepper, peppercorn, piper, true pepper

Pepper is a woody vine that can grow up to sixteen feet long. Its heavily veined leaves are slightly heart shaped with a pointed tip. Growing in long pendulous clusters, berries start out green and turn red at maturity. Depending on when they are harvested and how they are processed, peppercorns can be black, white, green, or red.

History and Lore

The ancient Romans were crazy about pepper and kept great storehouses filled with it. In the home, it was often kept in ornate gold and silver pepper pots. Pepper was used regularly in many dishes and sometimes added to honeyed wine. It was common even in the far reaches of the Empire at Hadrian's Wall in Scotland and was customarily given as a gift at the festival of Saturnalia. While it was common to the Romans, throughout medieval Europe pepper was a symbol of wealth and so valuable that it served as payment for dowries and taxes. In addition, pepper was widely believed to be an aphrodisiac. Merchants called *pepperers* and *spicers* were the forerunners of apothecaries.[118]

Magical Connections

Element/s	Fire
Astrological influence	Aries; Mars
Other associations	Saturnalia

....
118. Duke, *Duke's Handbook of Medicinal Spices*, 24.

Powers and attributes	Banish, bind, challenges/obstacles, courage, defense, determination, dream work, healing, justice/legal matters, protection, release, renewal, strength
Available for purchase	Essential oil; whole peppercorns; ground pepper

Spells and Rituals

Diffuse a little essential oil as part of a defensive magic spell when seeking justice. Also diffuse it to get things going when you are in a rut or need to resolve a problem. Store a few peppercorns with your ritual gear to cleanse them after use to release old energy and provide protection.

Periwinkle

Greater Periwinkle, Big Leaf Periwinkle (*Vinca major*)

Lesser Periwinkle, Common Periwinkle (*V. minor*)

Both plants are also known as blue stars, fairy paintbrush, sorcerer's violet

Periwinkle's tube-shaped flowers range from light to violet-blue. Their five, slightly asymmetrical petals give the flower a pinwheel appearance. Greater periwinkle has rounded to slightly heart-shaped leaves. Lesser periwinkle has oblong leaves and forms a ground cover.

History and Lore

Periwinkle was one of the plants worn during Bacchanalia, the Roman festival celebrating the god of agriculture and wine. In medieval Italy, it was regarded as a plant of the dead and used for children's funeral wreaths. While periwinkle was considered unlucky in a nuptial bouquet in England, attitudes changed and brides wore it in their garters as a fertility charm. Periwinkle was believed to foster a happy marriage when grown in the garden. It was used for divination on Twelfth Night and faeries reputedly made charms with it. In medieval France periwinkle was used for love potions and charms as well as for divination on New Year's Eve. Throughout England, France, Belgium, and Germany, periwinkle's power was used to detect witches, break spells, and heal demonic possession. It also served as an amulet against the evil eye and ghosts.

Magical Connections

Element/s	Water
Astrological influence	Mercury, Venus
Deities	Aphrodite, Bacchus
Magical entities	Faeries
Other associations	New Year's Eve, Twelfth Night
Powers and attributes	Abundance, awareness, bind, clarity, divination, fertility, healing, hexes, knowledge, love, peace, prosperity/money, protection, security, spirit guides/spirits
Available for purchase	Flower essence; cut, dried leaves and stems; pressed, dried flowers; seeds

Spells and Rituals

To strengthen a love charm, wrap a trailing stem of lesser periwinkle around objects used in the spell. For increased levels of awareness during divination, wear a periwinkle circlet on your head. When contacting spirits, sprinkle dried leaves to cast a protective circle.

Pignut

Pignut, Earthnut (*Conopodium majus* syn. *C. denudatum*); also known as cuckoo potatoes, devil's bread, earth chestnuts, fairy potatoes, ground nut

Reaching only about a foot tall, pignut has feathery leaves that resemble carrot foliage. Its tiny, white flowers grow in umbrella-like clusters. The edible root is an irregularly round tuber that resembles a chestnut and is the size of a hazelnut. When the flowers finish blooming, the plant dies back leaving almost no trace above ground making it a challenge to find the tubers.

History and Lore

Although pignut roots were sometimes dried, roasted, and made into bread during the Middle Ages in Britain, by the Victorian era pignut was regarded as food fit only for, well, pigs. Perhaps because of their earthiness, English herbalist Nicholas Culpeper noted that they "provoke lust exceedingly."[119] Believed to be faery food in parts of England, in Ireland pignut was regarded as a plant of the leprechauns.

Magical Connections

Element/s	Earth
Astrological influence	Venus
Magical entities	Faeries, leprechauns

Powers and attributes	Abundance, challenges/obstacles, determination, family and home, luck, prosperity/money, protection, secrets, sex/sexuality
Available for purchase	Seeds (UK and Europe)

Spells and Rituals

When dealing with sexual issues, place a few seeds in your bedroom where their energy can aid the situation. For help in keeping a secret, place a picture of the plant where you will see it often and be reminded to hold your tongue.

Pimpernel

Pimpernel, Scarlet Pimpernel (*Anagallis arvensis* syn. *Lysimachia arvensis*); also known as bird's eye, eyebright, poor man's weather-glass, red chickweed, waywort

Pimpernel is a low-growing, sprawling plant with small, oval or egg-shaped leaves. The orange-red flowers have five rounded petals with a touch of red or lavender at the base of each. Occasionally, the flowers can be brick red or blue and even sometimes white.

Caution: All parts of the plant, especially the roots, are toxic if ingested.

History and Lore

A medicinal herb since the time of ancient Greece, in sixteenth-century Scotland pimpernel was used to determine whether a wounded person would survive. In medieval England, it was hung over doorways for protection from witchcraft. Because the flowers close on cloudy or rainy days, it was regarded as a weather forecaster. In Ireland,

---

119. Culpeper, *The English Physician*, 84.

pimpernel was believed to possess magical power. Holding the plant was said to give a person second sight, the ability to understand birds and animals, and to communicate with spirits. According to legend, pimpernel could help a person discern truth in any situation. Medieval Irish herbalists believed that the blue flowered form was female and the red, male.

Pimpernel

Magical Connections

Element/s	Air
Astrological influence	Gemini, Leo, Virgo; Mercury, Sun
Powers and attributes	Changes/transitions, clarity, protection, psychic abilities, truth
Available for purchase	Flower essence; seeds

Spells and Rituals

As part of a spell to create a buffer of protection, collect several handfuls of flower and leaf sprigs, and then end your magic work by throwing the pimpernel in the air as you visualize it forming a shield of energy around you as it falls to the ground.

Pine

Scots Pine (*Pinus sylvestris*); also known as Scotch pine

White Pine (*P. strobus*); also known as eastern white pine, northern pine, soft pine

Pine trees are cone-bearing evergreens with needles that grow in clusters. The cones have woody scales and hang down from the branches. The soft, flexible needles of the white pine are dark green. Scots pine has blue-green needles.

History and Lore

Pine was venerated by the Assyrians, Greeks, Romans, Egyptians, and Germanic peoples.

To the Greeks, pine represented victory and immortality. Both Greeks and Romans dedicated pine to a number of deities. To the Romans, the tree represented the power of male virility and the pinecone was a symbol of fertility. Also used as a funeral emblem and a symbol of resurrection, pine boughs were placed on graves and in front of homes during mourning. In Germany, branches were hung in homes to celebrate the winter solstice and to keep evil spirits at bay. On New Year's Eve in the Alsace of France, girls danced *a la* Maypole fashion around a decorated pine. On Walpurgis in the state of Tyrol, Austria, pine boughs were set alight and carried around villages to burn out witches. Throughout Europe and the British Isles, elves, faeries, and pixies were said to live in or gather around pine trees.

Magical Connections

Element/s	Air, earth, fire
Astrological influence	Aquarius, Cancer, Capricorn; Jupiter, Mars, Saturn

Deities	Aphrodite, Artemis, Astarte, Attis, Bacchus, Ceres, Cybele, Demeter, Diana, Dionysus, Faunus, Ishtar, Isis, Neptune, Osiris, Pan, Persephone, Poseidon, Rhea, Silvanus, Venus, Vulcan
Magical entities	Elves, faeries, pixies, satyrs
Ogham	Ailm ┼ Ifin 𐌟 Emancholl / Amhancholl / Mór ▦ Onn ╫
Other associations	Beltane, Litha, Midsummer's Eve, Yule
Powers and attributes	Abundance, banish, fertility, focus, happiness, healing, hexes, inspiration, justice / legal matters, negativity, prosperity / money, protection, psychic abilities, purification, spirit guides / spirits
Available for purchase	Dried pinecones; essential oil; flower essence

Spells and Rituals

To aid concentration during psychic work or to facilitate contacting spirits, diffuse a small amount of essential oil. Draw a circle in the air with a pine branch to stimulate energy for defense and to break a spell against you. Carry a few pinecone scales as an amulet.

Plantain

Greater Plantain (*Plantago major*); also known as broadleaf plantain, common plantain, waybread

Ribwort Plantain (*P. lanceolata*); also known as buckhorn plantain, English plantain, narrowleaf plantain

Greater plantain has a base rosette of wide, ribbed leaves with wavy edges. The upright stalk holds a long, cylindrical flower spike that is green to purplish green. Ribwort plantain has lance-shaped leaves that mostly stand upright. The short, dense flower spike grows atop a tall, thin stalk.

History and Lore

The Anglo-Saxons regarded greater plantain as a sacred plant that had been created by Woden and used it in healing charms to ward off demons and sickness. It was also used to enhance magical power. Medieval Welsh texts note that greater plantain was used to cure the bite of a mad dog. In Devonshire and Germany, it was believed that once every seven years it turned into a bird. According to Irish lore, ribwort was powerful enough to bring back the dead; however, picking it was dangerous because there was a chance that it could cause insanity. Nevertheless, it was used medicinally and as a good luck charm. In Scotland, both plants were used for love divination.

Magical Connections

Element/s	Earth
Astrological influence	Venus
Magical entities	Faeries
Powers and attributes	Courage, determination, divination, dream work, family and home, healing, luck, negativity, nightmares, protection, purification, sex / sexuality, strength, success, truth
Available for purchase	Cut, dried leaves

Spells and Rituals

As part of a spell for success, place a greater plantain leaf in each of the cardinal directions on your altar. For a protection amulet, dry a piece of root and keep it in a small pouch that you can carry with you. Ribwort flower stalks help to keep bad dreams at bay.

Poinsettia

Poinsettia (*Euphorbia pulcherrima*); also known as
Christmas flower, Christmas star, flame leaf

The poinsettia has a woody stem and large, dark green leaves with slightly wavy edges that are reminiscent of holly. What we think of as the flower are actually large, red bracts that surround clusters of tiny, yellow flowers. In addition to red, poinsettias can be pinkish, salmon, purple, yellowish, and white as well as marbled and speckled.

Caution: Poinsettia stems have a thick, milky sap that can cause skin irritation; it is mildly toxic if ingested.

History and Lore

Although the poinsettia had a few medicinal uses, the Aztec cultivated them for their beauty and brilliant red color, which was a spiritual symbol of purity and sacrifice.[120] In some rituals a red dye from the plant was used to represent blood. Poinsettias were used for trade in the markets of Tenochtitlan, present-day Mexico City. According to legend, seventeenth-century friars included the plant in nativity processions and thus began the poinsettia's association with Christmas as well as a range of Little Drummer Boy types of stories.

Magical Connections

Element/s	Fire
Astrological influence	Sun
Other associations	Yule
Powers and attributes	Purification, renewal, wishes
Available for purchase	The plant; seeds

Spells and Rituals

Although the poinsettia has had little magical use, it fits into Yule celebrations with a brilliant sunburst to welcome the returning sun. As part of your ritual, remove a red bract and hold it between your hands as you make a wish for the coming year.

Poke

Pokeweed, Poke Root (*Phytolacca americana* syn.
P. decandra); also known as American nightshade, coakum, crowberry, ink plant, pigeon berry, pocan, pokeberry

Reaching between four to ten feet tall, poke has reddish stems and bright green, oval to lance shaped leaves. Pinkish stems hold spikes of small, greenish white flowers that develop into dangling clusters of purple-black berries.

Caution: Pokeweed is highly toxic if ingested and can be fatal; handle the plant with gloves as toxins can be absorbed through the skin.

---

120. John, *A Christmas Compendium*, 91.

History and Lore

The name *poke* comes from the Algonquian word for the plant, *pocan*.[121] Poke was used medicinally for a range of ailments and as a dye by the Algonquian, Iroquois, Delaware, Micmac, and Ute peoples. The Iroquois used it for love medicine; however, the directions were vague: "tie in a poplar tree, then place among roots."[122] They also used it against bewitchment. The young shoots were used as food but had to be cooked in a certain way to avoid poisoning. Following their lead, European settlers used pokeweed medicinally. The berry juice was used for ink by the Pennsylvania Dutch and by soldiers during the Civil War. Despite being toxic, poke berries were used in Portugal to enhance the color of port. In the American magical tradition of hoodoo, the seeds and roots are used for breaking jinxes and curses.

Magical Connections

Element/s	Fire
Astrological influence	Mars, Uranus
Powers and attributes	Courage, hexes, negativity, spirit guides/spirits
Available for purchase	Flower essence; cut, dried roots; seeds

Spells and Rituals

Use the berry juice as ink when writing spells, especially when dealing with hexes. Hang a cluster of berries wherever you feel the presence of a negative spirit and tell it to leave. Carry a small pouch of dried root whenever you need to bolster your courage.

121. Small, *North American Cornucopia*, 539.

122. Moerman, *Medicinal Plants of Native America*, 337.

Pomegranate

Pomegranate (*Punica granatum* syn. *Malum punicum*)

Pomegranate has pointed, glossy leaves and orange-red, trumpet-shaped flowers that grow singly or in clusters. The leathery, yellowish-red fruit is divided into sections that contain juicy, fleshy pulp surrounding the seeds.

Pomegranate

History and Lore

The pomegranate was venerated by the Assyrians, Greeks, and Romans who dedicated it to a number of deities. It was a symbol of fertility in Persian, Greek, Roman, and Semitic lore. It represented passionate love to the Greeks and was regarded as an aphrodisiac. Roman brides wore crowns of pomegranate leaves. The Moroccans poured pomegranate juice on the horns of plow oxen in the belief that it would boost fertility of the fields. In the Greek myth of Demeter and Persephone, it represented the mysteries of death and rebirth. The Egyptians placed pomegranates in tombs to aid the deceased in the afterlife. The Persians made garlands of pomegranate leaves to ward off witches and demons. In Sicily, pomegranate branches were used as diving rods to find hidden treasure and if a witch or person who knew the right magic words used one, they would always come up lucky.

Magical Connections

Element/s	Earth, Fire
Astrological influence	Gemini, Scorpio, Virgo; Mercury, Saturn, Venus
Deities	Adonis, Aphrodite, Apollo, Astarte, Attis, Baal, Bacchus, Ceres, Cybele, Demeter, Dionysus, Hades, Hera, Hermes, Inanna, Ishtar, Juno, Mercury, Mithras, Persephone, Pluto, Sekhmet
Magical entities	Unicorns
Other associations	The afterlife, the otherworld, Samhain
Powers and attributes	Abundance, changes/transitions, death/funeral practices, divination, fertility, hope, loss/sorrow, luck, prosperity/money, protection, psychic abilities, renewal, sex/sexuality, wisdom, wishes
Available for purchase	Fruit; juice; flower essence; dried seeds; pomegranate oil

Spells and Rituals

When dealing with difficult transitions, hold a pomegranate during meditation to instill a sense of hope and security. For a good luck charm,

keep three dried seeds in a pouch. To honor the dead or to connect with the otherworld, place a pomegranate on your altar.

Poplar

Black Poplar (*Populus nigra*); also known as Italian poplar, Lombardy poplar
White Poplar (*P. alba*); also known as lady poplar, silver poplar, silverleaf poplar

Poplars have reddish male catkins and yellow-green female catkins that develop before the leaves open. The leaves are rounded, toothed, and pointed at the tips. Both trees have dark green leaves, but the white poplar's leaves are whitish underneath. The seeds are encased in white, cotton-like hairs called *seed wool* and *seed fluff*.

History and Lore

According to Greek mythology, black poplars lined the path to the underworld. With the duality of their leaves (light side, dark side), white poplars were said to grow in the underworld offering hope to new arrivals. This duality also symbolized the ever-present association of life and death. White poplar crowned the dead in Sumerian graves. Known as devil's fingers in England, a profusion of black poplar catkins in the spring indicated misfortune. In medieval Russia, poplar sticks were driven into the ground on the grave of suspected witches to keep them in place.

Magical Connections

Element/s	Water
Astrological influence	Moon (white), Saturn

Deities	Apollo, Asherah, Brahma, Cronus, Demeter, Hades, Hecate, Luna, Persephone, Pluto, Selene, Zeus
Magical entities	Hamadryads
Ogham (white)	Edad / Edhadh ╫╫
Other associations	The otherworld, Ostara, Beltane, Samhain
Powers and attributes	Ancestors, death/funeral practices, divination, hope (white), loss/sorrow, past-life work, prophecy (black), prosperity/money, renewal (white), spirit guides/spirits, spirituality
Available for purchase	Dried, cut bark; dried buds

Spells and Rituals

To deepen spiritual meditation or enhance a divination session, place a poplar twig or several dried leaf buds on your altar. For Ostara, place a few catkins on your ritual altar to symbolize renewal; for esbats, use white poplar buds or a photograph of them.

Poppy

Common Poppy, Red Poppy (*Papaver rhoeas*); also
   known as corn poppy, field poppy, goblin's
   eye, red hag
Opium Poppy, White Poppy (*P. somniferum*); also
   known as balewort, blue poppy

Poppies have deeply lobed, toothed leaves and cup-shaped flowers. The common poppy flower ranges from red to orange with a blackish base. Its seedpod is shaped like an ice cream cone. The opium poppy flower ranges from white to deep mauve with a purple spot at the base of each petal. Its seedpod is spherical. Poppy seeds are called *khus khus*.

Caution: Only processed poppy seeds are edible; they can cause a positive drug test.

History and Lore

Because of its narcotic effects, poppies have been associated with death for thousands of years. The Romans placed seeds with the dead so they would "sleep rather than walk."[123] The Greeks and Egyptians crowned their dead with wreaths of poppies. During the Middle Ages in Poland, seeds were scattered in coffins to ward off vampires. Seeds have also been found in burials in Spain. Medieval German magicians used opium poppy to manifest spirits. While the opium poppy was used to deter evil spirits and witches in Central Europe, in Ireland the common poppy was regarded as a witch's flower and in Wales it was associated with goblins.

Magical Connections

Element/s	Fire, water
Astrological influence	Cancer, Capricorn; Moon
Deities	Aphrodite, Artemis, Ceres, Demeter, Diana, Hera, Hermes, Mercury, Minerva, Modron, Morpheus, Persephone, Venus
Other associations	The afterlife

123. Watts, *Elsevier's Dictionary of Plant Lore*, 278.

Powers and attributes	Challenges/obstacles, death/funeral practices, defense, dream work, fertility, love, luck, prosperity/money, protection, renewal, support, wisdom
Available for purchase	Dried seedpods; whole or ground seeds; seed oil;

Spells and Rituals

To aid in dream work, place a vase of dried seedpods on your bedside table or a sachet of seeds under your pillow. When seeking wisdom, hold a seedpod in each hand while meditating, and then offer them to your chosen deity.

Pothos

Golden Pothos (*Epipremnum aureum* syn. *Scindapsus aureus*); also known as devil's ivy, devil's vine, hunter's robe, money plant, Solomon Islands ivy

This popular houseplant is a trailing vine that can reach up to ten feet long. Ranging from lance- to heart-shaped, the glossy leaves are medium green with creamy golden marbling. The plant produces small, white, hooded flowers, but rarely when grown indoors.

Caution: Pothos is moderately toxic if ingested; the sap may irritate the skin.

History and Lore

The names *devil's ivy* and *devil's vine* come from the fact that this plant is extremely hardy and nearly impossible to kill. It can also thrive in very low-light conditions. In the wild, pothos can be invasive. In India, it is known as *money plant* per-haps because of the veins of gold in its leaves. For a time, an Indian bank used it as a logo. The name *hunter's robe* may have come from its use in New Guinea where the leaves were stitched together to fashion a type of loincloth.

Magical Connections

Element/s	Air
Powers and attributes	Determination, negativity, prosperity, protection
Available for purchase	Houseplant

Spells and Rituals

Well known for its air-purifying properties, place one of these plants wherever you need to clear away any type of negativity and lift the energy of a room. As part of a prosperity spell, place a leaf with your bank statements and other financial papers.

Primrose

Common Primrose (*Primula vulgaris* syn. *P. acaulis*); also known as butter rose, English primrose, fairy cups, key flower
Polyanthus Primrose (*P.* x *polyantha*); also known as florists' primrose

A rosette of crinkled, green leaves forms the base of the primrose plant from which a short flower stem rises. The six-petaled, rose-like flowers grow in clusters at the top. The common primrose flower is pale yellow. The polyanthus primrose encompasses a group of hybrids with flower colors that can be blue, orange, pink, purple, white, or yellow.

History and Lore

According to Greek legend, it was customary for dryads to pick primroses during the new moon. In Germany, primrose was believed to be a gift from the gods to help people find treasure. Primroses hung over a door or scattered on the threshold on Walpurgis were believed to deter witches from entering a home. According to belief in Ireland, tying primrose flowers onto a cow's tail kept it from harm. In England the flowers were used like cowslip and tied into a sphere called a *tissy ball* for love divination. Mostly regarded as a faery plant, primrose was also used to deter their mischief. In Cheshire, a primrose blooming in winter was regarded as an omen of death.

Magical Connections

Element/s	Air, earth, fire
Astrological influence	Libra; Venus
Deities	Bertha, Freya
Magical entities	Faeries
Other associations	Walpurgis, Beltane
Powers and attributes	Banish, divination, dream work, fertility, focus, growth, healing, knowledge, loss/sorrow, love, peace, protection, relationships, see faeries, sex/sexuality, spirituality
Available for purchase	Flower essence; dried flowers

Spells and Rituals

When recovering from a broken relationship, hold a potted primrose and visualize its energy surrounding you with love and healing. To banish anything unwanted from your life, burn a couple of dried leaves, and then toss the ashes to the wind.

Pumpkin

Pumpkin

Field Pumpkin (*Cucurbita pepo* var. *pepo*)

The pumpkin is a variety of the plant that also produces yellow crookneck squash (var. *torticollia*), zucchini (var. *cylindrica*), acorn squash (var. *turbinata*), and others. The pumpkin plant is a coarse, creeping vine with winding tendrils and prickly stems. The rounded leaves are lobed and have serrated edges. Large, bright yellow or orange, trumpet-shaped flowers precede the fruit.

History and Lore

Originating in Central America thousands of years ago, the pumpkin was a source of food and medicine for Indigenous people throughout the region. Early explorers took plants back to Europe and by the time the Pilgrims set foot in Plymouth, pumpkins were a familiar crop. Although the jack-o-lantern was originally fashioned from a turnip in Ireland, the much larger pumpkin provided a more impressive result. In Central Europe, eating pumpkin was believed to increase male virility.

Magical Connections

Element/s	Earth
Astrological influence	Moon
Other associations	Samhain
Powers and attributes	Abundance, divination, family and home, fertility, prosperity/money, protection
Available for purchase	Fresh pumpkins; dried seeds; pumpkin seed oil

Spells and Rituals

To use pumpkin seeds for divination, hold a handful between your hands as you visualize a question for whatever you seek guidance. Toss them into the air, and then look for patterns or symbols they may form on the floor. Place a small pumpkin in the kitchen to attract prosperity.

Purslane

Common Purslane (*Portulaca oleracea*); also known as garden purslane, green purslane, pigweed, little hogweed

Golden Purslane (*P. sativa* syn. *P. oleracea* var. *sativa*); also known as golden pigweed, little golden hogweed

Purslane is a succulent plant with mostly prostrate stems. Common purslane has smooth, reddish stems and fleshy, oval leaves with reddish edges.

The small, yellow flowers have five heart-shaped petals. Golden purslane leaves are yellow-green and less fleshy. The seedpods are urn-shaped and contain tiny black seeds.

Caution: Purslane looks similar to various types of spurges (*Euphorbia* spp.), which are poisonous; spurge leaves and stems exude white sap if broken, purslane does not.

History and Lore

From the people of ancient China to the Maya of Central America, both types of purslane were used for medicinal and culinary purposes. The Cherokee and Iroquois used common purslane medicinally; the Iroquois also used it as an "antidote to bad medicine."[124] Called *porclaca* in Old English, golden purslane was used medicinally by the Anglo-Saxons for several types of ailments. Well known in medieval Europe, common purslane was considered an aphrodisiac and a protective herb to dispel nightmares and evil spirits. Soldiers carried it as a good luck charm for protection when going into battle. Medieval magicians used the seeds to create smoke and fumes for magical rites. This was also done to counteract negative magic.

Magical Connections

Element/s	Water
Astrological influence	Cancer, Libra, Pisces; Moon
Powers and attributes	Defense, nightmares, protection, purification
Available for purchase	Dried, cut stems and leaves; seeds

---

124. Hurst, *Hidden Natural Histories*, 151.

Spells and Rituals

Include purslane in defensive spells to counter negative magic sent your way. If you are prone to bad dreams, hang a small sachet of seeds on your bedpost. Burn a few dried leaves in your cauldron to purify outdoor ritual space.

Quassia

Jamaica Quassia (*Picrasma excelsa*); also known as
bitter apple, bitter ash, bitterwood
Suriname Quassia (*Quassia amara*); also known
as amargo, bitter ash, bitterwood, Suriname
wood

Suriname quassia is an evergreen shrub that
grows about nine feet tall and has pointed, elliptical leaflets. Growing in loose clusters, the red,
tubular flowers have five petals that are rounded
at the base with a sharply pointed tip. The small,
reddish brown fruit turns black when ripe.
Jamaica quassia grows about sixty-five feet tall
and has pointed, elliptical leaflets that are prominently veined. Its tiny, greenish white flowers
grow in small clusters and develop into round,
green fruit that ripens to black.

Caution: Quassia should not be ingested during pregnancy or breastfeeding.

History and Lore

Quassia amara was named for Graman Quassia
(c. 1692–c. 1787) a freed slave in Suriname, formerly Dutch Guiana, a plantation colony in South
America. Mr. Quassia used the bark of the tree
to treat fevers and became revered by those who
knew him. According to Swedish botanist Daniel
Rolander (1725–1793) who met the former slave
and introduced the shrub into Europe, Mr. Quassia was said to also practice magic. The wood of
both shrubs yields a compound called *quassin*,
which is used as a bittering agent for drinks. In the
American magical tradition of hoodoo, quassia is
used as an ingredient in mojo bags to draw money
and in spells to have control over a person.

Magical Connections

Element/s	Earth
Astrological influence	Saturn
Powers and attributes	Love, prosperity, release
Available for purchase	Wood and bark chips; powdered bark

Spells and Rituals

For a love charm to attract someone's attention, write the person's initials on several pieces of bark, place them in a small sachet, and keep it in a pocket or pinned inside your clothing. Release something by tossing a handful of powdered bark outside as you visualize letting go.

Queen Anne's Lace

Queen Anne's Lace

Queen Anne's Lace, Wild Carrot (*Daucus carota*); also known as bee's nest, bird's nest, devil's plague

Growing up to four feet tall, Queen Anne's lace has feathery leaves and wide, flat umbrella-shaped clusters of tiny, white flowers. Most flower clusters have a dark reddish purple floret at the center. After it sets seed, the flower head curls up forming a cup that resembles a bird's nest.

Caution: Queen Anne's lace is easily confused with the poisonous water hemlock (*Cicuta maculata*) and fool's parsley (*Aethusa cynapium*).

History and Lore

Wild carrot was mainly used for medicinal purposes by the ancient Greeks and Romans. The Greeks reputedly also used it for love potions. When wild carrot was introduced into the British Isles in the sixteenth century, the root became a popular vegetable and the flowers and leaves a trendy hair accessory. In Scotland, eating carrots was believed to increase a woman's fertility. Associated with sexual desire, menstruation, and fertility in Eastern Europe, the dark-colored floret in the middle of the flowerhead was referred to as girl's honor and girl's shame. In Transylvania, a missing or larger than usual reddish purple floret in the middle was said to indicate the modesty or promiscuity of women in the area.

Magical Connections

Element/s	Earth, fire
Astrological influence	Mars, Mercury
Deities	Aphrodite, Luna, Selene, Venus
Powers and attributes	Balance/harmony, changes/transitions, clarity, dream work, fertility, healing, love, negativity, purification, renewal, sex/sexuality
Available for purchase	Essential oil; flower essence; seeds

Spells and Rituals

For a pre-ritual purification bath, add an infusion of leaves. Use the flowers to decorate and energize your altar for love spells and esbat rituals. For fertility spells, use the "bird's nest" seed heads. Wrap a dried root in lace and put it under your pillow to enhance dream work.

Quince

Common Quince (*Cydonia oblonga*); also known as edible quince, fruiting quince, true quince
Japanese Quince (*Chaenomeles japonica*); also known as fairies' fire, Japanese flowering quince

The common quince is a multi-trunked tree with pale green leaves. Its five-petaled flowers are white with a tinge of pink. The yellow fruit is round to pear shaped and slightly knobby. Japanese quince is a low-growing shrub with dense branches and dark green leaves. The flowers are orange-red and have five overlapping petals. The branches are thorny.

Caution: Quince seeds contain trace amounts of cyanide and can be toxic in large amounts.

History and Lore

First cultivated in Mesopotamia, the earliest association of quince with marriage occurred in Greek writings from approximately 600 BCE.[125] As a symbol of fertility, the Greeks and Romans used the fruit and flowers to decorate wedding banquet tables and nuptial bedchambers. Into the eighteenth century, a piece of fruit was a token of

love from the groom to the bride at wedding celebrations in England and France. The bride or the couple consuming the quince at the banquet represented consummation of the marriage. In addition to its use as a love charm, Roman naturalist Pliny the Elder noted that quince provided protection from the evil eye. According to English herbalists John Gerard and Nicholas Culpeper, the scent of quince was an antidote to poison and eating the fruit during pregnancy would make a child wise.

Magical Connections

Element/s	Earth
Astrological influence	Moon, Saturn, Venus
Deities	Aphrodite, Venus
Magical entities	Elves, faeries
Powers and attributes	Balance/harmony, fertility, love, luck, negativity, peace, prosperity/money, protection, sex/sexuality (common)
Available for purchase	Fresh or dried fruit; flower essence; jam and jelly; seeds

Spells and Rituals

With a long tradition in wedding celebrations, include quince in a handfasting ceremony. To create a magical atmosphere and attract faeries, take a budding branch of Japanese quince indoors to bloom. To enhance a money spell, place a leaf between two paper bills on your altar.

125. Davidson, *The Oxford Companion to Food*, 664.

Ragwort

Common Ragwort, Tansy Ragwort (*Senecio jacobaea* syn. *Jacobaea vulgaris*); also known as dog stalk, fairy horse, ragged Jack, stinking Willie, yellow top

Ragwort leaves have deep lobes with uneven edges and an unpleasant odor when crushed. The flower stem is red at the base and branches at the top with a spray of flowers. The yellow, daisy-like flowers grow in clusters. The seeds have downy, white hairs that carry them on the wind. Do not confuse with ragweed (*Ambrosia artemisiifolia*).

Caution: All parts of the plant are toxic if ingested.

History and Lore

The ancient Romans used ragwort for protection against the evil eye. Centuries later in Ireland, faeries were said to turn ragwort into horses for travel to their midnight revels. It was also said to be a daytime disguise for a fairy horse and stepping on it would cause it to rear up and gallop off with the human on its back. In Scotland, witches were also believed to ride ragwort like horses. Harnessing a chariot of ragwort to the wind was another mode of transport for witches. In Dorset, picking ragwort was believed to make a person vulnerable to bewitchment. In other areas of England, it was used as a charm against witchcraft. Sprinkling water on a fire with a ragwort stem was said to bring good luck.

Magical Connections

Element/s	Water
Astrological influence	Venus
Magical entities	Faeries, leprechauns
Other associations	Samhain
Powers and attributes	Courage, divination, hexes, luck, negativity, prosperity/money, protection
Available for purchase	Flower essence

Spells and Rituals

To neutralize a spell, dab a little flower essence on a protective amulet before wearing it. For help in attracting prosperity, place a jar of dried flowers with your financial papers or on your desk. To boost energy for divination, place several sprigs of flowers and leaves on your altar.

Raspberry

Black Raspberry (*Rubus occidentalis*); also known as American black raspberry

Red Raspberry (*R. idaeus*); also known as hindberry, raspis

Growing about six feet tall and ten feet wide, raspberry bushes are thicket-forming shrubs with slender, arching canes (branches). The purplish red canes are covered with prickles. The leaves consist of three, heavily veined and coarsely toothed leaflets. Flat-topped clusters of white, five-petaled flowers develop into fruit. The berries are oblong with a bumpy texture.

History and Lore

Raspberry is associated with Mount Ida on Crete, the mythical birthplace of Zeus. According to Greek legend, raspberries were white until his nursemaid, the nymph Ida, scratched her breast while tending to the infant and her blood stained the fruit red. The botanical name of red raspberry means "bramble of Mount Ida."[126] The Greeks and Romans initially used raspberries only as a medicinal plant. The Cherokee, Chippewa, Dakota, Omaha, and Pawnee used them medicinally; the Iroquois also used black raspberries magically to prevent a wife from "fooling around."[127] In the American magical tradition of hoodoo, raspberries are used for luck and fidelity.

Magical Connections

Element/s	Water
Astrological influence	Leo, Taurus; Venus
Deities	Venus, Zeus
Powers and attributes	Fertility, love, loyalty/fidelity, luck, protection, security, trust
Available for purchase	Flower essence; cut, dried leaves; fresh fruit; wine; preserves

Spells and Rituals

Share a bowl of raspberries with your partner as you pledge your dedication to one another. When separated for a period, send your lover a letter with a pressed raspberry leaf. As part of a protection spell, place a wreath made from a prickly cane on your altar.

126. Staub, *75 Remarkable Fruits for Your Garden*, 198.

127. Moerman, *Medicinal Plants of Native America*, 417.

Reed and Rush

Common Reed (*Phragmites australis*); also known
　　as common reed grass, Dutch reed, Norfolk
　　reed, star-reed, water grass
Common Rush (*Juncus effusus*); also known as
　　bog rush, mat rush, soft rush

Common reed has bluish green, blade-like leaves
and plume-like flowers. It can reach thirteen feet
tall. Common rush is a grass that grows in large
clumps about four feet tall. Tiny florets form on
the sides of the stems and develop into brown
seed capsules.

Reed and Rush

History and Lore

Reeds were used for arrow shafts in Europe, Egypt,
and the Americas. The Egyptians and Romans also
used them as pens for writing. According to Italian legend, the Turabug was a spirit and guardian
of reeds who was attracted to the sound of a reed
flute. The enchanting music of the Greek god Pan
and the Pied Piper of Hamelin, Germany, may
have been played on instruments made of reed.
With a magical word, faeries in Ireland reputedly
turned rushes into horses to ride to their revels.
Green rushes were used as a charm to break a
faery spell that had been placed on milk. In Welsh
legend, faeries were said to dance across the tops
of rushes. In Scotland, when the kelpie, a shape-
shifting water horse, took human form it could be
identified by pieces of rush or reed tangled in its
hair if it came out of fresh water.

Magical Connections

Element/s	Water
Astrological influence	Pisces, Sagittarius, Scorpio; Mars, Pluto (reed)
Deities	Coventina, Geb, Inanna, Manan-nán Mac Lir, the Morrigan, Pan, Poseidon, Rhiannon
Magical entities	Faeries, Turabug
Ogham	Ngetal ‖‖‖
Other associations	Imbolc, Samhain

Powers and attributes	Abundance, ancestors, confidence, determination, family and home, focus, growth, inspiration, protection, security, spirit guides/spirits, support
Available for purchase	Rush floor mat; rush basket; reed flute; reed basket

Spells and Rituals

For a protection amulet, braid several green stems together. Carry it with you when you need a boost in confidence. To enhance rituals, cut six equal lengths of stems and lay them on your altar in the shape of a pentagram. Place plumes of reed flowers on your altar to honor ancestors.

Rhubarb

Chinese Rhubarb (*Rheum palmatum*); also known as Turkey rhubarb

Garden Rhubarb (*R. rhabarbarum* syn. *R. undulatum*); also known as pie plant

Wild Rhubarb (*R. rhaponticum*); also known as false rhubarb, rhapontic, Siberian rhubarb

Rhubarb has large, triangular leaves with wavy edges and stalks that look like over-sized celery. Small flowers grow in dense clusters on tall stems. Garden rhubarb has white, yellow, or pinkish-green flowers and red leaf stalks. Wild rhubarb has greenish white flowers and green leaf stalks. Chinese rhubarb has lobed leaves and loose clusters of yellow or white flowers that turn red.

Caution: Only the stalks are edible; the leaves and other parts of the plant are toxic if ingested.

History and Lore

Rhubarb was used medicinally for thousands of years by the Chinese, Siberians, Greeks, Romans, and people of India. In China and medieval Europe, rhubarb was believed to be a cure for the plague. Alchemists in France and Germany knew it by the secret name *zipar*.[128] Because of its phallic shape, rhubarb was believed to be an aphrodisiac in India and a cure for erectile problems. In England and America, the word *rhubarb* has been used as slang in reference to both the penis and impotence. According to Ozark folklore, it came to be known as pie plant because the word *rhubarb* had a sexual connotation.

Magical Connections

Element/s	Air, earth
Astrological influence	Gemini; Jupiter, Saturn, Venus
Powers and attributes	Abundance, love, loyalty/fidelity, sex/sexuality
Available for purchase	Flower essence; fresh leaf stalks; sliced, frozen leaf stalks; cut, dried root; powdered root

Spells and Rituals

As part of a spell to attract love, prepare a red candle with the flower essence or for sex magic include fresh leaf stalks. If your partner consents, share food made with rhubarb to enhance your devotion. Sprinkle powdered root outside your home to attract abundance.

128. Sédir, *Occult Botany*, 247.

Rose

Dog Rose (*Rosa canina*); also known as beach
   rose, dagger rose, pixy pears, wild briar,
   witches' briar
Sweet Briar Rose (*R. rubiginosa* syn. *R. eglanteria*);
   also known as briar rose, eglantine rose
Rose Gall; also known as: briar balls, fairy pincushions, Robin's pillows. A fuzzy ball called
   a *rose gall* is caused when a gall wasp lays
   eggs on a leaf bud.

These thicket-forming roses have arching stems
with thorns and simple, five-petaled flowers. Dog
rose flowers range from white to pale pink and the
sweet briar are pink with white centers. Another
name for the red rosehip/fruit is *rose haw*; from a
dog rose it is also called a *pixy pear*.

History and Lore

The Romans used the dog rose medicinally and
scattered rose petals along the streets on festival
days. During the feast of *Rosalia*, rose petals were
scattered on the graves of loved ones. The Greeks
also scattered rose petals and placed wreaths of
rose branches on graves. In Tudor England, rose
petals dusted with sugar were considered an aphrodisiac. During the Middle Ages in Germany,
Belgium, and France, dried rosehips were a charm
against enchantment and sorcery. Rosehips were
believed to provide protection from thunder and
lightning as well. Germanic peoples called the rose
Friggdorn, Frigg's thorn.[129] In Scandinavia, roses
were believed to be under the protection of elves

----
129. De Cleene and Lejeune, *Compendium of Symbolic and Ritual
   Plants in Europe*, 617.

and dwarves. Rose galls were used for magical
healing in England, Wales, Belgium, and Germany,
and often worn around the neck as an amulet.

Magical Connections

Element/s	Water
Astrological influence	Cancer, Libra, Sagittarius, Taurus; Venus
Deities	Adonis, Aphrodite, Athena, Cupid, Demeter, Eros, Flora, Freya, Frigg, Harpocrates, Hathor, Holle, Idunn, Isis, Odin, Venus
Magical entities	Dwarves, elves, faeries
Other associations	The afterlife, the otherworld, Midsummer's Eve, Rosalia
Powers and attributes	Banish, communication, consecrate/bless, death/funeral practices, divination, dream work, emotions, healing, intuition, love, luck, protection, psychic abilities, release (gall), secrets, sex/sexuality, spirit guides/spirits, trust
Available for purchase	Rosehip tea; rosehip seed oil; rosewater; flower essence

Spells and Rituals

For support in divination sessions or when working with spirits, string rosehips together to wear
as a necklace. Create a protective wreath for your
home by bending long rose canes into a circle. As
part of a banishing spell, crumble a handful of
dried rose hips and throw them on the ground.

Rosemary

Rosemary (*Rosmarinus officinalis*); also known as compass plant, elf leaf, sea dew

Rosemary is a shrubby, evergreen herb with short, stiff, needle-like leaves that grow along the stems. Its tubular flowers are pale blue and grow in small clusters of two or three. The plant can reach up to six feet tall.

History and Lore

First mentioned in Sumerian texts, rosemary was also sacred to the Egyptians, Greeks, and Romans. Used in funeral practices, it was placed in graves and carried by mourners. In addition, the Greeks and Romans associated rosemary with love and fertility and included it in wedding celebrations. This practice continued centuries later throughout Europe. In France, Belgium, Germany, and England rosemary was used in love magic, often for holding onto a lover. When grown in a garden in England, it was believed to keep a household safe from witches, faeries, and lightning. It was customary for the French, Germans, and Dutch to hang a twig over the door or burn rosemary like incense to repel demons and keep the plague at bay. The Portuguese sprinkled rosemary water on the head to cure the plague and in Spain, a sprig was worn for protection against the evil eye. The wizards of Belgium reputedly used a bundle of sprigs as an "anti-magic sprinkling brush."[130]

Magical Connections

Element/s	Fire
Astrological influence	Aquarius, Aries, Leo, Sagittarius, Virgo; Mercury, Moon, Sun

Deities	Aphrodite, the Lares, Venus
Magical entities	Elves, Faeries
Other associations	The afterlife, Walpurgis, Yule
Powers and attributes	Clarity, communication, consecrate/bless, creativity, death/funeral practices, defense, dream work, focus, healing, inspiration, love, loyalty/fidelity, negativity, nightmares, protection, purification
Available for purchase	Flower essence; essential oil; dried leaves; dried sprigs; infused oil

Spells and Rituals

To prepare space for ritual, magic, or healing work, diffuse a little essential oil. Also use it to consecrate charms and amulets. For help in remembering dreams, hang a sachet of dried flowers from the headboard of your bed. Use rosemary for clarity in communications and for inspiration.

Rowan

American Mountain Ash (*Sorbus americana*); also known as dogberry, wild ash

Rowan, European Mountain Ash (*S. aucuparia*); also known as quickbeam, roan tree, sorb apple, Thor's helper, witch beam, witch wood, witchen tree

Mountain ash trees have lance-shaped leaflets and dense, flattened clusters of white flowers. The orange-red berries grow in large clusters. The American tree has dark green leaves; the European leaves are light to medium green.

Caution: Rowanberries are only safe to eat when cooked.

---

130. Ibid., 648.

History and Lore

According to ancient Vedic legend in India, a bolt of lightning struck a rowan tree bringing the gift of fire to earth. In England, Germany, and other parts of Europe, branches were hung in homes or placed in windows for protection from lightning. In Sweden and Norway, a rowan growing parasitically on another tree was known as a flying rowan and believed to have especially potent magical properties. Throughout Europe and the British Isles, rowan was believed to take away the power of witches, however, in some areas of Germany witches reputedly used rowan. In addition to hanging a branch in the home or stable in England, Scotland, and Ireland, a piece of twig was carried in the pocket as a protective amulet. Because witches were thought to access homes via the chimney, in Scotland the support beams around fireplaces were often made of rowan and known as witch posts. Associated with Thor, it was customary in Scandinavia to include a piece of rowan when building a ship to garner his protection. Similarly, the Romani had a piece built into their caravans for protection against the devil. In Ireland, a rowan stick driven through a corpse was said to keep it from becoming a wandering ghost.

Magical Connections

Element/s	Earth, fire
Astrological influence	Aquarius, Capricorn, Sagittarius; Moon, Saturn, Sun, Uranus
Deities	Aphrodite, Brigantia, Brigid, Cerridwen, the Dagda, Hecate, Luna, Pan, Ran, Selene, Thor, Vulcan
Magical entities	Dragons, elves, faeries

Ogham	Luis ⊤⊤
Other associations	Imbolc, Beltane, Lughnasadh
Powers and attributes	Authority/leadership, consecrate/bless, creativity, divination, fertility, healing, hexes, inspiration, luck, protection, psychic abilities, see faeries, skills, spirit guides/spirits, strength, success, wisdom
Available for purchase	Dried berries; flower essence

Spells and Rituals

When seeking advice from spirits guides, hold a rowan branch to strengthen your contact. For defense and aid in breaking a hex, place a cluster of rowanberries on your altar. Place a handful of dried berries in your workspace to boost creativity or on your altar for healing rituals.

Rue

Common Rue, Wild Rue (*Ruta graveolens*); also known as herb of grace, herbgrass

Rue is a shrubby plant with oblong leaflets that are wider at the tips. They give off a pungent odor when bruised. The yellow or greenish yellow flowers have four to five stemmed petals and grow in small clusters. The plant reaches two to three feet tall and wide.

Caution: Rue may cause dermatitis and photosensitize the skin; it is unsafe to burn.

History and Lore

In Greek mythology, rue was the herb that cured Ulysses's companions from the enchantment by the sorceress Circe. According to lore in the Middle East, rue prevented abduction by jinn as well as the ability to escape from them. In the British Isles, the plant was believed to foster second sight and the power to see faeries; in the Austrian state of Tyrol, it was an ingredient in a potion to see witches. Grown in English gardens, rue was a good luck charm that kept evil at bay and it was believed that a witch could not enter a home where the floors had been washed with rue. Sprigs were hung in windows to ward off the plague and used it in potions to cure madness. The Italians called a sprig of rue *cimaruta*, from *cima di ruta*, meaning "a piece of rue."[131] It was worn as a protective amulet against the evil eye and witches and it was used to cure ailments caused by enchantment.

Magical Connections

Element/s	Fire
Astrological influence	Capricorn, Leo, Pisces; Mars, Saturn, Sun
Deities	Circe, Diana, Mars
Magical entities	Faeries, Turabug
Powers and attributes	Banish, clarity, consecrate/bless, defense, divination, emotions, healing, hexes, inspiration, love, luck, negativity, nightmares, protection, purification, relationships, release, see faeries, spirit guides/spirits, wisdom
Available for purchase	Cut, dried stems and leaves; seeds

Spells and Rituals

Prepare outdoor space for ritual by strewing crumbled, dried leaves around the area. To boost protective energy, grow rue near your front door or sprinkle seeds under the doormat. To keep divination tools energetically ready for use, store a small pouch of seeds with them.

Rue

131. Watts, *Elsevier's Dictionary of Plant Lore*, 74.

Sage

Common Sage (*Salvia officinalis*); also known as
European sage, garden sage, true sage

Sage is a bushy plant with square, woody base
stems that reaches up to three feet tall. Its oblong
leaves are light gray-green, veined, and appear
wrinkled. Leafy stalks bear whorls of small, blue-
purple flowers.

Caution: Abortifacient.

History and Lore

Used medicinally by the Greeks, Romans, and
Egyptians, the medieval herbalists of England
and France also praised its virtues. While the
Romans regarded sage as a sacred herb, they
also used it as a tonic for the brain and memory.

The Greeks believed that eating sage would promote longevity and the Arabs associated it with
immortality. The Anglo-Saxons used sage to
honor the dead and throughout the Middle Ages
it was planted on graves in some areas of England
to help mitigate grief. Sage was used for love and
marriage divination, especially around Midsummer's Eve, and if things didn't go well, a sprig was
carried in the pocket as an amulet to cure a broken heart. Medieval French and German magicians used the seeds to create smoke and fumes
in rituals to drive away evil spirits. In Spain and
Portugal, sage was used for protection from the
evil eye. Common sage is often used for smoke
cleansing in place of white sage (*S. apiana*), which
is a sacred herb to the Arapaho, Cheyenne, Chumash, Comanche, Creek, Navajo, Lakota, Ute,
and other tribes.

270   S

Magical Connections

Element/s	Air, earth
Astrological influence	Aquarius, Pisces, Sagittarius, Taurus; Jupiter, Mercury
Deities	Jupiter, Kupala, Zeus
Other associations	Mabon Midsummer's Eve, Samhain, Walpurgis, Yule
Powers and attributes	Consecrate/bless, death/funeral practices, divination, focus, healing, loss/sorrow, protection, psychic abilities, purification, secrets, spirit guides/spirits, truth, wisdom, wishes
Available for purchase	Essential oil; flower essence; extract; cut, dried leaves; powdered leaves

Spells and Rituals

Burn a small piece during meditation when seeking a spirit guide. Use sage to cleanse crystals and magic tools. To heighten concentration during divination and psychic work, especially clairvoyance, diffuse a little essential oil before sessions.

St. John's Wort

St. John's Wort (*Hypericum perforatum*); also
known as chase-devil, goat weed, rosin rose

St. John's wort is a shrubby plant with pale green, oblong leaves. Its star-shaped flowers are bright yellow and grow in clusters at the ends of the branches. The flowers have a light, lemon-like scent. The flowers and buds ooze a red liquid when squeezed or bruised.

History and Lore

The magical use of St. John's wort dates back to the Greeks who believed it could drive away evil spirits. In medieval England it was used to recover from and prevent demon attacks. It was placed under the bed pillow to keep witches away at night. At Midsummer, sprigs and garlands of St. John's wort were hung in homes and around villages throughout most of the British Isles for safety from witches, wicked spirits, and faeries. The Germans also used St. John's wort to ward off witches and evil spirits. In Wales, the roots were dug up on Midsummer's Eve and hung above doorways. It was customary in France to pick St. John's wort before sunrise and smoke it over the Midsummer bonfire to make it more potent. To keep evil spirits away at other times, a piece of the plant was carried in a pocket or worn under clothing in the Hebrides and in England it was picked on a Friday and worn around the neck as an amulet. St. John's wort was also used for love divination on Midsummer's Eve. In Scotland, it reputedly deterred second sight but could help gain it when used with other herbs.

Magical Connections

Element/s	Fire
Astrological influence	Leo, Sagittarius; Sun
Deities	Balder
Magical entities	Faeries
Other associations	Litha; Midsummer's Eve

Powers and attributes	Abundance, banish, consecrate/bless, defense, divination, dream work, fertility, happiness, healing, love, negativity, nightmares, protection, purification, release, renewal, security, see faeries, spirit guides/spirits, spirituality, strength
Available for purchase	Essential oil; flower essence; infused oil; extract; cut, dried leaves; powdered leaves; dried flowers; seeds

Spells and Rituals

Use the pungent smoke of a few burning leaves to prepare outdoor ritual space. To boost the power of love charms and fertility spells, use the flowers to infuse oil (it will turn red), and then dab a little on the objects you use.

Sandalwood

Australian Sandalwood (*Santalum spicatum*)
Indian Sandalwood (*S. album*); also known as true sandalwood, white sandalwood

Sandalwood is a small, evergreen tree with semi-parasitic roots and oval leaves. Clusters of small, maroon flowers grow at the ends of the branches and are followed by round, plum-like fruit. While the popularity and overuse of Indian sandalwood has made it a vulnerable species, Australian sandalwood works well as a powerful alternative in every aspect and its harvest has been carefully regulated for sustainability.

Caution: Purchase only sustainably harvested sandalwood products.

History and Lore

Throughout Southeast Asia and India, sandalwood was regarded as sacred and used for temple incense. Sandalwood oil was used to draw magic circles, squares, and other symbols during exorcism rituals in India. The wood was included on funeral pyres. The Parsi, followers of the Iranian prophet Zoroaster, used sandalwood to kindle sacred altar fires. In the Middle East and medieval Europe, sandalwood oil was a fixative base in perfumery. The combination of sandalwood and rose is one of the oldest aphrodisiacs. The Indigenous people of Australia burned sandalwood to drive out bad spirits that were said to make people sick.

Magical Connections

Element/s	Air, water
Astrological influence	Aquarius, Cancer, Leo, Pisces, Virgo; Mercury, Moon, Venus
Deities	Venus, Vishnu
Powers and attributes	Awareness, balance/harmony, banish, clarity, consecrate/bless, healing, hexes, manifest, past-life work, peace, protection, purification, sex/sexuality, spirit guides/spirits, spirituality, truth, wisdom, wishes
Available for purchase	Essential oil; incense; wood chips and powder

Spells and Rituals

Diffuse a little essential oil during past-life sessions to help break old ties and protect against emotional upset. Prepare a candle with the oil to enhance awareness for clairvoyance or for astral work. Place a small bowl of wood chips on your altar to aid in contacting spirit guides.

Sassafras

Common Sassafras (*Sassafras albidum* syn. *S. officinale*); also known as ague tree, cinnamon wood, mitten tree, saloop, sassafrax, white sassafras

Reaching about forty feet tall, sassafras is unique in that it has three typical leaf shapes that can occur on a single branch. Some leaves are oval and without lobes, others have two off-centered lobes and are called *mittens*. Leaves with three lobes are called *ghosts* because they look like someone wearing a sheet over their head with two arms in the air. The six-petaled flowers grow in clusters at the ends of branches and develop into small, oval, dark blue fruit.

Caution: As a potential carcinogen, sassafras is considered unsafe to ingest.

History and Lore

Regarded as a cure-all, sassafras was used by the Cherokee, Chippewa, Choctaw, Creek, Delaware, Mohegan, and Seminole people. The early French settlers in Florida and the English in Virginia adopted it as a medicinal plant. In later centuries throughout the United States and Europe, sassafras became widely used as a flavoring and was the original root in root beer. In seventeenth-century England, a beverage called *saloop*, which was customarily made with orchid root, was adapted to sassafras root and sold on the streets of London. According to Ozark legend, sassafras wood making popping sounds in a fireplace meant that someone in the room would die soon or that the devil was sitting on the roof. In North Carolina, bringing it into the house was said to bring bad luck although it could be burned outside. In the American magical tradition of hoodoo, sassafras is used to attract wealth and money.

Magical Connections

Element/s	Fire
Astrological influence	Leo; Jupiter, Saturn, Venus
Powers and attributes	Negativity, prosperity/money, protection
Available for purchase	Flower essence; cut, dried leaves; powdered leaves; dried roots

Spells and Rituals

To ward off negativity, collect two mitten leaves (right and left hand), place them wherever you feel they are needed. Make tea with the leaves, wash a few coins in it, and then keep them in your wallet to attract money. Place a bundle of roots near your front door for protection.

Savory

Savory

Summer Savory (*Satureja hortensis*); also known
   as garden savory, satyricon, stone basil
Winter Savory (*S. montana*); also known as
   mountain savory

Summer savory is an annual herb with narrow, oblong leaves. Whorls of small, white flowers grow amongst the leaves. Winter savory is a woody-stemmed, shrubby perennial with slightly stiff, lance-shaped leaves. Its flowers are white and tinged with lilac. Both plants grow up to eighteen inches tall.

History and Lore
Roman naturalist and historian Pliny the Elder gave these plants the genus name *Satureia*, meaning "for the satyrs," the mythical satyr man/goats who were equated with sexual vitality.[132] According to Greek legend, the satyrs wore crowns of savory at their celebrations. Summer savory was an herb of love to the Romans who regarded it as an aphrodisiac. Not grown in Italy but imported during Roman times, winter savory was thought to dampen down the libido.

Magical Connections

Element/s	Air, fire
Astrological influence	Virgo; Mercury
Deities	Pan
Magical entities	Satyrs

Powers and attributes	Abundance, challenges/obstacles, creativity, focus, happiness, healing, inspiration, sex/sexuality
Available for purchase	Essential oil; flower essence; fresh or powdered herb; cut, dried leaves; seeds

Spells and Rituals
Tuck a sprig of savory behind your ear to aid concentration and help tackle problems. Hang a bundle in your workspace to promote productivity and stoke the imagination. Savory also stokes the fires of passion and enhances sexual expression; diffuse a little in the bedroom.

Seaweed

Bladderwrack (*Fucus vesiculosus*); also known as
   lady wrack, rockweed, sea oak
Giant Kelp (*Macrosystis pyrifera*); also known as
   giant bladder kelp
Slender Wart Weed (*Gracilaria gracilis*); also
   known as fairy laces

Yellow to brownish green, bladderwrack has flattened, fan-shaped, branching fronds with spherical air bladders. Giant kelp creates forests in the sea with upright, branching stems that have wide frond blades with a round, hollow float at the base. Resembling shoestrings, the small, slender wart weed has cylindrical fronds that are purplish red. Seaweed is technically algae and not plants.

History and Lore
Attributed with healing powers, bladderwrack was also used to fertilize crops and feed cattle during the winter in Ireland and Scotland. On Samhain the people of Scotland's Western Isles poured a cup of ale into the ocean with a prayer to Shony,

132. Staub, *75 Exceptional Herbs for Your Garden*, 212

a sea god of the Hebrides, for an abundance of seaweed that they could gather for their crops. According to Scottish legend, the kelpie, a shape-shifting water horse, was often covered with sea-weed when it came ashore from the ocean. In Brittany and Cornwall, korrigans, dwarf-like faery beings, reputedly sailed in boats constructed of seaweed. In some folktales, mermaids were said to have hair of seaweed. Strands of seaweed was commonly hung on porches for weather proph-ecy. In Welsh lore, the magician Gwydion con-jured a ship using seaweed.

Magical Connections

Element/s	Water
Astrological influence	Cancer, Pisces; Moon, Neptune
Deities	Aegir, Amphitrite, Lir/Llyr, Manannán Mac Lir, Neptune, Njord, Poseidon, Ran, Sedna, Shony, Varuna
Magical entities	Kelpies, korrigans, mermaids, Nereides
Other associations	Imbolc, Samhain
Powers and attributes	Awareness, balance/harmony, banish, fertility, negativity, peace, prophecy, prosperity/money, protection, psychic abilities, skills, spirit guides/spirits, truth
Available for purchase	Fresh, dried, or powdered seaweed

Spells and Rituals

Include a long strand of seaweed in a money spell and wrap it around a piece of paper currency as you visualize prosperity coming into your life.

To boost psychic skills, place a handful of sea-weed on your altar. Seaweed is a powerful ally for working with sea deities.

Self Heal

Common Self Heal, All Heal (*Prunella vulgaris*); also known as blue curls, Cailleach's tea, car-penter's weed, heal all, heart's ease, prunella, woundwort

Self heal is a creeping plant with oval, gray-green leaves, and square, red-tinged stems. Dense clus-ters of flowers form a cylindrical spike at the top of the stems. The pink or violet-blue flowers have two lips: The lower lip has three lobes with the center one larger than the others and often fringed.

History and Lore

The names *self heal*, *all heal*, and *heal all* are vari-ously spelled as one or two words or hyphenated. Despite its name, the plant's medicinal uses were limited; however, it was widely popular in medi-eval Europe and Britain because people could use it to safely treat their own ailments. The Irish believed that self heal was so powerful that noth-ing natural or supernatural could harm it and used it to cure a child that had been fairy struck (enchanted). In parts of England, children were told that the plant belonged to the devil and they would be carried off by him in the middle of the night if they picked the flowers.

Magical Connections

Element/s	Earth
Astrological influence	Venus
Deities	Cailleach Bheur

Powers and attributes	Clarity, growth, healing, hope, peace, release, spirituality
Available for purchase	Flower essence; cut, dried leaves and stems; dried root

Spells and Rituals

Self heal is a plant that aids in focusing on yourself in a healthy (non-egotistical) way for personal growth and to deepen your spiritual beliefs. Crumble a handful of dried leaves into your cauldron as part of a ritual to let go of things that may be holding you back.

Senna

Alexandrian Senna (*Cassia senna* syn. *C. acutifolia*, *Senna alexandrina*); also known as true senna

Indian Senna (*C. angustifolia* syn. *S. alexandrina*); also known as Tinnevelly senna

Senna is a woody plant about three feet tall. The feathery leaflets are oval to lance shaped. The leaves of Alexandrian Senna are grayish green; Indian senna leaves are larger and yellowish green. Both plants have five-petaled flowers that grow in clusters and oval, flat seedpods. Because of the tangled botanical names, some sources vary as to whether Alexandrian and Indian senna are the same plant.

History and Lore

Senna has been used medicinally for over a thousand years in India, Egypt, and the Middle East. It was introduced into Europe by Arab physicians during the ninth or tenth century. In addition to standard medicinal applications, the Arabs used senna to remove illness caused by sorcery, influences of the evil eye, and possession by jinn. In India, the plant was used to foster cooperation among people and in sachets used for love magic.

Magical Connections

Element/s	Air, earth
Astrological influence	Taurus, Virgo; Mercury, Moon, Saturn, Sun
Powers and attributes	Hexes, love, loyalty/fidelity, protection
Available for purchase	Cut, dried leaves; powdered leaves; dried seed pods

Spells and Rituals

Seedpods can be used in love spells or tucked in a pocket or purse to attract love. Keep a few seedpods in the workplace to facilitate cooperation. Include dried leaves in counter-magic to remove unwanted influences.

Sesame

Sesame (*Sesamum indicum*); also known as benne, sum-sum

Sesame has oval, veined leaves growing along the length of its stalks, which can reach up to nine feet tall. The tube-shaped flowers can be white, light pink, or pinkish purple and grow at the base of the leaves. The seedpods form inside the flowers as they fade and burst open with a popping sound when they are ripe.

History and Lore

Sesame oil was used in Mesopotamia for ritual offerings and ceremonial anointing. According to Hindu legend, Yama, the god of death, created the sesame plant. In India, the oil was used as an offering in funeral rites as well as to anoint statues of deities. Cakes of sesame and honey called *melloi* in the shape of female genitalia were used as offerings to Demeter and Persephone during the three-day Thesmorphoria festival in Greece.[133] Regarded as an aphrodisiac and symbol of fertility, sesame cakes were included in Greek and Roman wedding celebrations. According to the folklore of northern Pakistan, sesame was cultivated by mountain faeries in the Hindu Kush region.

Magical Connections

Element/s	Fire
Astrological influence	Moon, Sun
Deities	Artemis, Demeter, Ganesh, Hecate, Persephone, Yama
Magical entities	Faeries
Other associations	Imbolc, Mabon
Powers and attributes	Banish, changes/transitions, consecrate/bless, defense, fertility, healing, negativity, prosperity/money, secrets, sex/sexuality, spirit guides/spirits, truth
Available for purchase	Seeds; sesame seed oil; tahini or sesame paste; sesame seed milk

Spells and Rituals

When seeking truth, place a dab of sesame seed oil on your third eye chakra, and then meditate on the situation. If you feel the urge to reveal a secret, eat a spoonful of tahini. Burn a few seeds as part of a banishing spell to get an unwanted spirit to move on.

133. Wilkins, *Food in the Ancient World*, 128.

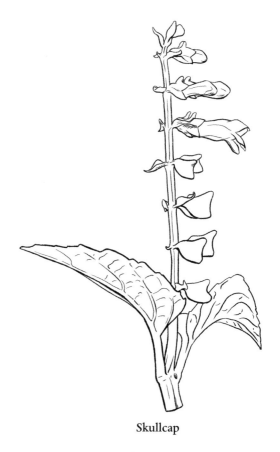

Skullcap

Skullcap

Common Skullcap (*Scutellaria galericulata*); also known as European skullcap, helmet flower, hoodwort, marsh skullcap

Mad-dog Skullcap (*S. lateriflora*); also known as American skullcap, blue skullcap, madweed, Virginia skullcap

Also spelled *scullcap*, these plants have toothed leaves that are rounded at the bottom and taper to a point. Growing from the leaf axils, the flowers are an irregular trumpet shape with a flared, larger lower lip and an upper lip that forms a rounded hood. The common skullcap flowers are blue to violet with a pattern of blue dots on the inside of the lower lip. Mad-dog skullcap flowers are usually blue, but sometimes pink.

History and Lore

Although the common name may seem slightly ghoulish, it comes from the resemblance that the upper flower petal has to the small, round, close-fitting medieval headgear worn on the top of the head. Despite expectations, it does not have a macabre history. Because of its sedative effects, common skullcap was used in England to treat everything from headache to madness. In the United States, New Jersey physician Lawrence Van Derveer (1740–1815) promoted the use of mad -dog skullcap as a treatment for rabies. The Cherokee, Delaware, Iroquois, Meskwaki, and Ojibwe used skullcap for a range of ailments but most frequently for menstruation issues. It was also used for purification in ceremonies for girls entering womanhood.

Magical Connections

Element/s	Water
Astrological influence	Aquarius, Capricorn, Virgo; Pluto, Saturn
Powers and attributes	Balance/harmony, creativity, emotions, family and home, focus, healing, love, loyalty/fidelity, peace, relationships
Available for purchase	Flower essence; cut, dried leaves; seeds

Spells and Rituals

Include skullcap in a ritual with your partner to mark your loyalty and strengthen your commitment. To bring emotions into balance after a family row, crumple dried leaves, sprinkle them in common areas of the house, and then vacuum them up as you focus on peace.

Snake Plant

Snake Plant (*Dracaena trifasciata* syn. *Sansevieria trifasciata*)

Variegated Snake Plant (*D. trifasciata* var. *laurentii* syn. *S. trifasciata* var. *laurentii*); also known as goldband sansevierias

Both plants are also known as bowstring hemp, devil's tongue, good luck plant, magic sword, mother-in-law's tongue, sword of St. George

Snake plants have a rosette of individual leaves that grow directly from the root. Reaching up to three feet tall, the stiff, sword-like leaves have a pointed tip and horizontal bands of gray-green and dark green. The variegated snake plant has golden-yellow leaf margins. Mature plants produce spikes of small, pale green flowers, but rarely as a houseplant.

History and Lore

In Africa and India, the snake plant has been used for its fibers and as first aid to treat snakebites. An important plant in Afro-Brazilian rituals, the snake plant was used to remove the evil eye and as a charm against bewitchment. In our homes, it is an excellent plant to help purify the air.

Magical Connections

Element/s	Earth
Powers and attributes	Hexes, luck, protection, purification, strength
Available for purchase	Houseplant

Spells and Rituals

To counteract a hex or any type of jinx against you, remove a leaf from the plant, and brandish it like a sword as you visualize sending the energy back to where it originated. Carry the plant when casting a circle to strengthen and enhance magic.

Snakeroot

Snakeroot (*Aristolochia rotunda*); also known as European birthwort, round-leaved birthwort, smearwort

Virginia Snakeroot (*A. serpentaria* syn. *Endodeca serpentaria*); also known as birthwort, snakeweed, Virginia Dutchman's pipe

Reaching about two feet tall, snakeroot stems zigzag from one rounded, heart-shaped leaf to the next. The leaves clasp the stem with basal lobes and from this axil a small, reddish purple, jack-in-the-pulpit-like flower grows. The stems of Virginia snakeroot also zigzag from one elongated, heart-shaped leaf to the next. However, its flowers grow under the leaves and close to the ground. The small, pale green to purplish brown flower has a long tube that curves down like a smoking pipe with the end opening horizontally. Like most species in this genus, these plants have malodorous flowers.

Caution: Both plants are poisonous if ingested; Virginia snakeroot is regarded as threatened or endanger in some areas.

History and Lore

Called *smerowyrt*, "smearwort," for its frequent use in salves, the Anglo-Saxons found snakeroot useful to treat the bites of snakes and rabid dogs.[134]

Reputedly, it could cure bewitchment and provide protection from demonic possession as well as elves. By medieval times in England, the plant was believed to have the power to ward off or kill serpents.

Magical Connections

Element/s	Earth
Astrological influence	Gemini, Virgo; Jupiter, Mars
Powers and attributes	Banish, hexes, luck, prosperity/money, secrets
Available for purchase	Seeds

Spells and Rituals

Gaining prosperity is not always a straightforward process; keep a piece of stem to remind you that you may need to zigzag your plans and make your own luck. For counter-magic to remove a hex or break knot magic take your cauldron outside and burn a handful of seeds.

Snapdragon

Common Snapdragon (*Antirrhinum majus*); also known as bunny rabbits, dragon's mouth, garden snapdragon, lady's slipper, snap Jacks

Snapdragons grow on spires up to three feet tall with flowers growing around the tops of the stems. The flower is tubular and two-lipped with a muzzle-like shape. They can be white, yellow, pink, red, orange, peach, or purple. Gently squeezing the sides of the flower opens the "mouth." The glossy, dark green leaves are lance shaped and grow in spirals around the stems.

---

134. Pollington, *Leechcraft*, 154.

History and Lore

Greek physician Dioscorides and Roman naturalist Pliny the Elder noted that wearing a bracelet of snapdragon flowers provided protection against illness and poisoning. According to ancient Greek magicians, sleeping with a flower under the tongue, and then reciting a certain incantation upon waking rendered a person invisible. Snapdragon has been a popular garden plant since medieval times in England where it was believed to protect against charms and enchantments. In parts of Ireland, snapdragon was grown on thatched roofs for luck and protection from fire. While Germans believed that the flowers provided shelter for elves, the plant was also said to have the power to break elven spells. In the American magical tradition of hoodoo, snapdragon is used against evil spirits, ghosts, and demonic possession.

Magical Connections

Element/s	Fire
Astrological influence	Gemini, Scorpio; Mars
Magical entities	Elves
Powers and attributes	Banish, hexes, negativity, nightmares, protection, release, truth
Available for purchase	Flower essence; dried flowers; seed oil; seeds

Spells and Rituals

Carry a small pouch of seeds as a charm against lies when you are going to be around a person who has previously deceived you. To aid in returning a jinx or negative energy to whomever sent it, place the flowers in front of a mirror as part of a protection spell.

Snowdrop

Common Snowdrop (*Galanthus nivalis*); also known as death's flower, drooping lily, fair maids, white bells, white queen

The snowdrop has narrow, grass-like leaves that surround the flower stems. Its drooping flowers are white with three inner and three outer petals. The inner petals have a touch of green at the tips. They often come up through a blanket of snow.

Caution: The bulbs are toxic if ingested.

History and Lore

According to Greek legend, Persephone brought the snowdrop with her when she returned from the underworld and like other flowers from that realm it was regarded as unlucky. Its association with death may also be attributed to the unopened flower looking like a little corpse in a shroud. Giving snowdrops to someone in the hospital in England was considered a death omen. Although unlucky to take indoors, if the cut flowers were kept in a vase just outside the house, they were said to ward off bad luck. In Wales, it was considered unlucky to take snowdrops indoors on Valentine's Day; however, in the Welsh Borders a bowl of flowers was taken in at Imbolc to drive out evil spirits and mark the beginning of spring. In England and Scotland, the snowdrop was considered a flower of hope because it heralded spring. To see a snowdrop blooming before New Year's Day in Scotland was said to bring luck for the year ahead.

Magical Connections

Element/s	Earth
Deities	Persephone
Magical entities	Faeries
Other associations	Imbolc
Powers and attributes	Adaptability, challenges/obstacles, changes/transitions, courage, death/funeral practices, determination, family and home, happiness, hope, loss/sorrow, negativity, release, trust, wishes
Available for purchase	Flower essence; dried flowers; bulbs

Spells and Rituals

To aid perseverance when going through a difficult period, carry a sachet of dried flowers with you or dab a little flower essence behind your ears. When dealing with trust issues, write the initials of the person on a picture of snowdrops and keep it on your altar until it is resolved.

Solomon's Seal

Common Solomon's Seal (*Polygonatum multiflorum*); also known as lady's lockets, sow's teats

Great Solomon's Seal (*P. biflorum*); also known as lady's seal, sealwort

Each plant has a single, elegantly arching stem with lance-shaped leaves growing on the upper side. The tubular flowers are creamy or waxy white and topped with yellowish green. They dangle beneath the stem under the leaves. Great Solomon's seal can reach up to seven feet tall.

Caution: All parts of these plants are toxic if ingested.

Solomon's Seal

History and Lore

King Solomon of Israel reputedly used a special signet/seal ring for magic and by medieval times in Europe he was regarded as a great wizard. According to legend in the Middle East, Solomon placed his seal upon this plant, which can be seen as circular scars on the roots. While the Greeks and Romans generally ignored the plant, by the Middle Ages herbalists and alchemists throughout Europe found it of value. The root was regarded as a powerful amulet if the design of the ancient seal ring could be discerned on it. In Germany, it was considered "a key to subterranean treasure chambers."[135] On May Day in France and Belgium, fronds of Solomon's seal were hung on houses and barns for luck.

....
135. Lust, *The Herb Book*, 589.

Magical Connections

Element/s	Water
Astrological influence	Capricorn, Gemini; Saturn
Other associations	Beltane
Powers and attributes	Banish, bind, focus, growth, intuition, luck, negativity, protection, purification, secrets, spirit guides/spirits, success, wisdom
Available for purchase	Flower essence; extract; dried root pieces and powdered; root oil

Spells and Rituals

To bind an oath, write it on paper, fold it, and then dip the bottom of a flower in ink and press it to the paper to make a seal. To develop inner wisdom, hold a piece of root as you meditate. To repel negative energy, sprinkle powdered root around the outside of your home.

Southernwood

Southernwood (*Artemisia abrotanum*); also known as lad's love, mother-wood, sweet Benjamin

Southernwood is a close cousin to mugwort and wormwood. Strongly aromatic, it releases a woodsy fragrance when brushed against. The fern-like, gray-green leaves retain their fragrance after drying and give off scent when burned. The flowers look like small, yellow buttons.

Caution: Southernwood is toxic if ingested in large amounts.

History and Lore

The ancient Greeks and Romans revered southernwood for its magical powers and effectiveness against sorcery, mundane ailments, and snakes. Roman naturalist Pliny the Elder designated it as an erotic herb and suggested placing it under the mattress to act as an aphrodisiac. Associated with courtship and flirting in Britain, women used southernwood in divination to discover whom they would marry; men used it as a buttonhole flower. A piece of the plant worn in a shoe was believed to attract a lover. In Germany, southernwood was used in love potions and in France it was placed in bouquets that lovers gave each other to symbolize fidelity. The Germans also used southernwood for protection from witches and spells. Reputedly in England, southernwood could cure faery-inflicted illness that befell a person after taking part in fae revels or eating their food.

Magical Connections

Element/s	Air
Astrological influence	Aries, Scorpio; Mercury
Deities	Artemis, Isis
Magical entities	Faeries
Powers and attributes	Challenges/obstacles, divination, fertility, healing, hexes, love, loyalty/fidelity, luck, negativity, protection, purification, renewal, sex/sexuality, strength, truth
Available for purchase	Cut, dried leaves and stems

Spells and Rituals

For a handfasting ceremony or renewal of vows, wrap a long stem around your wrists as you join hands. Tuck a few sprigs under the mattress to boost pleasure in the bedroom. To clear the energy and enhance your skills for divination, burn a few dried leaves before a session.

Speedwell

Common Speedwell (*Veronica officinalis*); also
  known as blue star, gypsy weed, heath speedwell, Veronica

Germander Speedwell (*V. chamaedrys*); also
  known as angel's eyes, bird's eye, blue eye,
  eyebright

Both plants are also known as bright-eye, cat's eyes, mother-die, poor man's tea, wish-me-well.

Speedwell has creeping stems and spikes of flowers that are tubular with four rounded, streaked petals. Common speedwell flowers can be pale blue, violet, or pinkish purple. The leaves are oval with toothed edges. Germander speedwell flowers can be various shades of blue, mauve, or pale violet with a white "eye" at the center. The oval leaves are slightly pointed.

History and Lore

In Ireland, speedwell was used to keep evil spirits away and to counteract spells. It was believed that the plant could not be harmed by anything natural or supernatural. Along with yarrow (*Achillea millefolium*) and other herbs, it was given to cows during calving to protect them against faeries and run-of-the-mill bad luck. With its name meaning "farewell" and "good luck," speedwell was tucked into clothing for protection from accidents while traveling. According to various legends in England, picking the flowers could result in a thunderstorm, bird's pecking your eyes out, or your mother dying.

Magical Connections

Element/s	Fire
Astrological influence	Aries; Mercury
Powers and attributes	Defense, intuition, loyalty/fidelity, luck, negativity, protection
Available for purchase	Flower essence; cut, dried leaves and stems; seeds

Spells and Rituals

For luck, tuck a sprig of flowers into your suitcase while traveling or keep it in the glove box of your car. Include it in a protective charm to counteract spells or to dispel any form of negativity. Place a picture of speedwell on your altar to enhance intuition.

Spider Plant

Spider Plant (*Chlorophytum comosum* syn. *Anthericum comosum*, *Hartwegia comosa*); also known
  as hen and chickens, ribbon plant, spider ivy,
  walking anthericum

This popular houseplant consists of a rosette of spreading, arching leaves. The narrow leaves taper to a point and can be solid green or variegated with lengthwise stripes of white or pale yellow. The drooping flower stems produce white, star-shaped flowers. The flowers develop into tiny plants that dangle from the mother like little spiders on a web.

History and Lore

Spider plants have been used medicinally by the Indigenous people of South Africa and Zimbabwe and as a charm for pregnant mothers to protect them and their infants from evil spirits. According to Polish folklore, a flowering plant in the home indicated a wedding in the making or a baby on the way.

Magical Connections

Element/s	Air
Powers and attributes	Abundance, adaptability, fertility, negativity, prosperity/money, protection
Available for purchase	Houseplant

Spells and Rituals

Good for clearing impurities from the air indoors, spider plants absorb negativity and give the energy of your home a boost. As part of a fertility spell, hang one in the bedroom if you are planning a pregnancy, or root one of the babies in its own pot and place it next to your bed.

Spikenard

American Spikenard (*Aralia racemosa*); also
    known as American sarsaparilla, Indian root,
    old man's root, spiceberry, wild licorice
Ploughman's Spikenard (*Inula conyza*); also
    known as cinnamon root, fly grass, great
    fleabane, poor man's spikenard
Spikenard (*Nardostachys jatamansi* syn. *N. grandi-
    flora*); also known as Indian nard, Indian root,
    nard, true spikenard

Spikenard has lance-shaped leaves and mauve- to pinkish purple, bell-shaped flowers that grow in rounded clusters at the top of the stems. Ameri-can spikenard has pointed oval leaves with serrated edges. Its tiny, green flowers grow in starburst clusters on branched stalks and develop into dark purple berries. Ploughman's spikenard has lance-shaped leaves with serrated margins and branching purplish stems. Growing in clusters, its thistle-like, barrel-shaped flowers are dull yellow and purplish. All three plants grow about three feet tall and have aromatic roots.

Caution: True spikenard is a critically endangered species.

History and Lore

The Egyptians, Hebrews, and Hindus used spikenard medicinally and ritually. The scented oil was highly prized by the ancient Greeks and Romans who used it for anointing prior to crowning with wreaths at festivals. Ploughman's spikenard was used medicinally by the Anglo-Saxons. In later centuries, the English hung roots in homes or burned them in alehouse fireplaces to scent the air and remove unpleasant odors. American spikenard was used medicinally by the Cherokee, Chippewa, Iroquois, Menominee, and Micmac for a wide range of ailments.

Magical Connections

Element/s	Water
Astrological influence	Venus
Powers and attributes	Balance/harmony, consecrate/bless, focus, love, loyalty/fidelity, luck, negativity, purification
Available for purchase	Cut, dried root; powdered root; seeds

Spells and Rituals

Because true spikenard is critically endangered it is best to work with it symbolically or use American or ploughman's spikenard instead. The strong cleansing properties of these plants negate negative energy bringing balance and fidelity between people.

Spindletree

Spindletree

Spindletree (*Euonymus europaeus*); also known as death alder, louse berry, pegwood, prickwood, spindle wood, spindleberry

Wahoo (*E. atropurpureus*); also known as burning bush, Indian arrow wood, purple spindletree

The spindletree has dull green, oval leaves and small, yellowish-green flowers. The reddish-pink fruit capsules contain orange berries. The wahoo has dark green, oval leaves, dark purple flowers, and scarlet-red fruit capsules.

Caution: All parts of these trees are toxic if ingested.

History and Lore

As might be expected, the name of the European tree comes from its use for making equipment for spinning and weaving. In England, Romani favored the wood for knitting needles. Since the time of the Anglo-Saxons, spindletree was used medicinally in England although in Buckinghamshire where it was known as death alder it was considered unlucky to take any part of it into the home. According to Roman naturalist Pliny the Elder, an abundance of flowers indicated an immanent outbreak of the plague. Used to make arrows, the name *wahoo* is from the Lakota Sioux word *wanhu*, meaning "arrow shaft."[136] Although all parts of the tree are poisonous, the Meskwaki and Winnebago used wahoo medicinally.

Magical Connections

Element/s	Water
Deities	Athena, the Fates, Freya, Frigg, Holle, Minerva, the Norns
Ogham	Ór / Oir ◇
Other associations	Imbolc
Powers and attributes	Challenges/obstacles, courage, creativity, divination, focus, healing, hexes, inspiration, manifest, purification, spirituality, success
Available for purchase	Dried bark from the wahoo tree

Spells and Rituals

Because the spindle is a symbol of magic and manifestation, wrap a piece of yarn around a branch like a spindle to add power to your spells. To aid

---

136. Homoya, *Wildflowers and Ferns of Indiana Forests*, 78.

in breaking or deterring a hex, crush a handful of dried berries underfoot, and then scatter them outside.

Spruce

Black Spruce (*Picea mariana*); also known as
    American spruce, bog spruce, swamp spruce
Norway Spruce (*P. abies* syn. P. *excelsa*); also
    known as mountain spruce, red fir, white fir
White Spruce (*P. glauca*); also known as Black
    Hills spruce, cat spruce, skunk spruce

Black spruce has stiff, blue-green needles and purplish-brown, egg-shaped cones that grow in clusters. Norway spruce has a pyramid shape and dark green needles. Its main branches arch upward with smaller branches drooping from them. The blue-green needles of white spruce have a waxy, white coating and a pungent odor when crushed.

History and Lore

In Germany and Belgium, spruce was regarded highly enough to be used for Maypoles and Yule logs. It was commonly believed in Bavaria that spirits inhabited spruce trees. Like pine, spruce was also used on Walpurgis in the Austrian state of Tyrol where boughs were set alight and carried around villages accompanied by the ringing of bells and beating on pans to burn out witches. Spruce was used as a nail tree for sympathetic medicine and magic in Germany and Austria. Making a request for healing was accompanied by driving a nail into the tree. In Sweden, spruce branches were included in burials to cover the dead. This was believed to also prevent the deceased from coming back to haunt the living.

Magical Connections

Element/s	Earth, water
Astrological influence	Cancer, Capricorn, Sagittarius (black spruce)
Deities	Attis, Cerridwen, Cybele, Danu, Poseidon
Other associations	Beltane, Yule
Powers and attributes	Adaptability, challenges/obstacles, emotions, growth, healing, hope (Norway), inspiration, intuition, prosperity/money, protection, psychic abilities, renewal, security, spirit guides/spirits, spirituality, wisdom (black)
Available for purchase	Essential oil is obtained from the needles and twigs of the black spruce

Spells and Rituals

To determine when to act on intuition, diffuse a little essential oil to aid you. To ground energy after ritual or magic work, hold a cone between your hands for a minute or two. For help with a problem, write keywords about it on a picture of spruce, visualize a resolution, and then burn it.

Spurge

Cypress Spurge (*Euphorbia cyparissias*); also
    known as graveyard weed, love-in-a-huddle,
    witch's milk, wolf's milk
Sun Spurge (*E. helioscopia*); also known as cat's
    milk, devil's milk, madwoman's milk, wart
    weed, witch's milk, wolf's milk

These plants have clusters of unusual cup-shaped flowers with large, rounded bracts underneath. Cypress spurge is bushy and about twelve inches tall with needle-like foliage. Its flowers are lime yellow and grow at the tops of the erect stems. Sun spurge has distinctive red stems and serrated, oblong leaves that are wider at the ends and taper at the base. The flowers are light green to pale yellow. Both plants contain a milky latex sap.

Caution: Spurge is toxic if ingested, sun spurge can be fatal; the white sap can be toxic to the skin and eyes; sun spurge may cause photosensitivity.

History and Lore

Mentioned in ancient Greek magical texts, spurge has been used throughout the centuries in Europe to ward off demons and cure bewitchment. Despite the plant's toxicity, it was used medicinally in Ireland and England. Herbalist Nicholas Culpeper also noted that it "provokes lust."[137] In England, cypress spurge was commonly planted in gardens and cemeteries. In Ireland, sun spurge was reputedly an aid for rescuing a woman who had been taken by faeries; however, to be effective the plant had to be gathered at a particular time during the month of August.

Magical Connections

Element/s	Fire
Astrological influence	Leo; Mars, Mercury
Powers and attributes	Defense, hexes, protection
Available for purchase	Essential oil; seeds

137. Culpeper, *The English Physician*, 188.

Spells and Rituals

Include spurge in a spell to break any type of jinx against you by placing a few dabs of essential oil on your magical tools. Use a picture of spurge as a protective charm. Scatter a few seeds on your altar to help raise defensive energy.

Star Anise

Chinese Star Anise (*Illicium verum*); also known as aniseed stars

Japanese Star Anise (*I. anisatum* syn. *I. religiosum*); also known as anise shrub

Chinese star anise is a small tree; the Japanese tree is more of a large, bushy shrub. Both have glossy, oval leaves that taper at both ends. The spidery, yellowish-white flowers have a pink to reddish tinge and grow on long stems that sprout from the base of the leaves. The Chinese flowers are solitary; Japanese flowers grow in clusters. The eight-pointed, star-shaped seedpod is brown and woody when mature.

Caution: Japanese star anise is toxic if ingested.

History and Lore

In Asia, Chinese star anise has been used medicinally and as an aphrodisiac for centuries. According to Chinese folklore, it was also used for protection against the evil eye. Finding a seedpod with more than eight points was regarded as lucky. Japanese star anise was used as a temple offering to deities in Japan. The seedpods are burned as incense in Buddhist religious ceremonies.

Magical Connections

Element/s	Air, water
Astrological influence	Aquarius, Pisces, Sagittarius; Jupiter, Mercury
Deities	Ishtar, Lakshmi
Other associations	The otherworld
Powers and attributes	Abundance, awareness, banish, consecrate/bless, divination, happiness, luck, protection, psychic abilities, purification, skills, spirituality, success
Available for purchase	Essential oil; whole or ground seed pods;

Spells and Rituals

Anoint each cardinal direction of your altar with the essential oil to amplify the power of ritual. Hold three seedpods between your hands for a minute before any type of psychic work to boost awareness. Use a seedpod as an amulet for success when taking an exam or for a job interview.

Stitchwort

Greater Stitchwort (*Stellaria holostea* syn. *Rabelera holostea*); also known as devil's nightcap, moon flower, morning stars, satin flower, starwort

Lesser Stitchwort, Common Stitchwort (*S. graminea* syn. *Alsine graminea*); also known as piskie flower, starwort

Stitchwort has grass-like leaves and white, five-petaled flowers with deep notches that make them appear to have ten petals. Greater stitchwort reaches up to a foot tall; its flowers are about an inch in diameter. Low-growing lesser stitchwort hides its smaller, half-inch-wide flowers among meadow grasses.

History and Lore

The Anglo-Saxons used stitchwort to cure elf shot and other unexplained pains, especially in the side. Elf shot was believed to be an invisible magical weapon used by elves to cause disease. Stitchwort was also used as an amulet against the evil eye. British children were warned not to pick the flowers because it would cause thunder and lightning and in Cornwall, they were told that they would be pixie-led or bitten by adders. According to English legend, stitchwort was guarded by pixies so it could not be used in charms against them. It was also said to be under the protection of faeries because they were fond of the flowers and liked to make garlands with them.

Magical Connections

Element/s	Water
Astrological influence	Moon
Magical entities	Elves, faeries, pixies
Powers and attributes	Adaptability, clarity, creativity, determination, emotions, fertility, healing, peace, renewal, strength, support
Available for purchase	Flower essence

Spells and Rituals

To boost lunar magic for esbat rituals, tie long flower stems into a circle to place on your altar. To create a sense of peace and tranquility, hold a picture of stitchwort between your hands as you visualize white light emanating from the flowers and surrounding you.

Stonecrop

Stonecrop

Stonecrop, Orpine (*Hylotelephium telephium* syn. *Sedum telephium*); also known as everlasting, life-everlasting, live-forever, love-forever, Midsummer men, witch's moneybags

Reaching up to two feet tall, stonecrop has succulent, oblong or rounded leaves that are toothed and bluish green. The flowers grow in dense, flat-topped to convex branching clusters at the top of the stems. The flowers are star-shaped with five, spreading petals in colors that range from pink to purplish red and sometimes white or greenish.

History and Lore

Stonecrop has been used medicinally since the time of the ancient Greeks and Romans and for centuries it was worn as a healing charm. Because the plant seemed to resist drying out and could grow in stony soil, it gained a wide-spread reputation of lasting forever. In Britain, Germany, and Switzerland, stonecrop was used for love divination on Midsummer's Eve. At other times, it was used to indicate whether or not a lover was faithful. The French believed that it was an indicator of sorcery and that it would wither if a witch were nearby. In England, keeping stonecrop in the house was said to bring good health, and in Massachusetts, growing it in the garden would bring prosperity. Stonecrop was grown on roofs in Scandinavia to protect houses from lightning and fire; however, a plant that suddenly died was an omen that someone in the household would also.

Magical Connections

Element/s	Water
Astrological influence	Moon
Powers and attributes	Divination, healing, love, loyalty/fidelity, protection, strength
Available for purchase	Seeds

Spells and Rituals

Incorporate several clusters of flowers to strengthen a love spell. Grow it in your garden as a protective charm and to foster a sense of fidelity in your household. Sprinkle a handful of seeds on your altar or table to enhance divination sessions.

Storax

Liquidambar, Levant Storax (*Liquidambar orientalis*); also known as Asian storax, Levant stracte, Oriental sweet gum, styrax, Turkish sweet gum

Storax (*Styrax officinalis*); also known as snowbell
    bush, snowdrop bush, stracte, styrax
Sweet Gum (*L. styraciflua*); also known as American storax, American styrax, witch's burr

Storax is a small, shrubby tree with oval leaves. White, bell-shaped flowers grow in small, drooping clusters at the ends of the branches and develop into round, creamy-yellow fruit. The *Liquidambar* trees have coarsely toothed leaves with five to seven lobes. Tiny, yellow-green flowers grow in upright clusters (male) and dangling, round clusters (female). The female flowers develop into the spiny fruiting clusters called *gumballs*.

Caution: The fruit of these trees is not edible.

History and Lore
The names *styrax* (Greek) and *storax* (Latin) have caused centuries of confusion. While the gum resin is called *storax*, it was often distinguished as "liquid storax" if it came from the *Liquidambar orientalis* tree and "solid storax" if it came from *Styrax officinalis*. However, scholars still debate over which one was the highly prized storax of the ancients. The Greeks and Romans burned the resin as offerings to deities and for centuries it was used as incense in churches and mosques throughout Europe and the Middle East. Storax was also burned in French medieval magical rites. The Aztec used sweet gum to flavor tobacco and in the Yucatan, it was used as temple incense.

Magical Connections

Element/s	Earth, fire, water
Astrological influence	Jupiter, Mercury, Moon, Sun

Deities	Demeter Dionysus, Hecate, Zeus
Powers and attributes	Divination, hexes, prosperity / money, protection, purification
Available for purchase	Essential oil; solid resin pieces

Spells and Rituals
Burn storax incense to raise psychic protection during divination and to aid in breaking hexes. Also include it in spells to increase their effectiveness. Diffuse a little essential oil to purify magic tools or to prepare space for ritual.

Strawberry
Cultivated Strawberry, Garden Strawberry
    (*Fragaria* x *ananassa*)
Wild Strawberry (*F. vesca*)

Strawberry leaves have three toothed leaflets and form a base rosette. The white, five-petaled flowers grow on separate stems. The cultivated strawberry grows about six inches tall; the wild strawberry looks like a smaller version of the garden plant.

History and Lore
According to Celtic legend, wild strawberries helped sustain the warrior band known as the Fianna when they were off fighting. While the Romans valued strawberries more for medicinal purposes, by the Middle Ages the French were happily eating them and in London they were prized treats sold by street vendors. Lovers in Germany traditionally exchanged bracelets of wild strawberry stems. Strawberries reputedly provided protection from demons and were a deterrent to witches and any illness caused by them. Drinking strawberry leaf tea was said to protect against

bewitchment. The first strawberry plants found in the summer were believed to have especially strong healing powers. In Bavaria, small baskets of strawberries were tied between the horns of cows so elves would bless them with abundant milk.

Magical Connections

Element/s	Water
Astrological influence	Libra; Venus
Deities	Freya, Frigg, Odin, Venus
Magical entities	Brownies, elves, faeries
Other associations	Full moon in June
Powers and attributes	Abundance, adaptability, balance/harmony, divination, happiness, healing, love, luck, manifest, peace, protection, relationships, sex/sexuality
Available for purchase	Fresh, dried, or frozen fruit; flower essence; cut, dried leaves; jam and preserves; wine

Spells and Rituals

To attract abundance, make a wreath with long stems and hang it in your kitchen. Sprinkle a handful of dried leaves across the threshold of your front door to invite happiness and harmony. Kindle passion with your lover by slowly and sensually feeding strawberries to each other.

Sunflower

Common Sunflower (*Helianthus annuus*); also known as annual sunflower

Reaching up to ten feet tall, this iconic sunflower has thick, branching stems and coarse, heart-shaped leaves covered with rough hairs. The yellow-rayed flower head can measure four to twelve inches wide. A large disk of seeds forms in the middle of the flower.

History and Lore

With its large flowerhead resembling radiant beams, the sunflower was venerated by the Inca and represented their sun god. Priests and priestesses wore gold pendant disks with the image of a sunflower on it. They were also depicted in carvings on temple stones. Sunflower seeds were used for food and medicine by the Iroquois, Ojibwe, Shoshoni, Ute, and others. As a symbol of strength and endurance, the sunflower was included in the Sun Dance, an important and sacred ceremony of the Lakota Sioux, Arapaho, Cheyenne, and Blackfoot. Imported into Europe in the sixteenth century, growing sunflowers in the garden was believed to bring luck in England.

Magical Connections

Element/s	Fire
Astrological influence	Leo; Sun
Deities	Apollo, Demeter, Helios, Inti
Other associations	Lughnasadh
Powers and attributes	Challenges/obstacles, clarity, determination, fertility, happiness, luck, manifest, negativity, peace, prosperity/money, release, spirituality, strength, wisdom, wishes
Available for purchase	Seeds; sunflower seed oil; flower essence; dried flowers; dried petals

Spells and Rituals

For help in manifesting your dreams and desires, float a handful of petals in your bath water as you visualize what you want. To bring clarity and solve a problem, prepare a candle with sunflower oil, and then burn it while you meditate on the situation.

Sweet Flag

Sweet Flag, Calamus (*Acorus calamus* syn. *Calamus aromaticus*); also known as calamus root, flagroot, gladden, gladdon, sweet grass, sweet rush, sweet sedge

Sweet flag is an aquatic plant that reaches about three feet tall. It has flat, iris-like stems with sword-like leaves growing from the base. An off-centered ridge runs along the length of each leaf. A cylindrical protrusion halfway up the stem contains tiny, yellowish-brown, or greenish yellow flowers.

Caution: The root is toxic if ingested.

History and Lore

The Sumerians used sweet flag in sacred incense mixtures. In addition to incense, the Egyptians placed the flowers and leaves in tombs. To the ancient Romans and Arabs, the scent of sweet flag was an aphrodisiac. The Anglo-Saxons used it medicinally as did the Cherokee, Dakota, Iroquois, Lakota, Menominee, Ojibwe, Omaha, and Pawnee, some of whom also used it for its hallucinogenic effects. In Europe, these properties gave sweet flag an association with witchcraft despite its common use as a strewing herb in churches. According to Japanese folklore, sweet flag provided protection from evil. In Borneo, it was used to contact spirit beings for divination and healing rituals. In Papua New Guinea, sweet flag was an aid for communicating with the spirit world.

Magical Connections

Element/s	Earth, water
Astrological influence	Virgo; Moon, Sun
Powers and attributes	Luck, prosperity/money, protection, spirit guides/spirits, wisdom
Available for purchase	Flower essence; essential oil; cut, dried or powdered root

Spells and Rituals

Diffuse sweet flag essential oil as you cast a circle to help contact and work with spirit guides. Also use the scent during meditation when seeking wisdom. To attract luck into your life, sprinkle powdered root under four stones that you place at the corners of your property.

Sweet Woodruff

Sweet Woodruff (*Galium odoratum* syn. *Asperula odorata*); also known as hay plant, master of the woods, sweet-scented bedstraw, wild baby's breath

Reaching eight to fifteen inches tall, whorls of six to eight leaves form around the stems. Growing in small clusters, the dainty, white flowers are funnel shaped with petals that splay open at the ends. While the plant seems to have little or no fragrance, it develops a sweet, hay-like scent that gets stronger as it dries.

History and Lore

During the Middle Ages in Germany, sweet woodruff was strewn on floors to deter odors, insects, and evil spirits. Because witches were allegedly afraid of the flowers, they served as a magic charm for children and placing blossoms in cradles protected the mother and infant from spells. Sweet woodruff was also carried in a linen pouch to keep poisonous animals at bay. During illness, Germans and Belgians hung little bouquets at the head of the bed for magical healing. In weather divination, the scent of sweet woodruff in a linen closet was said to be stronger before rain. Sweet woodruff is believed to be the plant called *matrysilva* that German scholar and occult writer Heinrich Cornelius Agrippa associated with the fixed star Aldebaran.[138]

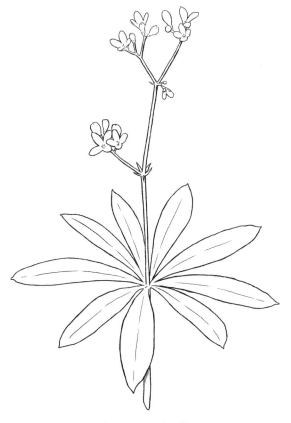

Sweet Woodruff

Magical Connections

Element/s	Fire
Astrological influence	Capricorn; Mars, Venus
Deities	Freya, Mars
Magical entities	Faeries
Other associations	Beltane, Walpurgis
Powers and attributes	Adaptability, changes/transitions, clarity, communication, consecrate/bless, divination, dream work, healing, negativity, peace, protection, purification, relationships, skills, success
Available for purchase	Cut, dried leaves; seeds

Spells and Rituals

To enhance dream work, drink woodruff tea before bed or place a sachet of dried leaves beside your pillow. For a boost to communication skills, keep a small jar of seeds in your workspace. As part of a spell for success, burn a few dried leaves.

Sweetgrass

Sweetgrass (*Hierochloe odorata*); also known as bison grass, buffalo grass, holy grass, Seneca grass, vanilla grass

Sweetgrass stems reach up to three feet tall and are often reddish purple at the base. The leaves are long and narrow with rough edges and shiny undersides. Tiny yellowish-brown flowers grow in branched, tapering clusters. A vanilla-like fragrance develops when the plant begins to dry.

138. Agrippa, *Three Books of Occult Philosophy*, 100.

Caution: Sweetgrass has potentially toxic properties and should not be ingested.

History and Lore

The genus name *Hierochloe* was derived from the Greek *hieros*, "sacred," and *chloë*, "grass."[139] Sweetgrass is regarded as a sacred plant by Native American tribes across North America including the Blackfoot, Passamaquoddy, Ojibwe, Cheyenne, Chippewa, Mohawk, Lakota, and Potawatomi. It is often worn in a medicine pouch for spiritual protection and used as an aid for removing evil spirits. Tribal elders are given sweetgrass as a sign of respect. Braided leaves are burned as incense for sacred smoke in purification ceremonies and to carry prayers. Also native to Europe, sweetgrass was used medicinally and as a strewing herb in Eastern Europe. It was used to flavor vodka in Poland.

Magical Connections

Element/s	Air, water
Astrological influence	Venus
Powers and attributes	Consecrate/bless, healing, purification, spirit guides/spirits, spirituality
Available for purchase	Essential oil; hydrosol; cut, dried leaves; braids; seeds; baskets

Spells and Rituals

Burn a small braid of sweetgrass and waft the smoke over you before any type of spiritual work or for healing. Burn a few leaves or diffuse the essential oil to consecrate and purify ritual space.

....

139. Small and Catling, *Canadian Medicinal Crops*, 69.

Also burn a little when contacting and working with spirit guides.

Sycamore

American Sycamore (*Platanus occidentalis*); also known as American plane tree, buttonwood, ghost tree

London Plane Tree (*P. x acerifolia* syn. *P. x hispanica*); also known as London planetree

Oriental Sycamore (*P. orientalis*); also known as ghost tree, oriental plane tree

The leaves of sycamore trees look like oversized maple leaves. Yellow and red flowers grow in small clusters that develop into fuzzy, brown seed balls. American sycamore seed balls grow singly, the London plane tree's grow in pairs, and the oriental sycamore's grow in clusters of two to six. Sycamore bark flakes or peels off revealing a lighter-colored inner bark sometimes giving the tree a ghostly appearance. A type of maple (*Acer pseudoplatanus*) is also known as sycamore.

History and Lore

A valued shade tree, the thick foliage of the sycamore provided cool, convenient meeting places for the ancient Greeks and Romans. The Greeks considered the tree a gift from the gods; the Romans poured libations of wine on the roots. Couples in Greece who had to be temporarily separated each took half of a sycamore leaf to symbolize their love and their eventual reunion. Although it had some medicinal use in medieval Europe, it was believed that sycamores growing in a village would deter the plague from entering. Revered in Syria well into the nineteenth century, it was customary to hang amulets on the tree's branches.

Magical Connections

Element/s	Air, water
Astrological influence	Jupiter, Venus
Deities	Artemis, Diana, Eos, Europa, Zeus
Other associations	Imbolc
Powers and attributes	Abundance, balance/harmony, challenges/obstacles, communication, determination, divination, love, peace, prophecy, protection, psychic abilities, purification, renewal, support, wisdom
Available for purchase	Flower essence

Spells and Rituals

For help in dealing with problems and to wipe the slate clean for a fresh start, crumble a seed ball, and then scatter the pieces outside. Keep a twig on your desk to aid you in everyday communications. To prepare outdoor ritual areas, strew dried leaves before casting a circle.

Tagetes

African Marigold (*Tagetes erecta*); also known as
American marigold, Aztec marigold, chry-
santhemum marigold, Mexican marigold
French Marigold (*T. patula*)

Growing from one to four feet tall, the African
marigold has large, rounded flowers in various
shades of yellow and orange. Its narrow, lance-
shaped leaves are coarsely toothed. The French
marigold is a compact plant between six and
twelve inches tall. It has toothed, lance-shaped leaflets. The flowers vary in shades of yellow, orange,
and mahogany-red. The leaves and flowers of both
plants are aromatic.

History and Lore

Despite a genus name derived from Tages, a
grandson of Jupiter, these marigolds did not reach
Europe until the sixteenth century. The Aztec
regarded the plants as sacred and used them for ritual and medicinal purposes. Considered the flower
of the dead by the Aztec, marigolds are used on
altars for Day of the Dead observances (November
2) in present-day Mexico and represent the tenu-
ousness of life. According to Mexican legend, the
reddish brown splotches on the flowers were from
the blood of people killed by Spanish conquista-
dors. In India, participants in religious celebrations
wear garlands of African marigolds. The magical
properties of the common marigold (*Calendula
officinalis*) are often confused with tagetes.

Magical Connections

Element/s	Air, fire
Astrological influence	Cancer, Leo; Sun
Deities	Tages, Xochiquetzal
Other associations	The afterlife, Beltane, Mabon, Samhain
Powers and attributes	Consecrate/bless, death/funeral practices, healing, justice/legal matters, loss/sorrow, skills, transformation
Available for purchase	Flower essence; essential oil; dried flowers; petals; seeds

Spells and Rituals

Sprinkle dried flower petals across your altar for your Samhain ritual. Leave them in place until November 2nd to acknowledge the Mexican Day of the Dead. Use a handful of leaves in a spell to bring success in legal matters. Sprinkle a circle of flower petals to consecrate ritual space.

Tamarisk

Athel Tamarisk (*Tamarix aphylla* syn. *T. articulata*); also known as athel pine, desert tamarisk, leafless tamarisk, salt cedar, salt tree

French Tamarisk (*T. gallica*); also known as common tamarisk, English tamarisk, salt cedar, sea cypress, tamarisk of Apollo

Tamarisk trees were known as salt cedars because their scale-like leaves resemble cedar foliage and they secrete salt. The Athel tamarisk has pale pink to whitish flowers that grow in clusters near the tips of the branches. The pink flowers of French tamarisk grow on spikes and resemble little bottlebrushes. Although their names are similar, tamarisk should not be confused with the tamarind tree (*Tamarindus indica*).

History and Lore

The tamarisk was regarded as a sacred tree by the Assyrians, Arabs, Greeks, Romans, and Egyptians. Persian priests used tamarisk branches to aid in divination and prophecy and Scythian magicians wore tamarisk wreaths when making predictions. The wood was used as a charm against the evil eye in Morocco. Legends vary in the resurrection story of Osiris, but he either turned into a tamarisk tree or a tamarisk grew around his coffin. The tree was regarded as a messenger of Yama, the Hindu god of death. Believing in the tree's magical power, water diviners in the island of Guernsey often used tamarisk for their rods.

Magical Connections

Element/s	Water
Astrological influence	Saturn
Deities	Anu, Aphrodite, Apollo, Cernunnos, Osiris, Pan, Wepwawet, Yama
Other associations	The afterlife, Samhain
Powers and attributes	Ancestors, banish, death/funeral practices, divination, hexes, hope, negativity, prophecy, protection, spirituality
Available for purchase	Flower essence

Spells and Rituals

For energetic protection of your home, hang a small sprig of leaves over the exterior doors. To honor your ancestors and loved ones at Samhain, write their names on a picture of a tamarisk tree and place it on your altar. Burn a few leaves or picture of the tree as part of a banishing spell.

Tansy

Tansy

Common Tansy, Garden Tansy (*Tanacetum vulgare* syn. *Chrysanthemum vulgare*); also known as bachelor's buttons, bitter buttons, golden buttons, hind heal, yellow buttons

Tansy leaves are deeply lobed and fern-like. Clusters of flat, bright yellow flowers resemble buttons or daisies without their white petals. The flower's strong scent is long lasting even when dried. Growing from one to four feet tall, the plant tends to sprawl.

Caution: All parts of the plant, especially the flowers, are toxic if ingested; abortifacient.

History and Lore

According to Greek legend, a drink brewed from tansy made Ganymede, the cupbearer of Zeus, immortal. The name *tansy* is a corruption of the Greek *athanasia*, meaning "immortality."[140] Tansy was one of the plants that the Anglo-Saxons believed a wounded deer would eat to heal itself. As a strewing herb, tansy was widely used in public places during the plague years in England. It was customary during medieval funeral preparations to rub tansy on a corpse to preserve it before burial. The flowers were also tucked into funeral shrouds and coffins. Wreaths were sometimes placed on the dead. In New England, tansy continued to be used for funerals well into the nineteenth century.

Magical Connections

Element/s	Water
Astrological influence	Venus
Other associations	Midsummer
Powers and attributes	Banish, death/funeral practices, defense, negativity, purification, release
Available for purchase	Flower essence; cut, dried leaves; dried flowers; dried bouquets; seeds

Spells and Rituals

Hang small tufts of tansy above your altar or front door to repel negativity. After they wilt and dry, burn them and sprinkle the ashes outside. Regarded as an antidote to black magic, place dried

140. Dobelis, *Magic and Medicine of Plants*, 318.

tansy flowers with your ritual and magic tools to cleanse them and banish negative energy.

Tarragon

French Tarragon (*Artemisia dracunculus*); also known as dragon's mugwort, little dragon, silky wormwood, wild tarragon

Tarragon is an erect herb with slender stems and narrow, lance-shaped leaves that are light to medium green. The drooping, yellowish-green flowers are semi spherical and grow in loose, branching clusters.

History and Lore

This culinary and medicinal herb is cousin to mugwort and wormwood. Tarragon's common name comes from the Arabic word for the plant, *tarkhum*, which like its species name *dracunculus* means "little dragon."[141] The reference describes the serpentine appearance of the plant's roots. Because of this, the Romans believed that wearing a sprig of leaves would provide protection against snakes and dragons. During the Middle Ages in Europe, tarragon was believed to be an effective remedy against the bites and stings of poisonous creatures. The French called it *herbe au dragon*.

Magical Connections

Element/s	Air, fire, water
Astrological influence	Aries; Mars, Venus
Deities	Aphrodite, Artemis, Diana, Lilith, Venus
Magical entities	Dragons

Other associations	Midsummer
Powers and attributes	Abundance, confidence, dream work, growth, justice/legal matters, knowledge, peace, protection, secrets, security
Available for purchase	Essential oil; cut, dried leaves; seeds

Spells and Rituals

Sprinkle tarragon seeds across your altar and visualize a dragon rising to your aid as part of a protection spell to instill confidence and a sense of security. Place a sachet of dried leaves under your pillow to enhance dream work and aid in understanding any knowledge you receive.

Tea Tree

Tea Tree (*Melaleuca alternifolia*); also known as narrow-leaved paperbark, ti tree

Tea tree is a shrubby, evergreen tree that reaches about twenty feet tall and ten feet wide. It has pale, papery bark and needle-like foliage that is smooth and soft. The tree produces frothy spikes of creamy white flowers that resemble bottlebrushes.

Caution: Tea tree should not be ingested.

History and Lore

Tea tree has been used in Australian traditional medicine for thousands of years and bark fibers have been used to make burial shrouds. British captain and explorer James Cook (1728–1779) is responsible for its common name. When he saw Aboriginal people making a brew with the leaves, he mistakenly thought they were preparing tea. Regarded as the strongest natural antiseptic, tea tree was a standard item in Australian Army

141. Staub, *75 Exceptional Herbs for Your Garden,* 221

kits during World War II. As its use proliferated through the ranks of other armies, it became known as the wonder from down under.

Magical Connections

Element/s	Earth
Powers and attributes	Emotions, healing, protection, purification
Available for purchase	Essential oil; cut, dried leaves

Spells and Rituals

Diffuse a little of the essential oil for healing that supports both physical and emotional recovery. Tea tree's powers of purification can be used to prepare space for ritual and magic work. Use a few dried leaves in a protection spell or dab the essential oil on an amulet.

Thistle

Blessed Thistle, Holy Thistle (*Cnicus benedictus* syn. *Carduus benedictus*)

Milk Thistle (*Silybum marianum* syn. *Carduus marianus*); also known as lady thistle

Scottish Thistle, Cotton Thistle (*Onopordum acanthium* syn. *Carduus acanthium*); also known as Scotch thistle

Thistles have prickly stems, leaves with spines, and pointed bracts around the flowers, which turn into tufts of white hairs known as thistledown. Blessed thistle has red stems and reddish bracts surrounding the yellow flowers. Milk thistle has pinkish purple flowers and white marbling on its leaves. The Scottish thistle stem has flat, spiny wings along the stems and dark pink to violet flowers.

History and Lore

Farmers in Estonia placed thistle in their grain fields to drive away demons. The Romans believed that carrying a piece of thistle provided protection from all types of harm. The seeds were burned in Poland to cure illnesses caused by evil spirits. A potion made with thistle seed and St. John's wort (*Hypericum perforatum*) was given to women on trial for witchcraft in England to make them tell the truth. Reputedly, witches used thistle with the spit of toads to become invisible and wizards used tall thistles as wands. In Cornwall, pixies were said to use thistle spines as swords and in Ireland faeries were believed to cast a spell so they could ride thistledown like a horse.

Magical Connections

Element/s	Fire
Astrological influence	Aries (blessed), Scorpio; Mars
Deities	Minerva, Pan (blessed), Thor, Tyr
Magical entities	Faeries, pixies
Other associations	Mabon, Yule
Powers and attributes	Banish, challenges/obstacles, clarity, confidence, courage, defense, determination, healing, hexes, negativity, nightmares, protection, release, spirit guides/spirits, strength, trust, truth, wishes
Available for purchase	Flower essence; dried flower heads; cut, dried leaves and stems; seed oil; seeds

Spells and Rituals

To boost the power of defensive spells or to break a hex, include a few thistle spines. If you find some thistledown, hold it in your hand, make a wish, and then blow it to the wind. To aid self-confidence, keep a sachet of dried flowers with you for encouragement.

Thorn Apple

Thorn Apple, Jimson Weed, Datura (*Datura stramonium*); also known as devil's apple, devil's trumpet, locoweed, mad apple, moonflower

Thorn apple is a branching, sprawling plant that can reach up to five feet tall. Its large, oval leaves have coarse, unevenly toothed edges. Blooming at night, the trumpet-shaped flower can be white or purplish and has pointed petals. The round, walnut-sized seedpod is covered with spines. The entire plant has an unpleasant odor.

Caution: All parts of the plant are toxic and can be fatal if ingested; wear gloves to handle.

History and Lore

The ancient Greeks, Romans, and Egyptians were familiar with this plant. Although the oracle at Delphi in Greece was noted as chewing a sacred laurel leaf, or eating some type of mint, she may have also eaten datura.[142] In addition, the vapors said to rise from the ground at Delphi could have been from burning datura. In medieval Germany, it was said to be an ingredient in a witches' salve that reputedly produced erotic sensations, vivid dreams, and hallucinations. The plant's introduction into a wide area of Europe in the early fifteenth century coincided with the rise of witch trials and investigations of demonology.[143] Along with physical torture, the use of potions and ointments for extracting confessions of sex with demons and the devil was fairly common. In the Americas, datura was used as a sacred hallucinogen by the Aztec and other people of Mexico and South America. The Navajo used it for prophecy, visions, and to find helping spirits.

Magical Connections

Element/s	Water
Astrological influence	Sagittarius; Jupiter, Saturn
Deities	Hades, Hecate
Powers and attributes	Banish, divination, dream work, hexes, protection
Available for purchase	Flower essence; seeds

Spells and Rituals

To banish something or someone from your life, write a few keywords on a piece of paper, and then sprinkle it with the flower essence. After visualizing the desired outcome, take it outside, burn the paper, and scatter the ashes.

Thyme

Common Thyme, Garden Thyme (*Thymus vulgaris*); also known as English thyme, sweet thyme

Wild Thyme, Creeping Thyme (*T. serpyllum*); also known as mother-thyme, shepherd's thyme

Thyme has oval, gray-green leaves and small, pink to lilac or bluish-purple flowers that grow in little

---

142. Hanson, Venturelli, and Fleckenstein, *Drugs and Society*, 368.

143. Sidky, *Witchcraft, Lycanthropy, Drugs and Disease*, 206.

clusters. The base stems become woody with age. Common thyme grows up to fifteen inches tall; wild thyme is a ground cover only two to four inches tall.

Thyme

burials. It was common practice in northern England to place thyme in coffins and in Wales to plant it on graves. Throughout England it was believed that smelling the scent of thyme where none grew indicated the ghostly presence of someone who had been murdered. Dried thyme was often burned as a fumigant against witchcraft. Regarded as a faery plant, brushing a sprig of thyme across the eyes reputedly enabled a person to see them. Customarily thrown into the bonfire on Midsummer's Eve, it was also used for love divination through dreams on that night.

Magical Connections

Element/s	Air, water
Astrological influence	Aries, Capricorn, Libra, Taurus; Venus
Magical entities	Elves, Faeries
Other associations	Midsummer's Eve, Walpurgis
Powers and attributes	Adaptability, authority/leadership, awareness, consecrate/bless, courage, divination, dream work, healing, love, luck, nightmares, peace, protection, psychic abilities, purification, renewal, see faeries
Available for purchase	Essential oil; flower essence; dried leaves; dried flowers; fresh or dried bunches

History and Lore

The ancient Greeks and Romans burned thyme as temple offerings and as a fumigant to purify sacred space. It was also included in ritual fires. Roman soldiers bathed in thyme-scented water to boost their courage. The Egyptians used it in the mummification process and the Greeks included it in

Spells and Rituals

To stimulate energy for divination and psychic work, sprinkle dried flowers on your altar. It will also enhance awareness for clairvoyance. For help in remembering and interpreting dreams, use a dream pillow stuffed with thyme. Wear a fresh sprig to aid in contacting faeries.

Ti Plant

Ti Plant (*Cordyline fruticosa* syn. *C. terminalis*);
    also known as good luck plant, Hawiian ti
    plant, ti tree

The ti plant grows about nine to fifteen feet tall
and three to eight feet wide. Its leathery, lance-
shaped leaves are up to thirty inches long and
grow spirally around the stems. The leaves can
be all green or shades of pale pink, green, purple,
or deep red. Mature plants lose their lower leaves.
Ti plant is also grown as a houseplant. It is sometimes mistakenly called a *Dracaena*.

History and Lore

Throughout Polynesia, the leaves of the ti plant
have been used to wrap food and to make grass
skirts and leis. On Easter Island, the ashes of burnt
leaves were used for tattooing. In Malaysia, it was
planted in graveyards and at the four corners of a
house to keep demons and ghosts away. The ends
of small, leafy branches were used as ceremonial
brushes for sprinkling water during protection rituals. A ti leaf was also worn as a protective amulet.
In Hawaii, ti plants are often grown around household altars and are believed to bring good luck.

Magical Connections

Element/s	Fire
Astrological influence	Jupiter
Deities	Kane-Hekili, Laka, Lono, Pele
Powers and attributes	Healing, luck, protection, purification
Available for purchase	Flower essence; houseplant

Spells and Rituals

Use the spiky end of a leafy branch like a fan to
purify and prepare ritual space or place a small
potted plant on your altar. Braid three narrow
leaves for a good luck charm or wrap a crystal in a
large leaf for a protective amulet.

Toadflax

Yellow Toadflax (*Linaria vulgaris*); also known
    as butter and eggs, dead-man's-bones,
    devil's flax, flaxweed, monkey flower, wild
    snapdragon

Reaching about two feet tall, toadflax resembles
common flax (*Linum usitatissimum*) with its long,
narrow leaves that grow in whorls around the
stems. The flowers are pale yellow to white with
orange throats and grow in clusters at the tops of
the stems. The two upper flower petals are erect;
the three lower petals have a straight spur at the
base.

Caution: Toadflax is mildly toxic if ingested.

History and Lore

Like the snapdragon, the flowers of toadflax can
be squeezed at the sides to open the "mouth."
Legends in England and America about the plant's
common name range from the flowers resembling toads or toad mouths to toads sheltering
underneath the plant. The most plausible is that
"toad" is a corruption of the German word *tot* or
todt (pronounced tote) meaning "dead" and associated with the plant because it was not useful for
weaving as are other types of flax.[144] In Scotland it
was believed that walking around the plant three
times could break a curse. For protection against

144. Watts, *Elsevier's Dictionary of Plant Lore*, 385.

evil in England, a piece of toadflax was threaded into linen clothing or three seeds were threaded onto a length of linen fiber and worn.

Magical Connections

Element/s	Earth, Fire
Astrological influence	Mars, Pluto
Powers and attributes	Defense, hexes, protection
Available for purchase	Flower essence; cut, dried leaves and flowers; seeds

Spells and Rituals

For a protective amulet, place three seeds in a small piece of white linen fabric, and then tie it into a bundle with black thread. To break a hex, burn a few dried leaves as you visualize the smoke dissolving the negativity.

Tobacco

Common Tobacco (*Nicotiana tabacum*); also
　　known as cultivated tobacco, Virginia
　　tobacco
Wild Tobacco (*N. rustica*); also known as Aztec
　　tobacco, rustic tobacco

Growing four to six feet tall, common tobacco has thick, hairy stems and large, broadly oval leaves. The tubular flowers can be white, pink, or red and widen at the end with a ruffle of petals. They grow in a large cluster at the top of the stems. Wild tobacco is smaller, reaching up to five feet tall; it has yellow flowers.

Caution: All parts of these plants are toxic if ingested or smoked.

History and Lore

Both types of tobacco were regarded as sacred by Indigenous peoples throughout the Americas and used for medicinal, spiritual, and magical purposes. The Winnebago, Chippewa, Pilaga of Paraguay, and Yecuana of Venezuela believed that the plant had mystical origins and power. Tapirapé shamans of Brazil, Warao of Venezuela, Pima of Mexico, and Yuman of the American Southwest used it in rituals to induce hallucinations and work with spirit helpers. The early Indigenous tobacco crops had much higher nicotine content than today's plants. The Aztec used tobacco for protection from poisonous snakes and evil spirits and the Chippewa to ward off bad storms. When it arrived in Europe, French fisherman believed tobacco had magical properties for attracting fish. In Ukraine, some regarded tobacco as an herb of the devil. In Scotland, growing or possessing it was enough to link a person with witchcraft.

Magical Connections

Element/s	Earth, Fire
Astrological influence	Virgo; Mars, Moon
Deities	Yacatecuhtli
Powers and attributes	Healing, purification, release, spirit guides/spirits
Available for purchase	Cut or whole dried leaves; seeds

Spells and Rituals

Include dried tobacco in a sachet with healing herbs and charge it with energy in the light of the full moon before giving to someone dealing with illness. Place a pinch of tobacco on your altar as an offering to your chosen deity or when communicating with spirits.

Tonka Bean

Tonka Bean (*Dipteryx odorata* syn. *Coumarouna odorata, Baryosma tongo*); also known as almendro, Brazilian teak, cumaru, Dutch tonka tree, kumaru, tonquin bean

The tonka bean comes from a large rainforest tree that has oblong, glossy leaves, and spiky clusters of two-tone pink flowers. The green fruit looks like a small mango and contains a single seed. The oblong seed/bean is dark brown to black and wrinkled. It has a vanilla-like fragrance with a hint of almond, cinnamon, and fresh-cut hay.

Caution: Tonka beans contain the chemical coumarin, which can cause liver damage if ingested in excessive amounts. The use of tonka beans in food is banned or regulated in a number of countries.

History and Lore

Imported into Europe by the French in the late eighteenth century, tonka beans were a sensation in the perfume industry. It was later used to flavor tobacco and then as a culinary substitute for vanilla in both Europe and America until the mid-twentieth century when coumarin was discovered to be toxic. In the Caribbean, the tonka seed was called *the love wishing bean* and used in spells to attract love. In the American magical tradition of hoodoo, it is used to foster luck and prosperity and to make wishes come true.

Magical Connections

Element/s	Earth, Water
Astrological influence	Jupiter, Venus
Powers and attributes	Courage, love, luck, prosperity/money, wishes
Available for purchase	Whole beans; absolute

Spells and Rituals

To bolster courage for a job interview or important meeting, carry a tonka bean in your pocket or purse. For luck, place three in a small white pouch to use as a talisman. As part of a love spell, write your love interest's name on a piece of paper and sprinkle it with a pinch of grated bean.

Tulip

Common Garden Tulip, Didier's Tulip (*Tulipa gesneriana*)
Wild Tulip, Woodland Tulip (*T. sylvestris*)

The garden tulip has broad, gray-green leaves that tend to flop over rather than stand upright. The cup-shaped flowers come in a range of pinks, reds, oranges, and yellows. The wild tulip has bright yellow, star-shaped flowers with a streak of green outside each pointed petal. It has gray-green, lance-shaped leaves.

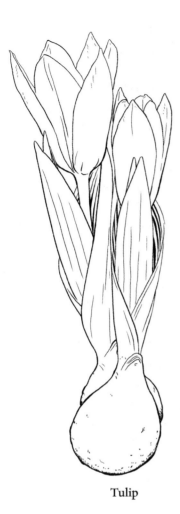

Tulip

History and Lore

According to Roman legend, a Dalmatian nymph was turned into a tulip to escape the advances of Vertumnus, a shape-shifting god of the changing seasons. To the Persians, the tulip was a symbol of passionate love. In addition to erotic associations, it was a symbol of wealth and status in the Turkish Ottoman Empire. Sultan Ahmed III (1673–1736) adored the flowers and held tulip festivals during the full moon. He also reputedly ate the bulbs to enhance his sexual prowess. Into the nineteenth century in Europe, tulips were considered an aphrodisiac. In England tulips were associated with faeries and it was regarded as bad luck to cut the flowers for a bouquet because it would upset them. According to legend, faeries placed their babies in tulips for safekeeping while dancing in the meadows at night.

Magical Connections

Element/s	Earth
Astrological influence	Venus
Magical entities	Elves, faeries, pixies
Powers and attributes	Abundance, banish, courage, divination, dream work, fertility, happiness, love, loyalty/fidelity, luck, peace, prosperity/money, protection, release, sex/sexuality
Available for purchase	Flower essence; dried petals; bulbs

Spells and Rituals

To bolster courage, sprinkle flower essence on a picture of tulips and keep it with you when you need it. Associated with love and sex, use tulip color for various purposes such as red for passion, pink for flirty romance, and white for fertility.

Turmeric

Turmeric (*Curcuma longa*); also known as curcuma, haldi, Indian saffron, Indian yellow root, yellow ginger

Turmeric grows in clumps up to four feet tall; the oblong leaves are veined and pointed. Growing on dense spike-like stalks, the yellow-white or pinkish flowers grow in ascending clusters protected by bracts. The thick, branched rhizome yields a bright yellow-orange spice.

History and Lore

In India turmeric is regarded as sacred and auspicious. Powdered turmeric root is used in Hindu and Buddhist practices as an offering to deities and sprinkled on temple statues to consecrate them. In addition to dyeing priests' robes, dabbing a little turmeric paste on the hem of a new garment was believed to make it auspicious. Reputedly an aphrodisiac, turmeric is an important component of Hindu wedding ceremonies. It is also used in the women's life-cycle ritual at puberty. Because of the belief that supernatural beings did not like the smell of burning turmeric, it was used to scare away ghosts. To ward off evil spirits, turmeric powder is combined with water and dabbed on the cheeks or a small piece of turmeric root is tied with a string and worn as a bracelet.

Magical Connections

Element/s	Earth, fire
Astrological influence	Mars, Mercury, Sun
Deities	Durga, Ganish, Kali, Krishna
Other associations	The otherworld
Powers and attributes	Banish, confidence, consecrate/bless, fertility, healing, hexes, luck, prosperity/money, protection, purification, secrets, spirituality
Available for purchase	Essential oil; whole or powdered root

Spells and Rituals

With strong powers of purification that enhance the flow of energy, use turmeric to protect a magic circle or to clear ritual space. To enhance the effectiveness of a banishing spell or to deter negative magic, sprinkle a circle of turmeric on your altar. Diffuse the essential oil for courage.

Turnip

Turnip, White Turnip (*Brassica rapa* var. *rapa*); also known as neep, Swede, Swedish turnip

The round, fleshy taproot of the turnip is white with a purplish top. Multiple stems sprout directly from the root with elongated, irregularly shaped leaves. Sometimes lobed, the leaves have jagged edges and prominent veining. Clusters of small, four-petaled, yellow flowers grow on branching stems. The narrow seedpods have pointed tips.

History and Lore

The turnip was a valuable vegetable cultivated by the Greeks, Romans, Celts, and Germans. After the introduction of the potato from the New World during the Middle Ages, the turnip became regarded as lower class and famine food. According to Irish legend, a ghost called Stingy Jack carried a turnip lantern. Neepie lanterns (hollowed out turnips with candles) were carved with faces to scare Jack and any other spirits away. The Welsh and Shetland Islanders used turnips for divination to determine a future marriage partner. In India, oil from the plant was used to determine whether someone was a witch. To ward off witches in the American South, turnip seeds were scattered around gardens and homes. Three seeds were used in a charm to protect a turnip crop from pests.

Magical Connections

Element/s	Earth, water
Astrological influence	Gemini, Scorpio; Moon

Other associations	Samhain
Powers and attributes	Love, protection
Available for purchase	Fresh roots; fresh greens; seeds

Spells and Rituals

To enhance lunar energy, carve a turnip with a waxing, full, and waning moon symbol for your esbat altar. Remove the outer skin of a turnip in one long peel to include in a love spell. Place three seeds in a small purple pouch as a protective amulet.

Unicorn Root

Unicorn Root, Ague Root (*Aletris farinosa*); also
  known as blazing star, colic root, crow corn,
  devil's bit, star grass, true unicorn root,
  white colic root

Unicorn root consists of a single, slender stalk
that grows up to three feet tall from a base of
grass-like, yellow-green leaves that spread out
like a star. A few small leaves grow on the lower
half of the stalk. Small, white, urn-shaped flowers grow along the top of the stalk. The outer
surface of the flowers has a rough, mealy texture.

Caution: Do not ingest during pregnancy
or breastfeeding; the fresh root is mildly toxic if
ingested. The plant is endangered or threatened
in some areas, check before gathering in the wild.

History and Lore

In North America, unicorn root was used medicinally by the Catawba, Cherokee, Lumbee, and
Waccamaw Siouan, and was adopted by early
European settlers in Appalachia. In the nineteenth
century it was listed as a therapeutic herb in the
U. S. Pharmacopeia, an annually published compendium of drug information. Through the centuries
this plant has been confused with fairy wand/false
unicorn root (*Chamaelirium luteum*) and the words
false and *true* were variously applied to both plants.

Magical Connections

Element/s	Earth
Astrological influence	Saturn

Magical entities	Unicorns
Powers and attributes	Banish, family and home, happiness, hexes, negativity, protection, psychic abilities, security, success
Available for purchase	Powdered root; seeds. As noted, this plant is endangered in the wild; check vendors' sources.

Spells and Rituals

To banish negativity, sprinkle powdered root around the exterior of your house as you visualize protective unicorns springing up and brandishing their horns. For help in reaching goals, write a few keywords on a picture of unicorn root and tuck it away until they are met.

Uva Ursi

Uva Ursi, Bearberry (*Arctostaphylos uva-ursi*); also known as bear whortleberry, bear's bilberry, bear's grape, crowberry, kinnikinnik, upland cranberry

Uva ursi is a creeping, evergreen shrub with long, trailing stems that form a dense mat. Its tapering, oval leaves are dark green and glossy on the topside. Clusters of drooping, urn-shaped white and pink flowers grow at the ends of branches. The small, round berries are smooth and bright red.

Caution: This plant can be toxic if ingested in high amounts; pregnant women should not use it.

History and Lore

The species and many common names for this plant come from the fact that bears are fond of the fruit. Although Greco-Roman physician Claudius Galen (129–c. 216 CE) mentioned the use of uva ursi, it was mostly ignored until the thirteenth century when it was noted in a Welsh herbal *The Physicians of Myddfai*, which was written by a number of doctors and herbalists. In Iceland, it was believed that carrying a bearberry in the pocket would provide protection from evil spirits and ghosts. The folk name *kinnikinnik* comes from the Algonquin language and means "mixture."[145] The dried leaves were mixed with tobacco in a pipe or smudge pot for spiritually significant ceremonies, to seal a pact, or to subdue a thunderstorm. In the American magical tradition of hoodoo, it is used in mojo bags and candle magic.

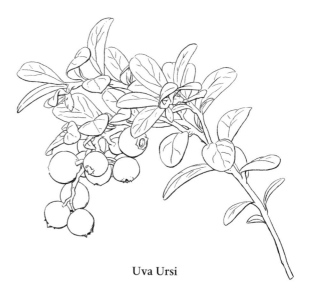

Uva Ursi

145. Watts, *Elsevier's Dictionary of Plant Lore*, 28.

Magical Connections

Element/s	Earth
Astrological influence	Scorpio; Mars, Pluto, Venus
Powers and attributes	Awareness, intuition, protection, psychic abilities, spirit guides/spirits, spirituality, strength
Available for purchase	Flower essence; cut or whole, dried leaves; seeds

Spells and Rituals

In preparation for astral work, place a handful of seeds in a small pouch and hold it against your forehead for a few minutes to open your mind. Prepare a candle with flower essence for aid in connecting with spirit guides as well as the true essence of your own spirit.

Valerian

Common Valerian (*Valeriana officinalis*); also
known as all-heal, cat valerian, garden heliotrope, vandalroot

Reaching up to five feet tall, valerian has dark green, deeply lobed base leaves and lance-shaped leaves on the stems. The small flowers are white or pale pink and grow in small, umbrella-shaped clusters. The sweet fragrance of the flowers is usually overwhelmed by the odor of the leaves and stems, which have been described as smelling like dirty socks.

History and Lore

Valerian was used medicinally by the Greeks and Romans and Greco-Roman physician Galen was the first to note its sedative properties. The Anglo-Saxons used it medicinally and to deter witches. In the Balkans, it was sewn into children's clothing to ward off witches. In medieval Britain and Europe, valerian was believed to protect against the plague. Despite the plant's odor, it was regarded as an invitation to romance and in Wales women wore it in their bodices in the hopes of holding a man's attention. In England, wearing a sprig was supposed to attract a lover or sometimes a number of suitors. The root was placed in cupboards to scent clothing and was sometimes referred to as English orris. The fragrance appeals to cats and rodents and according to some accounts the Pied Piper used valerian to lure the rats away from the city of Hamelin, Germany.

Magical Connections

Element/s	Water
Astrological influence	Scorpio, Virgo; Mercury, Venus
Deities	Epona, Kupala
Powers and attributes	Challenges/obstacles, consecrate/bless, family and home, healing, love, peace, prosperity/money, protection, purification, secrets, spirit guides/spirits, truth
Available for purchase	Essential oil; flower essence; cut, dried root; ground root; seeds

Spells and Rituals

To purify magic tools, store them with a sachet of seeds. To protect the home and invite prosperity, hang a sprig of flowers over an exterior door. Prepare a candle with the essential oil to aid in working with spirit guides. Prepare a love charm with the flower essence.

Vanilla

Common Vanilla (*Vanilla planifolia* syn. *V. fragrans*); also known as Bourbon vanilla, flat-leaved vanilla, Mexican vanilla

The vanilla orchid is a vine with fleshy, aerial roots that cling to trees. The waxy, greenish yellow flowers are trumpet shaped and only last a day. Its bright green leaves are flat and pointed and its seedpods are long and thin. The vanilla "bean" is technically a pod: A pod holds seeds; a bean is a seed.

Caution: Handling the vanilla plant may cause skin irritation.

History and Lore

Although the phrase *plain vanilla* means boring or simple, vanilla's fragrance and taste has been adored and considered exotic for centuries. Either the Maya or Totonac are believed to have domesticated the plant in Mexico. According to a Totonac legend, the daughter of a fertility goddess transformed herself into a vanilla vine to be a reminder of happiness and sacred love. The Aztec used vanilla to flavor chocolate. When the Spanish imported vanilla to Europe in the early sixteenth century, the French and English went crazy over it. Vanilla was a luxury item and regarded as an aphrodisiac in Elizabethan England. The word *vanilla* comes from the Spanish *vainilla*, meaning "little vagina."[146]

Magical Connections

Element/s	Water
Astrological influence	Libra, Scorpio, Taurus; Venus
Magical entities	Faeries
Powers and attributes	Balance/harmony, focus, happiness, inspiration, love, luck, peace, sex/sexuality, success
Available for purchase	Flower essence; whole or powdered "beans"; absolute; extract

Spells and Rituals

Dab a little vanilla absolute behind your ears before meditation to bring your body into balance and your mind to peace. To aid in working with faeries or to just feel a little magical, mix up

---

146. Morton, *Cupboard Love*, 320.

a cup of fairy mead: warm milk with honey and a drop of vanilla extract.

Vervain

Common Vervain, Verbena (*Verbena officinalis*); also known as Druid's weed, enchanter's weed, herb of grace, holy herb, vervine, wizard's herb

Reaching up to three feet tall and wide, vervain is a sprawling, branching plant. The base leaves are lobed, heavily veined, and toothed. Its small, lavender or mauve, five-petaled flowers grow on purple-tinged spikes.

History and Lore

From the ancient Greeks and Romans to the Druids of Britain, vervain was regarded as sacred and used for consecrating ritual or temple spaces and for prophecy. It was also regarded as sacred by the Egyptians, Persians, and Germanic peoples. The Persians used vervain as an aphrodisiac. It was used in love potions and charms in England, France, the Netherlands, Germany, and Italy. Vervain was also believed to offer protection and was planted on graves in Romania to keep the deceased from becoming a vampire. In France it was used for protection from witches, lightning, demons, and thieves. The herb was sewn into baby clothes in Scotland for protection against faeries. While vervain was used against witches, in Britain and the Netherlands it was also believed to be used by them, too. In Wales it was known as wizard's herb and in the Isle of Man it was sometimes known as Nan Wade after a famous local wise woman and healer. Vervain was also used as a good luck charm in the Isle of Man.

Magical Connections

Element/s	Air, earth, fire
Astrological influence	Capricorn, Gemini, Sagittarius; Sun, Venus
Deities	Aphrodite, Cerridwen, Demeter, Diana, Epona, Hera, Hermes, Isis, Juno, Jupiter, Mars, Mercury, Persephone, Thor, Venus, Zeus
Magical entities	Faeries
Other associations	Litha
Powers and attributes	Abundance, banish, consecrate/bless, defense, divination, dream work, healing, hexes, inspiration, love, luck, manifest, negativity, peace, prophecy, prosperity/money, protection, purification, see faeries, sex/sexuality, spirit guides/spirits
Available for purchase	Flower essence; essential oil; cut, dried leaves and stems; extract

Spells and Rituals

To attract abundance and prosperity, grow vervain in your garden or scatter dried leaves around your property. Place leaves on your altar to empower rituals. To combat negative magic, cast a circle of dried leaves, as part of a spell for defense and protection.

Vetch

Common Vetch, Garden Vetch (*Vicia sativa*); also known as fitches, poor man's peas, tare, thetch

Vetch is a semi-erect, climbing plant. It has flat, elliptical leaflets that are indented at the tip with a small spine-like projection. The leaflets grow along stems that end in tendrils. Pink to purple flowers grow from the upper leaf axils. The upper flower petal is broad and notched in the center; oval and wing like, the two lower petals are often a darker color. Below the leaf axil is a pair of leafy appendages with two or more sharp teeth. The flat pea pod is light brown when ripe.

History and Lore

Vetch seeds have been identified in Neolithic and Bronze Ages sites in Bulgaria, Hungary, Slovakia, and Turkey. Since ancient Roman and Egyptian times, vetch was grown for animal fodder but consumed by humans during famine. Pulses (peas, lentils, beans, and vetch) were important crops during the Middle Ages throughout Europe and Britain. Vetch is so hardy that it was regarded as indestructible in eighteenth-century England. Vetch flowers can be found as decorative illustrations in medieval manuscripts of the Netherlands, Germany, and England. The words *vetch* and *Vicia* come from the Latin *vincire*, which means "to twist or bind" and describes the plant's growing pattern.[147]

Magical Connections

Element/s	Air
Astrological influence	Gemini, Virgo; Moon
Powers and attributes	Bind, love, loyalty/fidelity, negativity
Available for purchase	Flower essence; seeds

147. Martin, *Wildflower Folklore*, 52.

Spells and Rituals

Wrap a length of vetch vine around a broomstick or other item used in a handfasting ceremony as you pledge your love and devotion to each other. Of course, vetch is perfect to boost the energy of a binding spell.

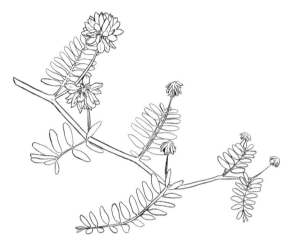

Vetchling

Vetchling

Bitter Vetch, Bitter Vetchling (*Lathyrus linifolius* syn. *L. montanus*); also known as fairies' corn, heath pea
Sweet Pea (*L. odoratus*); also known as wild pea

Also known as peavines, vetchlings are slender, climbing plants with wings, protrusions that form along the sides of the stems. Growing in clusters, their distinctive flowers have two upright and two lower petals. Bitter vetch has pointed leaves and veined flowers that are pink to red or purple and turn blue as they age. Sweet pea has oblong leaves and tendrils that help it climb. Its highly fragrant flowers can be white, pink, purple, blue, violet, red, lavender, or orange.

Caution: All parts of bitter vetch, especially the seeds, are toxic if ingested; sweet pea seeds are toxic if ingested.

History and Lore

While bitter vetch roots have been used to flavor whiskey in the Hebrides and the Scottish Highlands, in the Isle of Mull the roots were chewed to prevent drunkenness. In France, sweet pea flowers in a wedding bouquet were believed to make people speak only truth to the bride. According to Irish legend, faeries used the small tubers of bitter vetch as food. The fragrant sweet pea flowers were said to be faery favorites.

Magical Connections

Element/s	Water
Astrological influence	Gemini; Mars, Moon, Venus (sweet pea)
Magical entities	Faeries
Powers and attributes	Balance/harmony, courage, creativity, emotions, family and home, happiness, love, loyalty/fidelity, negativity, peace, psychic abilities, relationships, skills, spirituality, strength, truth, wisdom
Available for purchase	Flower essence; seeds

Spells and Rituals

In a new home, place a few sweet pea seeds in various locations around the house to foster a sense of belonging and to invite new friends. For aid in developing new skills, especially psychic ones, place a picture of bitter vetch where you will see it as you practice.

Vetiver

Vetiver (*Chrysopogon zizanioides* syn. *Vetiveria zizanioides*); also known as khus, moras, vetivergrass, vetivert

Vetiver is a tropical grass that grows in wide clumps and reaches about five or six feet tall. The erect, narrow leaves have rough margins. The small, brownish purple flowers grow in tufts at the tops of long, straight stems. The fragrant roots can grow ten feet deep.

History and Lore

The large, fibrous roots of vetiver have been woven into household items and used in perfumery in India for several thousand years. When used as floor mats, it was customary to sprinkle them with water to cool and scent the air. Vetiver is mentioned in the *Atharva-Veda*, an ancient Sanskrit text concerning the curative powers of herbs that also contains hymns (possibly charms) for success and love. Vetiver leaves were made into garlands for adorning statues in Hindu temples. Known as the oil of tranquility in India, vetiver is commonly used in modern aromatherapy blends.[148] In the American magical tradition of hoodoo, it is used in oil blends for hexes, quickly bringing about changes, and to strengthen spirituality.

Magical Connections

Element/s	Earth, fire
Astrological influence	Capricorn, Libra, Taurus; Jupiter, Saturn, Venus
Deities	Ganesh, Oshun, Shiva, Yemaya

---

148. Neil, *Gardener's Latin* 135

Powers and attributes	Defense, emotions, family and home, hexes, love, luck, peace, prosperity/money, protection, secrets, spirituality
Available for purchase	Essential oil; hydrosol; incense; basket

Spells and Rituals

Include vetiver in defensive magic to amplify your energy and break a hex. Sprinkle the hydrosol around your home to foster prosperity and protection. Diffuse the essential oil to calm emotional turmoil. Vetiver promotes balance between the spiritual and mundane.

Violet

Common Blue Violet (*Viola sororia*); also known
   as gypsy violet, meadow violet, wood violet
Sweet Violet, English Violet (*V. odorata*); also
   known as garden violet, sweet pansy

Violet flowers consist of five rounded petals: two upper petals, two on the sides, and one lower. The leaves are wide, oval to heart shaped, and gently serrated. The flowers of the common blue violet are bluish violet or white with purple veining. The flowers of the sweet violet are most often dark purple but occasionally white.

History and Lore

From ancient Roman through medieval times, the dark purple color of violet flowers linked them with death and they were placed on graves in commemoration. However, because of the seductively alluring scent, the Greeks and Romans also associated the sweet violet with love. The Greeks scattered them across nuptial beds; the Romans added them to wine. Centuries later in Europe, dried violets were sent as mementos in love letters. In Germany, it was believed that the first three violets of spring brushed lightly across the eyes provided protection from the evil eye. Although violets were used for healing, in parts of Germany and France it was believed that smelling violets would cause madness. Despite any negative association, violets have been so popular that they were sold in the markets of ancient Athens and on the streets of Victorian London.

Violet

Magical Connections

Element/s	Air, water
Astrological influence	Aquarius, Cancer, Libra, Scorpio, Taurus, Virgo; Saturn, Venus
Deities	Aphrodite, Attis, Cybele, Demeter, Jupiter, Persephone, Venus, Zeus
Magical entities	Elves, faeries
Other associations	Ostara
Powers and attributes	Banish, changes/transitions, death/funeral practices, emotions, happiness, healing, hexes, hope, love, luck, negativity, peace (common blue), protection, psychic abilities, relationships, sex/sexuality, wishes
Available for purchase	Flower essence; dried violet leaves; dried flowers; seeds

Spells and Rituals

For help in dealing with major transitions and unsettled emotions caused by them, gaze at a picture of violets as you sit quietly in front of your altar. As part of a banishing spell or to help break negative magic, burn a few dried leaves in your cauldron.

Walnut

Black Walnut (*Juglans nigra*); also known as
   American black walnut, eastern black walnut
English Walnut (*J. regia*); also known as Persian
   walnut

These trees have lance-shaped leaves and long,
slender male catkins that hang from the branches
while the female catkins grow on short spikes near
the ends of the branches. The round nuts of the
black walnut are encased in yellow-green husks.
The English walnut produces the familiar brown
nuts sold in stores.

History and Lore

According to Roman naturalist and historian Pliny
the Elder, walnuts were associated with fertility
because they resembled testicles. As a symbol of
marriage, walnuts were customarily scattered on
tables at Roman wedding feasts. In his writings,
Catalan physician and alchemist Arnold de Villeneuve (1240–1311) noted that walnuts were an
aphrodisiac and used in sexual magic. While Italians believed that demons lived near walnut trees
and witches gathered under them on Midsummer's
Eve, the French gathered walnut leaves before
dawn on Midsummer's Day for protection against
lightning. In the Middle East, walnut root and bark
were combined with henna (*Lawsonia inermis*) for
protection against supernatural forces. In Switzerland, a small, perfectly formed walnut was carried
for good luck.

Magical Connections

Element/s	Air, fire
Astrological influence	Gemini, Leo, Virgo; Jupiter, Sun
Deities	Aphrodite, Apollo, Artemis, Astarte, Diana, Dionysus, Freyr, Jove, Jupiter, Persephone, Pomona, Rhea, Thor, Zeus
Magical entities	Elves
Other associations	Midsummer's Eve, Yule
Powers and attributes	Abundance, changes/transitions, clarity, fertility, healing, inspiration, love, luck, manifest, prosperity/money, protection, sex/sexuality, spirit guides/spirits, success, transformation, wishes
Available for purchase	Nuts; walnut oil; flower essence

Spells and Rituals

For a love spell, separate a walnut shell, write your name and the other person's name on each half, and then tie them back together with red thread. Raise energy for healing by burning a few dried leaves. To achieve clarity for making decisions, hold a leaf in each hand while meditating.

Water Lily

American White Water Lily (*Nymphaea odorata*); also known as fragrant water lily

White Water Lily (*N. alba*); also known as white lotus

Yellow Pond Lily (*Nuphar lutea*); also known as cow lily, spatter dock

The white water lily has round leaves that are reddish when young, then turn medium green. The American white water lily has dark green leaves that are round to heart shaped. The flowers of both are bowl shaped. The yellow pond lily has waxy, yellow flowers that are cup shaped. Its leaves are oval.

Caution: The yellow pond lily is toxic if ingested.

History and Lore

While the ancient Egyptians sometimes referred to the white water lily as a lotus, they also called it *bride of the Nile*. Representing the spiritual power of the pharaohs, the fresh flowers were sometimes placed in graves. In India, the water lily was a symbol of the moon and associated with Shiva. In Europe, both the white and yellow water lilies were regarded as magical plants. According to German lore, water faeries called *nixies* hid underneath them. In the Rhineland, it was believed that picking a water lily while reciting the appropriate incantation could take away a witch's power. According to Scottish legend, faeries used water lilies to strengthen magical spells.

Magical Connections

Element/s	Water
Astrological influence	Cancer; Moon, Sun
Deities	Hathor, Horus, Isis, Osiris, Ra, Shiva
Magical entities	Faeries, nixies

Powers and attributes	Clarity, communication, courage, growth, happiness, inspiration, love, luck, manifest, peace, protection, psychic abilities, purification
Available for purchase	Flower essence

Spells and Rituals

When you want to draw something into your life, write keywords on a picture of a water lily, and then carry it with you from one full moon to the next. To enhance psychic skills, dab a little flower essence on your third eye chakra.

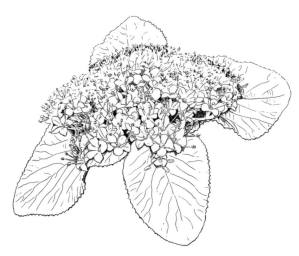

Wayfaring Tree

Wayfaring Tree

Wayfaring Tree (*Viburnum lantana*); also known as coven tree, hoar withy, wayfarer, whip crop

The wayfaring tree is a large, multi-stemmed shrub. Its oval slightly pointed leaves are heavily veined and serrated. The dull green color and gray downy hairs on the underside of the leaves gives them a dusty appearance. In autumn the leaves turn reddish to purplish. Creamy white flowers grow in wide, flat-topped clusters and develop into berry-like fruit. The green fruit turns red, and then black when ripe. All three colors may appear on the bush at the same time.

Caution: The leaves and fruit are mildly toxic if ingested.

History and Lore

This shrub's common name comes from its frequent location in hedgerows along pathways in England and because of its somewhat dusty appearance, like someone who has been traveling dirt roads. Like willow, its long flexible branches were used to make baskets and to bind sheaves or other agricultural items. The supple branches were popular for making whips and thicker ones for arrow shafts. The wood was used as pins to fasten oxen yokes and believed to provide magical protection for the animals. Planting the tree close to a house and cowshed reputedly protected both family and livestock from goblins and witches.

Magical Connections

Element/s	Air
Astrological influence	Moon
Powers and attributes	Bind, defense, protection
Available for purchase	Flower essence; seeds

Spells and Rituals

Carve the rune *raido* (it resembles the letter *R*) on a piece of branch to carry as a travel charm. Tie a long, supple branch into a circle to place on your altar for esbat rituals. Also use thin branches for knot magic and binding spells.

Willow

European Willow, White Willow (*Salix alba*); also known as European willow, withy

Pussy Willow, American Willow (*S. discolor*); also known as sallow, sally

Weeping Willow (*S. babylonica*)

Willow trees have narrow, lance-shaped leaves. The white undersides of the European willow leaves give the tree its whitish appearance. The pussy willow has fuzzy, gray catkins that resemble the pads of cat's feet. The weeping willow is widely loved for its long, graceful branches that sweep to the ground.

History and Lore

In Ireland, a solitary pussy willow was regarded as a faery tree. On the moors of Somerset, it was said that willows had the ability to follow people at night. Because sawn willow wood was used for gallows, builders in the Fenlands of eastern England used hand-cut willow. In addition to witches prowling around willows, German lore associates the tree with the will-o'-the-wisp, a sprite carried by or existing as a mist of light. Knot magic with willow branches was believed to have the power to kill an enemy. For healing cattle in central Germany, farmers touched their sick cattle with an elf's rod, a willow branch with three twigs left on one end. Associated with immortality, the Chinese used willow branches to honor the dead. In Japan, willow was associated with ghosts. While willow was a symbol of death to the Victorians, it also had the power to relieve grief.

Magical Connections

Element/s	Fire, water
Astrological influence	Aries, Capricorn, Pisces, Taurus; Moon, Venus
Deities	Artemis, Athena, Bel/Belenus, Brigid, Ceres, Cerridwen, Circe, Danu, Demeter, Diana, Hecate, Hera, Hermes, Ishtar, Juno, Loki, Luna, Mercury, the Morrigan, Osiris, Persephone, Poseidon, Rhiannon, Saturn, Zeus
Magical entities	Elves, faeries, water sprites, will-o-the-wisp
Ogham	Sail ᚄ
Other associations	The afterlife, the otherworld, Beltane, Samhain
Powers and attributes	Adaptability, bind, death/funeral practices, divination, fertility, healing, inspiration, intuition, knowledge, loss/sorrow (weeping), love, prophecy, protection, sex/sexuality, spirit guides/spirits, strength
Available for purchase	Pieces or powdered bark; willow baskets; flower essence

Spells and Rituals

As part of a binding spell, tie a long, thin branch into a knot. To help draw down lunar energy, place a circle of pussy willow catkins around the base of a white candle. Sprinkle willow leaves on a loved one's grave to wish them well in the afterlife.

Witch Hazel

Common Witch Hazel (*Hamamelis virginiana*); also known as American witch hazel, fall-blooming witch hazel, snapping alder, snapping hazelnut, winterbloom

Blooming in the autumn or winter after the leaves have dropped, witch hazel's yellow flowers look like crinkled ribbons tied to the bare branches. The bright green leaves are oblong and coarsely toothed. The greenish seed capsules turn light brown and when ripe they burst open shooting seeds up to twenty feet away.

History and Lore
Like wych elm, the word *witch* in this plant's name comes from Old English meaning "to bend" in reference to its pliant branches.[149] Because of its leaves, early settlers in North America confused it with hazel. In the American Colonies, dowsing became known as water witching and witch hazel diving rods reputedly had the power to reveal witches as well as underground water. European settlers learned and adopted the medicinal applications of witch hazel used by the Cherokee, Iroquois, Chippewa, Mohegan, and Potawatomi. In medicine ceremonies, the Menominee used the seeds as sacred beads.

Magical Connections

Element/s	Earth, fire, water
Astrological influence	Libra; Saturn, Sun
Ogham	Emancholl / Amhancholl also called Mór ▦
Other associations	Samhain

149. Martin, *The Folklore of Trees & Shrubs*, 207.

Powers and attributes	Ancestors, banish, challenges/obstacles, communication, courage, divination, healing, inspiration, knowledge, loss/sorrow, love, loyalty/fidelity, peace, protection, release, sex/sexuality, wisdom
Available for purchase	Witch hazel; witch hazel water; dried leaves in pieces or powdered; dried bark

Spells and Rituals
To clear energy for ritual and magic, sprinkle a little witch hazel water beforehand. For mental focus, place a twig on your altar or table during divination sessions. For help in letting go of something or someone, scatter a handful of dried leaves outdoors as you visualize the release.

Woad
Woad (*Isatis tinctoria*); also known as dyer's woad, glastum, pastel

Growing three to five feet tall and three feet wide, woad has a base rosette of gray-green, lance shaped leaves. Smaller, arrow-shaped leaves grow on the flower stalks, which branch near the top. The yellow, four-petaled flowers grow in small clusters. The flat, oblong seedpods are dark brown to black and suspended from small stalks.

Caution: Regarded as an invasive species in some areas.

History and Lore
Woad is most commonly known from Roman descriptions of Britons and Picts using it as war paint to create a fearsome appearance in battle. Used as a dye plant by the Egyptians and Romans, woad was the dominant source of blue dye for

many centuries. The Egyptians used it to color cloth for clothing and mummy wrappings. Woad was used medicinally by the Greeks and Romans to treat wounds and the Anglo-Saxons favored it for snakebites. In the Hallstatt culture of Central Europe (the ancestors of British Celts) it was used for dyeing cloth. During the Middle Ages throughout Europe, woad was used as a pigment by artists. An important crop plant in Ireland, eighth-century law noted that as part of a divorce settlement a woman was due half of any woad held by the couple. Meaning "place where woad grows," the name *Glastonbury* was derived from the ancient Celtic and British names for woad, *glas* and *glasto*, respectively.[150]

Magical Connections

Element/s	Fire
Astrological influence	Mars, Pluto, Saturn
Powers and attributes	Courage, prosperity/money, protection, strength
Available for purchase	Dried leaves; seeds; powdered woad pigment I have found conflicting information about using woad for any type of tattooing. Because it is an astringent, using it on broken skin may be painful.

Spells and Rituals

Include dried leaves in a spell to boost courage and give you the strength of a warrior to deal with whatever life throws at you. Sprinkle a pinch of dried leaves or powdered woad in the cardinal directions on your property to invite prosperity

---

150. Loudon, *British Wild Flowers*, 51 and Watts, *Elsevier's Dictionary of Plant Lore*, 431.

Wood Sorrel

Common Wood Sorrel (*Oxalis acetosella*); also known as evening twilight, fairy bells, shamrock, sour trefoil

Wood sorrel creates a soft carpet of color with its white flowers that sometimes have a blush of pink. They are lightly veined with purple or lilac. When the cup-like flowers droop as they close at night they look more like bells. After blooming, wood sorrel produces a second type of flower that is bud-like and stays hidden under the leaves. The shamrock-like leaves fold up at night and when it rains.

History and Lore

In parts of England, wood sorrel was a weather forecaster. An abundance of flowers meant a rainy season and few flowers meant it would be dry. Because of its leaves, wood sorrel was believed by some to be the true shamrock. In Ireland, clovers in the *Trifolium* genus are shamrocks; however, like the four-leaf clover, a four-leaf wood sorrel was regarded as a lucky charm. A leaf worn in a shoe was said to enable a person to see faeries. In France, if two lovers stepped on wood sorrel while out for a walk, their marriage plans would be delayed. In Wales, faeries and elves were said to ring the flowers like bells at midnight as a call to revelry.

Magical Connections

Element/s	Earth
Astrological influence	Taurus; Venus
Magical entities	Elves, faeries

Powers and attributes	Defense, happiness, healing, luck, peace, prosperity/money, protection, secrets, see faeries
Available for purchase	Flower essence; cut, dried leaves; seeds

Spells and Rituals

More than anything, wood sorrel is a faery plant and you may find contact easy to establish in places where it grows. The plant's three heart-shaped leaflets are ideal to use on your altar when honoring triple goddesses. Like a four-leaf clover, a wood sorrel leaf can be carried for luck.

Wormwood

Wormwood (*Artemisia absinthium*); also known as absinthe, the green fairy, madderwort, sagewort, wormit

Wormwood is an erect, bushy plant that can reach up to five feet tall. Its lacy, deeply lobed leaves are gray-green on top and whitish underneath. They have a strong, sage-like odor when crushed. The small, yellowish flowers are disc shaped and grow in clusters.

Caution: All parts of the plant are toxic if ingested and fatal in large amounts.

History and Lore

Wormwood was used medicinally by the ancient Egyptians, Romans, Greeks, Arabs, and Celts. The Romans tied long stems around the waist like a belt for protection during travel. Into the twentieth century, a sprig was placed on a car windshield in Italy for the same purpose. During the Middle Ages, Germans used wormwood to decorate funeral biers and gravestones. In addition to exorcism, bunches were hung above doors for protection from sorcery, witches, and evil spirits. Sprigs were hung on children's beds to protect them from bewitchment and elves.

Along with marjoram and thyme, wormwood was used in love charms in England. It was also believed to ward off sea dragons. The Romans used it for making wine, before hops were popular the English used it to flavor beer, and in the eighteenth century the French created an absinthe liqueur that became known as the green fairy.

Wormwood

Magical Connections

Element/s	Fire
Astrological influence	Cancer, Gemini; Mars, Pluto
Deities	Artemis, Diana, Isis
Other associations	The afterlife; Midsummer's Eve
Powers and attributes	Banish, bind, challenges/obstacles, death/funeral practices, divination, hexes, love, loyalty/fidelity, protection, psychic abilities, purification, renewal, sex/sexuality, spirit guides/spirits
Available for purchase	Flower essence; cut, dried leaves and stems; seeds

Spells and Rituals

To banish an unwanted spirit, hang a sachet of dried leaves in the highest place in your home or wherever you sense its presence. To aid psychic abilities during divination, sprinkle a little flower essence on your tools or altar cloth. Include dried leaves when countering negative magic.

Yarrow

Common Yarrow (*Achillea millefolium*); also
   known as angel flower, bloodwort, devil's
   nettle, devil's plaything, dog daisy, knight's
   milfoil, thousand leaf, woundwort

Yarrow's fern-like leaves give the plant a delicate,
lacy appearance. Its small, white, yellow, or pink
flowers grow in clusters of flat-topped flower heads.
The plant has a pleasant, sweet-herby aroma.

History and Lore

Famed for treating wounds, yarrow was used
medicinally by the ancient Greeks and Chinese
and almost everywhere else ever since. The
ancient Chinese used yarrow stems as *I Ching*
divination sticks. Throughout the British Isles
yarrow was used for marriage prophecy and to
find out if a lover was faithful. It was also used
as a love charm. On Midsummer's Eve yarrow
was hung over doorways and on baby cradles to
avert disease and spells. In England, it was strewn
across thresholds to keep witches from entering
a house, in the Scottish Highlands it was a charm
against the evil eye, and in Ireland against faery
mischief. The Anglo-Saxons wore it as an amulet
to keep poisonous animals at bay. In the Hebrides, brushing yarrow over the eyes was said to
bring second sight. When used for healing in Ireland, it had to be cut with a black-handled knife.
Carried in the pocket, yarrow was believed to
bring luck and protection against enemies.

Magical Connections

Element/s	Air, water
Astrological influence	Cancer, Gemini, Libra; Venus

Deities	Achilles, Cernunnos
Magical entities	Faeries
Other associations	Midsummer's Eve
Powers and attributes	Awareness, banish, consecrate/bless, courage, defense, divination, dream work, healing, hexes, intuition, love, loyalty/fidelity, negativity, prophecy, protection, psychic abilities, purification, relationships, see faeries, spirit guides/spirits
Available for purchase	Essential oil; flower essence; cut, dried leaves and stems; seeds

Spells and Rituals

Prepare ritual space by diffusing essential oil. Sprinkle a handful of dried leaves on your altar or table to stimulate intuition and open awareness for divination and psychic work, especially clairvoyance. Place a sprig on your altar for aid in working with spirits.

Yew

American Yew (*Taxus canadensis*); also known as Canada yew

English Yew (*T. baccata*); also known as common yew

Yews are evergreen trees with multiple trunks and reddish bark. They have dark green, needle-like leaves that are glossy on top and gray to pale green underneath. The red, cup-shaped berry contains seeds, which ripen in the autumn.

Caution: The seeds and foliage are toxic if ingested and can be fatal.

History and Lore

Associated with the underworld and death by the Greeks and Romans yew was also symbolic of hope and rebirth. The tree was sacred to the Celts of Gaul and the Druids in Britain. According to Greek myth, Artemis poisoned her arrows with yew sap as did Celtic warriors. The English and Welsh favored yew wood for longbows. French mourners carried yew branches at funerals, the English tucked sprigs of yew in burial shrouds. To the people of northern Europe, the yew was associated with rune magic and used for protection against witches. An amulet of yew wood was worn by Germanic people for protection from bewitchment. Placing yew twigs at the entrance to caves was believed to drive dwarfs away. In the Fenlands of eastern England, witches were said to lurk near yews. The Slavs and Bosnians used yew for protection from sorcery, the Spanish for safety from lightning, and Hebrideans from fire. In Welsh legend faeries could be seen when they walked under a yew tree, and in Scotland they were said to live under them.

Magical Connections

Element/s	Air, fire, water
Astrological influence	Capricorn; Jupiter, Mars, Saturn
Deities	Artemis, Bacchus, Badb, Banba, Cailleach Bheur, the Dagda, Dionysus, Dôn, the Furies, Hecate, Hermes, Holle, Loki, Lugh, Odin, Saturn
Magical entities	Elves, faeries
Ogham	Iodhadh ⵌ

Other associations	The afterlife, the otherworld, Ostara, Samhain, Yule
Powers and attributes	Ancestors, changes/transitions, communication, death/funeral practices, divination, dream work, hexes, justice/legal matters, knowledge, loss/sorrow, negativity, nightmares, protection, psychic abilities, see faeries, skills, spirit guides/spirits
Available for purchase	Boxes and other objects made from the wood; flower essence

Spells and Rituals

For aid in warding off bad dreams, place a sachet of dried berries on your bedside table. Invite your ancestors to be close on Samhain by writing their names on a picture of a yew and placing it on your sabbat altar. Include yew berries on your altar during divination.

Yucca

Adam's Needle (*Yucca filamentosa*); also known as devil's shoestring, needle palm, Spanish bayonet

Banana Yucca (*Y. baccata*); also known as blue yucca, datil, soapweed

The banana yucca has sword-like, spine-tipped leaves up to thirty inches long and pendant, fleshy white flowers with a reddish purple tinge. The fruit looks like little green bananas. Adam's Needle has pointed, blue-green leaves that are dagger-like and up to three feet long. The six-foot flower stalk has loose, nodding clusters of white, bell-shaped flowers.

History and Lore

In addition to food and medicine, the Indigenous people of the American Southwest and Mexico have used the yucca plant, especially its fibers, to make a wide range of domestic goods such as sandals, rope, and baskets. Some of these tribes include the Hopi, Mescalaro, Zuni, and Pima. The long, central yucca stalks were used in rituals and various other parts of the plant served as offerings to deities. Ribbons of fiber were worn as bracelets and anklets. The Tewa people used the banana yucca for name-giving ceremonies. The Navajo used roots to make a natural soap for ceremonial purification and the leaf fibers to make masks for particular rites.

Magical Connections

Element/s	Earth, fire
Astrological influence	Mars, Pluto
Deities	Gaia, Pachamama
Powers and attributes	Awareness, hexes, negativity, protection, purification, transformation
Available for purchase	Flower essence; cut or whole dried root.

Spells and Rituals

Pull fibers from the leaves to make a wreath for your front door and decorate it with other plants associated with protection. Two leaves can be hung like crossed swords as a protective talisman. Include the root in spells to counter jinxes or to purify ritual space.

Zedoary

Zedoary (*Curcuma zedoaria* syn. *Amomum zedoaria*); also known as Indian arrowroot, white turmeric, wild turmeric

Growing in clumps up to three feet tall, zedoary has broad, lance-shaped leaves with a reddish purple center vein. A red, pinkish white, or greenish white cone-like structure grows on separate spikes and holds the tubular white or yellow flowers within. Its rhizome looks like turmeric and tastes like ginger.

History and Lore

Considered an aphrodisiac by the Arabs, zedoary was introduced into Europe in the sixth century. Derived from the Arabic *zadwar*, it was called *sideware* in Old English and used medicinally by the Anglo-Saxons.[151] Zedoary was used to cure elf enchantment and elf-siden, which is thought to refer to nightmares possibly of a sexual nature. By Hildegard von Bingen's time, zedoary was known as zituar and she recommended it as a powerful healing herb. During the seventeenth century in Britain and Europe it was used against the plague. English poet Geoffrey Chaucer (1340–1400) mentioned adding zedoary to ale. German scholar and occult writer Heinrich Cornelius Agrippa noted that it was used in medieval magic.

Magical Connections

Element/s	Fire
Astrological influence	Mars, Sun

151. Quattrocchi, *CRC World Dictionary of Medicinal and Poisonous Plants*, 4006; Pollington, Leechcraft, 167.

Powers and attributes	Healing, hexes, nightmares, renewal, support
Available for purchase	Essential oil; fresh root; powdered root

Spells and Rituals

Sprinkle a circle of powdered root on your altar to boost the power of healing rituals. Conclude by sweeping the powder up with your hands, taking it outside, and blowing it away. Hang a sachet of dried root on your bedpost to ward off bad dreams.

Zinnia

Common Zinnia (*Zinnia elegans*); also known as
    elegant zinnia, garden zinnia
Wild Zinnia (*Z. grandiflora* syn. *Crassina grandiflora*); also known as plains zinnia, prairie zinnia, Rocky Mountain zinnia

Reaching up to four feet tall, common zinnia is an upright, bushy plant with hairy, branching stems. The leaves are oval to lance shaped. The flowers may have one or several rows of petals leaving the center visible or they may have many rows of petals that hide the center. Colors include shades of pink, rose, red, yellow, orange, lavender, green, and white. The wild zinnia is a low-growing plant with a woody base, branching stems, and needle-like leaves. The flowers are bright yellow with an orange center. The petals have a slight notch at the tips and curve back away from the center.

History and Lore

Healers in Brazil used common zinnia in ritual baths as cures and a leaf placed on top of a person's head was believed to be a remedy for madness. The Aztec held the zinnia in high regard and cultivated several varieties. In addition to its use as dye and paint, the Navajo and Zuni used zinnias as medicinal and ritual herbs and as an important fumigant for healing sweat baths. The zinnia is regarded as a symbol of wisdom by some Pueblo tribes.

Zinnia

Magical Connections

Element/s	Air
Astrological influence	Sun
Powers and attributes	Abundance, healing, purification, strength, wisdom
Available for purchase	Flower essence; dried flowers; seeds

Spells and Rituals

Grow zinnias in your garden or in a pot on your
porch to attract abundance to your home. Place
a vase of flowers on your altar to aid in seeking
wisdom. The petals of common zinnia can be
used magically by color.

Appendix A
Powers and Attributes

This listing provides a quick reference to help you find the plants to suit your purposes.

Abundance

Acacia, African violet, allspice, almond, apple, avens, avocado, barberry and Oregon grape, bay, bedstraw, beech, blackberry, bloodroot, bracken, bryony, buttercup, cactus, camellia, catnip, cattail, cedar, chamomile, cherry, chestnut (sweet), chicory, coconut, comfrey, crabapple, date, elder, fig, figwort, flax, garlic, gooseberry, grain, grape, grass, hackberry, harebell, hazel, hickory, hollyhock, honeysuckle, jasmine, juniper, lemon, maidenhair fern, maple, mesquite, milkwort, oak, olive, orange, periwinkle, pignut, pine, pomegranate, pumpkin, reed and rush, rhubarb, St. John's wort, savory, spider plant, star anise, strawberry, sycamore, tarragon, tulip, vervain, walnut, zinnia

Adaptability

Bamboo, bogmyrtle, buttercup, butterwort, forget-me-not, hackberry, heather and heath, honeysuckle, iris, snowdrop, spider plant, spruce, stitchwort, strawberry, sweet woodruff, thyme, willow

Ancestors

Acacia, apple, aspen, beech, birch, Bodhi tree, boxwood, cattail, cedar, crabapple, cypress, eucalyptus, fig, fumitory, hawthorn, henbane, immortelle, kava, oak, poplar, reed and rush, tamarisk, witch hazel, yew

Authority/Leadership

Blackthorn, cinquefoil, dandelion, heliotrope, high John, larkspur, mandrake, masterwort, mugwort, mullein, myrtle, oak, rowan, thyme

Awareness
(Expand, Heighten)

Acacia, almond, anise, ash, benzoin, blackberry, Bodhi tree, borage, butterwort, camellia, carnation, catnip, celery, cherry, cinnamon, cypress, daisy, dandelion, deer's tongue, fir, flax, fly agaric, forget-me-not, foxglove, frankincense, galangal, hazel, heather and heath, heliotrope, hemp, henbane, lady's mantle, lady's slipper, larkspur, lavender, lemon, lotus, mimosa, morning glory and moonflower, mugwort, mullein, mushroom, myrrh, nutmeg, oak, periwinkle, sandalwood, seaweed, star anise, thyme, uva ursi, yarrow, yucca

Balance/Harmony

Acacia, African violet, agrimony, aloe, amaranth, anemone, angelica, apricot, bamboo, blackberry, Bodhi tree, burdock, cardamom, carnation, cherry, columbine, coriander, cow parsley, cumin, dandelion, evening primrose, fig, forget-me-not, forsythia, foxglove, gardenia, geranium, harebell, hickory, ivy, jelly fungus, jojoba, lady's mantle, lavender, lily, lily of the valley, locust, lords and ladies, lotus, meadowsweet, milkwort, morning glory and moonflower, Queen Anne's lace, quince, sandalwood, seaweed, skullcap, spikenard, strawberry, sycamore, vanilla, vetchling

Banish

Agrimony, alder, angelica, anise, asafoetida, bay, benzoin, betony, birch, bittersweet, blackthorn, broom, buckthorn, burdock, camphor, centaury, chestnut (horse), chicory, Chinaberry, clove, comfrey, crocus, cumin, date, devil's shoestring, dill, dogwood, dragon's blood, elder, eucalyptus, evening primrose, fairy wand, fly agaric, frankincense, fumitory, galangal, garlic, gorse, hazel, hellebore, hemlock, holly, hollyhock, horehound, hornbeam, jelly fungus, juniper, knotgrass, life everlasting, maidenhair fern, mallow, mandrake, mint (peppermint), mistletoe, moonwort, morning glory and moonflower, mugwort, mullein, myrrh, nettle, onion, patchouli, peach and nectarine, pearlwort, peony, pepper, pine, primrose, rose, rue, St. John's wort, sandalwood, seaweed, sesame, snakeroot, snapdragon, Solomon's seal, star anise, tamarisk, tansy, thistle, thorn apple, tulip, turmeric, unicorn root, vervain, violet, witch hazel, wormwood, yarrow

Bind

Angelica, apple, bindweed, bistort, comfrey, dodder, dragon's blood, flax, forget-me-not, grape, honeysuckle, hop, ivy, jasmine, knotgrass, licorice, locust, mallow, mandrake, morning glory and moonflower, pear, pearlwort, pepper, periwinkle, Solomon's seal, vetch, wayfaring tree, willow, wormwood

Challenges/Obstacles
(Overcome)

Betony, bistort, black cohosh, blackberry, blackthorn, bluebell, broom, butterwort, campion, celandine, cherry, chicory, chili pepper, daisy, date, deadnettle, devil's bit scabious, dragon's blood, foxglove, galangal, goldenrod, gooseberry, grass, harebell, hawthorn, hellebore, knotgrass, lady's mantle, lily of the valley, locust, mallow, mandrake, mistletoe, mulberry, pennyroyal, pepper, pignut, poppy, savory, snowdrop, southernwood, spindletree, spruce, sunflower, sycamore, thistle, valerian, witch hazel, wormwood

Changes/Transitions (Initiate, Carry Through)

Apricot, ash, belladonna lily, benzoin, bindweed, birch, bistort, borage, caraway, cardamom, Chinaberry, cinnamon, coriander, cumin, dill, elm, evening primrose, fennel, fir, flax, forsythia, goosefoot, hackberry, hazel, heather and heath, hickory, hollyhock, hornbeam, hyssop, lady's mantle, lily, linden, mistletoe, morning glory and moonflower, nutmeg, parsley, pimpernel, pomegranate, Queen Anne's lace, sesame, snowdrop, sweet woodruff, violet, walnut, yew

Clarity (Enhance, Foster)

Alder, aster, barberry and Oregon grape, bee balm, betony, birch, campion, cardamom, chicory, cypress, daffodil, dandelion, eyebright, fennel, forget-me-not, frankincense, harebell, heather and heath, honesty, honeysuckle, horehound, lemon, lemon balm, lemongrass, lily of the valley, magnolia, marsh marigold, mastic and pistachio, milkwort, orange, pansy, passionflower, periwinkle, pimpernel, Queen Anne's lace, rosemary, rue, sandalwood, self heal, stitchwort, sunflower, sweet woodruff, thistle, walnut, water lily

Communication

Adder's tongue, ash, aspen, blackberry, broom, cinquefoil, dandelion, elecampane, fir, forget-me-not, foxglove, geranium, grass, iris, jasmine, linden, maple, rose, rosemary, sweet woodruff, sycamore, water lily, witch hazel, yew

Confidence

Arnica, bergamot, camellia, caraway, cardamom, carnation, cattail, chamomile, cyclamen, dragon's blood, fennel, geranium, heather and heath, knapweed, nettle, oak, passionflower, reed and rush, tarragon, thistle, turmeric

Consecrate/Bless

Acacia, aconite, African violet, allspice, angelica, anise, apple, aster, carnation, cattail, centaury, chamomile, chestnut, chrysanthemum, cinnamon, coconut, columbine, comfrey, coriander, cress, cypress, daffodil, daisy, dragon's blood, elder, fairy wand, frankincense, fumitory, galangal, ginger, goldenseal, grain, grape, hawthorn, henbane, henna, holly, hyssop, juniper, lily, lily of the valley, lime, lotus, marigold, milkwort, mimosa, mugwort, mulberry, myrrh, oak, olive, patchouli, pear, rose, rosemary, rowan, rue, sage, St. John's wort, sandalwood, sesame, spikenard, star anise, sweet woodruff, sweetgrass, tagetes, thyme, turmeric, valerian, vervain, yarrow

Courage

Adder's tongue, allspice, anemone, angelica, aspen, bamboo, basil, bean, black cohosh, bloodroot, borage, camellia, campion, cardamom, catnip, chili pepper, columbine, cow parsley, date, fennel, forsythia, frankincense, galangal, garlic, geranium, hellebore, holly, hop, lady's mantle, larkspur, life everlasting, lily of the valley, mandrake, masterwort, mullein, mushroom, nettle, oak, onion, pansy, pepper, plantain, poke, ragwort, snowdrop, spindletree, thistle, thyme, tonka bean, tulip, vetchling, water lily, witch hazel, woad, yarrow

Creativity

Almond, anemone, apple, apricot, ash, aster, bay, bean, beech, broom, campion, cardamom, celery, cherry, clove, columbine, daisy, dill, dogwood, elder, evening primrose, fig, fir, fly agaric, foxglove, geranium, grape, hackberry, hazel, hibiscus, jasmine (winter), lilac, lords and ladies, lotus, meadowsweet, mulberry, mushroom, nightshade, pea, pear, rosemary, rowan, savory, skullcap, spindletree, stitchwort, vetchling

Death/Funeral Practices

Acacia, aconite, alder, aloe, amaranth, apple, aspen, basil, bean, birch, bistort, bittersweet, blackberry, boxwood, broom, camellia, caraway, carnation, celery, chrysanthemum, crabapple, cypress, daffodil, elder, fig, fir, fly agaric, grain, hellebore, hemp, henbane, holly, immortelle, lily, mistletoe, myrrh, myrtle, olive, onion, oregano and marjoram, parsley, pea, peach and nectarine, pomegranate, poplar, poppy, rose, rosemary, sage, snowdrop, tagetes, tamarisk, tansy, violet, willow, wormwood, yew

Defense

Apricot, bay, black cohosh, blackthorn, bog myrtle, boxwood, buckthorn, burdock, chicory, chili pepper, cinquefoil, cypress, devil's bit scabious, devil's shoestring, dill, dodder, dogwood, dragon's blood, elder, feverfew, frankincense, globeflower, goosefoot, gorse, hawthorn, hazel, heather and heath, hemlock, hickory, high John, holly, iris, jasmine, juniper, lemongrass, lilac, lily of the valley, linden, locust, lotus, maidenhair fern, moonwort, motherwort, mugwort, mullein, nettle, oak, oregano and marjoram, patchouli, pepper, poppy, purslane, rosemary, rue, St. John's wort, sesame, speedwell, spurge, tansy, thistle, toadflax, vervain, vetiver, wayfaring tree, wood sorrel, yarrow

Determination

Allspice, anemone, apricot, aspen, bog myrtle, broom, butterwort, cactus, campion, cattail, deadnettle, dragon's blood, edelweiss, elm, eucalyptus,

gorse, hop, hornbeam, iris, knapweed, knotgrass, locust, mallow, mesquite, mimosa, oak, pepper, pignut, plantain, pothos, reed and rush, snowdrop, stitchwort, sunflower, sycamore, thistle

Divination

Acacia, adder's tongue, alder, almond, angelica, anise, apple, apricot, arnica, ash, aspen, bamboo, basil, bay, birch, bistort, bloodroot, borage, boxwood, bracken, burdock, buttercup, camphor, cardamom, celery, chamomile, cherry, chestnut (horse), chicory, cinquefoil, coltsfoot, coriander, cornflower, cowslip, crabapple, crocus, cyclamen, cypress, daisy, dandelion, dill, dittany, dock, dodder, elecampane, elm, eyebright, fennel, fir, flax, fly agaric, goldenrod, gorse, grain, grape, grass, hazel, hemp, hibiscus, holly, honeysuckle, hop, ivy, juniper, kava, knapweed, lady's mantle, lady's smock, lavender, lemon, lemongrass, lilac, maidenhair fern, mandrake, maple, marigold, meadowsweet, mistletoe, moonwort, morning glory and moonflower, mugwort, mulberry, mullein, mushroom, nettle, nightshade, nutmeg, onion, orange, pansy, pea, periwinkle, plantain, pomegranate, poplar, primrose, pumpkin, ragwort, rose, rowan, rue, sage, St. John's wort, southernwood, spindletree, star anise, stonecrop, storax, strawberry, sweet woodruff, sycamore, tamarisk, thorn apple, thyme, tulip, vervain, willow, witch hazel, wormwood, yarrow, yew

Dream Work

Adder's tongue, agrimony, alder, anise, apple, ash, aster, bamboo, bay, betony, bilberry, bog myrtle, bracken, buttercup, butterwort, catnip, cedar, celandine, chamomile, cinquefoil, coltsfoot, coriander, cress, crocus, daisy, elder, elm, eucalyptus, eyebright, fly agaric, frankincense, heather and heath, heliotrope, holly, honeysuckle, hop, jasmine, juniper, lady's slipper, lavender, lilac, linden, lobelia, magnolia, mallow, mandrake, maple, marigold, mimosa, mistletoe, morning glory and moonflower, mugwort, mulberry, myrtle, onion, orange, passionflower, peony, pepper, plantain, poppy, primrose, Queen Anne's lace, rose, rosemary, St. John's wort, sweet woodruff, tarragon, thorn apple, thyme, tulip, vervain, yarrow, yew

Emotions
(Deal With, Support)

Adder's tongue, amaranth, anemone, anise, bittersweet, borage, buttercup, chamomile, chickweed, clove, columbine, coriander, cow parsley, crocus, cumin, dogwood, eucalyptus, fairy wand, feverfew, forsythia, foxglove, gardenia, geranium, ginger, hackberry, hollyhock, hyacinth, juniper, lemon balm, lily of the valley, myrtle, parsley, passionflower, rose, rue, skullcap, spruce, stitchwort, tea tree, vetchling, vetiver, violet

Family and Home

African violet, agrimony, aloe, bilberry, bittersweet, bloodroot, butterwort, catnip, cattail, chestnut, chickweed, chrysanthemum, coconut, coltsfoot, columbine, comfrey, cow parsley, crocus, cumin, daffodil, daisy, deadnettle, evening primrose, fennel, flax, forsythia, fumitory, heather and heath, holly, hollyhock, houseleek, iris, masterwort, meadowsweet, milkwort, morning glory and moonflower, mugwort, myrtle, olive, oregano and marjoram, pennyroyal, pignut, plantain, pumpkin, reed and rush, skullcap, snowdrop, unicorn root, valerian, vetchling, vetiver

Fertility

Allspice, almond, amaryllis, apple, apricot, asafoetida, ash, avocado, bedstraw, beech, birch, black cohosh, blackberry, boxwood, broom, bryony, cabbage, carnation, catnip, cherry, chickweed, coriander, crocus, cyclamen, daisy, date, dock, fairy wand, fennel, fig, fly agaric, forsythia, ginseng, gooseberry, grain, grape, hawthorn, hazel, hemp, henna, hogweed, hop, hyssop, lady's mantle, lady's smock, lemon, lemon balm, lords and ladies, lovage, mallow, mandrake, meadowsweet, mistletoe, mugwort, mushroom, mustard, myrtle, nutmeg, oak, olive, onion, orange, orchid, patchouli, pea, peach and nectarine, periwinkle, pine, pomegranate, poppy, primrose, pumpkin, Queen Anne's lace, quince, raspberry, rowan, St. John's wort, seaweed, sesame, southernwood, spider plant, stitchwort, sunflower, tulip, turmeric, walnut, willow

Focus
(The Mind, Energy)

Ash, aster, basil, bee balm, benzoin, birch, bog myrtle, bracken, broom, camphor, campion, cardamom, cypress, eucalyptus, fennel, forget-me-not, frankincense, geranium, groundsel, hibiscus, iris, lady's mantle, lemon balm, lemongrass, lilac, maidenhair fern, milkwort, mint, moonwort, myrrh, nutmeg, orange, oregano and marjoram, pansy, parsley, pine, primrose, reed and rush, rosemary, sage, savory, skullcap, Solomon's seal, spikenard, spindletree, vanilla

Growth
(Personal, Spiritual)

African violet, allspice, angelica, birch, blackberry, cattail, cypress, eucalyptus (lemon), forsythia, frankincense, geranium, grape, hawthorn, hop, ivy, lotus, mandrake, marsh marigold, patchouli, primrose, reed and rush, self heal, Solomon's seal, spruce, tarragon, water lily

Happiness

Alkanet, almond, apple, apricot, bamboo, basil, blackberry, borage, boxwood, buttercup, cacao, catnip, celandine, cherry, chervil, chrysanthemum, clove, cornflower, crocus, cyclamen, elecampane, eyebright, figwort, fir, forsythia, frankincense, grape, grass, hawthorn, henna, hibiscus, high John, hollyhock, honesty, hyacinth, juniper, lady's mantle, lemon, lilac, lily of the valley, marigold, meadowsweet, mimosa, morning glory and moonflower, motherwort, mugwort, mushroom, orange, oregano and marjoram, parsley, peach and nectarine, peony, pine, St. John's wort, savory, snowdrop, star anise, strawberry, sunflower, tulip, unicorn root, vanilla, vetchling, violet, water lily, wood sorrel

Healing

Acacia, adder's tongue, agrimony, alder, allspice, aloe, amaranth, anemone, angelica, apple, asafoetida, ash, aspen, avocado, barberry and Oregon grape, basil, bay, beech, betony, bilberry, birch, bittersweet, blackberry, broom, burdock, butterwort, cactus, campion, cardamom, carnation, catnip, cattail, cedar, celery, centaury, chamomile, chestnut, Chinaberry, cinnamon, clove, coconut, coltsfoot, comfrey, coriander, cow parsley, cowslip, crabapple, crocus, cypress, daisy, dandelion, date, deadnettle, dock, dogwood, dragon's blood, elder, elecampane, elm, eucalyptus, evening primrose, fairy wand, fennel, feverfew, fir, forsythia, foxglove, frankincense, gardenia, garlic, ginger, ginseng, goldenrod, goldenseal, gooseberry, grape, groundsel, hackberry, hazel, heather and

heath, heliotrope, hemp, henna, hogweed, hop, horehound, hyssop, iris, jasmine, jelly fungus, jojoba, juniper, knapweed, lady's mantle, lady's smock, larch, lavender, lemon, lemon balm, licorice, life everlasting, lily of the valley, lime, maidenhair fern, mallow, marigold, marsh marigold, mastic and pistachio, meadowsweet, mesquite, milkwort, mint, mullein, mustard, myrrh, myrtle, nettle, nutmeg, oak, olive, onion, oregano and marjoram, pansy, peach and nectarine, pear, pennyroyal, peony, pepper, periwinkle, pine, plantain, primrose, Queen Anne's lace, rose, rosemary, rowan, rue, sage, St. John's wort, sandalwood, savory, self heal, sesame, skullcap, southernwood, spindletree, spruce, stitchwort, stonecrop, strawberry, sweet woodruff, sweetgrass, tagetes, tea tree, thistle, thyme, ti plant, tobacco, turmeric, valerian, vervain, violet, walnut, willow, witch hazel, wood sorrel, yarrow, zedoary, zinnia

Hexes
(Break, Protect From)

Agrimony, angelica, anise, asafoetida, ash, aspen, avens, bamboo, basil, bay, benzoin, bilberry, bittersweet, black cohosh, blackthorn, boxwood, bracken, buckthorn, butterwort, cedar, celery, chamomile, chestnut, chili pepper, cinquefoil, clove, clover, cow parsley, devil's shoestring, dill, dock, dragon's blood, elder, fir, fumitory, galangal, garlic, ginger, globeflower, gorse, grain, grass, heliotrope, hellebore, hemlock, hemp, hogweed, holly, horehound, hyssop, jelly fungus, juniper, knotgrass, lilac, lobelia, maidenhair fern, mallow, mandrake, moonwort, mullein, myrrh, nettle, nutmeg, onion, oregano and marjoram, patchouli, peach and nectarine, pearlwort, pennyroyal, peony, periwinkle, pine, poke, ragwort, rowan, rue, sandalwood, senna, snake plant, snakeroot, snapdragon, southernwood, spindle-tree, spurge, storax, tamarisk, thistle, thorn apple, toadflax, turmeric, unicorn root, vervain, vetiver, violet, wormwood, yarrow, yew, yucca, zedoary

Hope

Almond, birch, celandine, coconut, cornflower, fir (silver), gorse, grain, hawthorn, hop, lily, marigold, olive, pomegranate, poplar (white), self heal, snowdrop, spruce (Norway), tamarisk, violet

Inspiration

Acacia, anemone, angelica, ash, aster, birch, bog myrtle, borage, campion, cattail, chrysanthemum, cinquefoil, columbine, dogwood, fairy wand, fir, gorse, grape, groundsel, hackberry, hazel, iris, ivy, lilac, lily of the valley, lotus, marsh marigold, meadowsweet, mulberry, oak, pansy, pine, reed and rush, rosemary, rowan, rue, savory, spindle-tree, spruce, vanilla, vervain, walnut, water lily, willow, witch hazel

Intuition

Alder, almond, ash, aster, bay, birch, blackberry, broom, centaury, chamomile, coconut, elecampane, elm, eyebright, foxglove, hazel, holly, honeysuckle, larch, lavender, lemongrass, masterwort, mimosa, rose, Solomon's seal, speedwell, spruce, uva ursi, willow, yarrow

Justice/Legal Matters

Bay, buckthorn, cedar, celandine, chestnut, coltsfoot, cypress, elm, frankincense, galangal, hickory, high John, larch, linden, marigold, mustard, nettle, nutmeg, oak, pear, pepper, pine, tagetes, tarragon, yew

Knowledge (Seek, Acquire)

Alder, almond, angelica, apricot, aspen, beech, bistort, blackberry, Bodhi tree, campion, celandine, centaury, cherry, crabapple, cress, cumin, cypress, fly agaric, hazel, iris, ivy, juniper, larch, moonwort, oak, parsley, periwinkle, primrose, tarragon, willow, witch hazel, yew

Loss/Sorrow (Ease, Recover From)

Aloe, amaranth, anemone, betony, borage, chervil, chrysanthemum, cypress, eucalyptus, fairy wand, forget-me-not, goldenrod, hackberry, harebell, hyacinth, knotgrass, maple, morning glory and moonflower, pansy, pearlwort, peony, pomegranate, poplar, primrose, sage, snowdrop, tagetes, willow (weeping), witch hazel, yew

Love

Acacia, African violet, allspice, almond, aloe, amaryllis, anemone, anise, apple, apricot, arnica, ash, aster, avens, avocado, bamboo, basil, bay, bedstraw, belladonna lily, benzoin, betony, bilberry, birch, black cohosh, bloodroot, bluebell, boxwood, bracken, burdock, buttercup, butterwort, cacao, camellia, campion, caraway, cardamom, carnation, catnip, cedar, chamomile, cherry, chestnut, chickweed, chili pepper, chrysanthemum, cinnamon, clove, clover, coltsfoot, columbine, coriander, cornflower, cow parsley, cowslip, crabapple, crocus, cumin, cyclamen, daffodil, daisy, damiana, dandelion, date, deadnettle, deer's tongue, dill, dittany, dock, dodder, dragon's blood, edelweiss, elder, elecampane, elm, fairy wand, feverfew, fig, forget-me-not, frankincense, gardenia, geranium, ginger, ginseng, goldenrod, gorse, grain, grape, harebell, hawthorn, heather and heath, hemp, henna, hibiscus, high John, honeysuckle, hornbeam, houseleek, hyacinth (pink), iris, ivy, jasmine, jojoba, juniper, knapweed, lady's mantle, lady's slipper, lady's smock, lavender, lemon, lemon balm, licorice, lilac, lily (white), lily of the valley, lime, linden, lobelia, locust, lotus, lovage, magnolia, maidenhair fern, mallow, mandrake, maple, mastic and pistachio, Mayapple, meadowsweet, mimosa, mint, mistletoe, moonwort, motherwort, mugwort, mullein, myrtle, nettle, nutmeg, olive, orange, orchid, oregano and marjoram, pansy, pea, peach and nectarine, pear, pearlwort, periwinkle, poppy, primrose, quassia, Queen Anne's lace, quince, raspberry, rhubarb, rose, rosemary, rue, St. John's wort, senna, skullcap, southernwood, spikenard, stonecrop, strawberry, sycamore, thyme, tonka bean, tulip, turnip, valerian, vanilla, vervain, vetch, vetchling, vetiver, violet, walnut, water lily, willow, witch hazel, wormwood, yarrow

Loyalty/Fidelity

Blackthorn, bluebell, caraway, cattail, cedar, celery, chickweed, chili pepper, clover, cornflower, cumin, daisy, dogwood, edelweiss, elder, fairy wand, forget-me-not, harebell, hickory, honeysuckle, larkspur, lavender, lemon, lemongrass, licorice, linden, locust, magnolia, myrtle, nutmeg, olive, orange, orchid, peach and nectarine, raspberry, rhubarb, rosemary, senna, skullcap, southernwood, speedwell, spikenard, stonecrop, tulip, vetch, vetchling, witch hazel, wormwood, yarrow

Luck

Alder, alkanet, allspice, almond, aloe, anemone, apple, ash, bamboo, basil, bean, beech, bergamot, bilberry, black cohosh, blackberry, bog myrtle, boxwood, bracken, bryony, butterwort, cabbage, cactus, carnation, catnip, centaury, cherry, chestnut, chicory, chili pepper, Chinaberry, cinnamon, cinquefoil, clover (four-leaf and red), club moss, daffodil, daisy, date, deadnettle, devil's bit scabious, devil's shoestring, edelweiss, elecampane, fly agaric, forget-me-not, frankincense, fumitory, galangal, garlic, ginseng, goldenrod, gorse, grain, grass, hawthorn, hazel, heather and heath, henna, high John, holly, honesty, honeysuckle, houseleek, hyacinth, iris, ivy, jelly fungus, Joe Pye weed, kava, lady's mantle, larch, lavender, lemongrass, lichen, lilac, lily of the valley, maidenhair fern, mandrake, marsh marigold, meadowsweet, mimosa, mint, mistletoe, moonwort, moss, mugwort, mulberry, myrtle, nettle, nutmeg, oak, olive, orchid, pea, peach and nectarine, pear, pearlwort, peony, pignut, plantain, pomegranate, poppy, quince, ragwort, raspberry, rose, rowan, rue, snake plant, snakeroot, Solomon's seal, southernwood, speedwell, spikenard, star anise, strawberry, sunflower, sweet flag, thyme, ti plant, tonka bean, tulip, turmeric, vanilla, vervain, vetiver, violet, walnut, water lily, wood sorrel

Manifest
(Desires, Dreams, Will)

Angelica, beech, bilberry, bittersweet, bluebell, buttercup, camellia, campion, cherry, crocus, dill, dogwood, dragon's blood, elm, grass, hackberry, hawthorn, hazel, heather and heath, holly, lavender, lily (Turk's cap), masterwort, myrrh, patchouli, peach and nectarine, pear, sandalwood, spindletree, strawberry, sunflower, vervain, walnut, water lily

Negativity
(Remove, Ward Off)

Acacia, aconite, agrimony, alder, allspice, angelica, anise, asafoetida, ash, aspen, aster, bamboo, barberry and Oregon grape, basil, bay, bean, betony, birch, bistort, blackthorn, bloodroot, bracken, broom, buckthorn, burdock, butterwort, camphor, centaury, chamomile, chickweed, chili pepper, chive, cinquefoil, clove, coltsfoot, columbine, cornflower, cow parsley, cumin, cyclamen, daffodil, dandelion, date, devil's bit scabious, devil's shoestring, dragon's blood, elm, eucalyptus, frankincense, fumitory, galangal, ginger, globeflower, goldenseal, gorse, grass, groundsel, hackberry, harebell, hawthorn, hemlock, henbane, hornbeam, hyacinth, hyssop, ivy, jelly fungus, Joe Pye weed, juniper, larkspur, lavender, lemongrass, lichen, lilac, lily, linden, locust, lovage, marigold, marsh marigold, masterwort, Mayapple, mistletoe, mugwort, mullein, myrrh, nettle, onion, pansy, patchouli, peach and nectarine, pearlwort, pennyroyal, peony, pine, plantain, poke, pothos, Queen Anne's lace, quince, ragwort, rosemary, rue, St. John's wort, sassafras, seaweed, sesame, snapdragon, snowdrop, Solomon's seal, southernwood, speedwell, spider plant, spikenard, sunflower, sweet woodruff, tamarisk, tansy, thistle, unicorn root, vervain, vetch, vetchling, violet, yarrow, yew, yucca

Nightmares
(Alleviate, Ward off)

Anise, betony, bluebell, carnation, chervil, crocus, cyclamen, daffodil, evening primrose, hyacinth, mallow, mandrake, marigold, mullein, peony, plantain, purslane, rosemary, rue, St. John's wort, snapdragon, thistle, thyme, yew, zedoary

Past-life Work

Camphor, cyclamen, cypress, eucalyptus, frankincense, hazel, lemon balm, lilac, myrrh, poplar, sandalwood

Peace

Aconite, aloe, angelica, apricot, arnica, aspen, bamboo, basil, bay, bedstraw, bee balm, bittersweet, Bodhi tree, bog myrtle, borage, burdock, carnation, catnip, chamomile, cherry, chestnut, clover, coltsfoot, columbine, comfrey, coriander, cornflower, cow parsley, cowslip, crocus, cypress, daffodil, elecampane, fig, figwort, fir, foxglove, gardenia, gooseberry, harebell, hawthorn, heather and heath, hop, hyacinth, hyssop, jelly fungus, lady's mantle, lady's slipper, lavender, licorice, lilac, lily (white), lily of the valley, linden, loosestrife, lotus, maidenhair fern, mallow, meadowsweet, mimosa, morning glory and moonflower, motherwort, mugwort, myrtle, nettle, olive, orange, oregano and marjoram, pansy, passionflower, pennyroyal, peony, periwinkle, primrose, quince, sandalwood, seaweed, self heal, skullcap, stitchwort, strawberry, sunflower, sweet woodruff, sycamore, tarragon, thyme, tulip, valerian, vanilla, vervain, vetchling, vetiver, violet (common blue), water lily, witch hazel, wood sorrel

Prophecy

Aconite, alder, anise, apricot, ash, bay, beech, bilberry, boxwood, bracken, butterwort, celandine, crabapple, dandelion, date, elm, fly agaric, grain, grape, ivy, lilac, maple, marigold, poplar (black), seaweed, sycamore, tamarisk, vervain, willow, yarrow

Prosperity/Money

Acacia, alkanet, allspice, almond, amaranth, apple, ash, aspen, avocado, barberry and Oregon grape, basil, bay, bee balm, beech, bergamot, bilberry, blackberry, bog myrtle, boxwood, bryony, buttercup, cacao, camellia, cedar, chamomile, chestnut, chicory, cinnamon, cinquefoil, clove, clover, club moss, coltsfoot, cowslip, crabapple, cypress, dill, dock, elder, fig, flax, fumitory, galangal, garlic, ginger, goldenrod, goldenseal, gorse, grain, grape, hawthorn, hazel, heliotrope, henna, hickory, high John, hollyhock, honesty, honeysuckle, hornbeam, iris (blue flag), jasmine, juniper, lichen, mandrake, maple, marsh marigold, Mayapple, mint, moonwort, moss, mustard, nutmeg, oak, olive, onion, orange, oregano and marjoram, parsley, patchouli, pea, pear, pennyroyal, peony, periwinkle, pignut, pine, pomegranate, poplar, poppy, pothos, pumpkin, quassia, quince, ragwort, sassafras, seaweed, sesame, snakeroot, spider plant, spruce, storax, sunflower, sweet flag, tonka bean, tulip, turmeric, valerian, vervain, vetiver, walnut, woad, wood sorrel

Protection

Acacia, aconite, agrimony, alder, alkanet, almond, aloe, amaranth, anemone, angelica, anise, arnica, asafoetida, ash, aspen, aster, avens, bamboo, barberry and Oregon grape, basil, bay, beech, benzoin, bergamot, betony, bilberry, birch, bittersweet, black cohosh, blackberry, blackthorn, bloodroot, bog myrtle, borage, boxwood, bracken, broom, bryony, buckthorn, burdock, butterwort, cactus, campion, caraway, carnation, catnip, cattail, cedar, celandine, celery, centaury, chamomile, chestnut, chili pepper, chive, chrysanthemum, cinnamon, cinquefoil, clove, clover, club moss, coconut, colts-

foot, comfrey, coriander, cornflower, cow parsley, cowslip, crabapple, cress, crocus, cumin, cyclamen, cypress, daffodil, daisy, dandelion, date, deadnettle, deer's tongue, devil's bit scabious, devil's shoestring, dill, dock, dogwood, dragon's blood, edelweiss, elder, elecampane, elm, eucalyptus, evening primrose, fairy wand, fennel, feverfew, fig, figwort, fir, flax, fly agaric, forget-me-not, foxglove, frankincense, fumitory, garlic, geranium (red), ginger, ginseng, goosefoot, gorse, grain, grass, groundsel, hackberry, hawthorn, hazel, heather and heath, heliotrope, hellebore, hemlock, hemp, henna, hickory, high John, holly, honesty, honeysuckle, horehound, hornbeam, houseleek, hyacinth, hyssop, iris, ivy, juniper, kava, lady's slipper, larch, larkspur, lavender, lemon, life everlasting, lilac, lily, lily of the valley, lime, linden, locust, loosestrife, lovage, magnolia, maidenhair fern, mallow, mandrake, marigold, marsh marigold, masterwort, Mayapple, mesquite, milkwort, mimosa, mint, mistletoe, moonwort, motherwort, mugwort, mulberry, mullein, mustard, myrrh, myrtle, nettle, oak, olive, onion, orange, oregano and marjoram, parsley, pea, pear, pearlwort, pennyroyal, peony, pepper, periwinkle, pignut, pimpernel, pine, plantain, pomegranate, poppy, pothos, primrose, pumpkin, purslane, quince, ragwort, raspberry, reed and rush, rose, rosemary, rowan, rue, sage, St. John's wort, sandalwood, sassafras, seaweed, senna, snake plant, snapdragon, Solomon's seal, southernwood, speedwell, spider plant, spruce, spurge, star anise, stonecrop, storax, strawberry, sweet flag, sweet woodruff, sycamore, tamarisk, tarragon, tea tree, thistle, thorn apple, thyme, ti plant, toadflax, tulip, turmeric, turnip, unicorn root, uva ursi, valerian, vervain, vetiver, violet, walnut, water lily, wayfaring tree, willow, witch hazel, woad, wood sorrel, wormwood, yarrow, yew, yucca

Psychic Abilities

Acacia, anise, arnica, aster, basil, bay, bean, beech, bistort, Bodhi tree, borage, bracken, catnip, cedar, celery, centaury, chamomile, cinnamon, coltsfoot, comfrey, cornflower, cress, crocus, damiana, dandelion, deer's tongue, dittany, elecampane, elm, eucalyptus, eyebright, fennel, fig, flax, fly agaric, frankincense, geranium, ginger, grape, grass, hazel, heather and heath, heliotrope, hemp, hibiscus, honeysuckle, immortelle, jasmine, juniper, larkspur, lavender, lemon, lemongrass, lichen, lilac, maidenhair fern, mandrake, mimosa, mint (peppermint), moonwort, mugwort, mulberry, mullein, mushroom, nettle, nutmeg (mace), orange, orchid, oregano and marjoram, pimpernel, pine, pomegranate, rose, rowan, sage, seaweed, spruce, star anise, sycamore, thyme, unicorn root, uva ursi, vetchling, violet, water lily, wormwood, yarrow, yew

Purification

Acacia, agrimony, allspice, aloe, anise, apricot, arnica, asafoetida, avens, bay, bee balm, belladonna lily, benzoin, betony, birch, bistort, blackberry, blackthorn, bloodroot, bog myrtle, broom, burdock, camphor, cedar, chamomile, chickweed, cinnamon, clove, coconut, columbine, cumin, dill, elder, elecampane, eucalyptus, evening primrose, fairy wand, fennel, feverfew, fir, frankincense, fumitory, geranium, ginger, gorse, hawthorn, hemlock, hyssop, iris, juniper, lady's mantle, lavender, lemon, lemongrass, life everlasting, lime, lobelia, lotus, lovage, magnolia, masterwort, mastic and pistachio, mesquite, mimosa, mint, mistletoe, moonwort, mugwort, myrrh, myrtle, nettle, oak, olive, orange, oregano and marjoram, parsley, passionflower, patchouli, pennyroyal, pine, plantain, poinsettia, purslane, Queen Anne's lace, rosemary, rue, sage, St. John's wort, sandalwood, snake plant, Solomon's seal, southernwood, spikenard, spindletree, star anise, storax, sweet woodruff, sweetgrass, sycamore, tansy, tea tree, thyme, ti plant, tobacco, turmeric, valerian, vervain, water lily, wormwood, yarrow, yucca, zinnia

Relationships

Acacia, aconite, allspice, amaranth, anemone, apple, apricot, bean, bog myrtle, caraway, cardamom, carnation, chickweed, cinquefoil, clove, crocus, cyclamen, daffodil, deadnettle, elecampane, forget-me-not, foxglove, geranium, ginger, hawthorn, jojoba, lady's mantle, lavender, lemon, lemon balm, lovage, marigold, meadowsweet, passionflower, primrose, rue, skullcap, strawberry, sweet woodruff, vetchling, violet, yarrow

Release (Let Go, Move On)

Agrimony, amaranth, bay, bistort, bittersweet, bloodroot, bracken, broom, burdock, celandine, chamomile, chicory, chrysanthemum, columbine, comfrey, cumin, deadnettle, dragon's blood, foxglove, groundsel, heliotrope, hemlock, hollyhock, hornbeam, iris, maidenhair fern, maple, moonwort, mugwort, mullein, myrrh, nettle, oregano and marjoram, peony, pepper, quassia, rose (gall), rue, St. John's wort, self heal, snapdragon, snowdrop, sunflower, tansy, thistle, tobacco, tulip, witch hazel

Renewal

Alder, almond, angelica, apple, apricot, aspen, beech, belladonna lily, birch, bittersweet, bluebell, boxwood, carnation, cherry, chervil, cumin, cypress, daffodil, elm, fennel, fir, flax, fly agaric, gorse, grain, hickory, hogweed, holly, ivy, lemon balm, marsh marigold, milkwort, mimosa, mistletoe, pansy, parsley, peach and nectarine, pepper, poinsettia, pomegranate, poplar (white), poppy, Queen Anne's lace, St. John's wort, southernwood, spruce, stitchwort, sycamore, thyme, wormwood, zedoary

Secrets

Caraway, chicory, coriander, cowslip, deadnettle, elecampane, flax, fly agaric, forget-me-not, galangal, ginger, globeflower, hazel, ivy, juniper, lemon, locust, marsh marigold, moonwort, mulberry, mushroom, nightshade, oak (white), onion, pignut, rose, sage, sesame, snakeroot, Solomon's seal, tarragon, turmeric, valerian, vetiver, wood sorrel

Security

Aloe, apple, arnica, bay, borage, comfrey, coriander, daffodil, dragon's blood, eucalyptus, evening primrose, fennel, geranium (pink), hickory, ivy, maidenhair fern, Mayapple, meadowsweet, mimosa, moonwort, morning glory and moonflower, mullein, nettle, oregano and marjoram, periwinkle, raspberry, reed and rush, St. John's wort, spruce, tarragon, unicorn root

See Faeries

Alder, ash, bluebell, clover (four-leaf), elder, grass, harebell, hawthorn, hazel, hollyhock, lavender, marigold, mullein, primrose, rowan, rue, St. John's wort, thyme, vervain, wood sorrel, yarrow, yew

Sex/Sexuality

Adder's tongue, almond, aloe, amaryllis, anise, apple, apricot, arnica, avocado, cacao, caraway, cardamom, carnation, cattail, celery, chili pepper, cinnamon, clove, coconut, coriander, crocus,

damiana, date, deer's tongue, dill, dodder, dragon's blood, elecampane, fairy wand, flax, galangal, geranium, ginger, ginseng, grape, hawthorn, hemp, henna, hibiscus, high John, hogweed, hop, hyssop, jasmine, lady's smock, lemongrass, licorice, lords and ladies, lotus, lovage, magnolia, mallow, mandrake, mistletoe, mushroom, myrtle, nettle, oak, olive, onion, patchouli, pear, pennyroyal, pignut, plantain, pomegranate, primrose, Queen Anne's lace, quince (common), rhubarb, rose, sandalwood, savory, sesame, southernwood, strawberry, tulip, vanilla, vervain, violet, walnut, willow, witch hazel, wormwood

Skills

Aconite, bean, centaury, daisy, dandelion, eyebright, flax, hop, lily of the valley, masterwort, patchouli, rowan, seaweed, star anise, sweet woodruff, tagetes, vetchling, yew

Spirit Guides/Spirits

Agrimony, alder, almond, amaranth, anise, apple, arnica, asafoetida, benzoin, bergamot, betony, blackberry, catnip, cedar, chervil, chicory, cowslip, daffodil, dandelion, dittany, elder, elecampane, eucalyptus, fennel, fir, fly agaric, frankincense, gardenia, garlic, grass, harebell, heather and heath, hellebore, henbane, high John, holly, hyssop, immortelle, jasmine, jelly fungus, Joe Pye weed, juniper, kava, larkspur, lavender, lemon, lemon balm, lemongrass, lichen, lilac, mallow, mandrake, marsh marigold, masterwort, mistletoe, moonwort, mugwort, mullein, mushroom, myrrh, oak, onion, orange, patchouli, peony, periwinkle, pine, poke, poplar, reed and rush, rose, rowan, rue, sage, St. John's wort, sandalwood, seaweed, sesame, Solomon's seal, spruce, sweet flag, sweetgrass, thistle, tobacco, uva ursi, valerian, vervain, walnut, willow, wormwood, yarrow, yew

Spirituality

Acacia, adder's tongue, African violet, allspice, almond, angelica, bean, benzoin, Bodhi tree, buttercup, camellia, cedar, cherry, chicory, cinnamon, clove, coconut, columbine, cumin, date, dragon's blood, elder, eucalyptus, fir, forsythia, frankincense, gardenia, henna, holly, hyssop, ivy, jasmine, lady's mantle, larch, lavender, lemon balm, lemongrass, lilac, lily of the valley, lotus, mallow, myrrh, olive, passionflower, patchouli, poplar, primrose, St. John's wort, sandalwood, self heal, spindletree, spruce, star anise, sunflower, sweetgrass, tamarisk, turmeric, uva ursi, vetchling, vetiver

Strength

Aconite, adder's tongue, alder (black), angelica, apple, ash, avocado, bamboo, bean, bindweed, black cohosh, blackthorn, bloodroot, borage, broom, camellia, cardamom, carnation, catnip, centaury, chestnut, chili pepper, cinnamon, comfrey, cow parsley, cowslip, cypress, daisy, fennel, feverfew, flax, forget-me-not, garlic, gorse, hickory, high John, hogweed, horehound, hornbeam, knapweed, linden, locust, marsh marigold, masterwort, meadowsweet, mint, morning glory and moonflower, mugwort, mushroom, oak, onion, pennyroyal, pepper, plantain, rowan, St. John's wort, snake plant, southernwood, stitchwort, stonecrop, sunflower, thistle, uva ursi, vetchling, willow, woad, zinnia

Success

Alkanet, aloe, angelica, apple, aspen, avocado, basil, bay, bee balm, bilberry, buttercup, celandine, cinnamon, clover, coconut, date, dragon's blood, evening primrose, forget-me-not, frankincense, galangal, ginger, gooseberry, high John, hollyhock, iris, Joe Pye weed, larch, lemon balm, lily of the valley, masterwork, mesquite, morning glory and moonflower, mulberry, oak, orchid, pear, plantain, rowan, Solomon's seal, spindletree, star anise, sweet woodruff, unicorn root, vanilla, walnut

Support (Provide, Receive)

Aconite, aloe, bistort, butterwort, campion, cattail, chickweed, columbine, fairy wand, jelly fungus, mullein, poppy, reed and rush, stitchwort, sycamore, zedoary

Transformation

Alder, beech, Bodhi tree, cedar, cherry, cypress, date, fir, flax, frankincense, ivy, juniper, lotus, maple, myrrh, tagetes, walnut, yucca

Trust

Basil, bracken, camellia, columbine, cowslip, grain, heather and heath, lemongrass, mint, pennyroyal, raspberry, rose, snowdrop, thistle

Truth

Aster, bean, bittersweet, blackthorn, bluebell, Bodhi tree, buttercup, camellia, carnation, chrysanthemum, cornflower, daisy, elecampane, evening primrose, eyebright, foxglove, grain, grape, harebell, hazel, honesty, lotus, magnolia, meadowsweet, moonwort, pimpernel, plantain, sage, sandalwood, seaweed, sesame, snapdragon, southernwood, thistle, valerian, vetchling

Wisdom

Acacia, almond, aloe, apple, ash, bamboo, bay, bean, beech, birch, Bodhi tree, buttercup, campion, cherry, crabapple, elder, elm, eucalyptus, fumitory, goldenrod, goldenseal, hawthorn, hazel, henna, iris, kava, larkspur, lilac, lotus, mulberry, oak, peach and nectarine, pear, pomegranate, poppy, rowan, rue, sage, sandalwood, Solomon's seal, spruce (black), sunflower, sweet flag, sycamore, vetchling, witch hazel, zinnia

Wishes

Anemone, bamboo, bay, beech, buckthorn, camellia, chestnut, cinnamon, dandelion, dogwood, elm, fairy wand, ginseng, grass, hawthorn, hickory (pecan), horehound, juniper, loosestrife, pea, peach and nectarine, pear, poinsettia, pomegranate, sage, sandalwood, snowdrop, sunflower, thistle, tonka bean, violet, walnut

Appendix B
Plants by Other Associations

This listing provides a quick reference to find the plants associated with the four elements, astrological signs, and planetary/solar system connections.

Plants by Element

Air
Acacia, agrimony, alder, almond, anemone, anise, apple, ash, aspen, bamboo, bay, bean, bee balm, benzoin, bergamot, bindweed, bittersweet, Bodhi tree, borage, bracken, broom, camphor, caraway, catnip, cedar, chamomile, chervil, chestnut, chicory, clove, clover, coconut, comfrey, crabapple, dandelion, date, deadnettle, dill, dock, dogwood, elder, elecampane, elm, eucalyptus, eyebright, fig, fir, fly agaric, forget-me-not, forsythia, frankincense, goldenrod, goosefoot, grape, hawthorn, hazel, hickory (pecan), holly, hop, horehound, houseleek, hyssop, immortelle, ivy, jasmine, lavender, lemon, lemon balm, lemongrass, lily of the valley, linden, lords and ladies, lotus, maidenhair fern, maple, mastic and pistachio, meadowsweet, mesquite, mimosa, mint (spearmint), mistletoe, mugwort, mulberry, myrrh, nutmeg (mace), oak, olive, orange, oregano and marjoram, parsley, patchouli, pear, pimpernel, pine, pothos, primrose, rhubarb, sage, sandalwood, savory, senna, southernwood, spider, plant, star anise, sweetgrass, sycamore, tagetes, tarragon, thyme, vervain, vetch, violet, walnut, wayfaring tree, yarrow, yew, zinnia

Earth
Agrimony, alkanet, amaryllis, ash, avocado, barberry and Oregon grape, bistort, blackthorn, bluebell, boxwood, bracken, camphor, campion, cardamom, cedar, celandine, Chinaberry, cinquefoil, clove, clover, comfrey, cornflower, cypress, devil's bit scabious, dock (yellow), dogwood, elder,

elm, eucalyptus, fairy wand, figwort, fir, fumitory, galangal, ginger, grain, grass, henbane, henna, hickory, high John, hogweed, holly, honeysuckle, hop, horehound, houseleek, ivy, jasmine, juniper, knotgrass, lemon, lichen, life everlasting, locust, lotus, lovage, magnolia, maidenhair fern, mandrake, maple, mugwort, mushroom, oak, olive, orange, patchouli, pea, pear, pignut, pine, plantain, pomegranate, primrose, pumpkin, quassia, Queen Anne's lace, quince, rhubarb, rowan, sage, self heal, senna, snake plant, snakeroot, snowdrop, spruce, storax, sweet flag, tea tree, toadflax, tobacco, tonka bean, tulip, turmeric, turnip, unicorn root, uva ursi, vervain, vetiver, witch hazel, woad, wood sorrel, yucca

Fire

Alder, allspice, almond, amaranth, anemone, angelica, asafoetida, ash, avens, basil, bay, beech, betony, bilberry, black cohosh, blackthorn, bloodroot, borage, bryony, buckthorn, cacao, camellia, camphor, caraway, cardamom, carnation, cedar, celandine, celery, centaury, cherry, chestnut, chili pepper, chive, chrysanthemum, cinnamon, cinquefoil, clove, coconut, coriander, cow parsley, cress, crocus (saffron), cumin, damiana, date, deer's tongue, devil's shoestring, dill, dragon's blood, edelweiss, elder, evening primrose, fennel, fir, flax, forsythia, frankincense, fumitory, galangal, garlic, ginger, ginseng, goldenseal, gorse, grape, hackberry, hawthorn, hazel, heliotrope, hickory, high John, holly, hornbeam, hyssop, juniper, larch, lime, lotus, lovage, mandrake, marigold, masterwort, Mayapple, mesquite, mint (peppermint), mullein, mustard, nettle, nutmeg, oak, olive, onion, orange, oregano and marjoram (oregano), parsley, pennyroyal, peony, pepper, pine, poinsettia, poke, pomegranate, poppy, primrose, Queen Anne's lace,

rosemary, rowan, rue, St. John's wort, sassafras, savory, sesame, snapdragon, speedwell, spurge, storax, sunflower, sweet woodruff, tagetes, tarragon, thistle, ti plant, toadflax, tobacco, turmeric, vervain, vetiver, walnut, willow, witch hazel, wormwood, yew, yucca, zedoary

Water

Aconite, adder's tongue, African violet, alder, alkanet, aloe, apple, apricot, arnica, ash, aspen, aster, bean, bedstraw, beech, belladonna lily, benzoin, bilberry, bindweed, birch, blackberry, bloodroot, bluebell, Bodhi tree, bog myrtle, buckthorn, burdock, buttercup, butterwort, cabbage, cacao, cactus, camellia, camphor, cardamom, catnip, cattail, cedar, celery, chamomile, cherry, chestnut, chickweed, club moss, coltsfoot, columbine, comfrey, cornflower, cowslip, crabapple, cress (watercress), crocus, cyclamen, cypress, daffodil, daisy, dittany, dodder, elder, elm, eucalyptus, feverfew, fig, figwort, foxglove, frankincense, gardenia, geranium, globeflower, gooseberry, grape, groundsel, hackberry, harebell, hazel, heather and heath, hellebore, hemlock, hemp, henbane, hibiscus, hollyhock, honesty, hop, hornbeam, hyacinth, iris, ivy, jasmine, Joe Pye weed, jojoba, juniper, kava, knapweed, lady's mantle, lady's slipper, lady's smock, larkspur, lemon, lemon balm, lichen, licorice, lilac, lily, lime, lobelia, locust, loosestrife, lotus, magnolia, mallow, marsh marigold, meadowsweet, mesquite, milkwort, mimosa, mint (spearmint, water mint), moonwort, morning glory and moonflower, moss, motherwort, mugwort, myrrh, myrtle, nightshade, olive, orange, orchid, pansy, passionflower, peach and nectarine, pear, pearlwort, periwinkle, poplar, poppy, purslane, ragwort, raspberry, reed and rush, rose, sandalwood, seaweed, skullcap, Solomon's seal, spikenard, spindletree, spruce, star anise, stitchwort, stonecrop, storax, strawberry, sweet flag, sweetgrass, sycamore, tamarisk, tansy, tarragon, thorn apple, thyme, tonka bean, turnip, valerian, vanilla, vetchling, violet, water lily, willow, witch hazel, yarrow, yew

Plants by Astrological Sign

Aquarius

Acacia, almond, amaranth, apple, aspen, bindweed, bistort, bittersweet, borage, cherry, cornflower, crabapple, cypress, dandelion, foxglove, frankincense, hawthorn, hellebore, hop, iris, knapweed, lemon, mimosa, mullein, myrrh, olive, parsley, patchouli, pine, rosemary, rowan, sage, sandalwood, skullcap, star anise, violet

Aries

Alder, allspice, anemone, angelica, basil, betony, blackberry, blackthorn, broom, buttercup, cardamom, carnation, cedar, celandine (lesser), cherry, chicory, chili pepper, cinnamon, clove, coriander, cowslip, cress, cumin, dandelion, deer's tongue, dragon's blood, eyebright, fennel, fir, fly agaric, frankincense, fumitory, galangal, geranium, ginger, gorse, hawthorn, holly, honeysuckle, juniper, locust, lords and ladies, mushroom, mustard, nettle, olive, orange, oregano and marjoram, pepper, rosemary, southernwood, speedwell, tarragon, thistle (blessed), thyme, willow

Cancer

Agrimony, alder, aloe, apple, betony, bluebell, cabbage, camphor, cardamom, catnip, chamomile, chestnut, crabapple, daisy, dill, eucalyptus, figwort, gardenia, geranium, holly, honesty, honey-

suckle, hyssop, jasmine, lemon, lemon balm, lotus, maple, mimosa, moonwort, mugwort, myrrh, oak, pine, poppy, purslane, rose, sandalwood, seaweed, spruce, tagetes, violet, water lily, wormwood, yarrow

Capricorn

Aconite, ash, aspen, benzoin, birch, bryony, carnation, cinnamon, comfrey, cornflower, cypress, elm, fumitory, hellebore, holly, jasmine, kava, magnolia, mimosa, myrrh, patchouli, pine, poppy, rowan, rue, skullcap, Solomon's seal, spruce, sweet woodruff, thyme, vervain, vetiver, willow, yew

Gemini

Almond, anise, asafoetida, bay, bean, bee balm, beech, bindweed, bracken, caraway, chestnut, chickweed, clover (white), comfrey, dill, dittany, eyebright, fennel, hawthorn, hazel, hickory, horehound, iris, ivy, lemon, lemongrass, lily, lily of the valley, linden, mandrake, mint, moss, mugwort, mulberry, oak, oregano and marjoram, parsley, pimpernel, pomegranate, rhubarb, snakeroot, snapdragon, Solomon's seal, turnip, vervain, vetch, vetchling, walnut, wormwood, yarrow

Leo

Acacia, amaranth, angelica, anise, basil, bay, borage, bryony, celandine (greater), celery, centaury, chamomile, chrysanthemum, cinnamon, clove, coconut, coriander, crocus, cyclamen, daffodil, date, dill, edelweiss, eyebright, frankincense, goldenseal, hazel, heliotrope, holly, juniper, lime, marigold, mistletoe, motherwort, nutmeg, oak, olive, orange, peony, pimpernel, raspberry, rosemary, rue, St. John's wort, sandalwood, sassafras, spurge, sunflower, tagetes, walnut

Libra

Aloe, apple, ash, aspen, avocado, bean, bluebell, buckthorn, burdock, catnip, cherry, chickweed, coltsfoot, cornflower, crabapple, cyclamen, dandelion, devil's bit scabious, dittany, figwort, foxglove, grape, hazel, hollyhock, lilac, magnolia, maple, mugwort, mullein, nightshade, orchid, oregano and marjoram, parsley, passionflower, pennyroyal, primrose, purslane, rose, strawberry, thyme, vanilla, vetiver, violet, witch hazel, yarrow

Pisces

Alder, aloe, anise, avens, bay, bilberry, camphor, cardamom, catnip, cattail, chickweed, clove, cypress, eucalyptus, gardenia, heliotrope, hemp, houseleek, hyacinth, jasmine, lemon, lily, lovage, meadowsweet, mimosa, nutmeg, purslane, reed and rush, rue, sage, sandalwood, seaweed, star anise, willow

Sagittarius

Aster, beech, bilberry, birch, burdock, carnation, cattail, cedar, centaury, chestnut, chive, clove, clover (red), coconut, cress, daffodil, date, deer's tongue, dragon's blood, feverfew, frankincense, ginger, holly, houseleek, hyssop, juniper, linden, mugwort, myrtle, nutmeg, oak, orange, reed and rush, rose, rosemary, rowan, sage, St. John's wort, spruce, star anise, thorn apple, vervain

Scorpio

Allspice, anemone, barberry and Oregon grape, basil, black cohosh, blackberry, blackthorn, cabbage (green), camellia, cattail, clove, coconut, crocus (saffron), cumin, date, deer's tongue, dill, galangal, gardenia, ginger, heather and heath, hop, horehound, ivy, lily, myrrh, nettle, nightshade, orchid, patchouli, pomegranate, reed and rush, snapdragon, southernwood, thistle, turnip, uva ursi, valerian, vanilla, violet

Taurus

Agrimony, alkanet, apple, apricot, ash, barberry and Oregon grape, blackberry, burdock, cardamom, cedar, cherry, Chinaberry, cinquefoil, coltsfoot, cornflower, crabapple, cumin, cypress, daisy, dandelion, devil's bit scabious, figwort, hawthorn, heather and heath, hibiscus, hornbeam, lilac, lily of the valley, linden, lovage, magnolia, mandrake, moss, mugwort, myrtle, patchouli, raspberry, rose, sage, senna, thyme, vanilla, vetiver, violet, willow, wood sorrel

Virgo

Almond, ash, aster, bean, bee balm, beech, bistort, caraway, chestnut, chicory, cypress, dill, eyebright, fennel, grain, hazel, hickory, horehound, houseleek, hyacinth, lily, lily of the valley, maple, mimosa, mulberry, oak, oregano and marjoram, patchouli, pimpernel, pomegranate, rosemary, sandalwood, savory, senna, skullcap, snakeroot, sweet flag, tobacco, valerian, vetch, violet, walnut

Plants by Planetary/Solar System Association

Jupiter

Agrimony, alkanet, almond, aloe, anise, apple, avens, barberry and Oregon grape, beech, betony, bilberry, birch, Bodhi tree, borage, cabbage (red), carnation, cedar, centaury, chervil, chestnut, chickweed, cinnamon, cinquefoil, clove, coconut, comfrey, dandelion, date, devil's shoestring, dock, dogwood (cornelian), edelweiss, elecampane, fig, fir, fumitory, goosefoot, grape, henna, hickory, honeysuckle, houseleek, hyssop, immortelle, Joe Pye weed, jojoba, larch, lavender (spike), lemon balm, lichen, licorice, linden, magnolia, maple, mastic and pistachio (pistachio), meadowsweet, nutmeg, oak, olive, pea, pear, peony, pine, rhubarb, sage, sassafras, snakeroot, star anise, storax, sycamore, thorn apple, ti plant, tonka bean, vetiver, walnut, yew

Mars

Acacia, aconite (wolfsbane), alder, allspice, almond, anemone, anise, asafoetida, barberry and Oregon grape, basil, benzoin, black cohosh, blackthorn, bloodroot, boxwood, broom, bryony, buckthorn, buttercup, cacao, cactus, campion, caraway, cattail, celandine, chili pepper, chive, clove, coconut, coriander, cow parsley, cress, cumin, cyclamen (wild), damiana, date, deer's tongue, dogwood, dragon's blood, fir, galangal, garlic, geranium, ginger, gorse, hawthorn, hellebore, high John, holly, honeysuckle, hop, hyacinth, juniper, larkspur, loosestrife, lords and ladies, masterwort, mustard, nettle, onion, oregano and marjoram (oregano), patchouli, pennyroyal, pepper, pine, poke, Queen Anne's lace, reed and rush, rue, snakeroot, snapdragon, spurge, sweet woodruff, tarragon, thistle, toadflax, tobacco, turmeric, uva ursi, vetchling, woad, wormwood, yew, yucca, zedoary

Mercury

Agrimony, almond, anise, ash, aspen, bean, bee balm, benzoin, bergamot, betony, bindweed, bittersweet, bracken, bryony, caraway, catnip, cedar, celery, chamomile, cherry, chervil, chicory, chrysanthemum, cinnamon, cinquefoil, clove, clover, dandelion, devil's bit scabious, dill, elder, elecampane, elm, eucalyptus, fennel, flax, fly agaric, harebell, hazel, hickory, honeysuckle, horehound, jasmine, juniper, lavender, lemon, lemongrass, lichen, licorice, lilac, lily of the valley, lime, linden, maidenhair fern, mandrake, mastic and pistachio (pistachio), Mayapple, mint (peppermint), mistletoe, mulberry, mushroom, nutmeg (mace), olive, oregano and marjoram, parsley, periwinkle, pimpernel, pomegranate, Queen Anne's lace, rosemary, sage, sandalwood, savory, senna, southernwood, speedwell, spurge, star anise, storax, turmeric, valerian

Moon

Adder's tongue, alder, aloe, bee balm, belladonna lily, birch, blackberry, bloodroot, bluebell, cabbage, cacao (white chocolate), camellia, camphor, celery, chickweed, club moss, coconut, cress (watercress), daisy (ox-eye), date, dittany, dogwood, eucalyptus, figwort, frankincense, gardenia, ginger, grape, hackberry, hibiscus (white flower), hogweed, honesty, hyssop, iris, jasmine, jojoba, juniper, knotgrass, lady's smock, lemon, lemon balm, lichen, lilac, lily, loosestrife, lotus, mallow, mesquite, milkwort, moonflower, moonwort, morning glory and moonflower (moonflower), mugwort, mushroom, myrrh, myrtle, nutmeg, olive, pear, pearlwort, poplar (white), poppy, pumpkin, purslane, quince, rosemary, rowan, sandalwood, seaweed, senna, sesame, stitchwort, stonecrop, storax, sweet flag, tobacco, turnip, vetch, vetchling, water lily, wayfaring tree, willow

Neptune

Apricot, ash, hemp, immortelle, kava, lobelia, mugwort, seaweed

Pluto

Asafoetida, basil, bittersweet, black cohosh, cypress, dragon's blood, hop, mandrake, nettle, nightshade, parsley, patchouli, reed and rush (reed), skullcap, toadflax, uva ursi, woad, worm-wood, yucca

Saturn

Aconite, amaranth, arnica, aspen, bean, beech, benzoin, bindweed, bistort, bittersweet, black-thorn, bluebell, buckthorn, carnation, cattail, centaury, Chinaberry, comfrey, coriander, cornflower, cypress, dodder, elm, eucalyptus, fir, fumitory, hellebore, hemlock, hemp, henbane, holly, hornbeam, hyacinth, ivy, Joe Pye weed, kava, knapweed, knotgrass, lady's slipper, lichen, life everlasting, lobelia, magnolia, mandrake, mesquite, mimosa, morning glory and moonflower (morning glory), moss, mullein, nightshade, pansy, patchouli, pine, pomegranate, poplar, quassia, quince, rhubarb, rowan, rue, sassafras, senna, skullcap, Solomon's seal, tamarisk, thorn apple, unicorn root, vetiver, violet, witch hazel, woad, yew

Sun

Acacia, almond, amaranth, angelica, apricot, ash, bamboo, bay, benzoin, bergamot, birch, broom, carnation, cedar, celandine (greater), centaury, chamomile, chestnut, chicory, chrysanthemum, cinnamon, clove, coconut, crocus (saffron), cyclamen, daffodil, daisy, date, dittany, eucalyptus, eyebright, forsythia, frankincense, galangal, ginseng, goldenseal, gorse, grain (maize, rice), grape, hazel, heliotrope, hickory, high John, juniper, knotgrass, lemongrass, lime, linden, lotus, lovage, marigold, marsh marigold, mastic and pistachio (mastic), mistletoe, myrrh, oak, olive, orange, peach and nectarine, pear, peony, pimpernel, poinsettia, rose-mary, rowan, rue, St. John's wort, senna, sesame, storax, sunflower, sweet flag, tagetes, turmeric, vervain, walnut, water lily, witch hazel, zedoary, zinnia

Uranus

Ash, chicory, fir, mandrake, marsh marigold, poke, rowan

Venus

African violet, alder, alkanet, almond, aloe, amaranth, apple, apricot, aspen, aster, avocado, barberry and Oregon grape, basil, bedstraw, bee balm, benzoin, birch, blackberry, Bodhi tree, bog myrtle, burdock, cacao, camellia, cardamom, catnip, cherry, coltsfoot, columbine, coriander, cornflower, cowslip, crabapple, crocus, cumin, cyclamen, daffodil, daisy, deadnettle, devil's bit scabious, dittany, elder, evening primrose, fairy wand, feverfew, fig, figwort, forget-me-not, foxglove, geranium, goldenrod, gooseberry, grain, groundsel, harebell, heather and heath, hibiscus, hollyhock, houseleek, hyacinth, iris, ivy, lady's mantle, larkspur, lemongrass, licorice, lilac, lovage, magnolia, maidenhair fern, mallow, mimosa, mint, motherwort, mugwort, mulberry, myrtle, orchid, passionflower, pea, peach and nectarine, pear, pennyroyal, periwinkle, pignut, plantain, pomegranate, primrose, quince, ragwort, raspberry, rhubarb, rose, sandalwood, sassafras, self heal, spikenard, strawberry, sweet woodruff, sweetgrass, sycamore, tansy, tarragon, thyme, tonka bean, tulip, uva ursi, valerian, vanilla, vervain, vetchling (sweet pea), vetiver, violet, willow, wood sorrel, yarrow

Appendix C

Deities

Following is a list of deities who have more than one plant associated with them. All deities can be found in the index.

Adonis: anemone, bay, centaury, dill, fennel, marigold, myrrh, pomegranate, rose

Aine: gorse, meadowsweet, moonwort

Amaterasu: chrysanthemum, grain (rice), heliotrope, olive

Amun: betony, date, olive

Aphrodite: allspice, anemone, apple, apricot, benzoin, boxwood, cardamom, cinnamon, crabapple, daisy, date, dittany, frankincense, hazel, hibiscus, hyacinth, lotus, magnolia, maidenhair fern, mandrake, marigold, myrrh, myrtle, oregano and marjoram, patchouli, peach and nectarine, pear, periwinkle, pine, pomegranate, poppy, Queen Anne's lace, quince, rose, rosemary, rowan, tamarisk, tarragon, vervain, violet, walnut

Apollo: anise, apple, aspen, bay, bean, beech, bluebell, boxwood, centaury, chrysanthemum, cinnamon, clove, crabapple, cyclamen, cypress, date, frankincense, hazel, heliotrope, hyacinth, larkspur, lily of the valley, lotus, marigold, mistletoe, olive, pear, pomegranate, poplar, sunflower, tamarisk, walnut

Ares: ash, holly, maple, oak

Ariadne: grape, moonwort

Arianrhod: cedar, gorse, hazel, heather, ivy, linden, mistletoe, moonwort

Artemis: amaranth, bay, caraway, cedar, cherry, chestnut, cypress, daisy (ox-eye), date, dittany, fir, hazel, hyacinth, lemon balm, lily, marigold, mastic and pistachio, moonwort, mugwort, myrtle, pine, poppy, sesame, southernwood, sycamore, tarragon, walnut, willow, wormwood, yew

Asclepius: bay, cinnamon, lily of the valley, mistletoe, mustard

Asherah: date, lily, peach and nectarine, poplar

Astarte: acacia, almond, cedar, crocus, cypress, date, frankincense, lily, myrtle, pine, pomegranate, walnut

Athena: apple, beech, chrysanthemum, crabapple, feverfew, fir, flax, grape, hyacinth, maple, mulberry, myrtle, olive, patchouli, pear, rose, spindletree, willow

Attis: almond, pine, pomegranate, spruce, violet

Baal: cedar, frankincense, pomegranate

Bacchus: bay, beech, daffodil, dill, fig, fir, grape, hemp, ivy, mastic and pistachio, orchid, periwinkle, pine, pomegranate, yew

Badb: apple, crabapple, yew

Balder: apple, bay, chamomile, juniper, mistletoe, oak, St. John's wort

Banba: blackthorn, yew

Bast: catnip, frankincense, gooseberry

Bel/Belenus: ash, blackthorn, frankincense, gorse, hawthorn, henbane, willow

Bertha: blackthorn, cowslip, elder, flax, primrose

Blodeuwedd: hawthorn, meadowsweet

Boann: chestnut, elder, hazel

Brahma: acacia, licorice, lotus, olive, poplar

Brigid: anemone, blackberry, blackthorn, cedar, coltsfoot, dandelion, figwort, flax, grain, hawthorn, oak, rowan, willow

Buddha: Bodhi, lotus, patchouli

Cailleach Bheur: alder, crabapple, elder, holly, self heal, yew

Ceres: apple, bay, bean, chervil, daffodil, elm, fig, grain, lily, linden, lotus, pine, pomegranate, poppy, willow

Cernunnos: asafoetida, bay, campion, chamomile, gooseberry, holly, ivy, oak, tamarisk, yarrow

Cerridwen: beech, birch, elm, honeysuckle, locust, rowan, spruce, vervain, willow

Chiron: centaury, cornflower

Circe: boxwood, cardamom, garlic, mandrake, nightshade, rue, willow

Coventina: cattail, reed and rush

Cronus: bluebell, hellebore, poplar

Cupid: cypress, rose

Cybele: almond, boxwood, fir, lemon balm, myrrh, pine, pomegranate, spruce, violet

Dagda: ash, betony, birch, blackberry, blackthorn, elder, gorse, hawthorn, holly, oak, rowan, yew

Danu: aspen, blackberry, elder, elm, hawthorn, hazel, holly, ivy, meadowsweet, spruce, willow

Demeter: amaranth, apple, daffodil, elm, fig, fumitory, grain, hazel, hyacinth, lady's mantle, lemon balm, lotus, mint, mistletoe, myrrh, myrtle, pennyroyal, pine, pomegranate, poplar, poppy, rose, sesame, storax, sunflower, vervain, violet, willow

Diana: acacia, apple, bay, beech, chestnut, crabapple, cypress, date, dittany, fir, gardenia, hazel, hibiscus, jasmine, juniper, lily, mandrake, marigold, mastic and pistachio, moonwort, mugwort, mulberry, pine, poppy, rue, sycamore, tarragon, vervain, walnut, willow, wormwood

Dionysus: apple, bay, bean, beech, cinnamon, crabapple, daffodil, dill, elm, fennel, fig, fir, grape, hemp, ivy, mastic and pistachio, myrtle, orchid, pine, pomegranate, storax, walnut, yew

Dôn: oak, yew

Durga: lemon, turmeric

Eos: crocus, sycamore

Eostre: lily, linden

Epona: coltsfoot, valerian, vervain

Eros: apple, crabapple, myrtle, rose

Fates: cypress, daffodil, flax, mandrake, spindletree

Faunus: grape, pine

Flora: anemone, cherry, cornflower, crabapple, hawthorn, olive, rose

Freya: alder, apple, beech, birch, blackberry, cowslip, crabapple, daisy, elder, flax, goosefoot, ivy, lady's mantle, linden, mistletoe, moss, primrose, rose, spindletree, strawberry, sweet woodruff

Freyr: ash, elder, gorse, holly, walnut

Frigg: ash, aspen, bedstraw, beech, birch, fir, flax, hawthorn, lady's mantle, linden, mistletoe, rose, spindletree, strawberry

Furies: cypress, juniper, yew

Gaia: aspen, bay, elder, elm, holly, honeysuckle, lady's mantle, orange, patchouli, peach and nectarine, yucca

Ganesh: coconut, hibiscus, sesame, turmeric, vetiver

Geb: cattail, reed and rush

Gwydion: fly agaric, meadowsweet

Hades: boxwood, celery, cypress, daffodil, fumitory, henbane, mint, mistletoe, pomegranate, poplar, thorn apple

Harpocrates: peach and nectarine, rose

Hathor: fig, grape, heliotrope, lotus, mandrake, myrtle, rose, water lily

Hecate: aconite, anise, arnica, aspen, bittersweet, cardamom, chrysanthemum, cress, cyclamen, cypress, dandelion, date, feverfew, fumitory, garlic, hemlock, henbane, juniper, lavender, locust, mandrake, mint, moonwort, mugwort, myrrh, nightshade, pennyroyal, poplar, rowan, sesame, storax, thorn apple, willow, yew

Helios: bay, cinnamon, date, frankincense, heliotrope, hellebore, pear, sunflower

Hera: apple, celery, crabapple, crocus, henbane, iris, lily, olive, orange, parsley, peach and nectarine, pear, pomegranate, poppy, vervain, willow

Hermes: almond, anise, bay, caraway, date, fig, hazel, ivy, lemon, lotus, mulberry, olive, pomegranate, poppy, vervain, willow, yew

Hina: bamboo, coconut

Holda: grain, linden

Holle: ash, beech, blackthorn, elder, elm, flax, holly, ivy, juniper, rose, spindletree, yew

Horus: centaury, cinnamon, clove, horehound, iris, lotus, myrrh, olive, water lily

Idunn: apple, rose

Indra: hemp, olive

Inanna: cattail, date, fir, grain, grape, pomegranate, reed and rush

Iris: fig, iris

Ishtar: acacia, myrtle, pine, pomegranate, star anise, willow

Isis: acacia, date, fir, gardenia, grain, heather, iris, lily, lotus, mugwort, myrrh, onion, peach and nectarine, pine, rose, southernwood, vervain, water lily, wormwood

Juno: celery, dittany, elm, fig, grape, iris, lily, myrrh, orange, parsley, pear, pomegranate, vervain, willow

Jupiter: carnation, cinnamon, cypress, gorse, henbane, houseleek, mistletoe, mullein, oak, olive, orange, parsley, sage, vervain, violet, walnut

Kali: asafoetida, coconut, hibiscus, turmeric

Kane-Hekili: kava, ti plant

Krishna: basil, camphor, cardamom, turmeric

Kuan Yin: bamboo, camellia, camphor, lily, lotus

Kupala: fennel, galangal, lemon balm, oregano and marjoram, sage, valerian

Lakshmi: basil, galangal, lotus, star anise

Lilith: garlic, tarragon

Loki: beech, blackthorn, elm, ivy, juniper, moss, willow, yew

Lono: kava, ti plant

Lugh: bilberry, birch, crabapple, gorse, grain, holly, yew

Luna: bluebell, eucalyptus, gardenia, moonwort, poplar, Queen Anne's lace, rowan, willow

Macha: apple, ash, blackthorn, crabapple, nightshade

Manannán Mac Lir: alder, apple, ash, blackberry, crabapple, hazel, reed and rush, seaweed

Mars: ash, bay, cherry, fig, myrtle, rue, sweet woodruff, vervain

Medea: aconite, cardamom, chrysanthemum, cress, henbane

Mercury: almond, anise, bay, caraway, cinnamon, date, eucalyptus, fig, hazel, mulberry, pomegranate, poppy, vervain, willow

Minerva: alder, apple, ash, flax, geranium, hibiscus, mulberry, olive, pear, poppy, spindletree, thistle

Mithras: cypress, heliotrope, pomegranate

Modron: patchouli, poppy

Morpheus: elm, poppy

Morrigan: aspen, cattail, cherry, gooseberry, henbane, honeysuckle, juniper, locust, reed and rush, willow

Neptune: ash, pine, seaweed

Norns: flax, spindletree

Odin: ash, aspen, beech, cedar, elm, fennel, fly agaric, hazel, lemon, linden, mistletoe, oak, rose, strawberry, yew

Ogma: hazel, ivy

Oshun: allspice, vetiver

Osiris: acacia, cedar, clove, dittany, fig, fir, fumitory, grain, ivy, licorice, lotus, pine, tamarisk, water lily, willow

Pachamama: damiana, yucca

Pan: alder, asafoetida, campion, cattail, cherry, dittany, fir, hemp, ivy, mulberry, oak, orchid, patchouli, peony, pine, reed and rush, rowan, savory, tamarisk, thistle (blessed)

Parvati: camellia, henna, lemon

Pele: olive, ti plant

Persephone: aspen, cedar, cherry, daffodil, dittany, fig, fir, fumitory, grain, ivy, lemon balm, mint, mistletoe, parsley, pennyroyal, pine, pomegranate, poplar, poppy, sesame, snowdrop, vervain, violet, walnut, willow

Pluto: boxwood, celery, cypress, mint, mistletoe, pomegranate, poplar

Pomona: pear, walnut

Poseidon: ash, celery, olive, pine, reed and rush, seaweed, spruce, willow

Quetzalcoatl: cacao, mesquite

Ra: acacia, bay, cedar, centaury, chamomile, cinnamon, clove, fig, frankincense, heliotrope, lotus, myrrh, olive, water lily

Ran: blackthorn, elm, juniper, rowan, seaweed

Rhea: elder, fir, grape, ivy, lady's mantle, myrrh, oak, pine, walnut

Rhiannon: apple, cattail, crabapple, jasmine, maple, moonwort, reed and rush, willow

Saturn: bluebell, cypress, fig, grape, hellebore, holly, ivy, lavender, mandrake, myrrh, olive, orchid, willow, yew

Sekhmet: catnip, pomegranate

Selene: bluebell, eucalyptus, gardenia, moonwort, poplar, Queen Anne's lace, rowan

Shiva: aconite, almond, camphor, coconut, hemp, moonwort, patchouli, vetiver, water lily

Silvanus: grape, pine

Thor: aconite, ash, beech, birch, cherry, daisy, fumitory, gorse, grape, hazel, holly, houseleek, mugwort, nettle, oak, pea, rowan, thistle, vervain, walnut

Thoth: almond, bamboo, crocus, fig, forget-me-not, hawthorn, lemon, lotus

Tyr: aspen, linden, thistle

Venus: alder, allspice, almond, anemone, angelica, apple, apricot, aster, basil, benzoin, boxwood, cinnamon, crabapple, daisy, dittany, elder, eucalyptus, frankincense, hazel, heather, honeysuckle, lady's mantle, lily, linden, magnolia, maidenhair fern, maple, mint, mistletoe, mulberry, myrtle, oregano and marjoram, peach and nectarine, pear, pine, poppy, Queen Anne's lace, quince, raspberry, rose, rosemary, sandalwood, strawberry, tarragon, vervain, violet

Vesta: bay, hemp, lavender

Vishnu: basil, Bodhi, camphor, coconut, jasmine, lotus, patchouli, sandalwood

Vulcan: elder, pine, rowan

Woden: fennel, fly agaric, mugwort, nettle

Yama: sesame, tamarisk

Yemaya: allspice, vetiver

Zeus: almond, apple, aspen, beech, betony, carnation, crabapple, crocus, daisy, hawthorn, houseleek, mint, mistletoe, oak, olive, orange, parsley, poplar, raspberry, sage, storax, sycamore, vervain, violet, walnut, willow

Bibliography

Albala, Ken. *Beans: A History*. New York: Berg, 2007.

Alexander, Leslie M., and Walter C. Rucker, eds. *Encyclopedia of African American History*. Santa Barbara, CA: ABC-CLIO, LLC, 2010.

Anderson, Graham. *Greek and Roman Folklore*. Westport, CT: Greenwood Press, 2006.

Athanassakis, Apostolos N., and Benjamin M. Wolkow, trans. *The Orphic Hymns*. Baltimore, MD: The Johns Hopkins University Press, 2013.

Austin, Daniel F. *Florida Ethnobotany*. New York: CRC Press, 2004.

Baker, Margaret. *Discovering the Folklore of Plants*, 3rd. ed. Oxford, England: Shire Publications, 2021.

Bane, Theresa. *Encyclopedia of Spirits and Ghosts in World Mythology*. Jefferson, NC: McFarland & Company, Inc., 2016.

Barceloux, Donald G. *Medical Toxicology of Natural Substances: Foods, Fungi, Medicinal Herbs, Plants, and Venomous Animals*. Hoboken, NJ: John Wiley & Sons, Inc., 2008.

Barnhart, Robert K., ed. *The Barnhart Concise Dictionary of Etymology*. New York: HarperCollins, 1995.

Bäumler, Siegfried. *Heilpflanzenpraxis Heute: Arzneipflanzenporträts*. Munich, Germany: Elsevier GmbH, 2021.

Berens, E. M. *Myths and Legends of Ancient Greece and Rome*. Irvine, CA: Xist Publishing, 2015.

Bernhardt, Peter. *Gods and Goddesses in the Garden: Greco-Roman Mythology and the Scientific*

Names of Plants. New Brunswick, NJ: Rutgers University Press, 2008.

Betz, Hans Dieter, ed. *The Greek Magical Papyri in Translation, Including the Demotic Spells, vol.1, 2nd ed*. Chicago: The University of Chicago Press, 1996.

Bincsik, Monika. *Japanese Bamboo Art: The Abbey Collection*. New York: The Metropolitan Museum of Art, 2017.

Binney, Ruth. *The Gardener's Wise Words and Country Ways*. Newton Abbot, England: David & Charles, 2011.

———. *Plant Lore and Legend: The Wisdom and Wonder of Plants and Flowers Revealed*. Mineola, NY: Dover Publications, Inc., 2019.

Boas, Franz, ed. *Journal of American Folklore*, vol. 30, No. 115. New York: American Folk-Lore Society, 1917.

Bonar, Ann. *Herbs: A Complete Guide to the Cultivation and Use of Wild and Domesticated Herbs*. New York: MacMillan Publishing Co., 1985.

Bovery, Rodney W. *Mesquite: History, Growth, Biology, Uses, and Management*. College Station, TX: Texas A&M University Press, 2016.

Breverton, Terry. *Breverton's Complete Herbal: A Book of Remarkable Plants and Their Uses*. New York: Quercus, 2011.

Britten, James, and Robert Holland. *A Dictionary of English Plant-names*. London: Trübner & Co., 1886.

Brodo, Irwin M., Sylvia Duran Sharnoff, and Stephen Sharnoff. *Lichens of North America*. New Haven, CT: Yale University Press, 2001.

Cameron, John. *Gaelic Names of Plants (Scottish and Irish)*. London: William Blackwood and Sons, 1883.

Cameron, Ken. *Vanilla Orchids: Natural History and Cultivation*. Portland, OR: Timber Press, Inc., 2011.

Casas, Starr. *Old Style Conjure: Hoodoo, Rootwork & Folk Magic*. Newburyport, MA: Weiser Books, 2017.

Castleman, Michael. *The New Healing Herbs*, 4th ed. New York: Rodale, Inc., 2017.

Chapman, Baylor. *Decorating with Plants*. New York: Artisan, 2019.

Charles, Denys J. *Antioxidant Properties of Spices, Herbs and Other Sources*. New York: Springer Science + Business Media, 2013.

Chevallier, Andrew. *The Encyclopedia of Medicinal Plants*. New York: Dorling Kindersley, 1996.

Chichoke, Anthony J. *Secrets of Native American Herbal Remedies*. New York: Penguin Putnam Inc., 2001.

Chormaic, Sanas. *Cormac's Glossary. Translated by John O'Donovan. Edited by Whitley Stokes*. Dublin, Ireland: The Irish Archaeological and Celtic Society, 1868.

Chwalkowski, Farrin. *Symbols in Arts, Religion and Culture: The Soul of Nature*. Newcastle upon Tyne, England: Cambridge Scholars Publishing, 2016.

Clarke, Philip A. *Australian Plants as Aboriginal Tools*. Sydney, Australia: Rosenberg Publishing, 2012.

Clarke, Robert C., and Mark D. Merlin. *Cannabis: Evolution and Ethnobotany*. Berkeley, CA: University of California Press, 2013.

Collins, David J., ed. *The Cambridge History of Magic and Witchcraft in the West: From Antiquity to the Present*. New York: Cambridge University Press, 2015.

Coombes, Allen. *Dictionary of Plant Names*. Portland, OR: Timber Press, Inc., 1985.

Crawford, Suzanne J., and Dennis F. Kelley. *American Indian Religious Traditions: An Encyclopedia*, vol. 1. Santa Barbara, CA: ABC CLIO, 2005.

Craze, Richard. *The Spice Companion: The Culinary, Cosmetic, and Medicinal Uses of Spices*. Allentown, PA: People's Medical Society, 1997.

Cruden, Loren. *Medicine Grove: A Shamanic Herbal*. Rochester, VT: Destiny Books, 1997.

Culpeper, Nicholas. *The English Physician*. London: B. & R. Crosby & Co., 1814.

Cumo, Christopher, ed. *Encyclopedia of Cultivated Plants: From Acacia to Zinnia*. Santa Barbara, CA: ABC-CLIO, 2013.

Cunningham, Scott. *Cunningham's Encyclopedia of Magical Herbs*. St. Paul, MN: Llewellyn Publications, 1998.

Curtin, Jeremiah, and J. N. B. Hewitt. "Seneca Fiction, Legends, and Myths," *Thirty-Second Annual Report of the Bureau of American Ethnology* (1910–1911): 694–701. Washington, DC: Government Printing Office, 1918.

Damodaran, Vinita, Anna Winterbottom, and Alan Lester, eds. *The East India Company and the Natural World*. London: Palgrave Macmillan, 2014.

Daniels, Cora Linn, and C. M. Stevans, eds. *Encyclopedia of Superstitions, Folklore, and the Occult Sciences of the World*, vol. 2. Honolulu, HI: University Press of the Pacific, 2003.

Davies, Owen. *America Bewitched: The Story of Witchcraft After Salem*. New York: Oxford University Press, 2013.

Davidson, Alan. *The Oxford Companion to Food*, 3rd ed. Edited by Tom Jaine. Oxford, England: Oxford University Press, 2014.

Dawson, Adele G. *Herbs: Partners in Life*. Rochester, VT: Healing Arts Press, 2000.

De Cleene, Marcel, and Marie Claire Lejeune. *Compendium of Symbolic and Ritual Plants in Europe*, vols. 1 and 2. Ghent, Belgium: Man & Culture Publishers, 2003.

Deas, Lizzie. *Flower Favourites: Their Legends, Symbolism and Significance*. London: Chiswick Press, 1898.

Dendle, Peter, and Alain Touwaide, eds. *Health and Healing from the Medieval Garden*. Woodbridge, England: The Boydell Press, 2015.

Denker, Joel S. *The Carrot Purple and Other Curious Stories of the Food We Eat*. New York: Rowman & Littlefield Publishers, 2015.

Dobelis, Inge N., ed. *Magic and Medicine of Plants: A Practical Guide to the Science, History, Folklore, and Everyday Uses of Medicinal Plants*. Pleasantville, NY: The Reader's Digest Association, Inc., 1986.

Dorsey, Lilith. *Orishas, Goddesses, and Voodoo Queens: The Divine Feminine in the African Religious Traditions*. Newburyport, MA: Red Wheel/Weiser, 2020.

Drury, Nevill. *The Watkins Dictionary of Magic: Over 3000 Entries on the World of Magical Formulas, Secret Symbols and The Occult*. London: Watkins Publishing, 2005.

Duke, James A. *Duke's Handbook of Medicinal Spices*. Boca Raton, FL: CRC Press, Ltd., 2003.

Dundes, Alan, ed., *The Evil Eye: A Casebook*. Madison, WI: The University of Wisconsin Press, 1992.

Durkin, Philip. *The Oxford Guide to Etymology*. New York: Oxford University Press, 2009.

Eastman, John. *Wildflowers of the Eastern United States: An Introduction to Common Species of*

Woods, Wetlands and Field. Mechanicsburg, PA: Stackpole Books, 2014.

Editorial Staff. *Webster's Third New International Dictionary, Unabridged*, vol. 2. Chicago: Encyclopedia Britannica, Inc., 1981.

Ellena, Jean-Claude. *The Atlas of Perfumed Botany*. Translated by Erik Butler. Boston: The MIT Press, 2022.

English, Ali. *Wild Medicine: Summer*. London: Aeon Books, Ltd. 2019.

Euser, Barbara J., ed. *Bay Area Gardening: 64 Practical Essays by Master Gardeners*. Palo Alto, CA: Solas House, 2005.

Everett, Thomas H., ed. *New York Botanical Garden Illustrated Encyclopedia of Horticulture*, vol. 4. New York: Garland Publishing, Inc., 1980.

Fischer-Rizzi, Susanne. *The Complete Aromatherapy Handbook*. New York, NY: Sterling Publishing Company, Inc., 1991.

Flynn, Paula. "Witches' Brooms on Trees," Hortnews.extension.iastate.edu. Ames, IA: Iowa State University Extension and Outreach, 2/23/05. https://hortnews.extension.iastate .edu/2005/2-23-2005/witchesbroom.html . accessed 5/25/21.

Folkard, Richard. *Plant Lore, Legends, and Lyrics: Embracing the Myths, Traditions, Superstitions, and Folklore of the Plant Kingdom*, 2nd ed. London: Sampson, Low, Marston, & Company, 1892.

Foster, Steven, and Rebecca L. Johnson. *National Geographic Desk Reference to Nature's Medicine*. Washington, DC: National Geographic Society, 2008.

Foxwood, Orion. *The Candle and the Crossroads: A Book of Appalachian Conjure and Southern Root-Work*. Newburyport, MA: Weiser Books, 2012.

Frazer, James George. *The Golden Bough: A Study in Magic and Religion*. New York: The Macmillan Company, 1951.

Friend, Hilderic. *Flowers and Flower Lore*, vol. 2. London: W. Swan Sonnenschein and Company, 1884.

Fry, Susan Leigh. *Burial in Medieval Ireland 900-1500: A Review of the Written Sources*. Dublin, Ireland: Four Courts Press, 1999.

Ganeri, Anita. *Mesoamerican Myth: A Treasury of Central American Legends, Art, and History*. New York: Taylor & Francis, 2016.

Gerard, John. *The Herball or Generall Historie of Plantes*. London: John Norton, 1597.

Gibson, Marion, ed. *Witchcraft and Society in England and America*, 1550–1750. London: Continuum, 2003.

Gledhill, David. *The Names of Plants*, 4th ed. New York: Cambridge University Press, 2008.

Goll, James W., and Michal Ann Goll. *Dream Language: The Prophetic Power of Dreams*. Shippensburg, PA: Destiny Image Publishers, Inc., 2006.

Goodman, Jordan. *Tobacco in History: The Cultures of Dependence*. New York: Routledge, 2005.

Gordh, Gordon, comp. *A Dictionary of Entomology*, 2nd ed. Cambridge, MA: CABI Publishing, 2011.

Grady, Wayne, *The Great Lakes: The Natural History of a Changing Region*. Vancouver, Canada: Greystone Books, 2007.

Greene, Stephanie L., Karen A. Williams, Colin K. Khoury, Michael B. Kantar, and Laura F. Marek, eds. *North American Crop Wild Relatives*, vol. 2. Cham, Switzerland: Springer Nature Switzerland AG, 2019.

Grieve, Margaret. *A Modern Herbal*, vols. 1 and 2. Mineola, NY: Dover Publications, 1971.

Hall, John R. Clark. *Concise Anglo-Saxon Dictionary: For the Use of Students*. New York: Macmillan & Co., 1894.

Hallowell, Barbara G. *Mountain Year: A Southern Appalachian Nature Notebook*. Winston-Salem, NC: John F. Blair, Publisher, 1998.

Hancock, James F. *Plant Evolution and the Origin of Crop Species*, 3rd ed. Cambridge, MA: CABI, 2012.

Hand, Wayland D., ed. *The Frank C. Brown Collection of North Carolina Folklore*, vol. 7. Durham, NC: Duke University Press, 1964.

Hanif, Muhammad Asif, Haq Nawaz, Muhammad Mumtaz Khan, and Hugh J. Byrne, eds. *Medicinal Plants of South Asia*. Cambridge, MA: Elsevier, 2020.

Hanson, Glen R., Peter J. Venturelli, and Annette E. Fleckenstein. *Drugs and Society*, 11th ed. Burlington, MA: Jones & Bartlett Learning, 2012.

Hatfield, Gabrielle. *Encyclopedia of Folk Medicine: Old World and New World Traditions*. Santa Barbara, CA: ABC-CLIO, Inc., 2004.

———. *Hatfield's Herbal: The Curious Stories of Britain's Wild Plants*. New York: Penguin Books, 2009.

Hedera, Via. *Folkloric American Witchcraft and the Multicultural Experience: A Crucible at the Crossroads*. Alresford, England: Moon Books, 2021.

Heilmeyer, Marina. *Ancient Herbs*. Los Angeles: Getty Publications, 2007.

Henderson, Peter. *Henderson's Handbook of Plants and General Horticulture*. New York: Peter Henderson & Company, 1910.

Homoya, Michael A. *Wildflowers and Ferns of Indiana Forests: A Field Guide*. Bloomington, IN: Indiana University Press, 2012.

Hooke, Della. *Trees in Anglo-Saxon England: Literature, Lore and Landscape*. Woodbridge, England: The Boydell Press, 2010.

Hourihane, Colum, ed. *The Routledge Companion to Medieval Iconography*. New York: Routledge, 2017.

Hulme, Frederick Edward. *Wild Fruits of the Country-side*. London: Hutchinson & Co., 1902.

Hurst, Kim. Hidden Natural History. *Herbs: The Secret Properties of 150 Plants*. Chicago: University of Chicago Press, 2015.

Hutchings, Anne, Alan Haxton Scott, Gillian Lewis, and Anthony Cunningham. *Zulu Medicinal Plants*. Scottsville, South Africa: University of KwaZulu-Natal Press, 1996.

Jacob, Dorothy. *A Witch's Guide to Gardening*. Marlboro, NJ: Taplinger Publishing Company, 1965.

Jameson, John H., and Sergiu Musteaţă, eds. *Transforming Heritage Practice in the 21st Century*. Cham, Switzerland: Springer Nature, 2019.

Jamieson, John. *Supplement to the Etymological Dictionary of the Scottish Language*, vol. 1. Edinburgh, Scotland: Edinburgh University Press, 1825.

Janick, Jules, and James N. Moore, eds. *Fruit Breeding: Tree and Tropical Fruits*, vol. 1. New York: John Wiley & Sons, Inc., 1996.

John, J. *A Christmas Compendium*. New York: Continuum Books, 2005.

Jones, David E. *Poison Arrows: North American Indian Hunting and Warfare*. Austin, TX: University of Texas Press, 2009.

Jones, Julia, and Barbara Deer. *The Country Diary of Garden Lore*. London: Dorling Kindersley Ltd., 1987.

Kail, Tony. *A Secret History of Memphis Hoodoo: Rootworkers, Conjurers & Spirituals*. Charleston, SC: The History Press, 2017.

Kaplan, Matt. *Science of the Magical: From the Holy Grail to Love Potions to Superpowers*. New York: Scribner, 2015.

Kear, Katherine. *Flower Wisdom: The Definitive Guidebook to the Myth, Folklore, and Healing Powers of Flowers*. London: Thorsons, 2000.

Khory, Rustomjee Naserwanjee, and Nanabhai Navrosji Katrak. *Materia Medica of India and Their Therapeutics*. Bombay, India: Caxton Works, 1903.

Kieckhefer, Richard. *Magic in the Middle Ages*, 2nd ed. Cambridge, England: Cambridge University Press, 2014.

Kiple, Kenneth F. *The Cambridge World History of Food*, vol. 1 and 2. New York: Cambridge University Press, 2000.

Kivelson, Valerie A., and Christine D. Worobec, eds. *Witchcraft in Russia and Ukraine, 1000-1900*. Ithaca, NY: Northern Illinois University Press, 2020.

Klaniczay, Gábor, and Éva Pócs, eds. *Witchcraft Mythologies and Persecutions*, vol. 3. New York: Central European University Press, 2008.

Kowalchik, Claire, and William H. Hylton, eds. *Rodale's Illustrated Encyclopedia of Herbs*. Emmaus, PA: Rodale Press, Inc., 1998.

Lang, Andrew. *Tales of Troy and Greece*. Mineola, NY: Dover Publications, Inc., 2006.

Lawless, Julia. *The Essential Aromatherapy Garden: Growing and Using Scented Plants and Herbs*. Charlottesville, VA: Hampton Roads Publishing Company, Inc., 2019.

Lawrence, Sandra. *Witch's Garden: Plants in Folklore, Magic and Traditional Medicine*. London: Welbeck, 2020.

Lebot, Vincent, Mark Merlin, and Lamont Lindstrom. *Kava: The Pacific Elixir*. Rochester, VT: Healing Arts Press, 1992.

Lecouteux, *Encyclopedia of Norse and Germanic Folklore, Mythology, and Magic*. Translated by Jon E. Graham. Edited by Michael Moynihan. Rochester, VT: Inner Traditions, 2016.

Lehner, Ernst, and Johanna Lehner. *Folklore and Symbolism of Flowers, Plants and Trees*. Garden City, NY: Dover Publications, Inc., 2003.

Leland, Charles Godfrey. *Legends of Florence*. New York: Macmillan and Company, 1895.

Loudon, Jane. *British Wild Flowers*. London: William Smith, 1846.

Lucas, Susanne. *Bamboo*. London: Reaktion Books Ltd. 2013.

Luck, George, ed. *Arcana Mundi: Magic and the Occult in the Greek and Roman Worlds*, 2nd ed. Baltimore: The Johns Hopkins University Press, 2006.

Lust, John. *The Herb Book*. Mineola, NY: Dover Publications, Inc., 2009.

Mac Coitir, Niall. *Ireland's Trees: Myths, Legends and Folklore*. Wilton, Ireland: The Collins Press, 2015.

———. *Ireland's Wild Plants: Myths, Legends and Folklore*. Wilton, Ireland: The Collins Press, 2015.

MacLeod, Sharon Paice. *Celtic Myth and Religion. A Study of Traditional Belief with Newly Translated Prayers, Poems and Songs.* Jefferson, NC: McFarland & Company, Inc., 2011.

Magner, Lois N., and Oliver J. Kim. *A History of Medicine,* 3rd ed. Boca Raton, FL: CRC Press, 2017.

Mallows, Lucy, and Paul Brummell. *Romania: Transylvania,* 3rd ed. Guilford, CT: The Globe Pequot Press, Inc., 2018.

Markale, Jean. *Merlin: Priest of Nature.* Translated by Belle N. Burke. Rochester, VT: Inner Traditions, 1995.

Marley, Greg A. *Chanterelle Dreams, Amanita Nightmares: The Love, Lore, and Mystique of Mushrooms.* White River Junction, VT: Chelsea Green Publishing, Inc., 2010.

Martin, Laura C. *Wildflower Folklore.* New York: The East Woods Press, 1984.

———. *The Folklore of Trees & Shrubs.* Chester, CT: The Globe Pequot Press, 1992.

———. *A Naturalist's Book of Wildflowers: Celebrating 85 Native Plants of North America.* Taftsville, VT: Countryman Press, 2021.

McAleavy, Tony. *The Last Witch Craze: John Aubrey, the Royal Society and the Witches.* Stroud, England: Amberley Publishing, 2022.

McNeill, F. Marian. *The Silver Bough, Scottish Folklore and Folk-belief,* vol. 1. New York: Cannongate Books, Ltd., 2001.

Medina, Barbara F., and Victor Medina. *Central Appalachian Wildflowers.* Guilford, CT: The Globe Pequot Press, 2002.

Mercer, John Edward. *Alchemy, Its Science and Romance.* New York: The Macmillan Co., 1921.

Metzner, Ralph. *The Well of Remembrance: Rediscovering the Earth Wisdom Myths of Northern Europe.* Boston: Shambhala Publications, Inc., 1994.

Miller, Richard Alan, and Iona Miller. *The Magical and Ritual Use of Perfumes.* Rochester, VT: Destiny Books, 1990.

Minford, John, trans. *I-Ching: The Book of Change.* New York: Penguin Books, 2015.

Moerman, Daniel E. *Medicinal Plants of Native America,* vols. 1 and 2. Ann Arbor, MI: The University of Michigan Press, 1986.

Morton, Mark. *Cupboard Love: A Dictionary of Culinary Curiosities,* 2nd revised ed. Toronto, Canada: Insomniac Press, 2004.

Murray, Michael T., and Joseph Pizzorno. *The Encyclopedia of Healing Foods.* New York: Atria Books, 2005.

Nassau, Robert Hamill. *Fetichism in West Africa.* New York: Charles Scribner's Sons, 1904.

Neal, Bill. *Gardener's Latin: Discovering the Origins, Lore & Meanings of Botanical Names.* Chapel Hill, NC: Algonquin Books of Chapel Hill, 1992.

Németh, Éva, ed. *Caraway: The Genus Carum. Reading,* England: Harwood Academic Publishers, 1999.

Orr, Stephen. *The New American Herbal.* New York: Crown Publishing Group, 2014.

Pamita, Madame. *The Book of Candle Magic: Candle Spell Secrets to Change Your Life.* Woodbury, MN: Llewellyn Publications, 2010.

Pandit, Bansi. *Explore Hinduism.* Loughborough, England: Explore Books, 2005.

Parish, Helen L., ed. *Superstition and Magic in Early Modern Europe*. New York: Bloomsbury Publishing Plc., 2015.

Pauwels, Ivo, and Gerty Christoffels. *Herbs*. Translated by Milton Webber. Antwerp, The Netherlands: Struik Publishers, 2006.

Peattie, Donald Culross. *A Natural History of Trees of Eastern and Central North America*. New York: Houghton Mifflin, 1966.

Pereira, Jonathan. *The Elements of Materia Medica and Therapeutics*, vol. 2, 3rd ed. Philadelphia: Blanchard and Lea, 1854.

Phaneuf, Holly. *Herbs Demystified*. New York, NY: Marlowe & Company, 2005.

Pintchman, Tracy, and Corinne G. Dempsey, eds. *Sacred Matters: Material Religion in South Asian Traditions*. Albany, NY: State University of New York Press, 2015.

Pollington, Stephen. *Leechcraft: Early English Charms, Plantlore and Healing*. Ely, England: Anglo-Saxon Books, 2008.

Porteous, Alexander. *The Forest in Folklore and Mythology*. Mineola, NY: Dover Publications, Inc., 2002.

Porter, Enid. *Routledge Library Editions: Folklore*. Cambridgeshire Customs and Folklore, vol. 4. New York: Routledge, 2015.

Prance, Ghillean, and Mark Nesbitt. *The Cultural History of Plants*. New York: Routledge, 2005.

Pratt, Christina. *An Encyclopedia of Shamanism*, vol. 1. New York: The Rosen Publishing Group, Inc., 2007.

Quattrocchi, Umberto. *CRC World Dictionary of Plant Names: Common Names, Scientific Names, Eponyms, Synonyms, and Etymology*, vol. 1. Boca Raton, FL: CRC Press, LLC, 2000.

———. *CRC World Dictionary of Medicinal and Poisonous Plants: Common Names, Scientific Names, Eponyms, Synonyms, and Etymology*. Boca Raton, FL: CRC Press, 2012

Randolph, Vance. *Ozark Magic and Folklore*. New York: Dover Publications, Inc., 2012.

Ransome, Hilda M. *The Sacred Bee in Ancient Times and Folklore*. Mineola, NY: Dover Publications, Inc., 2012.

Rassool, G. Hussein. *Evil Eye, Jinn Possession, and Mental Health Issues: An Islamic Perspective*. New York: Taylor & Francis, 2018.

Rätsch, Christian. *The Encyclopedia of Psychoactive Plants: Ethnopharmacology and Its Applications*. Translated by John R. Baker. Rochester, VT: Park Street Press, 2005.

Ray, Meredith K. *Daughters of Alchemy: Women and Scientific Culture in Early Modern Italy*. Cambridge, MA: Harvard University Press, 2015.

Rhind, Jennifer Peace. *Fragrance and Wellbeing: Plant Aromatics and Their Influence on the Psyche*. Philadelphia: Singing Dragon, 2014.

Rich, Vivian A. *Cursing the Basil and Other Folklore of the Garden*. Victoria, Canada: Horsdal & Schubart Publishers, Ltd., 1998.

Richardson, Rosamond. *Britain's Wild Flowers: A Treasury of Traditions, Superstitions, Remedies and Literature*. London: National Trust Books, 2017.

Roberts, Peter, and Shelley Evans. *The Book of Fungi: A Life-Size Guide to Six Hundred Species from Around the World*. Chicago: University of Chicago Press, 2014.

Róbertsdóttir, Anna Rósa. *Icelandic Herbs and Their Medicinal Uses*. Translated by Shelagh Smith. Berkeley, CA: North Atlantic Books, 2016.

Rosenthal, Bernard. *Salem Story: Reading the Witch Trials of 1692*. New York: Cambridge University Press, 1995.

Salmón, Enrique. *Iwígara: American Indian Ethnobotanical Traditions and Science*. Portland, OR: Timber Press, Inc., 2020.

Sanders, Jack. *Secrets of Wildflowers: A Delightful Feast of Little-Known Facts, Folklore, and History*. Guilford, CT: Globe Pequot Press, 2014.

Sédir, Paul. *Occult Botany: Sédir's Concise Guide to Magical Plants*. Translated and edited by R. Bailey. Rochester, VT: Inner Traditions, 2021.

Shipley, Joseph T. *Dictionary of Early English*. Lanham, MD: Rowman & Littlefield Publishers, Inc., 2014.

Sidky, Homayun. *Witchcraft, Lycanthropy, Drugs and Disease: An Anthropological Study of the European Witch-Hunt*. Eugene, OR: Wipf and Stock Publishers, 1997.

Silverman, Deborah Anders. *Polish-American Folklore*. Chicago: University of Illinois Press, 2000.

Simpson, Jacqueline, and Steve Roud. *A Dictionary of English Folklore*. New York: Oxford University Press, 2000.

Skinner, Charles M. *Myths and Legends of Flowers, Trees, Fruits and Plants*. Philadelphia, J. B. Lippincott Company, 1925.

Small, Ernest. *Top 100 Food Plants: The World's Most Important Crops*. Ottawa, Canada: NRC Press, 1999.

———. *Culinary Herbs*. Ottawa, Canada: NRC Research Press, 2006.

———. *Top 100 Exotic Food Plants*. Boca Raton, FL: CRC Press, 2011.

———. *North American Cornucopia: Top 100 Indigenous Food Plants*. Boca Raton, FL: CRC Press, 2014.

Small, Ernest, and Paul M. Catling. *Canadian Medicinal Crops*. Ottawa, Canada: NRC Research Press, 1999.

Smith, Andrew F. *Food and Drink in American History: A "Full Course" Encyclopedia*, vol. 1. Santa Barbara, CA: ABC-CLIO, LLC, 2013.

Smith, Pamela H., and Paula Findlen, eds. *Merchants and Marvels: Commerce, Science, and Art in Early Modern Europe*. New York: Routledge, 2002.

Sonnedecker, Glenn. *History of Pharmacy*. Philadelphia: J. B. Lippincott Company, 1976.

Spearing, Sinéad. *Old English Medical Remedies: Mandrake, Wormwood and Raven's Eye*. Barnsely, England: Pen and Sword Books, Ltd., 2018.

Stanley, Autumn. *Mothers and Daughters of Invention: Notes for a Revised History of Technology*. New Brunswick, NJ: Rutgers University Press, 1995.

Staub, Jack. *75 Remarkable Fruits for Your Garden*. Layton, UT: Gibbs Smith, Publisher, 2007.

———. *75 Exceptional Herbs for Your Garden*. Layton, UT: Gibbs Smith, Publisher, 2008.

Stevenson, Matilda Coxe. "Ceremonial Uses of Plants," *Annual Report of the Bureau of American Ethnology to the Secretary of the Smithsonian Institution*, vol. 30. (1915): 87–99. Washington, DC: Government Printing Office.

Stork, Kent, and Joyce Stork. *You Can Grow African Violets*. New York: iUniverse, Inc., 2008.

Storl, Wolf D. *The Herbal Lore of Wise Women and Wortcunners: The Healing Power of Medicinal*

Plants. Berkeley, CA: North Atlantic Books, 2012.

———. *A Curious History of Vegetables: Aphrodisiacal and Healing Properties, Folk Tales, Garden Tips, and Recipes*. Berkeley, CA: North Atlantic Books, 2016.

Swinnen, Johan, and Devin Briski. *Beeronomics: How Beer Explains the World*. New York: Oxford University Press, 2017.

Tenenbaum, Frances, ed. *Taylor's Encyclopedia of Garden Plants*. New York: Houghton Mifflin Company, 2003.

Thoreau, Henry David. *The Writings of Henry D. Thoreau: Journal*, vol. 5. Edited by Patrick F. O'Connell. Princeton, NJ: Princeton University Press, 1997.

Thorpe, Benjamin. *Northern Mythology: Popular Traditions and Superstitions of Scandinavia, North Germany and the Netherlands*. London: Edward Lumley, 1851.

Torre, Dan. *Cactus*. London: Reaktion Books, Ltd., 2017.

Toussaint-Samat, Maguelonne. *A History of Food*, 2nd ed. Translated by Anthea Bell. Malden, MA: Wiley-Blackwell, 2009.

Tucker, Arthur O., and Jules Janick. *Flora of the Codes Cruz-Badianus*. Cham, Switzerland: Springer Nature Switzerland AG, 2020.

Turner, Jack. *Spice: The History of a Temptation*. New York: Alfred A. Knopf, 2004.

Turner, Patricia, and Charles Russell Coulter. *Dictionary of Ancient Deities*. New York: Oxford University Press, 2001.

Vickery, Roy, ed. *Oxford Dictionary of Plant-Lore*. Oxford, England: Oxford University Press, 1997.

———. *Vickery's Folk Flora: An A–Z of the Folklore and Uses of British and Irish Plants*. London: Weidenfeld & Nicolson, 2019.

von Bingen, Hildegard. *Hildegard von Bingen's Physica*. Translated by Priscilla Throop. Rochester, VT: Healing Arts Press, 1998.

Waltz, Lisa. *The Herbal Encyclopedia: A Practical Guide to the Many Uses of Herbs*. New York: iUniverse, Inc., 2004.

Waters, Marcus Woolombi. *Indigenous Knowledge Production: Navigating Humanity Within a Western World*. New York: Routledge, 2018.

Watts, D. C. *Elsevier's Dictionary of Plant Names and Their Origin*. New York: Elsevier, 2000.

———. *Elsevier's Dictionary of Plant Lore*. Burlington, MA: Academic Press, 2007.

Weaver, William Woys, ed. *Sauer's Herbal Cures: America's First Book of Botanic Healing 1762-1778*. Translated by William Woys Weaver. New York: Rutledge, 2001.

Weiss, E. A. *Spice Crops*. New York: CABI Publishing, 2002.

Wells, Diana. *Lives of the Trees: An Uncommon History*. Chapel Hill, NC: Algonquin Books of Chapel Hill, 2010.

Westermarck, Edward. *Ritual and Belief in Morocco*, vol. 1. London: Macmillan and Co., Limited, 1926.

Wilkins, John M., and Shaun Hill. *Food in the Ancient World*. Malden, MA: Blackwell Publishing, 2006.

Wilkinson, John Gardner. *The Manners and Customs of the Ancient Egyptians*, vol. 5, 3rd ed. London: John Murray, 1847.

Woolf, Jo. *Britain's Trees: A Treasury of Traditions, Superstitions, Remedies and Literature*. London: The National Trust, 2020.

Wood, J. Maxwell. *Witchcraft and Superstitious Record in the South-Western District of Scotland*. Dumfries, Scotland: J. Maxwell & Son, 1911.

Wood, Matthew. *The Book of Herbal Wisdom: Using Plants as Medicine*. Berkeley, CA: North Atlantic Books, 1997.

Wright, John. *Hedgerow*. London: Bloomsbury Publishing Plc., 2010.

Zohary, Daniel, Maria Hopf, and Ehud Weiss. *Domestication of Plants in the Old World*, 4th ed. New York: Oxford University Press, 2012.

Index

A

Abenaki, 173

abortifacient, 43, 50, 121, 137, 222, 241, 269, 297

absinthe, 327

acacia, 9, 10, 196, 210, 212, 337–340, 342, 343, 345–347, 349–351, 353, 355, 356, 358–362

Achilles, 18, 330

aconite, 10, 11, 339, 340, 345–349, 352, 353, 355, 356, 360–362

Adam and Eve, 101, 197, 233

Adam's needle, 331

Adam, Eve and Son root, 233

adder's tongue, 11, 339–342, 348, 349, 352, 355

adderwort, 43

Adonis, 20, 34, 71, 104, 120, 206, 223, 250, 265, 357

Aegir, 274

Africa, 9, 17, 19, 38, 65, 77, 87, 132, 277, 282

African evergreen, 139

African violet, 12, 337–339, 341, 343, 349, 352, 356

afterlife, the, 18, 22, 95, 98, 141, 192, 224, 230, 238, 250, 265, 324, 331

agrimony, 12, 13, 338, 340–342, 345–348, 351, 353–355

Agni, 150

Agrippa, Heinrich Cornelius, 3, 25, 29, 292, 333

ague root, 309

ague tree, 272

Aine, 140, 210, 215, 357

alchemist(s), 3, 25, 69, 70, 78, 81, 87, 92, 150, 152, 153, 181, 189, 192, 206, 215, 217, 226, 236, 264, 280, 321

alchemy, 3, 181

alder(s), 13, 14, 55, 284, 325, 338–340, 342–349, 351–356, 358, 359, 361, 362

Algonquin, 45, 48, 173, 310

alkanet, 14, 15, 342, 344, 346, 349, 351, 352, 354, 356

All Saints' Day, 167, 217

All Souls' Day, 167

all heal (all-heal), 213, 274, 313

aller, 13, 14, 55, 284, 325, 338–340, 342–349, 351–356, 358, 359, 361, 362

alligator pear, 29, 337, 341–343, 346, 348, 349, 351, 354, 356

allspice, 15, 16, 337, 339–347, 349, 352–355, 357, 361, 362

al-mais, 145

almendro, 304

almond, 4, 16, 208, 304, 337–344, 346–356, 358–362

aloe, 17, 338, 340–350, 352–356

alpine cudweed, 111

althea, 155, 159, 203

Althea (goddess), 128, 141, 252, 304

amara dulcis, 44

amaranth, 17, 18, 338, 340–343, 346–348, 352, 353, 356, 358, 359

amargo, 257

amaryllis, 18, 19, 38, 341, 343, 348, 351

Amaterasu, 79, 141, 150, 231, 357

ambergris, 113

American boxwood, 51, 107

American evergreen, 139

American mandrake, 209

American nightshade, 248

American sarsaparilla, 283

American valerian, 182

American wayfaring tree, 103

Amun, 40, 101, 231, 357

Anat, 154

anemone, 19, 20, 338–344, 346, 347, 350–355, 357–359, 362

angel flower, 329

angel's eyes, 282

angel's hair, 107

angelica, 20, 21, 338–347, 349, 352, 353, 356, 362

Anglo-Saxons, 4, 5, 11, 13, 20, 40, 41, 59, 69, 71, 72, 74, 85, 90, 91, 101, 106, 113, 120, 121, 123, 133, 138, 149, 150, 153, 161, 162, 179, 181, 189, 199, 205, 210, 219, 220, 225, 226, 241, 243, 247, 254, 269, 278, 283, 284, 287, 291, 297, 313, 326, 329, 333

Angus Mac Og, 43

anise, 21, 73, 120, 137, 189, 286, 337–349, 351, 353–355, 357, 360, 361

anise shrub, 286

aniseed, 21, 286

aniseed stars, 286

anodyne necklace, 243

Anu, 296

Anubis, 187

Apache, 68, 102, 115

aphrodisiac, 11, 21, 22, 24, 29, 31, 33, 35, 51, 61, 64–66, 70, 77, 78, 83, 87, 93, 94, 99, 101, 107, 131, 134, 136, 145, 177, 185, 190, 198, 199, 204, 205, 208, 213, 222, 225, 227, 231–233, 235, 236, 238, 243, 249, 254, 264, 265, 273, 276, 281, 286, 291, 305, 306, 314, 315, 321, 333

Aphrodite, 15, 20, 22, 23, 39, 52, 65, 80, 90, 99, 101, 105, 129, 148, 155, 165, 199, 202, 204, 206, 223, 224, 234, 238–240, 244, 247, 250, 251, 258, 259, 265–267, 296, 298, 315, 318, 322, 357

Apollo, 21, 22, 27, 34, 35, 37, 49, 52, 71, 79, 80, 82, 90, 94, 101, 129, 148, 150, 165, 185, 193, 199, 206, 214, 231, 240, 250, 251, 290, 296, 322, 357

apple, 22, 73, 90, 204, 209, 229, 257, 266, 300, 337–344, 346–362

apricot, 23, 24, 227, 237, 338–343, 345, 347, 348, 352, 354–357, 362

apricot vine, 237

archangel, 101

Arapaho, 269, 290

Ariadne, 142, 215, 357

Armenian plum, 23

arnica, 24, 339, 340, 343, 345–348, 352, 356, 360

Ares, 26, 158, 205, 230, 357

Arianrhod, 69, 140, 148, 149, 169, 195, 214, 215, 357

arrowhead vine, 139

arrowroot, 197, 333

Artemis, 18, 34, 64, 69, 73, 74, 94, 99, 101, 105, 124, 148, 165, 188, 192, 206, 209, 215, 218, 224, 247, 251, 276, 281, 294, 298, 322, 324, 328, 330, 358

asafetida, 24

asafoetida, 24, 25, 338, 341, 342, 345–348, 352, 353, 355, 358, 360, 361

Asclepius, 34, 80, 193, 214, 222, 358

ash, 25, 266, 338, 350–352, 355

Asherah, 101, 192, 239, 251, 358

Ashmole, Elias, 3

Ashtoreth, 231

aspen, 26, 337, 339, 340, 342, 343, 345–347, 349, 351–357, 359–362

ass ear, 86

Assyrians, 1, 101, 129, 198, 246, 249, 296

Astarte, 10, 16, 69, 92, 94, 101, 129, 192, 224, 247, 250, 322, 358

aster, 27, 28, 339–341, 343, 345–347, 349, 352, 354, 356, 362

Atharva-Veda, 317

athel pine, 296

Athena, 22, 37, 79, 90, 121, 124, 142, 165, 205, 219, 224, 231, 238, 240, 265, 284, 324, 358

Athena Parthenos, 121

Attis, 16, 247, 250, 285, 318, 358

Atum, 199

Australia, 2, 115, 271, 298

Avalon, 22

avens, 28, 337, 342, 343, 346, 347, 352, 354

avocado, 29, 337, 341–343, 346, 348, 349, 351, 354, 356

awa, 177

Awd Goggie, 139

Aztec, 2, 5, 15, 18, 29, 60, 61, 99, 201, 210, 211, 216, 248, 289, 295, 300, 303, 314, 334

B

Baal, 69, 129, 250, 358

Babylonians, 1, 25, 129, 142

Bacchus, 34, 37, 98, 104, 122, 124, 142, 153, 169, 209, 233, 244, 247, 250, 330, 358

bachelor's buttons, 63, 87, 121, 178, 297

Badb, 22, 90, 330, 358

bairnwort, 98

Balder, 22, 34, 72, 174, 214, 230, 270, 358

Balder's brow, 72

balewort, 251

Balkans, 46, 47, 108, 113, 133, 153, 169, 313

balm mint, 187, 213, 361

bamboo, 31, 32, 337–340, 342–346, 349–351, 356, 360, 362

Banba, 47, 330, 358

banewort, 226

banyan fig, 49

Barbados lily, 18

barberry, 32, 337, 339, 342, 345, 346, 351, 354–356

barley, 140, 141, 242

barleycorn, 140

basil, 33, 273, 339–347, 349, 352–356, 360, 362

basswood, 194

Bast, 67, 129, 138, 139, 358

bachelor's buttons, 63, 87, 121, 178, 297

bay, 34, 73, 134, 201, 246, 248, 266, 268, 292, 329, 337–340, 342, 343, 345–354, 356–362

bayberry, 50, 51

bead tree, 77

beads, 11, 33, 49, 50, 55, 77, 78, 84, 181, 240, 241, 243, 325

bean, 34, 35, 60, 61, 173, 196, 210, 211, 304, 314, 316, 339, 340, 344–359

bear whortleberry, 310

bearberry, 310

bearbind, 42

bear's bilberry, 310

bear's grape, 310

bedstraw, 35, 36, 291, 337, 341, 343, 345, 352, 356, 359

bee balm, 36, 187, 339, 341, 345–347, 349, 351, 353–356

bee bread, 51

bee nettle, 101

bee tree, 194

bee's nest, 258

beech, 4, 37, 38, 163, 337, 339, 341–347, 349, 350, 352–354, 356–362

beggar weed, 157

Bel/Belenus, 26, 47, 129, 140, 147, 154, 324, 358

Belgium/Belgians, 13, 22, 35, 37, 72, 73, 98, 141, 193, 218, 223, 240, 244, 265, 266, 280, 285, 292

belladonna, 18, 19, 38, 81, 226, 227, 339, 343, 347, 352, 355

belladonna lily, 18, 19, 38, 339, 343, 347, 352, 355

Beltane, 16, 20, 22, 26, 43, 46, 47, 49, 52, 69, 71, 74, 75, 81, 83, 88, 90, 99, 108, 112, 124, 126, 138–140, 146–148, 161, 169, 192, 193, 195, 198, 203, 206, 207, 211, 221, 230, 247, 251, 253, 267, 281, 285, 292, 296, 324

benne, 275

Benjamin tree, 38

bennet, 28

benzoin, 38, 39, 338, 339, 341–343, 346–349, 351–353, 355–357, 362

berberry, 32

bergamot, 36, 39, 339, 344, 346, 348, 351, 355, 356

bergamot mint, 36

bergamot orange, 36, 39

berry-bearing alder, 55

Bertha, 47, 89, 112, 124, 253, 358

besom, 53

betony, 40, 338–340, 342, 343, 345–348, 352–355, 357, 359, 362

bilberry, 40, 41, 310, 340–346, 349, 352, 354, 361

Bilé, 148

Billy buttons, 56

bindweed, 41, 42, 54, 338, 339, 349, 351–353, 355, 356

bindwood, 169

birch, 42, 43, 337–343, 345–347, 350, 352–356, 358, 359, 361, 362

bird pepper, 76

bird weed, 75, 178

bird's eye (s), 7, 14, 75, 116, 205, 240, 245, 282

bird's nest, 258

birdseed, 143

birthwort, 278

bisabol, 222

bishop's wort, 40

bison grass, 292

bistort, 43, 338–340, 343, 345, 347, 349, 351, 353, 354, 356

bitter apple, 257

bitter ash, 257

bitter buttons, 297

bitter herb, 70

bitter nightshade, 44

bittercress, 91, 183

bittersweet, 44, 45, 338, 340–342, 344–347, 349, 351, 353, 355, 356, 360

bittersweet nightshade, 44

bitterwood, 257

black bindweed, 54

black cohosh, 45, 46, 338–344, 346, 349, 352, 354, 355

black dogwood, 55

black haw, 47

black heg, 46

black knobs, 13

black nightshade, 153, 226

black nisewort, 151

black pepper, 15, 243

black snakeroot, 45

black sugar, 189

blackberry, 7, 46, 47, 219, 226, 337–344, 346–348, 352–356, 358, 359, 361

Blackfoot, 290, 293

blackthorn, 47, 337, 338, 340, 342, 344–347, 349, 351–356, 358–362

blackwort, 86

bladderpod, 195

bladderwrack, 273

blaeberry, 40

blazing star, 119, 309

blessed herb, 28

Blodeuwedd, 147, 210, 358

blood weed, 178, 179

bloodroot, 48, 337, 339–341, 343, 345–347, 349, 352, 355

bloodwort, 48, 329

blue beech, 163

blue bobs, 103

blue bonnets, 103

blue button, 103

blue crown, 237

blue curls, 274

blue eye, 282

blue ginger, 131

blue mountain tea, 137

blue pipe, 191

blue rocket, 10

blue sailors, 75

blue star(s), 244, 282

blue wattle, 212

bluebell, 48, 49, 146, 338, 343–345, 347–349, 351–358, 361, 362

bluebottle, 87

bo tree, 49

Boann, 74, 112, 148, 358

Bodhi tree, 49, 77, 337, 338, 343, 345, 347,
    349–352, 354, 356

bog myrtle, 50, 51, 337, 340, 341, 343–347, 352,
    356

bog violet, 57

Bona Dea, 142

boneset, 86, 173

borage, 51, 338–343, 345–349, 351–354

bottleweed, 178

bowstring hemp, 277

box, 32, 51, 52, 107, 282

boxwood, 51, 52, 107, 337, 340–347, 351, 355,
    357–362

bracken, 52, 337, 340–347, 349, 351, 353, 355

Brahma, 10, 190, 199, 231, 251, 358

brake fern, 52

bramble, 46, 262

bramble thorn, 46

brambleberry, 46

Brazil, 61, 202, 303, 304, 334

Brazilian teak, 304

bread, 51, 64, 65, 93, 140, 141, 245

briar balls, 265

bride of the Nile, 322

bridewort, 209

bright-eye, 282

Brigantia, 267

Brigid, 20, 46, 47, 69, 84, 100, 123, 124, 141, 147,
    230, 267, 324, 358

briony, 54

Britain, 11, 13, 25, 41, 43, 44, 46, 49, 59, 63, 67,
    74, 92, 97, 99, 100, 107, 124, 125, 128, 140–143,
153, 169, 172, 198, 203, 213, 216, 218, 221, 245,
    246, 258, 267, 268, 270, 274, 281, 287, 288, 298,
    313, 315, 316, 326, 329, 330, 333

British Isles, 13, 43, 44, 46, 49, 59, 63, 67, 100, 107,
    124, 125, 128, 141, 143, 153, 169, 172, 203, 213,
    216, 218, 221, 246, 258, 267, 268, 270, 329

Brittany, 46, 52, 274

broad buttercup, 206

broad vetch, 34

broom, 53, 54, 99, 139, 140, 166, 213, 338–343,
    345–347, 349, 351, 353, 355, 356

broom straw, 53

brownies, 222, 290

brownwort, 122

bryony, 54, 55, 337, 341, 344, 346, 352, 353, 355

buckthorn, 55, 338, 340, 342, 343, 345, 346, 350,
    352, 354–356

Buddha, 49, 199, 238, 358

Buddhism, 198

buffalo grass, 292

bugbane, 45

bugloss, 14, 15, 51

bugwort, 45

bull bay, 201

bull's blood, 162

bunny rabbits, 7, 190, 278

burr, 13, 28, 56, 289

burdock, 56, 338, 340, 342, 343, 345–347, 352, 354,
    356

burning bush, 284

burrage, 51

Burry Man, the, 56

burweed, 56

butter and eggs, 17, 29, 40, 56, 57, 60, 61, 106, 114, 140, 156, 172, 173, 223, 229, 237, 252, 265, 302

butter flower, 56

butter pear, 29

butter rose, 252

butterbur, 84

buttercup, 56, 57, 206, 337, 340–344, 346, 349, 350, 352, 353, 355

butterwort, 57, 58, 212, 241, 337, 338, 340–346, 349, 352

button-bur, 56

buttonweed, 203

buttonwood, 293

C

cabbage, 59, 60, 136, 341, 344, 352–355

cacao, 60, 61, 342, 343, 346, 348, 352, 355, 356, 362

cactus, 61, 211, 337, 340, 342, 344, 346, 352, 355

Cailleach Bheur, 14, 90, 112, 158, 274, 330, 358

Cailleach's tea, 274

calamus, 108, 291

calamus root, 291

calendula, 205, 206, 212, 295

Cambridgeshire, 55, 153, 158, 198

camellia, 62, 66, 337–340, 343, 344, 346, 349, 350, 352, 354–356, 360, 361

camphor, 62, 63, 338, 340, 341, 345, 347, 351–355, 360, 362

campion, 63, 64, 338–344, 346, 349–351, 355, 358, 361

candle of the woods, 89

candle tree, 74

candleberry, 50

candlewick, 220

cannabis, 152

Cape belladonna, 38

Cape jasmine, 132

capsicum, 76, 77

caraway, 64, 65, 73, 93, 339, 340, 343, 344, 346–348, 351–355, 358, 360, 361

cardamom, 65, 91, 338–343, 347–349, 351–354, 356–358, 360, 361

cardamom of Hecate, 91

cardinal flower, 195

Carna, 35

carnation, 65, 66, 338–349, 352–354, 356, 360, 362

carpenter's square, 122

carpenter's weed, 274

carrot, 23, 242, 245, 258

cassia, 79, 80, 275

cat claw, 9

Catawba, 309

catechu, 212

catmint, 66

catnip, 66, 67, 337–349, 351–356, 358, 362

cat-o-nine-tails, 67

cat's eyes, 282

cat's fancy, 66

cat's milk, 285

cattail, 67, 68, 337, 339–344, 346, 348, 349, 352, 354–356, 358–362

catwort, 66

cayenne, 76, 77

cedar, 68, 69, 296, 337, 340, 342–344, 346–349, 351–358, 361, 362

celandine, 69, 70, 338, 340, 342, 343, 345–347, 349, 351–353, 355, 356 celery, 20, 70, 129, 199, 264, 338–340, 342, 344, 346–348, 352, 353, 355, 360–362

Celts, 5, 22, 40, 74, 123, 147, 229, 306, 326, 327, 330

centaur, 2, 70, 71, 87

centaur's hoof, 70

centaury, 70, 71, 87, 338, 339, 342–349, 352–354, 356–358, 360, 362

Centéotl, 141

Cerberus, 11

Ceres, 22, 34, 35, 74, 98, 114, 122, 141, 192, 195, 199, 247, 250, 251, 324, 358

Cernunnos, 25, 34, 63, 72, 139, 158, 169, 230, 296, 330, 358

Cerridwen, 37, 43, 114, 161, 196, 267, 285, 315, 324, 358

Ceylon, 79

Chalchiuhtlicue, 18

chamomile, 71, 72, 121, 337, 339–343, 345–347, 351–353, 355, 356, 358, 362

changeling, 52, 159, 168, 214

Channel Islands, 147, 160

chase-devil, 270

Chaucer, Geoffrey, 333

cheese plant, 203

Cherokee, 20, 36, 45, 48, 102, 104, 115, 119, 138, 191, 195, 196, 201, 209, 254, 262, 272, 277, 283, 291, 309, 325

cherry, 54, 72, 73, 107, 108, 226, 337–345, 347, 349, 350, 352–356, 358, 359, 361, 362

chervil, 73, 74, 88, 89, 342, 343, 345, 347, 348, 351, 354, 355, 358

chestnut, 74, 75, 245, 337–346, 349–354, 356, 358, 359

chewing John, 131

Cheyenne, 191, 269, 290, 293

chi chi sticks, 31

chicory, 75, 76, 337–340, 344, 346–349, 351, 353–356

chickweed, 75, 143, 245, 341, 343–345, 347, 349, 352–355

childbirth, 36, 42, 94, 105, 154, 217

China (Chinese), 1, 5, 23, 27, 31, 62, 65, 77–81, 86, 107, 128, 131, 132, 136, 152, 155, 159, 171, 189, 198, 219, 222, 232, 238, 239, 254, 264, 286, 324, 329

China rose, 155

Chinaberry, 77, 338, 339, 342, 344, 351, 354, 356

Chinese ginger, 131

Chinese leek, 78

Chinese parsley, 86

Chicomecoatl, 18

chili pepper, 76, 194, 338–340, 342–346, 348, 349, 352, 353, 355

chipotle, 76

Chippewa, 36, 191, 262, 272, 283, 293, 303, 325

chives, 78

Chiron, 2, 71, 87, 88, 358

chocolate, 60, 61, 314, 355

Choctaw, 102, 201, 272

Christmas flower, 248

Christmas rose, 151

Christmas star, 248

chrysanthemum, 79, 98, 121, 295, 297, 339–343, 346, 347, 349, 352, 353, 355–358, 360, 361

Chumash, 269

cilantro, 86, 87

cimaruta, 268

Cinderella, 101, 183

cinquefoil, 80, 81, 337, 339, 340, 342–347, 351, 352, 354, 355

cinnamon, 62, 79, 80, 272, 283, 304, 338, 339, 342–344, 346–350, 352–362

cinnamon root, 283

cinnamon wood, 272

Circe, 2, 52, 65, 133, 204, 226, 267, 268, 324, 358

citronella grass, 188

clairvoyance, 34, 80, 92, 105, 150, 188, 189, 192, 215, 270, 271, 301, 330

clove, 28, 65, 81, 82, 338, 339, 341–343, 345–349, 351–357, 360–362

clove root, 28

clover, 82, 125, 326, 327, 342–346, 348, 349, 351, 353–355

club moss, 82, 83, 344, 346, 352, 355

clubweed, 178

coakum, 248

cobnut, 148

cockle buttons, 56

cocklebur, 12, 56

cocoa, 60, 61

coconut, 83, 84, 337, 339, 341–343, 346–349, 351–356, 359, 360, 362

coffee bush, 173

coffeeweed, 75

colewort, 28, 59

colic root, 309

colt pixies, 22

coltsfoot, 84, 340–343, 345–347, 352, 354, 356, 358, 359

columbine, 85, 86, 338, 339, 341, 343, 345, 347, 349, 352, 356

Comanche, 269

comfrey, 86, 337–339, 341, 342, 345–349, 351–354, 356

common balm, 187

compass plant, 266

conkers, 74

Cook, James, 298

coriander, 4, 86, 87, 338–343, 345, 346, 348, 352, 353, 355, 356

corn, 140, 251, 309, 316

cornflower, 87, 88, 340, 342–347, 349, 351–354, 356, 358, 359

cornelian tree, 107

Cornwall, 56, 92, 274, 287, 299

corpse straw, 141

cottonweed, 190

coughwort, 84

coven tree, 323

Coventina, 68, 263, 358

cow lily, 322

cow parsley, 88, 89, 338, 339, 341–343, 345, 346, 349, 352, 355

cow parsnip, 157

cow weed, 88

cowbane, 152

cowslip, 48, 89, 253, 340, 342, 343, 345, 346, 348, 349, 352, 353, 356, 358, 359

cowthwort, 217

crabapple, 90, 337, 340, 342, 343, 345, 346, 350–354, 356–362

crazies, 56, 69

Creek, 102, 191, 195, 269, 272

creeping Jenny, 41

cress, 90, 91, 183, 339, 340, 343, 346, 347, 352–355, 360, 361

Crete, 33, 105, 262

crocus, 91, 92, 338, 340–348, 352–354, 356, 358–360, 362

Crone, the, 112, 113, 152

Cronus, 49, 251, 358

crow corn, 309

crow flower, 56

crowberry, 40, 248, 310

crowfoot, 69

crown daisy, 79

crown of Venus, 213

Crusaders, 51, 76, 86, 194

Cú Chulainn, 210

cuckoo flower, 183, 197

cuckoo potatoes, 245

cudweed, 111, 190

Culpeper, Nicholas, 2, 34, 66, 78, 179, 181, 235, 245, 259, 286

culverwort, 85

cumin, 21, 64, 93, 338, 339, 341, 343–347, 349, 352–356

cumaru, 304

Cunningham, Scott, 6

Cupid, 94, 265, 359

cudweed, 111, 190

curcuma, 305, 333

curdwort, 35

curl-doddy, 103

curry plant, 167

cutch tree, 212

Cybele, 16, 52, 124, 187, 188, 223, 247, 250, 285, 318, 359

cyclamen, 93, 94, 339–343, 345–347, 352–357, 360

cypress, 94, 95, 285, 286, 296, 337–343, 345–347, 349, 351–362

D

daff-a-down-dilly, 97

daffodil, 97, 98, 339–341, 343–348, 352–354, 356, 358–361

Dagda, the, 26, 40, 43, 46, 47, 112, 140, 147, 158, 230, 267, 330, 359

daisy, 24, 27, 58, 79, 87, 98, 99, 113, 121, 167, 297, 329, 338–344, 346, 348, 349, 352–359, 362

damiana, 99, 100, 343, 347, 348, 352, 355, 361

dancing fairies, 85

dandelion, 4, 76, 84, 100, 113, 143, 212, 337–340, 342, 343, 345–348, 350, 351, 353–355, 358, 360

Danu, 27, 46, 112, 114, 147, 148, 158, 169, 210, 285, 324, 359

Daphne, 34

date, 5, 100, 101, 204, 210, 270, 337–339, 341–346, 348, 349, 351–361

datil, 331

datura, 300

Day of the Dead, 61, 295, 296

day's eye, 98

de Villeneuve, Arnold, 321

deadly amanita, 125

deadly nightshade, 38, 81, 226

dead man's bells, 127

dead-man's-bones, 302

deadnettle, 101, 102, 338, 340–344, 346–348, 351, 356

death alder, 284

death cap, 221

death's flower, 279

deer ear, 102

deer nut, 173

deer's tongue, 102, 103, 338, 343, 346–348, 352–355

Delaware, 20, 45, 48, 68, 136, 196, 209, 249, 272, 277

Delphi, 34, 187, 300

Demeter, 18, 22, 98, 114, 122, 130, 141, 148, 165, 182, 187, 188, 199, 213, 214, 223, 224, 241, 242, 247, 249–251, 265, 275, 276, 289, 290, 315, 318, 324, 359

demon(s), 3, 28, 39, 55, 64, 73, 74, 81, 87, 91, 120, 134, 141, 150, 160, 174, 194, 221, 225, 239, 240, 247, 250, 266, 270, 286, 289, 299, 300, 302, 315, 321

Denmark, 13, 112, 124, 218, 225

devil's apple, 204, 209, 300

devil's bit, 103, 119, 309, 338, 340, 344–346, 351, 354–356

devil's bit scabious, 103, 338, 340, 344–346, 351, 354–356

devil's bite, 19

devil's bread, 245

devil's cherry, 54, 226

devil's claw, 9

devil's dung, 24

devil's eye, 153

devil's fingers, 250

devil's flax, 302

devil's flower, 63

devil's garters, 42

devil's grass, 213

devil's guts, 41, 107

devil's incense, 24

devil's ivy, 252

devil's leaf, 225

devil's milk, 69, 285

devil's milk-pale, 100

devil's net, 107

devil's nettle, 329

devil's nightcap, 287

devil's oatmeal, 157

devil's parsley, 88

devil's penny, 160

devil's plague, 258

devil's plaything, 40, 329

devil's posy, 132

devil's shoestring, 103, 104, 331, 338, 340, 342, 344–346, 352, 354

devil's snuffbox, 221

devil's tongue, 11, 277

devil's tree, 49

devil's trumpet, 300

devil's turnip, 54

devil's vine, 252

devil's wort, 225

devil-daisy, 121

Devonshire, 49, 78, 247

dew cup, 181

Dian Cécht, 75

Diana, 10, 22, 34, 37, 74, 90, 94, 101, 105, 124, 132, 148, 155, 172, 174, 188, 192, 204, 206, 209, 215, 218, 219, 247, 251, 268, 294, 298, 315, 322, 324, 328, 359

dill, 104, 338–340, 342–344, 346–348, 351–355, 357–359

dilly, 104

Dionysus, 22, 34, 35, 37, 80, 90, 98, 104, 114, 120, 122, 124, 142, 153, 169, 209, 224, 233, 247, 250, 289, 322, 330, 359

Dioscorides, Pedanius, 2, 165, 187, 197, 198, 279

dittany, 105, 340, 343, 347, 348, 352–362

divine flower, 66

divining rod(s), 250, 325

dock, 106, 113, 322, 340–343, 346, 351, 354

docken, 106

dodder, 107, 338, 340, 343, 348, 352, 356

Dodona, 37

dog berry, 138

dog daisy, 329

dog grass, 143

dog stalk, 261

dog's dick, 197

dog's stones, 233

dogberry, 103, 266

dog-tongue, 102

dogtooth violet, 11

dogwood, 55, 107, 108, 338–344, 346, 350, 351, 354, 355

dollar plant, 160

Dôn, 230, 330, 359

Donar, 226

Dorset, 198, 261

draconis resina, 108

dragon grape, 32

dragon's blood, 108, 109, 185, 193, 338–340, 342–349, 352–355

dragon's mouth, 278

dragon's mugwort, 298

dragon(s), 31, 32, 77, 78, 108, 109, 140, 174, 185, 193, 195, 267, 278, 298, 327, 338–340, 342–349, 352–355

dragonwort, 43

Dreaming, the, 115

Druid's weed, 315

Druid(s), 83, 210, 213, 315, 330

drooping lily, 279

duck foot leaf, 209

Dumuzi, 101

Durga, 187, 306, 359

Dutch, 35, 59, 141, 174, 249, 257, 263, 266, 304

Dutchman's pipe, 278

dwarf(s), 64, 69, 80, 81, 93, 120, 124, 174, 195, 204, 238, 239, 241, 242, 265, 330

dyer's bugloss, 14, 15

E

Ea, 69

earth chestnuts, 245

earthnut, 245

Ebers Papyrus, 1

edelweiss, 111, 112, 340, 343, 344, 346, 352–354

Egypt, 1, 5, 9, 17, 19, 23, 32, 33, 35, 39, 62, 68, 71, 72, 74, 79–81, 87, 91–94, 97, 104, 122, 124, 126, 128, 134, 138, 140, 142, 154, 162, 169, 171, 188–190, 198, 203, 204, 208, 213, 223, 224, 230, 231, 239, 246, 250, 251, 263, 266, 269, 275, 283, 291, 296, 300, 301, 315, 316, 322, 325–327

Egyptian privet, 154

Egyptian sycamore, 122

elder, 2, 15, 51, 83, 93, 94, 112, 113, 123, 134, 187, 243, 259, 273, 279, 281, 284, 321, 337–340, 342–344, 346–352, 355, 356, 358–360, 362

elderberry, 112

elecampane, 113, 339, 340, 342–349, 351, 354, 355

Eleusinian Mysteries, 122, 213, 241

elf dock, 113

elf enchantment, 333

elf gloves, 127

elf goblets, 56

elf leaf, 185, 266

elf shot, 13, 20, 57, 106, 113, 181, 225, 287

elf sickness, 189, 199

elf's rod, 324

elf-bonds, 133

elf-siden, 333

elf-wand, 164

elfwort, 113

elkweed, 102, 103

ellhorn, 112

ellum, 114

elm, 114, 163, 325, 339, 340, 342–347, 350–353, 355, 356, 358–362

eltrot, 157

elven, 114, 279

elves, 13, 14, 20, 26, 34, 46, 57, 69, 73, 74, 82, 89, 90, 94, 95, 106, 112–114, 123–126, 128, 136, 143, 146, 148, 158, 162, 181, 186, 189, 195, 199, 204, 214, 225, 226, 230, 246, 247, 259, 265–267, 278, 279, 287, 290, 301, 305, 319, 322, 324, 326, 327, 330

Elysian Fields, 97

enchanter's weed, 315

English orris, 313

England/English, 2–5, 11, 14, 19–22, 24–26, 28, 29, 32–38, 40, 42–44, 46–48, 50–57, 59, 61, 63, 64, 66, 68, 72–76, 78, 81–90, 94, 98, 100, 101, 103, 105, 112–114, 117, 120, 121, 123, 124, 126–128, 132, 134, 136–141, 143, 144, 146–148, 150–152, 157–162, 164, 165, 167, 169, 172–174, 178, 179, 181, 183, 185, 186, 190–193, 196, 198, 199, 202, 205–218, 222, 223, 225, 227, 229–239, 241–245, 247, 250, 252–254, 259, 261, 264–270, 272, 274, 277–279, 281–284, 286–288, 290, 296,

297, 299–303, 305, 313–316, 318, 321, 323–327, 329, 330, 333

Eos, 92, 294, 359

Eostre, 192, 195, 359

Epona, 84, 85, 314, 315, 359

Eros, 22, 90, 224, 265, 359

Erzulie, 99, 100

Estonia, 174, 299

eucalyptus, 114, 115, 337, 338, 340–343, 345–356, 361, 362

Europa, 294

Europe/Europeans, 1, 2, 9, 11–15, 18, 19, 23–28, 32, 33, 36–40, 42–47, 49, 51, 52, 54, 55, 59, 61, 62, 64–66, 68, 70, 72–74, 76–81, 84, 86, 87, 89, 90, 93, 94, 101, 103–105, 107, 108, 112, 115, 119, 121–127, 129–131, 133, 134, 136–138, 140–143, 145, 150–153, 158–161, 163–165, 167, 174, 182, 184, 185, 187, 189–194, 196, 198, 199, 203, 204, 206, 208, 213, 214, 216–219, 223, 225, 226, 230, 231, 233, 234, 238–241, 243, 245, 246, 249, 251, 253, 254, 257, 258, 263–267, 269, 271, 272, 274–276, 278, 280, 284, 286, 289–291, 293, 295, 298, 300, 303–305, 309, 313, 314, 316, 318, 322, 324–326, 330, 333

European blueberry, 40

European cornel, 107

evening primrose, 115, 116, 338, 339, 341, 342, 345–349, 352, 356

evening star, 115

evening twilight, 19, 326

everlasting, 167, 190, 191, 288, 338, 339, 342, 346, 347, 352, 356

evil eye, the, 21, 55, 77, 103, 117, 143–145, 154, 161, 165, 181, 184, 186, 187, 194, 202, 205, 212, 213, 241, 244, 259, 261, 266, 268, 269, 275, 277, 286, 287, 296, 318, 329 exorcism, 56, 271, 327

eye of the star, 162

eyebright, 116, 117, 195, 245, 282, 339–343,
    347–349, 351, 353, 354, 356

eyewort, 116

eyeroot, 137

F

faeries, 3, 5, 13, 14, 16, 20, 22, 25, 26, 28, 34–36,
    41, 43, 46, 47, 49, 50, 52–54, 56–60, 63, 67–69,
    72, 74, 78, 81–83, 85, 87, 89, 90, 92, 94, 95,
    98–102, 106, 112–114, 116, 119, 123–128, 134,
    138–140, 142, 143, 146–149, 152, 157–159, 161,
    166, 168, 169, 172, 174, 181–184, 186, 191–193,
    195, 202, 203, 205–207, 210, 212, 214–218, 220,
    221, 226, 235, 236, 240, 241, 243–247, 253, 259,
    261–263, 265–268, 270, 271, 274, 276, 280–282,
    286, 287, 290, 292, 299, 301, 305, 314, 315, 317,
    319, 322, 324, 326, 327, 329–331, 348

fair maids, 279

fairies, 5, 7, 12, 19, 43, 45, 47, 48, 56, 63, 67, 85,
    88, 89, 99–101, 112, 116, 117, 119, 124, 125,
    127, 140, 143, 146, 159, 172, 174, 193, 197, 202,
    203, 205, 206, 211, 214, 221, 230, 244, 245, 252,
    259, 261, 265, 273, 274, 309, 315, 316, 326, 327,
    338, 339, 341–344, 346–350, 352, 356

fairy basins, 56, 89

fairy bells, 5, 48, 89, 127, 146, 326

fairy boots, 101

fairy bubbles, 206

fairy butter, 172

fairy caps, 127, 146

fairy candles, 45

fairy chains, 99

fairy cheese, 203

fairy circle, 143

fairy circles, 174

fairy clocks, 100

fairy cups, 5, 89, 193, 252

fairy feet, 101

fairy fern, 202

fairy flax, 5, 116, 124

fairy flower, 89

fairy gold, 140

fairy grass, 143

fairy horse, 5, 261

fairy lace, 88

fairy laces, 273

fairy ladder, 193

fairy lamps, 197

fairy lint, 124

fairy mead, 315

fairy paintbrush, 244

fairy petticoats, 127

fairy pincushions, 265

fairy potatoes, 245

fairy ring, 5, 143, 221

fairy soap, 211

fairy stool, 221

fairy struck, 274

fairy table, 221

fairy tables, 125

fairy tree, 47, 112

fairy wand, 7, 119, 309, 338, 339, 341–344,
    346–350, 352, 356

fairy windflower, 19

fairy woman's flax, 124

fairy woman's spindle, 67

fairy's wand, 7, 12

fairies' corn, 316

fairies' fire, 259

fairies' pinks, 63

false acacia, 196

false box, 107

false bulrush, 67

false unicorn root, 119, 309

Fates, the, 94, 98, 124, 204, 284, 359

Faunus, 142, 247, 359

fawn lily, 11

fayberry, 138, 139

featherfew, 121

felon herb, 218

female fern, 52

Fenlands, 75, 144, 153, 158, 161, 198, 324, 330

fennel, 64, 104, 120, 189, 339–342, 346–349,
    352–355, 357, 359–362

fern, 11, 14, 52, 53, 202, 203, 214, 284, 337, 338,
    340–342, 344–348, 351, 352, 355–357, 362

fever grass, 188

fever tea, 188

fever tree, 114

feverfew, 121, 340–343, 346, 347, 349, 352, 354,
    356, 358, 360

feverwort, 70

Fianna, 289

Fides, 231

field balm, 66

fig, 49, 122, 337–341, 343, 345–347, 351, 352, 354,
    356, 358–362

figwort, 122, 123, 337, 342, 345, 346, 352–356, 358

filbert, 148

fir, 82, 83, 123, 124, 285, 338–340, 342, 343,
    345–349, 351–356, 358–362

fir moss, 82

fire of Venus, 65

Fírinne, Donn, 41

fitches, 315

five-fingers, 80

five-leaf grass, 80

flag, 168, 169, 291, 344, 346, 348, 350, 352–356

flag lily, 168

flagroot, 291

flame leaf, 248

flannel leaf, 220

flax, 5, 116, 124, 125, 302, 337–341, 346–349, 352,
    355, 358–361

flaxweed, 302

fleabane, 241, 283

fleawort, 35

Flora, 20, 56, 73, 88, 90, 147, 201, 231, 265, 359

flower of the dead, 19, 79, 295

flower of the heart, 201

flowering onion, 78

fly agaric, 125, 126, 338–341, 343–348, 351, 353,
    355, 359, 361, 362

fly grass, 283

flying ointment, 11, 81, 125, 146, 226, 227

flying rowan, 267

foalswort, 84

folk's glove, 127

food of the gods, 25, 60, 125

forget-me-not, 126, 235, 337–339, 341, 343, 344,
    346–349, 351, 356, 362

forsythia, 127, 338, 339, 341, 342, 349, 351, 352,
    356

Fortuna, 232

fothram, 122, 123

fox bells, 127

foxglove, 4, 127, 128, 338, 339, 341–343, 345–347, 349, 352–354, 356

foxstones, 233

foxtail, 17, 18, 82, 197

France/French, 16, 22, 23, 25, 28, 32–35, 39, 43, 50, 59, 66, 71, 73, 76, 81, 98, 100, 115, 120, 134, 141, 143, 147, 150–152, 158, 163, 165, 168, 187, 191–194, 196, 198, 204, 214, 218, 220, 221, 224, 226, 227, 236, 238, 240, 244, 246, 259, 264–266, 269, 270, 272, 280, 281, 288, 289, 295, 296, 298, 303, 304, 314, 315, 317, 318, 321, 326, 327, 330

frankincense, 108, 128, 129, 338–349, 351–358, 360, 362

Frau Ellhorn, 112

French parsley, 73

Freya, 14, 22, 37, 43, 46, 89, 90, 99, 112, 139, 169, 182, 195, 202, 214, 217, 253, 265, 284, 290, 292, 359

Freya's hair, 202

Freyr, 26, 112, 140, 158, 322, 359

friar's cap, 10

Frigg, 26, 27, 35–37, 43, 124, 147, 182, 195, 214, 265, 284, 290, 359

Frigg's grass, 35

Frigg's thorn, 265

fumitory, 129, 130, 337–339, 341, 342, 344–347, 350, 352–354, 356, 359–362

fumus, 129, 130

Furies, the, 94, 174, 330, 359

furze, 139

G

Gaia, 27, 34, 112, 114, 158, 161, 182, 232, 238, 239, 331, 359

galangal, 131, 132, 338, 339, 342–346, 348, 349, 352–356, 360

galangale, 131

gale, 50

Galen, Claudius, 310, 313

gall, 229, 265, 347

gallow-grass, 152

Ganesh, 84, 155, 276, 317, 359

Ganymede, 297

garden heliotrope, 150, 313

garden mum, 79

garden myrrh, 73

gardenia, 132, 338, 341, 342, 345, 348, 349, 352–355, 359–362

garlic, 78, 132, 133, 231, 337–339, 342, 344, 346, 348, 349, 352, 355, 358, 360, 361

Gathon, Elaby, 159

Gauls, the, 330

Gautama, Siddhartha, 49

Geb, 68, 263, 359

geranium, 133, 134, 338–341, 344, 346–348, 352, 353, 355, 356, 361

Gerard, John, 11, 26, 36, 162, 235, 259

Germany/Germans/Germanic, 3, 11–13, 16, 19, 22, 24, 25, 28, 37, 42, 47, 52, 53, 55, 59, 66, 69–73, 76, 81, 83, 87, 89, 92, 93, 97, 99, 104, 108, 111, 112, 115, 117, 120, 123, 125–127, 129, 130, 133, 137, 138, 140, 141, 143, 147–150, 152, 153, 158, 163, 168, 174, 181, 184, 185, 187, 189, 192–195, 203–205, 208, 214, 215, 217, 218, 221, 223, 225–227, 229, 230, 233, 234, 236, 238, 240, 242, 244, 246, 247, 251, 253, 263–267, 269, 270, 279–281, 285, 288, 289, 291, 292, 300, 302, 306, 313, 315, 316, 318, 322, 324, 327, 330, 333

Glastonbury, 326

glastum, 325

goat nut, 173

goat weed, 270

ghost tree, 293

ghost(s), 17, 25, 34, 40, 44, 46, 47, 68, 120, 124, 186, 191, 192, 195, 214, 218, 226, 234, 244, 267, 272, 279, 293, 302, 306, 310, 324

gillyflower, 65

gin berry, 174

ginger, 131, 134, 135, 138, 305, 333, 339, 341, 342, 344–349, 352–355

ginseng, 135, 136, 341, 342, 344, 346, 348, 350, 352, 356

glacier queen, 111

gladden, 291

gladdon, 291

globeflower, 136, 137, 340, 342, 345, 348, 352

gnome(s), 125, 126, 133, 221

goat leaf, 160

goat nut, 173

goat weed, 270

goblin flower, 136, 206

goblin's eye, 251

goblin's gloves, 127

goblin's shaving brush, 143

goblin(s), 40, 52, 84, 127, 136, 143, 162, 206, 221, 234, 243, 251, 323

gold bells, 97

gold Melissa, 36

gold star, 28

gold thread, 107

goldband sansevierias, 277

golden apples of Hera, 23, 232

golden bell, 127

golden bough, 213

golden buttons, 297

golden dust, 137

golden eternal flower, 167

golden rod, 12, 53

golden stars, 69

golden sun, 100

golden willow, 50

goldenrod, 137, 338, 340, 342–344, 346, 350, 351, 356

goldenseal, 137, 138, 339, 342, 345, 346, 350, 352, 353, 356

goldins, 205

good luck plant, 277, 302

Goodfellow, Robin, 63

gooseberry, 138, 139, 337, 338, 341, 342, 345, 349, 352, 356, 358, 361

goosefoot, 139, 339, 340, 346, 351, 354, 359

goosegogs, 138

gorse, 53, 57, 139, 140, 338, 340, 342–347, 349, 352, 353, 355–362

Gothic/Goths, 149

gowan, 136

Graces, the, 117

grain(s), 32, 128, 140, 141, 223, 299, 337, 339–347, 349, 352, 354, 356–361

Grand Albert, the, 3, 66

granny's bonnet, 85

grannyvine, 216

grape, 32, 54, 138, 141, 142, 310, 337–349, 351, 352, 354–360, 362

grape-fern, 214

grass, 31, 35, 80, 126, 141, 143, 150, 185, 188, 197, 213, 241, 263, 283, 287, 291–293, 302, 309, 317, 337–340, 342, 344–348, 350, 352

grave brooms, 43

Graves, Robert, 8, 9, 17, 52, 55, 62, 70, 126, 153, 167, 191, 196, 203, 224, 230, 236, 239, 246, 250, 265, 266, 269, 301, 315, 318, 322

gravel root, 173

graveyard weed, 285

great fleabane, 283

great golden maidenhair, 216

great reed mace, 67

Grecian windflower, 19

Greece/Greeks, 2, 5, 11–13, 16–19, 21, 23, 25, 27, 32–35, 37, 38, 47, 51, 52, 59, 66, 70–72, 77–81, 84, 86, 87, 91–94, 97, 101, 104, 105, 107, 108, 113, 114, 116, 120, 122, 123, 125, 129, 130, 133, 134, 140, 142, 147, 148, 151–153, 157, 162, 164, 165, 167–169, 174, 185, 187, 188, 190, 192, 194, 197–199, 202–206, 208, 213, 214, 217, 219–225, 229–234, 236, 239–242, 245, 246, 249–251, 253, 258, 259, 262–267, 269, 270, 273, 276, 279–281, 283, 286, 288, 289, 293, 296, 297, 300, 301, 306, 313, 315, 318, 326, 327, 329, 330

green almond, 208

green fairy, the, 327

Green Man, the, 56, 230

ground nut, 245

ground pine, 82

ground raspberry, 137

groundsel, 143, 144, 341–343, 345–347, 352, 356

grundy swallow, 143

Guaycura, 99

Guernsey, 13, 17, 46, 113, 296

Guernsey pigweed, 17

gum Arabic, 9, 10

gum Benjamin, 38

gum mastic, 208, 209

gum tree, 114

gumballs, 289

Gwydion, 82, 126, 210, 274, 359

gypsy lace, 88

gypsy weed, 282

gypsy's lace, 157

H

hackberry, 72, 145, 146, 337, 339–346, 352, 355

hackmatack, 184

Hades, 52, 70, 94, 98, 130, 154, 213, 214, 250, 251, 300, 360

haeg, 147

hag brier, 145

hag's taper, 220

hagberry, 72, 145

hagthorn, 147

hair of Venus, 202

haldi, 305

Hallstatt culture, 326

hard beam, 163

hardheads, 178

hare's bells, 146

harebell, 48, 146, 337–339, 343–345, 348, 349, 352, 355, 356

haricot, 34

Harpocrates, 239, 265, 360

hartsthorn, 55

Hathor, 122, 142, 150, 199, 204, 224, 265, 322, 360

Hawaii/Hawaiian, 31, 155, 177, 302

haw bush, 147

haws, 147, 148

hawthorn, 25, 74, 147, 337–348, 350–355, 358, 359, 362

hay, 143, 291, 304

hay plant, 291

hazel, 13, 148, 149, 161, 173, 324, 325, 337–362

heal all, 274

healing wreath, 161

heart's ease, 274

heartsease, 235, 236

heartwort, 217

heath, 40, 149, 211, 282, 316, 337–342, 344–349, 352, 354, 356

heath berry, 40

heath pea, 316

heather, 41, 149, 150, 337–342, 344–349, 352, 354, 356, 357, 360, 362

Hebrew(s), 9, 80, 162, 223, 230, 283

Hebrides/Hebridean, 123, 217, 270, 274, 317, 329

Hecate, 11, 21, 24, 27, 44, 65, 79, 91, 94, 100, 101, 121, 130, 133, 152, 154, 174, 186, 196, 204, 213, 215, 218, 223, 226, 227, 242, 251, 267, 276, 289, 300, 324, 330, 360

hedder, 149

hedge bell, 42

hedge grape, 54

hedge parsley, 88

hedgenettle, 40

Hel, 130

Helen of Troy, 113

helichrysum, 167

Helios, 34, 80, 101, 129, 150, 151, 240, 290, 360

heliotrope, 150, 313, 337, 338, 341, 342, 346, 347, 352–354, 356, 357, 360–362

hellebore, 151, 338–340, 342, 346, 348, 352, 353, 355, 356, 358, 360, 362

hellweed, 41, 107

helmet flower, 10, 276

helonias root, 119

hemlock, 81, 88, 152, 258, 338, 340, 342, 345–347, 352, 356, 360

hemp, 152, 153, 277, 338, 340–342, 344, 346–348, 352, 354–356, 358–362

hen and chickens, 282

hen and chicks, 164

henbane, 4, 153, 154, 337–340, 345, 348, 352, 356, 358, 360, 361

henna, 14, 154, 155, 321, 339, 341, 342, 344, 346, 348–350, 352, 354, 361

Hera, 22, 23, 70, 90, 92, 154, 169, 192, 231, 232, 236, 239, 240, 250, 251, 315, 324, 360

herabol, 222

herb bennet, 28

herb of Beltane, 207

herb of gladness, 51

herb of grace, 267, 315

herbgrass, 267

Hercules, 70

Hermes, 16, 21, 34, 64, 101, 122, 148, 169, 187, 199, 219, 231, 250, 251, 315, 324, 330, 360

Herne, 230

hexenbaum, 73

hexenblumen, 19

hibiscus, 155, 340–342, 344, 347, 348, 352, 354–357, 359–361

hickory, 155, 156, 337–340, 343, 344, 346–356

high John, 42, 156, 157, 337, 340, 342–344, 346, 348, 349, 352, 355, 356

high man, 157

Hina (goddess), 32, 84, 360

hina, 32, 84, 154, 360

hind heal, 297

hindberry, 262

Hindu/Hindus, 9, 16, 25, 33, 63, 87, 154, 171, 198, 206, 275, 276, 283, 296, 306, 317

hing, 24

hoar withy, 323

hoarhound, 162

hobblebush, 103

hobgoblin, 221

hock herb, 203

hog apple, 209

hoggins, 147

hogweed, 157, 178, 254, 341, 342, 347–349, 352, 355

Holda, 141, 195, 360

holy grass, 292

holy herb, 165, 315

Holle, 26, 37, 47, 112, 114, 124, 158, 169, 174, 265, 284, 330, 360

Hollen, 126

hollin, 158

holly, 32, 44, 52, 99, 158, 248, 338–344, 346–349, 351–362

hollyhock, 159, 337–339, 341, 342, 346–349, 352, 354, 356

Homer, 240

honesty, 160, 339, 342, 344, 346, 349, 352, 353, 355

honey plant, 187

honeysuckle, 160, 161, 337–341, 343, 344, 346, 347, 352–355, 358, 359, 361, 362

hoodoo, 15, 45, 77, 99, 104, 108, 131, 138, 156, 157, 188, 190, 208, 249, 257, 262, 272, 279, 304, 310, 317

Hood, Robin, 63

hoodwort, 276

hop, 105, 161, 162, 338–343, 345, 348, 351–355

hop marjoram, 105

Hopi, 331

horehound, 162, 338, 339, 342, 346, 349–355, 360

hornbeam, 114, 163, 338–340, 344–347, 349, 352, 354, 356

horse knot, 178

horseheal, 113

horsehoof, 84

horsemint, 36

Horus, 71, 80, 82, 162, 169, 199, 223, 231, 322, 360

hot-foot charm, 77

hound's tongue, 102

houseleek, 164, 341, 344, 346, 351, 352, 354, 356, 360, 362

houseplant, 12, 139, 164, 252, 277, 282, 283, 302

Huitzilopochtli, 18

Hulda, 112

hunter's robe, 252

hyacinth, 48, 164, 165, 341–346, 352, 354–359

Hyacinthos, 165

Hyldemoer, 112

hyssop, 165, 166, 339, 341, 342, 345–349, 351–355

I

I Ching, 329

Iceland, 179, 210, 310

Idunn, 22, 265, 360

Imbolc, 20, 33, 43, 46, 47, 68, 69, 123, 141, 158, 263, 267, 274, 276, 279, 280, 284, 294

immortelle, 167, 168, 190, 337, 340, 347, 348, 351, 354, 355

Inanna, 68, 101, 124, 141, 142, 250, 263, 360

Inari, 141

Inca, 2, 5, 99, 290

incense tree, 128

incubus, 243

India, 1, 5, 9, 15, 25, 33, 49, 65, 77, 81, 84, 87, 108,
  128, 131, 134, 141, 152, 154, 155, 171, 187, 188,
  190, 194, 203, 212, 227, 231, 252, 264, 267, 271,
  275, 277, 295, 306, 317, 322

Indian arrow wood, 284

Indian arrowroot, 333

Indian lilac, 77

Indian moccasin, 182

Indian nard, 283

Indian nettle, 36

Indian paint, 137

Indian posy, 190

Indian root, 131, 283

Indian saffron, 305

Indian tobacco, 195, 196

Indian turmeric, 137

Indian yellow root, 305

Indonesia, 81, 171

Indra, 153, 231, 360

ink plant, 248

insane root, 153

Inti, 290

intoxicating pepper, 177

inula, 113, 283

Ireland, 25, 43, 44, 46, 47, 50, 53, 57, 59, 67, 71,
  74, 75, 82, 99, 103, 106, 117, 123, 128, 130, 133,
  140, 141, 146–149, 158, 161, 168, 181, 193, 206,
  210, 212, 220, 221, 229, 233, 245, 246, 251, 253,
  254, 261, 263, 267, 273, 279, 282, 286, 299, 324,
  326, 329

Iris (goddess), 168

iris (plant), 122, 168, 169, 337, 339–344, 346, 347,
  349, 350, 352, 353, 355, 356, 360

ironhead, 178

ironwood, 163, 210

Iroquois, 45, 48, 104, 138, 191, 195, 209, 249, 254,
  262, 277, 283, 290, 291, 325

Ishtar, 10, 224, 247, 250, 287, 324, 360

Isis, 10, 101, 124, 132, 141, 149, 169, 192, 199, 218,
  223, 231, 239, 247, 265, 281, 315, 322, 328, 360

Isle of Man, 63, 203, 207, 217, 218, 315

Italian starwort, 27

Italian strawflower, 167

Italy / Italians, 16, 27, 28, 33, 35, 39, 53, 66, 72, 79,
  85, 94, 133, 134, 160, 164, 167, 171, 185, 219,
  221, 225, 226, 229, 230, 232, 236, 241, 244, 250,
  263, 268, 273, 315, 321, 327

ivy, 169, 170, 217, 252, 282, 338, 340, 342–349,
  351–354, 356–362

Ixtlilton, 211

Izanami, 32

J

jacinth, 48, 164

jack-o-lantern, 254

jalap, 156

jalapeño, 76, 77

Jamaican pepper, 15

Jainism, 49

Japan / Japanese, 1, 62, 63, 79, 217, 259, 286, 291,
  324

jasmine, 132, 171, 337–342, 344, 346–349, 351–
  355, 359, 362

jelly fungus, 172, 338, 342, 344, 345, 348, 349

Jersey lily, 38

Jimson weed, 300

jinn, 87, 92, 94, 95, 267, 275

Joe Pye weed, 173, 344, 345, 348, 349, 352, 354, 356

John the conqueror, 131, 156

Johnny-jump-up, 235

jonquil, 97

jopi, 173

jojoba, 173, 174, 338, 342, 344, 347, 352, 354, 355

Jove, 322

joy flower, 116

joy of the mountain, 233, 234

juniper, 57, 68, 174, 337–350, 352–356, 358–362

Juno, 70, 105, 114, 122, 142, 169, 192, 223, 232, 236, 240, 250, 315, 324, 360

Juno's rose, 192

Jupiter (god), 230

Jupiter's beard, 164

Jupiter's eye, 164

kiss-me-at-the-garden-gate, 235

knapweed, 87, 178, 339, 340, 342, 344, 349, 352, 353, 356

knight's milfoil, 329

knight's spur, 185

knight's star, 18

knitbone, 86

knot magic, 42, 78, 107, 143, 190, 278, 323, 324

knotgrass, 178, 179, 338, 340, 342, 343, 352, 355, 356

knotweed, 178, 179

korrigans, 274

Krishna, 33, 63, 65, 306, 360

Kuan Yin, 31, 32, 62, 63, 192, 199, 360

Kukulcan, 61

kumaru, 304

Kupala, 120, 131, 188, 234, 270, 314, 360

K

Kali, 25, 84, 155, 306, 360

Kanaloa, 177

Kane-Hekili, 177, 302, 360

kava, 177, 178, 337, 340, 344, 346, 348, 350, 352, 353, 355, 356, 360, 361

kelp, 273

kelpies, 274

Kerry violet, 57

key flower, 89, 252

khus, 251, 317

khus khus, 251

king's cure-all, 115

kingcup, 206

kinnikinnik, 310

Kiowa, 68

L

lace flower, 152

Lada, 195

ladder to heaven, 193

lad's love, 281

lady of the woods, 42

lady thistle, 299

lady wrack, 273

lady's bedstraw, 35, 36

lady's chemise, 19

lady's finger, 143

lady's lockets, 129, 280

lady's mantle, 181–183, 338–342, 344, 345, 347, 349, 352, 356, 359, 362

lady's seal, 54, 280

lady's slipper, 182, 183, 278, 338, 341, 344–346, 352, 356

lady's smock, 183, 184, 340–342, 344, 348, 352, 355

lady's tuft, 65

Laka, 302

Lakota, 36, 68, 269, 284, 290, 291, 293

Lakshmi, 33, 131, 199, 287, 360

larch, 184, 342–344, 346, 349, 352, 354

Lares, the, 223, 266

lark's claw, 185

larkspur, 184, 185, 337–339, 344–348, 350, 352, 355–357

laurel, 34, 62, 300

lavender, 36, 77, 86, 91, 185, 186, 195, 245, 315, 316, 334, 338, 340–349, 351, 354, 355, 360, 362

Le Loup, Yvon, 25

lemon, 39, 89, 114, 115, 186, 187, 209, 337–342, 344–349, 351–355, 358–362

lemon balm, 187, 339, 341, 342, 344, 345, 347–349, 351–353, 355, 358–361

lemon gum tree, 114

lemongrass, 188, 339–341, 343–345, 347–349, 351, 353, 355, 356

lentisco, 208

lentisk, 208

leopard's bane, 24

leprechauns, 221, 245, 262

Leto, 101

lichen, 188, 189, 217, 344–348, 352, 355, 356

licorice, 21, 120, 189, 190, 283, 338, 342, 344, 345, 348, 352, 355, 356, 358, 361

Lieschi, 43

life everlasting, 190, 191, 338, 339, 342, 346, 347, 352, 356

life-everlasting, 288

lilac, 4, 77, 149, 168, 191, 213, 273, 300, 326, 340–350, 352, 354–356

Lilith, 133, 298, 361

lily, 11, 12, 18, 19, 38, 168, 192, 193, 198, 279, 322, 323, 338–349, 351–362

lily of the valley, 193, 338–346, 348, 349, 351, 353–355, 357, 358

lime, 193, 194, 286, 339, 342, 344, 346, 347, 352, 353, 355, 356

lime tree, 194

linden, 194, 195, 339–341, 343–346, 349, 351, 353–362

ling, 53, 149

Linnaeus, Carl, 3, 60, 101

linseed, 124

lint bells, 124

lion foot, 111

lion's ear, 217

lion's foot, 181

lion's tail, 217

liquidambar, 288, 289

liquorice, 189

Lir/Llyr, 14, 22, 26, 46, 90, 148, 263, 274, 361

Litha, 34, 37, 43, 72, 92, 112, 132, 149, 150, 158, 195, 214, 224, 230, 232, 247, 270, 315

Lithuania/Lithuanians, 162, 229

little blue heads, 87

little dragon, 298

little golden hogweed, 254

little hogweed, 254

live-forever, 288

liverwort, 12

lobelia, 195, 341, 342, 344, 347, 352, 355, 356

locoweed, 300

locust, 196, 338, 340, 344–346, 348, 349, 352, 353, 358, 360, 361

loggerheads, 178

Loki, 37, 47, 114, 169, 174, 216, 217, 324, 330, 361

Loki's oats, 216

Lono, 177, 302, 361

loosestrife, 197, 345, 346, 350, 352, 355

lords and ladies, 197, 198, 338, 340, 341, 348, 351, 353, 355

lotus, 198, 199, 322, 338–340, 342–345, 347–353, 355–362

louse berry, 284

lovage, 199, 341, 344–348, 352, 354, 356

love apple, 204

love bind, 160

love charm, 29, 38, 48, 77, 102, 103, 113, 184, 192, 193, 202, 209, 213, 241, 244, 258, 259, 314, 329

love herb, 11, 199

love potion, 14, 235

love root, 199

love vine, 107

love-forever, 288

love-in-a-huddle, 285

love-lies-bleeding, 17

low John, 131

luck flower, 89, 126

Lugh, 41, 43, 90, 140, 141, 158, 330, 361

Lughnasadh, 10, 22, 41, 46, 90, 140, 224, 230, 267, 290

Lumbee, 309

Luna, 17, 47, 49, 100, 108, 115, 132, 215, 251, 258, 267, 324, 361

Lunantishee, 47

lunary, 160, 215

lutins, 222

M

Ma'at, 187

Mabon, 27, 28, 46, 53, 69, 141, 142, 146, 148, 156, 169, 170, 196, 205, 224, 230, 242, 270, 276, 296, 299

Mabon (god), 142

Mabinogion, 210

mace, 67, 227, 228, 347, 351, 355

Macha, 22, 26, 47, 90, 226, 361

mad apple, 300

madderwort, 327

madweed, 276

madwoman's milk, 285

madwort, 152

magic lily, 38

magic sword, 277

magnolia, 201, 202, 339, 341, 344, 346–349, 352–357, 362

maid's hair, 35

maidenhair fern, 202, 203, 337, 338, 340–342, 344–348, 351, 352, 355–357, 362

maize, 140, 141, 356

mala beads, 49, 50

Malaysia, 39, 63, 84, 171, 194, 302

mallow, 159, 203, 338, 340–342, 344–346, 348, 349, 352, 355, 356

mandragora, 204, 209

mandrake, 54, 136, 204, 205, 209, 337–342, 344–348, 352–360, 362

mangetout, 238

Manannán Mac Lir, 14, 46, 90, 361

maple, 4, 25, 205, 217, 293, 337, 339–341, 343–347, 349, 351–355, 357, 358, 362

maplin tree, 205

marigold, 19, 205–207, 212, 295, 339–349, 352, 353, 356–359

marijuana, 152

marjoram, 105, 233, 234, 327, 340–342, 344–348, 351–355, 357, 360, 362

Mars (god), 122

marsh marigold, 206, 207, 339, 342–346, 348, 349, 352, 356

marsh parsley, 70

marsh violet, 57

marshmallow, 203

martagon, 215

marzipan, 16

master key oil, 208

master of the woods, 291

master root, 207

masterwort, 20, 207, 208, 337, 339, 341, 343–349, 352, 355

mastic, 208, 209, 339, 342, 344, 347, 351, 355, 356, 358, 359

matry-silva, 292

May (tree), 8, 147, 163, 205

May bells, 193

May buttercup, 206

May Day, 123, 161, 163, 183, 191, 193, 280

May Eve, 57, 81, 206

May lily, 193

Mayapple, 204, 209, 237, 344–346, 348, 352, 355

Mayblossom, 147

Mayday tree, 72

Maypop, 237

mays, 140, 145

maythe, 72

Maythorn, 147

mayweed, 71

mazer, 205

mazzard, 72

meadow cress, 183

meadowsweet, 209, 210, 338, 340–345, 347–349, 351, 352, 354, 355, 357–359

meadwort, 209, 210

meat of the goblins, 221

Mecca, 17

Medea, 11, 65, 79, 91, 154, 361

Medusa's head, 143

Megenberg, Konrad von, 129

Melissa, 36, 187

Menominee, 44, 182, 191, 283, 291, 325

Mercury (god), 16, 21, 34, 64, 80, 101, 115, 122, 148, 219, 250, 251, 315, 324, 361

meridian fennel, 64

Merlin, 22, 177

mermaids, 274

merry-tree, 72

Mescalaro, 331

Meskwaki, 36, 85, 136, 182, 195, 277, 284

mesquite, 210, 211, 337, 340, 342, 346, 347, 349, 351, 352, 355, 356, 362

Mexican holly, 99

Mexico, 18, 99, 141, 174, 201, 248, 295, 300, 303, 314, 331

Michaelmas daisy, 27

Micmac, 48, 249, 283

Midsummer daisy, 98, 121

Midsummer men, 288

Midsummer's Day, 36, 99, 108, 148, 195, 230, 236, 242, 321

Midsummer's Eve, 36, 37, 40, 43, 53, 57, 67, 72, 89, 100, 112, 113, 120, 123, 148, 153, 158, 164, 185, 186, 203, 214, 217, 218, 220, 230, 242, 247, 265, 269, 270, 288, 301, 321, 322, 328–330

milkmaids, 183

milkwort, 211, 212, 337–339, 341, 342, 346, 348, 352, 355

mimosa, 9, 210, 212, 338–348, 351–354, 356

Minerva, 14, 22, 26, 124, 134, 155, 219, 231, 240, 251, 284, 299, 361

mint, 36, 165, 187, 213, 234, 241, 300, 338, 341, 342, 344, 346, 347, 349, 351–353, 355, 356, 359–362

mistletoe, 9, 107, 145, 163, 204, 213, 214, 338–341, 344–348, 351, 353, 355–362

Mithras, 94, 150, 250, 361

mitten tree, 272

Moapa, 211

moccasin flower, 182

Modron, 238, 251, 361

Mohegan, 136, 191, 272, 325

Mohican, 173

mojo beans, 34

monarda, 36

money plant, 160, 252

monkey faces, 235

monkey flower, 302

monkshood, 10

monument plant, 102

moon fern, 214

moon flower, 287

moon of the faithful, 23

moon vine, 216

moonflower, 160, 216, 300, 338–343, 345, 348, 349, 352, 355, 356

moonshine, 171, 190

moonwort, 4, 160, 214, 215, 338, 340–344, 346–349, 352, 353, 355, 357–362

moor myrtle, 50

moorland tea, 41

mooseberry, 103

moras, 317

morning glory, 42, 156, 216, 338–343, 345, 348, 349, 352, 355, 356

morning stars, 287

Morocco/Moroccans, 87, 92, 241, 296, 375

Morpheus, 114, 251, 361

Morrigan, the, 27, 68, 73, 139, 154, 161, 174, 196, 263, 324

moss, 82, 83, 188, 189, 205, 216, 217, 344, 346, 352–356, 359, 361

mothan, 57, 240, 241

mother-die, 282

mother-in-law's tongue, 277

mother-wood, 281

motherwort, 217, 218, 340, 342, 344–346, 352, 353, 356

mountain daisy, 24

mountain mint, 234

mouse ear, 126

Mousse de Chene, 189

muggert, 218

muguet, 193

mugwort, 185, 218, 219, 281, 298, 337–342, 344–349, 351–356, 358–360, 362

mulberry, 122, 219, 220, 338–341, 343, 344, 346–351, 353–356, 358–362 mullein, 220, 337–340, 342, 344–349, 352–354, 356, 360

mums, 79

muscle wood, 163

mushroom, 125, 221, 338–342, 347–349, 352, 353, 355

mustard, 222, 341–343, 346, 352, 353, 355, 358

Mut, 39

myrrh, 73, 108, 222, 223, 338–342, 344–349, 351–357, 359, 360, 362

myrrhis, 73

myrtle, 15, 50, 51, 223, 224, 337, 340–348, 352, 354–362

myrtle pepper, 15

N

naked lady, 38

Nanna, 215

narcissus, 97

nard, 283, 353

Native American, 293

Navajo, 102, 269, 300, 331, 334

neck-weed, 152

nectarine, 239, 240, 338, 340–342, 344, 345, 348, 350, 352, 356–360, 362

needle palm, 331

neep, 306

Nefertum, 199

Neith, 10

Nemesis, 26

nephthytis, 139

Neptune (god), 26, 247, 274, 361

Nereides, 274

nerve-root, 182

Netherlands, 136, 143, 223, 315, 316

nettle, 36, 101, 145, 225, 226, 329, 338–340, 342–348, 352–355, 362

nettle tree, 145

night caps, 85

night light, 115

nightshade, 38, 44, 81, 153, 226, 248, 340, 348, 352, 354–356, 358, 360, 361

Nike, 101

nixies, 322

Njord, 274

nopal, 61

Norns, the, 124, 284, 361

Nut, 37, 122, 148, 156, 173, 208, 229, 245

nutmeg, 227, 228, 338–344, 346, 347, 351–355

O

oak, 4, 25, 37, 189, 213, 214, 229, 230, 273, 337–344, 346–362

oak apple, 229

oakmoss, 189

oat, 140, 141

Odin, 26, 27, 37, 69, 114, 120, 126, 148, 187, 195, 214, 230, 265, 290, 330, 361

ogham, 7, 8, 14, 22, 26, 27, 37, 43, 46–48, 90, 112, 114, 124, 140, 142, 147–149, 158, 161, 169, 230, 247, 251, 263, 267, 284, 324, 325, 330

Ogma, 148, 169, 361

Ojibwe, 36, 44, 48, 115, 182, 277, 290, 291, 293

oil of tranquility, 317

old man's beard, 188

old man's nightcap, 42

old man's root, 283

old woman's broom, 99

olibanum, 128

olive, 11, 86, 166, 230, 231, 337, 339–349, 351–353, 355–362

Olmec, 5, 60

Omaha, 85, 262, 291

onion, 78, 231, 232, 338–342, 345, 346, 348, 349, 352, 355, 360

oolong tea, 62

opium, 251

opopanax, 222

orange, 18, 36, 39, 44, 53, 79, 91, 107, 125, 128, 132, 145, 154, 192, 232, 233, 239, 251–253, 278, 284, 295, 302, 316, 334, 337, 339–342, 344–348, 351–354, 356, 359, 360, 362

orange lily, 18

orchanet, 14

orchid, 233, 272, 314, 341, 344, 347, 349, 352, 354, 356, 358, 359, 361, 362

oregano, 233, 234, 340–342, 344–348, 351–355, 357, 360, 362

Oregon grape, 32, 337, 339, 342, 345, 346, 351, 354–356

Orkney, 106

orpine, 288

orris root, 168

Osage, 209

Oshun, 15, 317, 361

Osiris, 9, 10, 69, 82, 105, 122, 124, 130, 141, 169, 190, 199, 239, 247, 296, 322, 324, 361

Ostara, 14, 16, 19, 26, 43, 44, 52, 98, 99, 108, 127, 140, 141, 161, 192, 195, 205, 220, 224, 251, 319, 331

Oswego tea, 36

otherworld, the, 11, 18, 22, 27, 66, 90, 95, 97, 98, 105, 114, 124, 130, 135, 141, 142, 147, 148, 154, 168, 169, 189, 192, 214, 224, 226, 230, 232, 236, 238, 242, 250, 251, 265, 287, 306, 324, 331

Ovid, 11, 35

Ozark/Ozarks, 68, 107, 264, 272

P

Pachamama, 100, 331, 361

pachupat, 237

Padma, 199

Pakistan, 87, 171, 276

palm, 83, 100, 101, 108, 135, 152, 237, 331

Pan, 14, 25, 63, 68, 73, 105, 124, 153, 169, 219, 230, 233, 238, 243, 247, 263, 267, 273, 296, 299, 361

pansy, 235, 318, 339–345, 348, 352, 356

paperbark, 298

paprika, 76, 77

Paracelsus, 3, 189, 217

Parsi, 271

parsley, 70, 73, 86, 88, 89, 129, 199, 236, 258, 338–343, 345–349, 351–355, 360–362

Parthenon, 121

Parvati, 62, 154, 187, 361

Passamaquoddy, 293

passion vine, 237

passionflower, 237, 339, 341, 345, 347, 349, 352, 354, 356

passionfruit, 237

Passover, 162

pastel, 325

patchouli, 237, 238, 338–342, 344–349, 351–359, 361, 362

Pawnee, 85, 136, 195, 262, 291

pea, 189, 238, 239, 316, 317, 340, 341, 344, 346, 350, 352, 355, 356, 362 peach, 239, 240, 278, 338, 340–342, 344, 345, 348, 350, 352, 356–360, 362

pear, 29, 39, 61, 240, 259, 265, 338–340, 342–344, 346, 348–352, 355–358, 360–362

pearlwort, 57, 240, 241, 338, 342–346, 352, 355

peavines, 316

pecan, 155, 156, 350, 351

pegwood, 107, 284

Pele, 231, 302, 361

Pennsylvania, 25, 59, 156, 249

penny flower, 160

pennyroyal, 241, 242, 338, 341, 342, 345–349, 352, 354–356, 359–361

Penobscot, 195, 209

peony, 242, 338, 341–348, 352, 353, 355, 356, 361

pepper, 15, 76, 77, 90, 93, 177, 194, 243, 244, 338–349, 352, 353, 355

peppermint, 213, 338, 347, 352, 355

pepperweed, 90

periwinkle, 244, 337–346, 348, 352, 355–358

Persia/Persians, 5, 25, 33, 64, 77, 93, 94, 142, 171, 208, 212, 219, 238, 249, 250, 296, 305, 315, 321

Persian cumin, 64

Persian lilac, 77

Persian silk tree, 212

Persian violet, 93

Persephone, 27, 69, 73, 97, 98, 105, 122, 124, 130, 141, 169, 187, 188, 213, 214, 236, 241, 242, 247, 249–251, 275, 276, 279, 280, 315, 318, 322, 324, 361

Perun, 230

Philyra, 195

Phoebe, 150

Phoenicians, 80, 92, 142, 198

phoenix, 69, 73, 77, 78, 80, 100, 101, 223

Physicians of Myddfai, 310

Picts, 149, 325

pie plant, 264

Pied Piper of Hamelin, 263

pigeon berry, 248

pignut, 173, 245, 337, 338, 340, 341, 344, 346, 348, 352, 356

pigweed, 17, 178, 254

pilewort, 69

Pima, 303, 331

pimenta, 15

pimento berry, 15

pimento leaf, 15

pimpernel, 245, 246, 339, 346, 347, 349, 351, 353–356

pine, 82, 83, 246, 247, 285, 296, 337, 338, 341–343, 345–348, 351–353, 355–362

pink, 16, 19, 33, 35, 38, 42, 43, 48, 61–63, 65, 66, 71, 76–78, 82, 86, 90, 93, 101, 103, 105, 126, 127, 129, 133, 134, 136, 147, 149, 155, 159, 160, 164, 165, 171, 179, 182, 183, 185, 187, 191, 193, 198, 203, 212, 213, 216, 217, 219, 233, 234, 237, 239, 240, 242, 252, 259, 265, 274–276, 278, 286, 288, 296, 299, 300, 302–305, 310, 313, 316, 326, 329, 334, 344, 348

pipal, 49

pipe tree, 112

piper, 177, 243, 263, 313

piskie flower, 287

pistachio, 208, 209, 339, 342, 344, 347, 351, 355, 356, 358, 359

pixie pears, 147

pixie stools, 125

pixie-led, 49, 287

pixies, 22, 49, 56, 126, 128, 146–149, 221, 246, 247, 287, 299, 305

pixy pears, 265

plague, the, 62, 73, 92, 103, 121, 134, 162, 165, 187, 211, 218, 227, 231, 241, 258, 264, 266, 268, 284, 293, 297, 313, 333

plane tree, 293

plantain, 247, 248, 339–342, 344–349, 352, 356

Pliny the Elder, 2, 15, 51, 83, 93, 94, 134, 187, 243, 259, 273, 279, 281, 284, 321

Plutarch, 169

Pluto (god), 25, 33, 44, 46, 52, 70, 94, 109, 162, 204, 213, 214, 226, 236, 238, 250, 251, 263, 277, 303, 311, 326, 328, 331, 355, 361

pocan, 248, 249

poinsettia, 248, 347, 348, 350, 352, 356

poke, 248, 249, 339, 342, 345, 348, 352, 355, 356

pokeberry, 248

pokeweed, 195, 248, 249

Poland/Polish, 83, 123, 184, 195, 236, 243, 251, 283, 293, 299

Polo, Marco, 232

pomegranate, 237, 249, 250, 337, 339–341, 343, 344, 346–348, 350, 352–362

Pomona, 240, 322, 362

Ponca, 48, 85

poor man's peas, 315

poor man's pepper, 90

poor man's salve, 122

poor man's tea, 282

poor man's treacle, 132

poor man's weather-glass, 245

poplar, 26, 249–251, 337, 340, 343, 345, 346, 348, 349, 352, 355–362

poppy, 19, 251, 338, 340, 341, 344, 346, 348–350, 352, 353, 355, 357–362

della Porta, Giambattista, 226

Poseidon, 26, 70, 231, 247, 263, 274, 285, 324, 362

pot mum, 79

Potawatomi, 44, 293, 325

pothos, 252, 340, 345, 346, 351

Powhatan, 48, 156

prickwood, 284

prickly bloom, 139

pride of India, 77

primrose, 89, 115, 116, 252, 253, 338–349, 351, 352, 354, 356, 358, 359

primrose tree, 115

prince's pear, 39

Prometheus, 120

prunella, 274

puccoon, 48, 137

puchaput, 237

pudding grass, 241

Pueblo, 334

puffball, 221

pumpkin, 253, 254, 337, 340, 341, 346, 352, 355

purple archangel, 101

purple boneset, 173

purple flag, 168

purple grass, 197

purslane, 254, 255, 340, 345–347, 352–355

Q

quaking poplar, 26

quassia, 257, 344, 346, 347, 352, 356

Queen Anne's lace, 64, 152, 258, 338, 339, 341, 342, 344, 345, 347, 348, 352, 355, 357, 361, 362

Queen of Sheba, 208

queen of spices, 65

queen of the meadow, 173, 209

Queen Victoria, 237

Quetzalcoatl, 61, 211, 362

quickbeam, 266

quicken, 114

quickthorn, 147

quince, 259, 338, 341, 344–346, 348, 352, 355–357,
    362

R

Ra, 10, 34, 69, 71, 72, 80, 82, 122, 129, 150, 199,
    223, 231, 322, 362

rabbit tobacco, 190

raccoon berry, 209

ragged Jack, 261

ragged Robin, 63

ragweed, 261

ragwort, 261, 339, 340, 342, 344–346, 352, 356

Raido, 323

Rama, 65

rams' foot, 28

ramsthorn, 55

Ran, 47, 114, 174, 267, 274, 362

raspberry, 137, 262, 341, 344, 346, 348, 349,
    352–354, 356, 362

raspis, 262

rattle weed, 45

raven's foot, 69

red Betty, 195

red cap, 125

red chickweed, 245

red chilies, 76, 194

red fir, 285

red hag, 251

red juniper, 68

red lily, 18

red puccoon, 48

red robin, 178

red root, 48

red sally, 197

reed, 67, 263, 264, 337, 339–343, 346, 348, 349,
    352, 354–356, 358–362

rhapontic, 264

Rhea, 112, 124, 142, 169, 182, 187, 223, 230, 247,
    322, 362

Rhiannon, 22, 68, 90, 172, 205, 215, 263, 324, 362

rhizotomoki, 2

rhubarb, 264, 337, 344, 348, 351–353, 355, 356

ribbon plant, 282

ribwort, 247, 248

rice, 140, 141, 238, 356, 357

roan tree, 266

Robin's pillows, 265

rock bells, 85

rock fern, 202

rockweed, 273

Rolander, Daniel, 257

Roman/Romans, 2, 5, 11, 13, 15, 17–19, 21, 23,
    25, 27, 32–35, 37, 38, 40, 51, 52, 59, 64, 66, 68,
    71, 72, 74, 78, 80, 81, 83, 84, 86, 87, 91–94, 101,
    104, 105, 114, 120, 122, 129, 130, 133, 134, 140,
    142–144, 147, 148, 151, 158, 164, 165, 167–169,
    174, 185, 187, 188, 190, 192, 194, 199, 202, 205,
    206, 208, 213, 214, 219, 220, 222–226, 229, 230,
    232–234, 239, 240, 243, 244, 246, 249, 251, 258,
    259, 261–266, 269, 273, 276, 279–281, 283, 284,

288, 289, 291, 293, 296, 298–301, 305, 306, 313, 315, 316, 318, 321, 325–327, 330

Roman candles, 74

Roman caraway, 93

Roman cumin, 64

Roman laurel, 34

Romania / Romanians, 123, 199

Romanov, Tsar Michael, 162

Romani, 20, 53, 78, 239, 267, 284

Rosalia, 265

rose gall, 265, 347

rose mallow, 159

rose of China, 155

rose of Sharon, 155

rose of winter, 62

rosemary, 266, 339–347, 352–357, 362

rosin rose, 270

rowan, 161, 266, 267, 337, 339–344, 346–350, 352–362

rue, 267, 268, 338–348, 350, 352–356, 358, 359, 361

running five-fingers, 80

rush, 263, 264, 291, 337, 339–343, 346, 348, 349, 352, 354, 355, 358–362

Russia / Russians, 26, 39, 148, 152, 162, 197, 219, 225, 240, 250

rye, 28, 32, 140, 141

S

saffron, 91, 92, 305, 352, 354, 356

sage, 269, 270, 339–343, 346–355, 360, 362

sagewort, 327

saguaro, 61

St. John's wort, 270, 299, 337–342, 344–349, 352–354, 356, 358

St. Joseph's lily, 18

Salem, 196

salep, 233

Salgfraulien, 184

Salingen, 184, 193

sallow, 324

sally, 197, 324

saloop, 233, 272

salt cedar, 296

salt tree, 296

samaras, 114, 205

Samhain, 10, 15, 20, 22, 33, 35, 37, 38, 44, 45, 47, 52–55, 59, 67, 68, 79, 83, 90, 95, 105, 122, 125, 130, 139–141, 148, 153, 154, 167–169, 178, 189, 196, 217, 218, 220, 234, 236–238, 250, 251, 254, 262, 263, 270, 273, 274, 296, 297, 307, 324, 325, 331

samurai, 62

sandalwood, 271, 338, 339, 342, 344–356, 362

sang, 135, 240

Sanskrit, 131, 222, 317

Sarasvati, 84

sassafras, 272, 345, 346, 352, 353, 355, 356

sassafrax, 272

satin flower, 75, 287

Saturn (god), 49, 94, 122, 142, 151, 158, 169, 186, 204, 223, 231, 233, 324, 330, 362

Saturnalia, 34, 158, 169, 243

satyricon, 273

satyrion root, 233

satyrs, 142, 169, 233, 247, 273

savin, 174

savory, 272, 273, 337, 338, 340–343, 348, 351, 352, 354, 355, 361 scabious, 103, 338, 340, 344–346, 351, 354–356

Scandinavia/Scandinavians, 22, 25, 36, 42, 65, 136, 141, 181, 195, 225, 265, 267, 288

scapes, 133

Scotland/Scottish, 13, 42–44, 49, 50, 53, 57, 59, 67, 69, 73, 82, 84, 91, 100, 103, 106, 112, 114, 117, 123, 136, 139, 141, 144, 147–149, 152, 157, 158, 161, 169, 174, 181, 207, 212, 214, 226, 233, 239, 241, 243, 245, 247, 258, 261, 263, 267, 270, 273, 274, 279, 299, 302, 303, 315, 317, 322, 329, 330

Scottish Highlands, 57, 82, 158, 317, 329

scrog, 90

scullcap, 276

scorpion grass, 126

scorpion's tail, 150

Scythian root, 190

Scythians, 104, 194

sea cypress, 296

sea dew, 266

sea oak, 273

seaweed, 273, 274, 338, 341, 345–349, 352–355, 361, 362

sealwort, 280

second sight, 38, 117, 246, 268, 270, 329

Sédir, Paul, 25, 66, 91, 264

Sedna, 274

seed fluff, 250

seed of Horus, 162

seed wool, 250

Sekhmet, 67, 250, 362

selago, 82, 83

Selene, 49, 115, 132, 215, 251, 258, 267, 362

self heal, 7, 211, 274, 275, 339, 342, 343, 345, 347, 349, 352, 356, 358

self-heal, 7

Seminole, 272

Seneca, 156, 292

Seneca grass, 292

senna, 275, 342, 344, 346, 351, 352, 354–356

sesame, 275, 276, 338–342, 345, 346, 348, 349, 352, 355, 356, 358–362

Shakespeare, 235

Shakti, 16

shamans, 43, 125, 303

shamrock, 82, 326

shepherd's thyme, 233, 300

she-vervain, 217

shillings, 160

shittah tree, 9

Shiva, 11, 16, 63, 84, 153, 215, 238, 317, 322, 362

shivering tree, 26

shoeblack plant, 155

Shony, 273, 274

shrub Althea, 155

Siamese ginger, 131

Siberia/Siberians, 43, 125, 264

Sif, 217

silk tree, 212, 213

silky acacia, 212

silky wormwood, 298

Silva Gadelica, 13

Silvanus, 142, 247, 362

silver bough, 22

silver button, 190

silver dollars, 160

silver leaf, 218

silver wattle, 212

silverleaf, 190, 250

skullcap, 276, 277, 338, 340–342, 344, 345, 347, 352–354, 356

slinkweed, 195

sloe plum, 47

sloes, 47, 48

smallage, 70

smearwort, 278

smoke-plant, 129

snake berry, 54

snake plant, 277, 342, 344, 346, 347, 349, 352

snakeroot, 43, 45, 278, 338, 343, 344, 346, 348, 352–355

snakeweed, 43, 278

snap Jacks, 278

snapdragon, 278, 279, 302, 338, 343, 345–347, 349, 352–355

snapping alder, 325

snapping hazelnut, 325

sneezewort, 24

snow flower, 111

snowdrop, 279, 289, 337–343, 345, 347, 349, 350, 352, 361

snowdrop bush, 289

soapweed, 331

Socrates, 152

Solomon Islands ivy, 252

Solomon's seal, 138, 280, 338, 341–350, 352, 353, 356

sorb apple, 266

sorcerer's berry, 226

sorcerer's root, 204

sorcerer's violet, 244

sour trefoil, 326

South Africa, 132, 282

southern blue gum, 114

southernwood, 281, 338, 340–349, 351, 353–355, 358, 360

sow berry, 32

sowbread, 93, 94

sow's teats, 280

Spain / Spanish, 14, 15, 19, 29, 73, 74, 108, 124, 189, 219, 236, 237, 251, 266, 269, 295, 314, 330, 331

Spanish bayonet, 331

Spanish bugloss, 14

Spanish marigold, 19

Spanish pear, 29

sparrow's tongue, 178

spatter dock, 322

spearmint, 213, 351, 352

speedwell, 282, 340, 343–346, 352, 353, 355

spiceberry, 283

spikenard, 283, 284, 338, 339, 341, 344, 345, 347, 356

spider ivy, 282

spider plant, 282, 337, 341, 345, 346, 351

spindleberry, 284

spindletree, 284, 338–344, 347, 349, 353, 358–361

spindle wood, 284

spotted gum, 114

spruce, 285, 337, 338, 341–343, 346–350, 352–354, 358, 359, 362

spurge, 254, 285, 286, 340, 343, 346, 352, 353, 355

squawroot, 45

staghorn moss, 82

stallions and mares, 197

star anise, 286, 337–340, 342, 344, 346–349, 351, 353–355, 360

star flower, 51

star grass, 309

starweed, 75

starwort, 27, 75, 119, 287

Stewart, Janet, 161

stitchwort, 287, 337, 339–342, 345, 348, 349, 353, 355

sticklewort, 12

stickwort, 12

Stingy Jack, 306

stinking gum, 24

stinking nightshade, 153

stinking rose, 132

stinking Willie, 261

stinkweed, 132

stitchwort, 287, 337, 339–342, 345, 348, 349, 353, 355

stone basil, 273

stonecrop, 288, 340, 342, 344, 346, 349, 353, 355

storkbill, 133

storax, 288, 289, 340, 343, 346, 347, 352, 353, 355, 356, 359, 360, 362

stracte, 288, 289

strangle weed, 107

straw, 53, 141

strawberry, 289, 290, 337, 338, 340, 342, 344–348, 353, 354, 356, 359, 361, 362

styrax, 38, 288, 289

succory, 75

sugarberry, 145

sum-sum, 275

sun flower, 113

sun turner, 150

sunflower, 205, 290, 291, 338–342, 344–347, 349, 350, 352, 353, 356, 357, 359, 360

Suriname wood, 257

swallowwort, 69

swamp bay, 201

Swede, 306

Sweden/Swedes, 3, 43, 60, 83, 101, 172, 208, 214, 257, 267, 285, 306

sweet balm, 187

sweet bean, 196

sweet Benjamin, 281

sweet cicely, 73

sweet cumin, 21

sweet everlasting, 190

sweet flag, 291, 344, 346, 348, 350, 352–356

sweet gale, 50

sweet grass, 291

sweet gum, 288, 289

sweet pansy, 318

sweet pea, 189, 316, 317, 356

sweet root, 189

sweet rush, 291

sweet sedge, 291

sweet weed, 203

sweet William, 65

sweet wood, 189

sweet woodruff, 291, 292, 337, 339–342, 345–349, 352, 353, 355, 356, 359, 361

sweetgrass, 292, 293, 339, 342, 347, 349, 351, 353, 356

sweet-scented bedstraw, 291

sword lily, 168

sword of St. George, 277

sycamore, 122, 293, 337–340, 344–351, 353, 355, 356, 358, 359, 362

T

Tages, 295, 296

tagetes, 205, 295, 339, 340, 342, 343, 348, 349, 351–353, 356

tamarack, 184

tamarisk, 296, 297, 337, 338, 340, 343, 345, 346, 349, 353, 356–358, 361, 362

tangle-foot, 103

tansy, 261, 297, 298, 338, 340, 345, 347, 353, 356

tansy ragwort, 261

tare, 315

tarragon, 298, 337, 339, 341–343, 345, 346, 348, 351–353, 355–359, 361, 362

Tasmanian blue gum, 114

tassel flower, 17

tea plant, 62

tea tree, 298, 299, 341, 342, 346, 347, 352

Teton Dakota, 36

tetterwort, 69

Tewa, 331

Thai ginger, 131

Theophrastus, 3, 21, 190

Thesmorphoria, 276

thetch, 315

thistle, 299, 300, 338–340, 342, 343, 345–347, 349, 350, 352–355, 361, 362

Thor, 11, 26, 37, 43, 73, 99, 130, 140, 142, 147, 148, 158, 164, 218, 226, 230, 239, 266, 267, 299, 315, 322, 362

Thor's beard, 164

Thor's helper, 266

Thoreau, Henry David, 191

thorn apple, 300, 338, 340, 341, 343, 346, 353–356, 360

thorn mimosa, 9

thorn tree, 196

Thoth, 16, 32, 92, 122, 126, 187, 199, 362

thousand leaf, 329

Trithemius, Johannes, 3

throatwort, 122

throw-wort, 217

thunder flower, 42, 63

thunder plant, 164

thunderbird, 68, 69

thunderbolts, 63

thunderer's plant, 130

thyme, 4, 233, 300, 301, 327, 337–342, 344–348, 351, 353, 354, 356

ti plant, 302, 342, 344, 346, 347, 352, 355, 360, 361

ti tree, 298, 302

Tinkerbelle, 4, 191

tinkle bell, 146

tissy ball, 90, 253

toad ointment, 24

toadflax, 302, 303, 340, 343, 346, 352, 355, 356

toadstool, 125, 126, 221

tobacco, 15, 102, 190, 195, 196, 289, 303, 304, 310, 342, 347, 349, 352, 354, 355

Tommies, 91

tonka bean, 304, 339, 344, 346, 350, 352, 353, 355, 356

Transylvania, 141, 258

tree moss, 188, 189

tree of death, 94

trefoil, 82, 326

trip-toe, 103

Troglodytes, 134

troll butter, 172

troll flower, 136

trolls, 136, 172, 214, 225

trout lily, 11, 12

trows, 52, 106

trows' caird, 52

true amaryllis, 18, 38

true laurel, 34

trumpet weed, 173

tsubaki oil, 62

Tuatha Dé Danann, 41, 148

tulasi, 33

tulip, 61, 304, 305, 337–342, 344–348, 352, 356

tulip prickly pear, 61

tulsi, 33

Turabug, 169, 263, 268

Turk's cap, 61, 192, 344

turmeric, 137, 305, 306, 333, 338, 339, 341–344,
    346–349, 352, 355, 356, 359, 360

turnip, 54, 254, 306, 307, 344, 346, 352–355

turn-sole, 150

Twelfth Night, 147, 148, 158, 174, 208, 214, 244

Tyr, 27, 195, 299, 362

Tyrol, 25, 66, 111, 148, 184, 208, 246, 268, 285

U

Ukraine, 303

Ulysses, 267

unicorn root, 119, 309, 310, 338, 341–343,
    345–349, 352, 356

unicorns, 14, 22, 77, 78, 119, 158, 231, 250, 310

upland cranberry, 310

Ute, 249, 269, 290

uva ursi, 310, 338, 343, 346, 347, 349, 352,
    354–356

V

Valentine's Day, 235, 236, 279

Valentine's flower, 57

valerian, 182, 313, 338, 339, 341, 342, 344–349,
    353–356, 359, 360

vampire, 47, 153, 315

Van Van oil, 188

vandalroot, 313

vanilla, 102, 292, 304, 314, 315, 338, 341–345, 348,
    349, 353, 354, 356

vanilla grass, 292

vanilla leaf, 102

Varuna, 274

Vedas, 1

Vedic, 267

vegetable sulfur, 82

velvet flower, 17

Venus, 12, 14–18, 20, 22, 23, 25, 26, 28, 29, 32, 33,
    36, 37, 39, 43, 46, 49, 50, 52, 56, 61, 62, 65, 67,
    73, 80, 84, 85, 87–90, 92–94, 98, 99, 102, 103,
    105, 107, 112, 115, 116, 119, 121–123, 126, 128,
    129, 134, 137, 139, 141, 144, 146, 148, 149, 155,
    159, 161, 164, 165, 169, 182, 185, 188, 190–192,
    195, 199, 201–203, 205, 212–214, 218, 219, 223,
    224, 233, 234, 237, 239, 240, 242, 244, 245, 247,
    250, 251, 253, 258, 259, 262, 264–266, 271, 272,
    274, 283, 290, 292–294, 297, 298, 301, 304, 305,
    311, 314, 315, 317, 318, 324, 326, 329, 356, 362

Venus of the woods, 25

Venus's hair, 107

verbena, 4, 217, 315

Veronica, 282

vervain, 4, 185, 217, 315, 337–349, 351–354, 356–362

vervine, 315

Vesta, 34, 153, 186, 362

vetch, 34, 315–317, 338, 344, 345, 351, 353–355

vetchling, 316, 338–342, 344, 345, 347–350, 353, 355, 356

vetiver, 317, 318, 340, 341, 343–346, 348, 349, 352–356, 359, 361, 362

vetivergrass, 317

vetivert, 317

Vikings, 65, 90

Vila, 26, 73

violet, 11, 12, 17, 27, 57, 93, 168, 189, 211, 244, 276, 282, 299, 316, 318, 319, 337–354, 356–362

Virgil, 28, 38, 114

Virginia cowslip, 48

Vishnu, 33, 49, 63, 84, 172, 199, 238, 271, 362

von Bingen, Hildegard, 24, 117, 163, 227, 242, 333

von Hohenheim, Theophrastus Bombastus, 3

voodoo, 99

Vulcan, 112, 247, 267, 362

W

Waccamaw Siouan, 309

Wade, Nan, 315

wahoo, 284

wake pintel, 197

wake Robin, 197

Wales / Welsh, 25, 50–53, 63, 74, 81, 82, 143, 157, 172, 174, 186, 202, 206, 210, 211, 214, 221, 230, 247, 251, 263, 265, 270, 274, 279, 301, 306, 310, 313, 315, 326, 330

walking anthericum, 282

walnut, 321, 322, 337, 339, 341–344, 346, 348–362

Walpurgis, 20, 21, 26, 43, 47, 53, 72, 104, 105, 112, 120, 125, 133, 134, 138–141, 148, 149, 174, 184, 194, 195, 204, 220, 229, 230, 242, 246, 253, 266, 270, 285, 292, 301

wart grass, 150

wart weed, 273, 285

wartwort, 69

wassail, 205

water beech, 163

water grass, 263

water lily, 198, 322, 323, 339, 342–347, 353, 355, 356, 360–362

water sprite(s), 324

water torch, 67

water witching, 325

wax dolls, 129

waybread, 247

wayfarer, 323

wayfaring tree, 103, 323, 338, 340, 346, 351, 355

waythorn, 55

waywort, 245

weapon salve, 189, 217

Wepwawet, 296

West Africa, 65

wheat, 32, 140, 141, 143

whin, 139

whip crop, 323

whippoorwill's shoe, 182

whistling thorn, 9

white-bane, 10

white bay, 201

white bells, 279

white bird's eye, 75

white colic root, 309

white fir, 285

white queen, 279

white turmeric, 333

white veratrum, 151

whitethorn, 9, 147

whortleberry, 40, 310

wild apple, 90

wild baby's breath, 291

wild briar, 265

wild carrot, 258

wild celery, 20, 70

wild chamomile, 71, 121

wild chervil, 88, 89

wild endive, 100

wild hazel, 173

wild heartsease, 235

Wild Hunt, the, 70

wild hyacinth, 48

wild jonquil, 97

wild lemon, 209

wild licorice, 283

wild morning glory, 42

wild pansy, 235

wild pea, 316

wild plum, 47

wild rye, 28

wild snapdragon, 302

wild turmeric, 333

wild vanilla, 102

wild wormwood, 218

will-o-the-wisp, 112, 324

willow, 26, 50, 197, 323, 324, 337, 338, 340–346, 348, 349, 352–356, 358–362

willow herb, 197

windflower, 19

Winnebago, 284, 303

winterbloom, 325

wintersweet, 105

winterweed, 75

wishes, 20, 32, 34, 38, 55, 62, 75, 80, 100, 108, 114, 120, 136, 143, 148, 156, 163, 175, 197, 239, 240, 248, 250, 270, 271, 280, 290, 299, 304, 319, 322, 350

wishing thorn, 47

wishing tree, 147

wish-me-well, 282

witch beam, 266

witch bells, 146

witch-gowan, 100

witch grass, 143

witch hazel, 324, 325, 337–340, 342–348, 350, 352–354, 356

witch pegs, 68

witch posts, 267

witch trial(s), 2, 153, 300, 372

witch wood, 266

witch's burr, 289

witch's butter, 172

witch's milk, 285

witchen tree, 266

witches' bells, 87, 127

witches' berry, 226

witches' briar, 265

witches' broom, 213

witches' candle, 220

witches' flying ointment, 81, 227

witches' gowan, 136

witches' hair, 107

witches' herb, 153

witches' milk, 136

witches' needles, 87

witches' nest, 213

witches' shoelaces, 107

witches' thimble, 146

witches' thimbles, 127

witches' tree, 72, 73

witches' whiskers, 188

witch-hobble, 103

witch's moneybags, 288

witchwood, 114

Withering, William, 128

withy, 323, 324

wizards, 230, 266, 299

wizard's herb, 315

woad, 325, 326, 339, 346, 349, 352, 355, 356

Woden, 91, 120, 218, 225, 226, 247, 362

wolf claw, 82

wolf farts, 221

wolf's bane, 24

wolf's milk, 285

wolfsbane, 4, 10, 11, 355

wolfsblume, 24

womandrake, 54, 204

wood bells, 48, 146

wood folk, 93, 205, 217

wood sorrel, 326, 327, 340, 342, 344–346, 348, 352, 354, 356

wood windflower, 19

woodbine, 160

woody nightshade, 44

wool flower, 111

wormit, 327

wormwood, 218, 281, 298, 327, 338, 340, 343, 344, 346–349, 352, 353, 355, 356, 358–360

wound weed, 137

woundwort, 40, 137, 274, 329

X

Xiuhtecutli, 18

Xochiquetzal, 296

Y

Yacatecuhtli, 303

Yama, 275, 276, 296, 362

yarrow, 4, 282, 329, 338–349, 351, 353, 354, 356, 358

yellow buttons, 281, 297

yellow flag, 168

yellow ginger, 305

yellow puccoon, 137

yellow top, 261

yellow trout lily, 11, 12

yellowroot, 137

Yemaya, 15, 317, 362

yew, 330, 331, 337, 339–341, 343, 345–349, 351–353, 355, 356, 358–362

Yggdrasil, 25

yoke elm, 163

yoni, 16, 198

Yorkshire, 50, 114, 221

yucca, 331, 338, 343, 345–347, 349, 352, 355, 356, 359, 361

Yule, 5, 22, 43, 69, 72, 75, 77, 90, 114, 123, 124, 129, 141, 158, 169, 214, 223, 228, 230, 247, 248, 266, 270, 285, 299, 322, 331

Yuma, 211

Z

zedoary, 333, 342, 343, 345, 348, 349, 352, 355, 356

Zeus, 16, 22, 27, 37, 40, 66, 90, 92, 99, 147, 164, 213, 214, 230–232, 236, 251, 262, 270, 289, 294, 297, 315, 318, 322, 324, 362

Zimbabwe, 282, 283

zinnia, 334, 335, 337, 342, 347, 349–351, 356

zipar, 264

Zoroaster, 271

Zuni, 331, 334

To Write to the Author

If you wish to contact the author or would like more information about this book, please write to the author in care of Llewellyn Worldwide Ltd. and we will forward your request. Both the author and the publisher appreciate hearing from you and learning of your enjoyment of this book and how it has helped you. Llewellyn Worldwide Ltd. cannot guarantee that every letter written to the author can be answered, but all will be forwarded. Please write to:

Sandra Kynes
℅ Llewellyn Worldwide
2143 Wooddale Drive
Woodbury, MN 55125-2989

Please enclose a self-addressed stamped envelope for reply,
or $1.00 to cover costs. If outside the U.S.A., enclose
an international postal reply coupon.

Many of Llewellyn's authors have websites with additional information and resources.

For more information, please visit our website at http://www.llewellyn.com